Loco Flee

CW00523293

TEN

The Complete List of Diesel and Electric Locomotives to run on BR and the National Rail Network

Tenth Anniversary Edition

ISBN   978 0 9564896 6 1

Compiled and researched by Lee Miller

For additional copies and details of other available titles and products
Please visit: www.locofleetshop.co.uk

For mail order instructions please contact: lee@locofleetshop.co.uk
or call 07855502212

Front Cover: 37401 passing Nethertown with a Carlisle to Lancaster service 08/08/2015 (Author)

Introduction

This publication gives a reference to all Diesel and Electric Locomotives which have operated on Britain's railways from the early experimental era right up until the present day.

This information has been put together to give an easy reference to the numbering and official naming of each locomotive and includes all withdrawn, preserved and currently operating locos in TOPS classification order.

This should prove to be very useful when identifying locos which have undergone considerable modifications resulting in numerous changes to the original series of allocated numbers.

Contents

1. Diesel Locomotives

2. DC Electric & Electro-Diesel Locomotives

3. AC Electric & Bi-Mode Locomotives

4. Eurotunnel Locomotives

5. Unclassified Locomotives

Message from the Author

Welcome to the tenth edition of Loco Fleet List and thank you for purchasing a copy of this publication.

This special anniversary edition has undergone a complete rewrite to include scrappage dates, locations and allocations of all preserved and operational locomotives.

I would like to take this opportunity in thanking all of our customers for their continued support since the release of our first edition back in 2009

A sincere thank you to Andy Prinsep for assistance with research and for the unlimited supply of tea and Jaffa Cakes throughout the diligent proof reading process.

We hope you enjoy this publication and welcome any feedback you may have which may help to enhance any future editions.

All information contained is thought to be correct and up to date at time of publication.

Kind Regards,

Lee Miller

Locomotives are listed in numerical order of original TOPS classification with any subsequent numbers contained alongside.

Below is an example of information contained throughout the book:

Original TOPS Number	Pre-1972 Number	Subsequent Re-numbering	Subsequent Re-numbering	Current Status	Location or Allocation
37001	D6701	37707	·	Scrapped	EMR, Kingsbury, 2011
37002	D6702	37351	·	Scrapped	T J Thomson, Stockton, 2007
37003	D6703	37360	·	Preserved	Mid-Norfolk Railway
37004	D6704	·	·	Scrapped	MC Metals, Springburn, 1996
37005	D6705	37501	37601	Operational	Rail Operations Group, Leicester
37006	D6706	37798	·	Scrapped	C F Booth, Rotherham, 2009
37007	D6707	37506	37604	Stored	DRS, Carlisle Kingmoor
37008	D6708	37352	·	Scrapped	MRJ Phillips, Crewe Works 1996
37009	D6709	37340	·	Preserved	Great Central Railway North
37010	D6710	·	·	Scrapped	C F Booth, Rotherham, 2007

Re-numbering:

Some locomotives have carried up to 5 numbers, usually a result of modification or in more recent years to coincide with the operators existing fleet.
Details on this can be found at the end of each class.
Locomotives built prior to 1972 carried a D or E prefix denoting it being a Diesel or Electric

Current Status:

Scrapped
Locomotives which are considered to have been cut up or beyond economic repair

Preserved
Locomotives which are being maintained and restored by heritage railways and preservation groups

Operational
Locomotives which are currently in regular commercial or industrial use

Stored
Locomotives which are not currently in traffic but may be brought back into service at any time

Location or Allocation:

Scrapped Locomotives - Details the location and year the locomotive was scrapped.

Preserved Locomotives - Details the latest location of where the locomotive is being maintained or restored.

Operational or Stored Locomotives - Detailing the latest operator and allocation.

09002 crossing Park Road, Stretford with an intermodal train from Felixstowe, 12/11/2011   **Lee Miller**

20227 & 20096 Crossing Selby Swing Bridge with 3S14 RHTT working, 29/10/2011   **Lee Miller**

31106 passing through Helsby on 3Q04 PLPR run from Crewe to Longsight, 11/07/2013 **Lee Miller**

33063 arriving into Groombridge during the Spa Valley Diesel Day, 5th June 2010 **Lee Miller**

D7017 Departing from Bishops Lydeard with a mixed freight, 05/06/2015 **Lee Miller**

37401 passing Nethertown with a Carlisle to Lancaster service, 08/08/2015 **Lee Miller**

D821 departing from Bewdley with a service to Bridgenorth, 09/10/2009 **Lee Miller**

43059 at Liverpool Lime Street with a service to Nottingham, 10/10/2015 **Lee Miller**

45128 Stands in York Station with a Newcastle to Liverpool service, 10/03/1987 **Andy Prinsep**

47292 arriving into Rushcliffe Halt during the GCR (North) Diesel Gala, 15th May 2010 **Lee Miller**

56094 with 6E07 Washwood Heath to Boston Dock at Stenson, 10/09/2012   **Lee Miller**

60074 passing Monks SB with 6F81 Liverpool Bulk Terminal to Fiddlers Ferry, 10/08/2012   **Lee Miller**

66434 Passing Winwick Junction with a Chirk to Carlisle working, 23rd April 2010   **Lee Miller**

67022 arriving into Helsby with a Manchester to Llandudno service, 04/06/2015   **Lee Miller**

68013 at London Marylebone with a service to Kidderminster, 26/04/2016 **Lee Miller**

73107 at Southport with a test train from Wigan Springs Branch to Hooton, 14/02/2012 **Lee Miller**

76029 Between duties at Wath Yard 12/07/1978 **Adam Brain**

86259 passing Daresbury with 1Z86 charter from London Euston to Carlisle, 14/06/2012 **Lee Miller**

1. DIESEL LOCOMOTIVES

CLASS 01

Total Built	5	Formation	0-4-0	Max T.E.	12,750 lbf
Date Built	1956/58	Max Speed	14.5 mph	P.A.R.	102 hp
Builder	Andrew Barclay, Kilmarnock	Weight	25 t	R.A.	1
Engine	Gardner 6L3, 153 hp	Brakes	Straight Air	Supply	N/A

01001	D2954	11504	·	·	Scrapped	O R Davies, Holyhead, 1982
01002	D2955	11505	·	·	Scrapped	O R Davies, Holyhead, 1982
·	D2953	11503	·	·	Preserved	Peak Rail
·	D2956	11506	·	·	Preserved	East Lancashire Railway
·	D2956*	Dep 81	·	·	Scrapped	Duport Steels, Briton Ferry, 1969

*Built in 1958 and renumbered in 1967 after the original D2956 had been withdrawn.

CLASS 02

Total Built	20	Formation	0-4-0	Max T.E.	15,000 lbf
Date Built	1960/61	Max Speed	19.5 mph	P.A.R.	100 hp
Builder	Yorkshire Engine Co, Sheffield	Weight	29 t	R.A.	1
Engine	Rolls-Royce C6NFL176, 170 hp	Brakes	Vacuum	Supply	N/A

02001	D2851	·	·	·	Scrapped	Arnott Young, Dudley Hill, 1975
02003	D2853	·	·	·	Preserved	Barrow Hill
02004	D2856	·	·	·	Scrapped	Redland, Mountsorrel, 1978
·	D2850	·	·	·	Scrapped	Hesslewoods, Attercliffe, 1971
·	D2852	·	·	·	Scrapped	Avon Transmission Allerton, 1970
·	D2854	·	·	·	Preserved	Peak Rail
·	D2855	·	·	·	Scrapped	Hesslewoods, Attercliffe, 1971
·	D2857	·	·	·	Scrapped	Birds, Long Marston, 1992
·	D2858	·	·	·	Preserved	Midland Railway Centre
·	D2859	·	·	·	Scrapped	Birds, Long Marston, 1971
·	D2860	·	·	·	Preserved	National Railway Museum, York
·	D2861	·	·	·	Scrapped	C F Booth, Rotherham, 1971
·	D2862	·	·	·	Scrapped	NCB Norton Colliery, 1979
·	D2863	·	·	·	Scrapped	Wards, Beighton, 1971
·	D2864	·	·	·	Scrapped	Hesslewoods, Attercliffe, 1971
·	D2865	·	·	·	Scrapped	Vic Berry, Leicester, 1985
·	D2866	AY1021	·	·	Preserved	Peak Rail
·	D2867	·	·	·	Preserved	Battlefield Line
·	D2868	·	·	·	Preserved	Peak Rail
·	D2869	·	·	·	Scrapped	Wards, Beighton, 1971

CLASS 03

Total Built	230	Formation	0-6-0	Max T.E.	15,650 lbf
Date Built	1957-62	Max Speed	28.5 mph	P.A.R.	152 hp
Builder	BR Swindon & Doncaster	Weight	30.3 t	R.A.	1
Engine	Gardner 8L3, 204 hp	Brakes	Vacuum / Air & Vac	Supply	N/A

03004	D2004	·	·	·	Scrapped	Cohen's, Kettering, 1976
03005	D2005	·	·	·	Scrapped	BR, Doncaster Works, 1977
03007	D2007	·	·	·	Scrapped	Cohen's, Kettering, 1976
03008	D2008	·	·	·	Scrapped	BR, Swindon Works, 1979
03009	D2009	·	·	·	Scrapped	Cohen's, Kettering, 1977

CLASS 03 (Continued)

03010	D2010	·	·	·	Scrapped	Trieste, Italy, 1976
03012	D2012	·	·	·	Scrapped	Mayer Parry, Snailwell, 1991
03013	D2013	·	·	·	Scrapped	BR, Doncaster Works, 1977
03014	D2014	·	·	·	Scrapped	BR, Doncaster Works, 1976
03016	D2016	·	·	·	Scrapped	BR, Swindon Works, 1979
03017	D2017	·	·	·	Scrapped	BR, Swindon Works, 1982
03018	D2018	·	·	·	Preserved	Mangapps Farm Railway Museum
03020	D2020	·	·	·	Preserved	Mangapps Farm Railway Museum
03021	D2021	·	·	·	Scrapped	BR, Swindon Works, 1983
03022	D2022	·	·	·	Preserved	Swindon & Cricklade Railway
03025	D2025	·	·	·	Scrapped	BR, Swindon Works, 1978
03026	D2026	·	·	·	Scrapped	C F Booth, Rotherham, 1984
03027	D2027	·	·	·	Preserved	Peak Rail
03029	D2029	·	·	·	Scrapped	BR, Doncaster Works, 1979
03034	D2034	·	·	·	Scrapped	C F Booth, Rotherham, 1983
03035	D2035	·	·	·	Scrapped	Cohen's, Kettering, 1977
03037	D2037	·	·	·	Preserved	Foxfield Railway
03044	D2044	·	·	·	Scrapped	Cohen's, Kettering, 1976
03045	D2045	·	·	·	Scrapped	BR, Doncaster Works, 1979
03047	D2047	·	·	·	Scrapped	BR, Doncaster Works, 1979
03050	D2050	·	·	·	Scrapped	C F Booth, Rotherham, 1979
03055	D2055	·	·	·	Scrapped	BR, Doncaster Works, 1974
03056	D2056	·	·	·	Scrapped	BR, Doncaster Works, 1981
03058	D2058	·	·	·	Scrapped	BR, Doncaster Works, 1977
03059	D2059	·	·	·	Preserved	Isle of Wight Steam Railway
03060	D2060	·	·	·	Scrapped	BR, Doncaster Works, 1983
03061	D2061	·	·	·	Scrapped	BR, Swindon Works, 1983
03062	D2062	·	·	·	Preserved	East Lancashire Railway
03063	D2063	·	·	·	Preserved	North Norfolk Railway
03064	D2064	·	·	·	Scrapped	BR, Doncaster Works, 1981
03066	D2066	·	·	·	Preserved	Barrow Hill
03067	D2067	·	·	·	Scrapped	BR, Doncaster Works, 1982
03068	D2068	·	·	·	Scrapped	Cohen's, Kettering, 1976
03069	D2069	·	·	·	Preserved	Vale of Berkeley Railway
03072	D2072	·	·	·	Preserved	Lakeside & Haverthwaite Railway
03073	D2073	·	·	·	Preserved	Crewe Heritage Centre
03075	D2075	·	·	·	Scrapped	BR, Doncaster Works, 1979
03076	D2076	·	·	·	Scrapped	Cohen's, Kettering, 1976
03078	D2078	·	·	·	Preserved	North Tyneside Steam Railway
03079*	D2079	97805	·	·	Preserved	Derwent Valley Light Railway
03080	D2080	·	·	·	Scrapped	BR, Swindon Works, 1981
03081	D2081	·	·	·	Preserved	Mangapps Farm Railway Museum
03084	D2084	·	·	·	Operational	WCRC, Carnforth
03086	D2086	·	·	·	Scrapped	BR, Doncaster Works, 1984
03089	D2089	·	·	·	Preserved	Mangapps Farm Railway Museum
03090	D2090	·	·	·	Preserved	National Railway Museum Shildon
03091	D2091	·	·	·	Scrapped	BR, Doncaster Works, 1977
03092	D2092	·	·	·	Scrapped	BR, Doncaster Works, 1978
03094	D2094	·	·	·	Preserved	Royal Deeside Railway
03095	D2095	·	·	·	Scrapped	Cohen's, Kettering, 1976
03096	D2096	·	·	·	Scrapped	BR, Doncaster Works, 1977
03097	D2097	·	·	·	Scrapped	BR, Doncaster Works, 1979
03098	D2098	·	·	·	Scrapped	Trieste, Italy, 1976
03099	D2099	·	·	·	Preserved	Peak Rail

CLASS 03 (Continued)

03102	D2102	·	·	·	Scrapped	Cohen's, Kettering, 1976
03103	D2103	·	·	·	Scrapped	BR, Doncaster Works, 1979
03104	D2104	·	·	·	Scrapped	BR, Doncaster Works, 1976
03105	D2105	·	·	·	Scrapped	Cohen's, Kettering, 1976
03106	D2106	·	·	·	Scrapped	Hesslewoods, Attercliffe, 1976
03107	D2107	·	·	·	Scrapped	BR, Doncaster Works, 1983
03108	D2108	·	·	·	Scrapped	BR, Doncaster Works, 1977
03109	D2109	·	·	·	Scrapped	BR, Doncaster Works, 1976
03110	D2110	·	·	·	Scrapped	Cohen's, Kettering, 1976
03111	D2111	·	·	·	Scrapped	BR, Swindon Works, 1981
03112	D2112	·	·	·	Preserved	Kent & East Sussex Railway
03113	D2113	·	·	·	Preserved	Peak Rail
03118	D2118	·	·	·	Preserved	Great Central Railway North
03119*	D2119	·	·	·	Preserved	Epping Ongar Railway
03120*	D2120	·	·	·	Preserved	Fawley Hill Railway
03121	D2121	·	·	·	Scrapped	BR, Swindon Works, 1985
03128	D2128	03901	·	·	Preserved	Peak Rail
03129	D2129	·	·	·	Scrapped	C F Booth, Rotherham, 1983
03134	D2134	·	·	·	Preserved	Royal Deeside Railway
03135	D2135	·	·	·	Scrapped	P Woods, Queenborough, 1976
03137	D2137	·	·	·	Scrapped	BR, Doncaster Works, 1977
03141*	D2141	·	·	·	Preserved	Pontypool & Blaenavon Railway
03142*	D2142	·	·	·	Scrapped	BR, Swindon Works, 1985
03144*	D2144	·	·	·	Preserved	Wensleydale Railway
03145*	D2145	·	·	·	Preserved	Moreton Business Park
03147	D2147			·	Scrapped	C F Booth, Doncaster, 1976
03149	D2149	·	·	·	Scrapped	BR, Doncaster Works, 1983
03151*	D2151	·	·	·	Scrapped	C F Booth, Rotherham, 1985
03152	D2152	·	·	·	Preserved	Swindon & Cricklade Railway
03153	D2153	·	·	·	Scrapped	Trieste, Italy, 1976
03154	D2154	·	·	·	Scrapped	BR, Doncaster Works, 1983
03155	D2155	·	·	·	Scrapped	BR, Doncaster Works, 1976
03156	D2156	·	·	·	Operational	Terlizzi, Italy
03157	D2157	·	·	·	Scrapped	Chiari Steelworks, Italy, 1997
03158	D2158	·	·	·	Preserved	Titley Junction Station
03159	D2159	·	·	·	Scrapped	BR, Swindon Works, 1978
03160	D2160	·	·	·	Scrapped	C F Booth, Rotherham, 1983
03161	D2161	·	·	·	Scrapped	C F Booth, Rotherham, 1983
03162	D2162	·	·	·	Preserved	Llangollen Railway
03163	D2163	·	·	·	Scrapped	Cohen's, Kettering, 1976
03164	D2164	·	·	·	Scrapped	Chiari Steelworks, Italy, 1997
03165	D2165	·	·	·	Scrapped	C F Booth, Doncaster, 1976
03166	D2166	·	·	·	Scrapped	C F Booth, Rotherham, 1976
03167	D2167	·	·	·	Scrapped	BR, Doncaster Works, 1976
03168	D2168	·	·	·	Scrapped	BR, Doncaster Works, 1982
03169	D2169	·	·	·	Scrapped	Drapers, Hull, 1976
03170	D2170	·	·	·	Preserved	Epping Ongar Railway
03171	D2171	·	·	·	Scrapped	Cohen's, Kettering, 1978
03172	D2172	·	·	·	Scrapped	Cohen's, Kettering, 1977
03174	D2174	·	·	·	Scrapped	C F Booth, Rotherham, 1976
03175	D2175	·	·	·	Scrapped	BR, Doncaster Works, 1983
03179*	D2179	97807	·	·	Preserved	Rushden Transport Museum
03180	D2180	·	·	·	Preserved	Battlefield Line
03189	D2189	·	·	·	Preserved	Ribble Steam Railway

CLASS 03 (Continued)

03196	D2196	·	·	·	Operational	WCRC, Carnforth
03197	D2197	·	·	·	Preserved	Lavender Line
03370	D2370	Dep 91	·	·	Scrapped	BR, Doncaster Works, 1983
03371	D2371	Dep 92	·	·	Preserved	Dartmouth Steam Railway
03382*	D2382	·	·	·	Scrapped	BR, Swindon Works, 1986
03386	D2386	·	·	·	Scrapped	Cohen's, Kettering, 1976
03389	D2389	·	·	·	Scrapped	C F Booth, Rotherham, 1983
03397	D2397	·	·	·	Scrapped	Vic Berry, Leicester, 1991
03399	D2399	·	·	·	Preserved	Mangapps Farm Railway Museum
·	D2000	·	·	·	Scrapped	Steelbreaking, Chesterfield, 1969
·	D2001	·	·	·	Scrapped	C F Booth, Rotherham, 1970
·	D2002	·	·	·	Scrapped	Ingot Metals, Kentish Town, 1969
·	D2003	·	·	·	Scrapped	Ingot Metals, Kentish Town, 1969
·	D2006	·	·	·	Scrapped	BR, Swindon Works, 1973
·	D2011	·	·	·	Scrapped	BR, Swindon Works, 1973
·	D2015	·	·	·	Scrapped	Cohen's, Kettering, 1972
·	D2019	·	·	·	Scrapped	Bresciia, Italy, 1973
·	D2023	·	·	·	Preserved	Kent & East Sussex Railway
·	D2024	No.4	·	·	Preserved	Kent & East Sussex Railway
·	D2028	·	·	·	Scrapped	BR, Doncaster Works, 1972
·	D2030	·	·	·	Scrapped	C F Booth, Rotherham, 1970
·	D2031	·	·	·	Scrapped	Pollocks, Southampton, 1969
·	D2032	·	·	·	Stored	Bresciia, Italy, 1973
·	D2033	·	·	·	Stored	Bresciia, Italy, 1973
·	D2036	·	·	·	Stored	Bresciia, Italy, 1973
·	D2038	·	·	·	Scrapped	Wards, Beighton, 1972
·	D2039	·	·	·	Scrapped	Wards, Beighton, 1977
·	D2040	·	·	·	Scrapped	C F Booth, Rotherham, 1970
·	D2041	·	·	·	Preserved	Colne Valley Railway
·	D2042	·	·	·	Scrapped	Ingot Metals, Kentish Town, 1969
·	D2043	·	·	·	Scrapped	P Woods, Queenborough, 1973
·	D2046	·	·	·	Preserved	Plym Valley Railway
·	D2048	·	·	·	Scrapped	BR, Swindon Works, 1973
·	D2049	·	·	·	Scrapped	NCB British Oak, 1985
·	D2051	·	·	·	Preserved	North Norfolk Railway
·	D2052	·	·	·	Scrapped	Drapers, Hull, 1973
·	D2053	·	·	·	Scrapped	Drapers, Hull, 1973
·	D2054	·	·	·	Scrapped	C F Booth, Rotherham, 1982
·	D2057	·	·	·	Scrapped	C F Booth, Rotherham, 1986
·	D2065	·	·	·	Scrapped	C F Booth, Rotherham, 1973
·	D2070	·	·	·	Scrapped	P Woods, Queenborough
·	D2071	·	·	·	Scrapped	Drapers, Hull, 1972
·	D2074	·	·	·	Scrapped	Drapers, Hull, 1973
·	D2077	·	·	·	Scrapped	BR, Swindon Works, 1973
·	D2082	·	·	·	Scrapped	BR, Doncaster Works, 1971
·	D2083	·	·	·	Scrapped	Pollocks, Southampton, 1969
·	D2085	·	·	·	Scrapped	BR, Doncaster Works, 1972
·	D2087	·	·	·	Scrapped	Pounds, Fratton, 1973
·	D2088	·	·	·	Scrapped	C F Booth, Rotherham, 1973
·	D2093	·	·	·	Scrapped	C F Booth, Rotherham, 1986
·	D2100	·	·	·	Scrapped	Cohen's, Kettering, 1972
·	D2101	·	·	·	Scrapped	Wards, Beighton, 1972
·	D2114	·	·	·	Scrapped	Birds, Long Marston, 1975
·	D2115	·	·	·	Scrapped	Cohen's, Kingsbury, 1968

CLASS 03 (Continued)

·	D2116	·	·	·	Scrapped	Marple & Gillott, Sheffield, 1973
·	D2117	L&HR 8	·	·	Preserved	Lakeside & Haverthwaite Railway
·	D2122	·	·	·	Scrapped	Cashmore's, Newport, 1975
·	D2123	·	·	·	Scrapped	Birds, Bristol, 1978
·	D2124	·	·	·	Scrapped	Slag Reduction Co, Barrow, 1970
·	D2125	·	·	·	Scrapped	Birds, Cardiff, 1976
·	D2126	·	·	·	Scrapped	P Woods, Queenborough
·	D2127	·	·	·	Scrapped	Cohen's, Kingsbury, 1968
·	D2130	·	·	·	Scrapped	C F Booth, Rotherham, 1973
·	D2131	·	·	·	Scrapped	Cohen's, Kettering, 1968
·	D2132	·	·	·	Scrapped	C F Booth, Rotherham, 1984
·	D2133	·	·	·	Preserved	West Somerset Railway
·	D2136	·	·	·	Scrapped	Robinsons, Blaydon, 1972
·	D2138	·	·	·	Preserved	Midland Railway Centre
·	D2139	D2000	·	·	Preserved	Peak Rail
·	D2140	·	·	·	Scrapped	BR, Swindon Works, 1972
·	D2143	·	·	·	Scrapped	Cashmore's, Newport, 1968
·	D2146	·	·	·	Scrapped	Birds, Long Marston, 1978
·	D2148	·	·	·	Preserved	Ribble Steam Railway
·	D2150	·	·	·	Scrapped	Cotswold Rail, Gloucester, 2001
·	D2173	·	·	·	Scrapped	BR, Doncaster Works, 1977
·	D2176	·	·	·	Scrapped	Cohen's, Kettering, 1971
·	D2177	·	·	·	Scrapped	Birds, Long Marston, 1970
·	D2178	2	·	·	Preserved	Gwili Railway
·	D2181	·	·	·	Scrapped	Marple & Gillott, Sheffield, 1987
·	D2182	·			Preserved	G & WR
·	D2183	·	·	·	Scrapped	Birds, Long Marston, 1969
·	D2184	·	·	·	Preserved	Colne Valley Railway
·	D2185	·	·	·	Scrapped	Birds, Long Marston, 1978
·	D2186	·	·	·	Scrapped	Cashmore's, Newport, 1981
·	D2187	·	·	·	Scrapped	Birds, Long Marston, 1978
·	D2188	·	·	·	Scrapped	Birds, Long Marston, 1978
·	D2190	·	·	·	Scrapped	Birds, Long Marston, 1969
·	D2191	·	·	·	Scrapped	Cohen's, Kingsbury, 1968
·	D2192	DVR No.2	·	·	Preserved	Dartmouth Steam Railway
·	D2193	·	·	·	Scrapped	Cashmore's, Newport, 1981
·	D2194	·	·	·	Scrapped	Birds, Long Marston, 1978
·	D2195	·	·	·	Scrapped	Duport Steels, Llanelli, 1981
·	D2198	·	·	·	Scrapped	BR, Doncaster Works, 1972
·	D2199	1	·	·	Preserved	Peak Rail
·	D2372	·	·	·	Scrapped	Cohen's, Kettering, 1971
·	D2373	·	·	·	Scrapped	NCB Manvers Main,1982
·	D2374	·	·	·	Scrapped	Cohen's, Kettering, 1968
·	D2375	·	·	·	Scrapped	Cohen's, Kettering, 1968
·	D2376	·	·	·	Scrapped	Cohen's, Kettering, 1968
·	D2377	·	·	·	Scrapped	BR, Swindon Works, 1970
·	D2378	·	·	·	Scrapped	BR, Swindon Works, 1972
·	D2379	·	·	·	Scrapped	BR, Swindon Works, 1970
·	D2380	·	·	·	Scrapped	Cohen's, Kettering, 1968
·	D2381	·	·	·	Operational	WCRC, Carnforth
·	D2383	·	·	·	Scrapped	Wards, Beighton, 1972
·	D2384	·	·	·	Scrapped	Cohen's, Kettering, 1968
·	D2385	·	·	·	Scrapped	C F Booth, Rotherham, 1973
·	D2387	·	·	·	Scrapped	C F Booth, Rotherham, 1973

CLASS 03 (Continued)

·	D2388	·	·	·	Scrapped	C F Booth, Rotherham, 1973
·	D2390	·	·	·	Scrapped	Cohen's, Kettering, 1968
·	D2391	·	·	·	Scrapped	Cohen's, Kettering, 1971
·	D2392	·	·	·	Scrapped	C F Booth, Rotherham, 1972
·	D2393	·	·	·	Scrapped	C F Booth, Rotherham, 1971
·	D2394	·	·	·	Scrapped	C F Booth, Rotherham, 1969
·	D2395	·	·	·	Scrapped	Cohen's, Kettering, 1968
·	D2396	·	·	·	Scrapped	Cohen's, Kettering, 1968
·	D2398	·	·	·	Scrapped	Pounds, Fratton, 1972

* Rebuilt with cut-down cabs for use on the Burry Port & Gwendraeth valley line

Class 03 Names:

03162   BIRKENHEAD SOUTH 1879 - 1985 | 03179   CLIVE

CLASS 04

Total Built	142	Formation	0-6-0	Max T.E.	16,850 lbf
Date Built	1948-61	Max Speed	27 mph	P.A.R.	152 hp
Builder	Drewry Car Co. at Vulcan and RS&H, Newcastle & Darlington	Weight	30.5 t	R.A.	1
Engine	Gardner 8L3, 204 hp	Brakes	Vacuum	Supply	N/A

·	D2200	11100	·	·	Scrapped	A Findlay, Worsborough, 1968
·	D2201	11101	·	·	Scrapped	A Findlay, Worsborough, 1968
·	D2202	11102	·	·	Scrapped	Cohen's, Kettering, 1968
·	D2203	11103	·	·	Preserved	Buckingham Railway Centre
·	D2204	11105	·	·	Scrapped	Duport Steels, Briton Ferry, 1979
·	D2205	11106	·	·	Preserved	Peak Rail
·	D2206	11107	·	·	Scrapped	Hughes Bolckows, Blyth, 1969
·	D2207	11108	·	·	Preserved	North Yorkshire Moors Railway
·	D2208	11109	·	·	Scrapped	NCB Silverwood, 1978
·	D2209	11110	·	·	Scrapped	NCB Kiverton, 1985
·	D2210	11111	·	·	Scrapped	R A Kings, Norwich, 1970
·	D2211	11112	·	·	Scrapped	Duport Steels, Llanelli, 1980
·	D2212	11113	·	·	Scrapped	C F Booth, Rotherham, 1972
·	D2213	11114	·	·	Scrapped	NCB Manvers Main,1978
·	D2214	11115	·	·	Scrapped	C F Booth, Rotherham, 1969
·	D2215	11121	·	·	Scrapped	Birds, Long Marston, 1970
·	D2216	11122	·	·	Stored	Bresciia, Italy, 1973
·	D2217	11123	·	·	Scrapped	C F Booth, Rotherham, 1973
·	D2218	11124	·	·	Scrapped	Steelbreaking, Chesterfield, 1969
·	D2219	11125	·	·	Scrapped	Geeson Ltd, Ripley, 1977
·	D2220	11126	·	·	Scrapped	Cohen's, Kettering, 1968
·	D2221	11127	·	·	Scrapped	C F Booth, Rotherham, 1969
·	D2222	11128	·	·	Scrapped	C F Booth, Rotherham, 1969
·	D2223	11129	·	·	Scrapped	Cohen's, Kettering, 1971
·	D2224	11130	·	·	Scrapped	Drapers, Hull, 1968
·	D2225	11131	·	·	Scrapped	NCB Wath, 1985
·	D2226	11132	·	·	Scrapped	Drapers, Hull, 1968
·	D2227	11133	·	·	Scrapped	Drapers, Hull, 1968
·	D2228	11134	·	·	Scrapped	Bowaters, Sittingbourne, 1979
·	D2229	11135	·	·	Preserved	Peak Rail
·	D2230	11149	·	·	Scrapped	Steelbreaking Chesterfield, 1969

CLASS 04 (Continued)

·	D2231	11150	·	·	Scrapped	Steelbreaking, Chesterfield, 1970
·	D2232	11151	·	·	Scrapped	Cohen's, Middlesborough, 1969
·	D2233	11152	·	·	Scrapped	Steelbreaking, Chesterfield, 1969
·	D2234	11153	·	·	Scrapped	Drapers, Hull, 1968
·	D2235	11154	·	·	Scrapped	A Findlay, Worsborough, 1968
·	D2236	11155	·	·	Scrapped	Cohen's, Kettering, 1968
·	D2237	11156	·	·	Scrapped	Hughes Bolckows, Blyth, 1970
·	D2238	11157	·	·	Scrapped	NCB Manvers Main,1982
·	D2239	11158	·	·	Scrapped	C F Booth, Rotherham, 1985
·	D2240	11159	·	·	Scrapped	R A Kings, Norwich, 1970
·	D2241	11160	·	·	Scrapped	Cohen's, Kettering, 1976
·	D2242	11212	·	·	Scrapped	C F Booth, Rotherham, 1970
·	D2243	11213	·	·	Scrapped	Cohen's, Middlesborough, 1973
·	D2244	11214	·	·	Scrapped	Cashmore's, Newport, 1981
·	D2245	11215	DVR 2	·	Preserved	Derwent Valley Light Railway
·	D2246	11216	·	·	Preserved	South Devon Railway
·	D2247	11217	·	·	Scrapped	Duport Steels, Briton Ferry, 1979
·	D2248	11218	·	·	Scrapped	C F Booth, Rotherham, 1987
·	D2249	11219	·	·	Scrapped	P Woods, Queenborough, 1971
·	D2250	11220	·	·	Scrapped	Pounds, Fratton, 1969
·	D2251	11221	·	·	Scrapped	Pollocks, Southampton, 1969
·	D2252	11222	·	·	Scrapped	Pollocks, Southampton, 1969
·	D2253	11223	·	·	Scrapped	Cohen's, Kettering, 1969
·	D2254	11224	·	·	Scrapped	BR, Selhurst, 1967
·	D2255	11225	·	·	Scrapped	Pollocks, Southampton, 1969
·	D2256	11226	·	·	Scrapped	Pollocks, Southampton, 1909
·	D2257	11227	·	·	Scrapped	Pollocks, Southampton, 1968
·	D2258	11228	·	·	Scrapped	C F Booth, Rotherham, 1986
·	D2259	11229	·	·	Scrapped	Bowaters, Sittingbourne, 1978
·	D2260	·	·	·	Scrapped	PD Fuels, Coed Bach, 1983
·	D2261	·	·	·	Scrapped	C F Booth, Rotherham, 1970
·	D2262	·	·	·	Scrapped	Ford Motors, Dagenham, 1978
·	D2263	·	·	·	Scrapped	Pollocks, Southampton, 1968
·	D2264	·	·	·	Scrapped	C F Booth, Rotherham, 1970
·	D2265	·	·	·	Scrapped	C F Booth, Rotherham, 1970
·	D2266	·	·	·	Scrapped	C F Booth, Rotherham, 1968
·	D2267	·	·	·	Scrapped	North Norfolk Railway, 2003
·	D2268	·	·	·	Scrapped	Wards, Beighton, 1968
·	D2269	·	·	·	Scrapped	Pounds, Fratton, 1969
·	D2270	·	·	·	Scrapped	Duport Steels, Briton Ferry, 1979
·	D2271	·	·	·	Preserved	West Somerset Railway
·	D2272	·	·	·	Preserved	Peak Rail
·	D2273	·	·	·	Scrapped	C F Booth, Rotherham, 1968
·	D2274	·	·	·	Scrapped	NCB Maltby Main, 1980
·	D2275	·	·	·	Scrapped	BR, Swindon Works, 1968
·	D2276	·	·	·	Scrapped	Cashmore's, Newport, 1977
·	D2277	·	·	·	Scrapped	Brahams, Bury St Edmunds, 1969
·	D2278	·	·	·	Scrapped	BR, Stratford, 1971
·	D2279	·	·	·	Preserved	East Anglia Railway Museum
·	D2280	·	·	·	Preserved	North Norfolk Railway
·	D2281	·	·	·	Scrapped	Duport Steels, Briton Ferry, 1971
·	D2282	·	·	·	Scrapped	P Woods, Queenborough, 1972
·	D2283	·	·	·	Scrapped	BR, Stratford, 1970
·	D2284	·	·	·	Preserved	Peak Rail

·	D2285	·	·	·	Scrapped	Brahams, Bury St Edmunds, 1970
·	D2286	·	·	·	Scrapped	Pounds, Fratton, 1969
·	D2287	·	·	·	Scrapped	Pounds, Fratton, 1969
·	D2288	·	·	·	Scrapped	Pollocks, Southampton, 1968
·	D2289	·	·	·	Operational	Lonato Steel Works, Italy
·	D2290	·	·	·	Scrapped	Pollocks, Southampton, 1968
·	D2291	·	·	·	Scrapped	Pollocks, Southampton, 1968
·	D2292	·	·	·	Scrapped	Pollocks, Southampton, 1968
·	D2293	·	·	·	Scrapped	P Woods, Queenborough, 1972
·	D2294	·	·	·	Scrapped	P Woods, Queenborough, 1985
·	D2295	·	·	·	Scrapped	P Woods, Queenborough, 1971
·	D2296	·	·	·	Scrapped	Brahams, Bury St Edmunds, 1970
·	D2297	·	·	·	Scrapped	Brahams, Bury St Edmunds, 1970
·	D2298	DVR 1	·	·	Preserved	Buckingham Railway Centre
·	D2299	·	·	·	Scrapped	C F Booth, Rotherham, 1984
·	D2300	·	·	·	Scrapped	NCB Manton, 1985
·	D2301	·	·	·	Scrapped	Steelbreaking, Chesterfield, 1969
·	D2302	·	·	·	Preserved	Moreton Business Park
·	D2303	·	·	·	Scrapped	BR, Doncaster Works, 1969
·	D2304	·	·	·	Scrapped	Duport Steels, Llanelli, 1977
·	D2305	·	·	·	Scrapped	Duport Steels, Llanelli, 1981
·	D2306	·	·	·	Scrapped	Duport Steels, Llanelli, 1981
·	D2307	·	·	·	Scrapped	Duport Steels, Llanelli, 1979
·	D2308	·	·	·	Scrapped	Duport Steels, Llanelli, 1980
·	D2309	·	·	·	Scrapped	C F Booth, Rotherham, 1969
·	D2310	04110	·	·	Preserved	Battlefield Line
·	D2311	·	·	·	Scrapped	Slag Reduction Co, Ickles, 1968
·	D2312	·	·	·	Scrapped	C F Booth, Rotherham, 1968
·	D2313	·	·	·	Scrapped	Slag Reduction Co, Ickles, 1968
·	D2314	·	·	·	Scrapped	Slag Reduction Co, Ickles, 1968
·	D2315	·	·	·	Scrapped	Hughes Bolckows, Blyth, 1968
·	D2316	·	·	·	Scrapped	C F Booth, Rotherham, 1968
·	D2317	·	·	·	Scrapped	NCB Cortonwood, 1986
·	D2318	·	·	·	Scrapped	Hughes Bolckows, Blyth, 1968
·	D2319	·	·	·	Scrapped	Arnott Young, Dinsdale, 1968
·	D2320	·	·	·	Scrapped	C F Booth, Rotherham, 1969
·	D2321	·	·	·	Scrapped	Cohen's, Middlesborough, 1968
·	D2322	·	·	·	Scrapped	NCB Kiverton, 1985
·	D2323	·	·	·	Scrapped	C F Booth, Rotherham, 1969
·	D2324	·	·	·	Preserved	Barrow Hill
·	D2325	·	·	·	Preserved	Mangapps Farm Museum
·	D2326	·	·	·	Scrapped	NCB Manvers Main,1978
·	D2327	·	·	·	Scrapped	Marple & Gillott, Sheffield, 1983
·	D2328	·	·	·	Scrapped	NCB Cortonwood, 1986
·	D2329	·	·	·	Scrapped	BR, York, 1970
·	D2330	·	·	·	Scrapped	M Turnbull, Thornaby, 1970
·	D2331	·	·	·	Scrapped	Wards, Beighton, 1968
·	D2332	·	·	·	Scrapped	NCB Dinnington, 1986
·	D2333	·	·	·	Scrapped	Ford Motors Dagenham, 1978
·	D2334	·	·	·	Preserved	Mid-Norfolk Railway
·	D2335	·	·	·	Scrapped	NCB Maltby Main, 1980
·	D2336	·	·	·	Scrapped	NCB Manvers Main,1978
·	D2337	·	·	·	Preserved	Peak Rail
·	D2338	·	·	·	Scrapped	Wards, Beighton, 1968

CLASS 04 (Continued)

·	D2339	·	·	·	Scrapped	Hughes Bolckows, Blyth, 1968
·	D2340	2593	·	·	Scrapped	Duport Steels, Briton Ferry, 1979
·	D2341*	2217	DS1173	·	Scrapped	Pollocks, Southampton, 1969

* Originally built for departmental use

CLASS 05

Total Built	79		Formation	0-6-0	Max T.E.	14,500 lbf
Date Built	1955-61		Max Speed	18 mph	P.A.R.	152 hp
Builder	Hunslet Engine Co, Leeds		Weight	31-32 t	R.A.	2
Engine	Gardner 8L3, 204 hp		Brakes	Vacuum	Supply	N/A

05001	D2554	11140	97803+	·	Preserved	Isle of Wight Steam Railway
·	D2400*	11177	·	·	Scrapped	Slag Reduction Co, Ickles, 1968
·	D2401*	11178	·	·	Scrapped	C F Booth, Rotherham, 1969
·	D2402*	11179	·	·	Scrapped	C F Booth, Rotherham, 1968
·	D2403*	11180	·	·	Scrapped	C F Booth, Rotherham, 1969
·	D2404*	11181	·	·	Scrapped	C F Booth, Rotherham, 1969
·	D2405*	11182	·	·	Scrapped	C F Booth, Rotherham, 1970
·	D2406*	11183	·	·	Scrapped	Wards, Beighton, 1968
·	D2407*	11184	·	·	Scrapped	C F Booth, Rotherham, 1969
·	D2408*	11185	·	·	Scrapped	Wards, Beighton, 1967
·	D2409*	11186	·	·	Scrapped	C F Booth, Rotherham, 1970
·	D2550	11136	·	·	Scrapped	BR, Doncaster Works, 1966
·	D2551	11137	·	·	Scrapped	C F Booth, Rotherham, 1968
·	D2552	11138	·	·	Scrapped	C F Booth, Rotherham, 1968
·	D2553	11139	·	·	Scrapped	C F Booth, Rotherham, 1968
·	D2555	11141	·	·	Scrapped	C F Booth, Rotherham, 1968
·	D2556	11142	·	·	Scrapped	Campbells, Airdrie, 1968
·	D2557	11143	·	·	Scrapped	C F Booth, Rotherham, 1968
·	D2558	11161	·	·	Scrapped	C F Booth, Rotherham, 1968
·	D2559	11162	·	·	Scrapped	Campbells, Airdrie, 1968
·	D2560	11163	·	·	Scrapped	Slag Reduction Co, Ickles, 1968
·	D2561	11164	·	·	Scrapped	Duport Steels, Llanelli, 1972
·	D2562	11165	·	·	Scrapped	Slag Reduction Co, Ickles, 1968
·	D2563	11166	·	·	Scrapped	C F Booth, Rotherham, 1968
·	D2564	11167	·	·	Scrapped	C F Booth, Rotherham, 1968
·	D2565	11168	·	·	Scrapped	C F Booth, Rotherham, 1968
·	D2566	11169	·	·	Scrapped	C F Booth, Rotherham, 1968
·	D2567	11170	·	·	Scrapped	Slag Reduction Co, Ickles, 1968
·	D2568	11171	·	·	Scrapped	Duport Steels, Briton Ferry, 1969
·	D2569	11172	·	·	Scrapped	Duport Steels, Briton Ferry, 1970
·	D2570	11173	·	·	Scrapped	Duport Steels, Briton Ferry, 1971
·	D2571	11174	·	·	Scrapped	BR, Glasgow Works, 1968
·	D2572	11175	·	·	Scrapped	Slag Reduction Co, Ickles, 1967
·	D2573	11176	·	·	Scrapped	J McWilliams, Shettleston, 1969
·	D2574	·	·	·	Scrapped	Campbells, Airdrie, 1968
·	D2575	·	·	·	Scrapped	Campbells, Airdrie, 1968
·	D2576	·	·	·	Scrapped	Machinery & Scrap Wishaw, 1968
·	D2577	·	·	·	Scrapped	Machinery & Scrap Wishaw, 1967
·	D2578	·	·	·	Preserved	Moreton Business Park
·	D2579	·	·	·	Scrapped	Campbells, Airdrie, 1969
·	D2580	·	·	·	Scrapped	Campbells, Airdrie, 1968

CLASS 05 (Continued)

·	D2581	·	·	·	Scrapped	Campbells, Airdrie, 1968
·	D2582	·	·	·	Scrapped	Campbells, Airdrie, 1969
·	D2583	·	·	·	Scrapped	Campbells, Airdrie, 1969
·	D2584	·	·	·	Scrapped	Hunslet, Leeds, 1968
·	D2585	·	·	·	Scrapped	Campbells, Airdrie, 1969
·	D2586	·	·	·	Scrapped	Slag Reduction Co, Ickles, 1967
·	D2587	·	·	·	Preserved	Peak Rail
·	D2588	·	·	·	Scrapped	Slag Reduction Co, Ickles, 1967
·	D2589	·	·	·	Scrapped	Campbells, Airdrie, 1968
·	D2590	·	·	·	Scrapped	Campbells, Airdrie, 1969
·	D2591	·	·	·	Scrapped	Slag Reduction Co, Ickles, 1969
·	D2592	·	·	·	Scrapped	Campbells, Airdrie, 1969
·	D2593	·	·	·	Scrapped	Hunslet, Leeds, 1968
·	D2594	·	·	·	Scrapped	Slag Reduction Co, Ickles, 1967
·	D2595	·	·	·	Preserved	Ribble Steam Railway
·	D2596	·	·	·	Scrapped	Campbells, Airdrie, 1969
·	D2597	·	·	·	Scrapped	Campbells, Airdrie, 1969
·	D2598	·	·	·	Scrapped	NCB Lambton Works, 1975
·	D2599	·	·	·	Scrapped	NCB Askern, 1981
·	D2600	·	·	·	Scrapped	Duport Steels, Briton Ferry, 1971
·	D2601	·	·	·	Scrapped	Duport Steels, Llanelli, 1979
·	D2602	·	·	·	Scrapped	Slag Reduction Co, Ickles, 1967
·	D2603	·	·	·	Scrapped	C F Booth, Rotherham, 1968
·	D2604	·	·	·	Scrapped	Cohen's, Swansea, 1968
·	D2605	·	·	·	Scrapped	Cohen's, Swansea, 1968
·	D2606	·	·	·	Scrapped	Slag Reduction Co, Ickles, 1967
·	D2607	·	·	·	Scrapped	Cooper's Metals, Sheffield, 1984
·	D2608	·	·	·	Scrapped	Campbells, Airdrie, 1969
·	D2609	·	·	·	Scrapped	C F Booth, Rotherham, 1968
·	D2610	·	·	·	Scrapped	C F Booth, Rotherham, 1968
·	D2611	·	·	·	Scrapped	NCB Yorkshire Main, 1976
·	D2612	Dep 88	·	·	Scrapped	Argosy Salvage Shettleston, 1967
·	D2613	·	·	·	Scrapped	NCB Bentley, 1977
·	D2614	·	·	·	Scrapped	Drapers, Hull, 1967
·	D2615	Dep 89	·	·	Scrapped	C F Booth, Rotherham, 1968
·	D2616	·	·	·	Scrapped	NCB Hatfield Main, 1973
·	D2617	·	·	·	Scrapped	Hunslet, Leeds, 1976
·	D2618	·	·	·	Scrapped	Campbells, Airdrie, 1969

* Originally Classified D2/5 Pre-TOPS and Built by Andrew Barclay & Co.
\+ Renumbered for departmental use

CLASS 06

Total Built	35	Formation	0-4-0		Max T.E.	19,800 lbf
Date Built	1958-60	Max Speed	22.5 mph		P.A.R.	152 hp
Builder	Andrew Barclay, Kilmarnock	Weight	37.3 t		R.A.	5
Engine	Gardner 8L3, 204 hp	Brakes	Vacuum		Supply	N/A

06001	D2413	·	·	·	Scrapped	Campbells, Airdrie, 1977
06002	D2414	·	·	·	Scrapped	BR, Swindon Works, 1982
06003	D2420	97804*	·	·	Preserved	Peak Rail
06004	D2421	·	·	·	Scrapped	BR, Glasgow Works, 1980
06005	D2422	·	·	·	Scrapped	BR, Dundee, 1983

CLASS 06 (Continued)

06006	D2423	·	·	·	Scrapped	BR, Dundee, 1983
06007	D2426	·	·	·	Scrapped	BR, Glasgow Works, 1979
06008	D2437	·	·	·	Scrapped	Campbells, Polmadie 1983
06009	D2440	·	·	·	Scrapped	Campbells, Airdrie, 1977
06010	D2444	·	·	·	Scrapped	BR, Glasgow Works, 1979
·	D2410	·	·	·	Scrapped	Campbells, Airdrie, 1969
·	D2411	·	·	·	Scrapped	Campbells, Airdrie, 1969
·	D2412	·	·	·	Scrapped	Campbells, Airdrie, 1969
·	D2415	·	·	·	Scrapped	Campbells, Airdrie, 1968
·	D2416	·	·	·	Scrapped	BR, Glasgow Works, 1973
·	D2417	·	·	·	Scrapped	Campbells, Airdrie, 1969
·	D2418	·	·	·	Scrapped	Campbells, Airdrie, 1968
·	D2419	·	·	·	Scrapped	Campbells, Airdrie, 1969
·	D2424	·	·	·	Scrapped	BR, Glasgow Works, 1974
·	D2425	·	·	·	Scrapped	Campbells, Airdrie, 1968
·	D2427	·	·	·	Scrapped	J McWilliams, Shettleston, 1971
·	D2428	·	·	·	Scrapped	Campbells, Airdrie, 1969
·	D2429	·	·	·	Scrapped	J McWilliams, Shettleston, 1971
·	D2430	·	·	·	Scrapped	Campbells, Airdrie, 1969
·	D2431	·	·	·	Scrapped	BR, Glasgow Works, 1972
·	D2432	·	·	·	Scrapped	Trieste, Italy, 1986
·	D2433	·	·	·	Scrapped	BR, Glasgow Works, 1973
·	D2434	·	·	·	Scrapped	J McWilliams, Shettleston, 1971
·	D2435	·	·	·	Scrapped	Campbells, Airdrie, 1974
·	D2436	·	·	·	Scrapped	BR, Glasgow Works, 1973
·	D2438	·	·	·	Scrapped	Campbells, Airdrie, 1974
·	D2439	·	·	·	Scrapped	BR, Glasgow Works, 1972
·	D2441	·	·	·	Scrapped	Slag Reduction Co, Ickles, 1967
·	D2442	·	·	·	Scrapped	Campbells, Airdrie, 1974
·	D2443	·	·	·	Scrapped	BR, Glasgow Works, 1973

* Renumbered for departmental use

CLASS 07

Total Built	14	Formation	0-6-0	Max T.E.	28,240 lbf
Date Built	1962	Max Speed	20 mph	P.A.R.	190 hp
Builder	Ruston & Hornsby, Lincoln	Weight	43 t	R.A.	6
Engine	Paxman 6RPHL, 275 hp	Brakes	Vacuum / Air & Vac	Supply	N/A

07001	D2985	·	·	·	Preserved	Barrow Hill
07002	D2986	·	·	·	Scrapped	P D Fuels, Kidwelly, 1986
07003	D2987	·	·	·	Scrapped	Operational Sand, Oakamoor, 85
07005	D2989	·	·	·	Preserved	Great Central Railway
07006	D2990	·	·	·	Scrapped	P D Fuels, Kidwelly, 1986
07007	D2991	·	·	·	Operational	AFS, Eastleigh
07009	D2993	·	·	·	Scrapped	Trieste, Italy, 1997
07010	D2994	·	·	·	Preserved	Avon Valley Railway
07011	D2995	·	·	·	Preserved	St Leonards Depot
07012	D2996	·	·	·	Preserved	Barrow Hill
07013	D2997	·	·	·	Preserved	East Lancashire Railway
·	D2988	·	·	·	Scrapped	BR, Eastleigh Works, 1973
·	D2992	·	·	·	Scrapped	BR, Eastleigh Works, 1976
·	D2998	·	·	·	Scrapped	BR, Eastleigh Works, 1976

CLASS 08

Total Built	996	Formation	0-6-0	Max T.E.	35,000 lbf
Date Built	1952-63	Max Speed	15 - 20 mph	P.A.R.	260 hp
Builder	BR Derby, Crewe, Darlington,	Weight	48 t	R.A.	5
	Doncaster & Horwich	Brakes	Vacuum / Air & Vac	Supply	N/A
Engine	English Electric 6KT, 400 hp				

08001	D3004	13004	·	·	Scrapped	BR, Swindon Works, 1979
08002	D3005	13005	·	·	Scrapped	BR, Swindon Works, 1978
08003	D3007	13007	·	·	Scrapped	BR, Glasgow Works, 1979
08004	D3008	13008	·	·	Scrapped	BR, Swindon Works, 1986
08005	D3009	13009	·	·	Scrapped	BR, Doncaster Works, 1979
08006	D3010	13010	·	·	Scrapped	BR, Swindon Works, 1980
08008	D3015	13015	·	·	Scrapped	BR, Swindon Works, 1986
08009	D3016	13016	·	·	Scrapped	BR, Swindon Works, 1976
08010	D3017	13017	·	·	Scrapped	BR, Eastleigh Works, 1978
08011	D3018	13018	·	·	Preserved	C & PRR
08014	D3021	13021	·	·	Scrapped	C F Booth, Rotherham, 1981
08015	D3022	13022	·	·	Preserved	Severn Valley Railway
08016	D3023	13023	·	·	Preserved	Peak Rail
08018	D3025	13025	·	·	Scrapped	BR, Swindon Works, 1985
08019	D3027	13027	·	·	Scrapped	BR, Swindon Works, 1986
08021	D3029	13029	·	·	Preserved	Tyseley Locomotive Works
08022	D3030	13030	·	·	Preserved	Cholsey & Wallingford Railway
08023	D3031	13031	·	·	Scrapped	BR, Swindon Works, 1987
08024	D3032	13032	·	·	Scrapped	BR, Doncaster Works, 1983
08025	D3033	13033	·	·	Scrapped	BR, Swindon Works, 1978
08026	D3036	13036	·	·	Scrapped	BR, Swindon Works, 1986
08027	D3039	13039	·	·	Scrapped	BR, Swindon Works, 1982
08028	D3040	13040	·	·	Scrapped	BR, Swindon Works, 1982
08029	D3041	13041	·	·	Scrapped	BR, Swindon Works, 1978
08030	D3042	13042	·	·	Scrapped	BR, Swindon Works, 1984
08031	D3043	13043	·	·	Scrapped	BR, Immingham, 1988
08032	D3044	13044	·	·	Preserved	Mid-Hants Railway
08033	D3046	13046	·	·	Scrapped	BR, Swindon Works, 1986
08035	D3048	13048	·	·	Scrapped	BR, Swindon Works, 1980
08036	D3049	13049	·	·	Scrapped	BR, Swindon Works, 1983
08037	D3050	13050	·	·	Scrapped	BR, Swindon Works, 1980
08041	D3054	13054	·	·	Scrapped	BR, Swindon Works, 1981
08042	D3055	13055	·	·	Scrapped	BR, Doncaster Works, 1979
08043	D3056	13056	·	·	Scrapped	BR, Swindon Works, 1977
08044	D3057	13057	·	·	Scrapped	BR, Doncaster Works, 1979
08045	D3058	13058	·	·	Scrapped	BR, Swindon Works, 1984
08046	D3059	13059	·	·	Preserved	Caledonian Railway
08047	D3060	13060	·	·	Scrapped	BR, Swindon Works, 1980
08048	D3061	13061	·	·	Scrapped	BR, Doncaster Works, 1979
08049	D3062	13062	·	·	Scrapped	BR, Swindon Works, 1985
08050	D3063	13063	·	·	Scrapped	BR, Swindon Works, 1983
08051	D3064	13064	·	·	Scrapped	BR, Swindon Works, 1986
08052	D3065	13065	·	·	Scrapped	C F Booth, March, 1982
08053	D3066	13066	·	·	Scrapped	BR, Swindon Works, 1981
08054	D3067	13067	·	·	Preserved	Embsay & Bolton Abbey Railway
08055	D3068	13068	·	·	Scrapped	BR, Swindon Works, 1983
08056	D3070	13070	·	·	Scrapped	Vic Berry, Leicester, 1989
08057	D3071	13071	·	·	Scrapped	BR, Doncaster Works, 1977
08058	D3072	13072	·	·	Scrapped	BR, Doncaster Works, 1983

08059	D3073	13073	·	·	Scrapped	BR, Swindon Works, 1985
08060	D3074	13074	·	·	Preserved	Cholsey & Wallingford Railway
08061	D3075	13075	·	·	Scrapped	BR, Doncaster Works, 1985
08062	D3076	13076	·	·	Scrapped	BR, Doncaster Works, 1985
08063	D3077	13077	·	·	Scrapped	BR, Doncaster Works, 1985
08064	D3079	13079	·	·	Preserved	National Railway Museum, York
08065	D3080	13080	·	·	Scrapped	BR, Doncaster Works, 1978
08066	D3081	13081	·	·	Scrapped	BR, Doncaster Works, 1978
08067	D3082	13082	TS1	·	Scrapped	BR, Swindon Works, 1986
08068	D3083	13083	·	·	Scrapped	BR, Swindon Works, 1986
08069	D3084	13084	·	·	Scrapped	BR, Doncaster Works, 1984
08070	D3085	13085	97801-	·	Scrapped	BR, Glasgow Works, 1980
08071	D3086	13086	·	·	Scrapped	BR, Doncaster Works, 1978
08074	D3089	13089	·	·	Scrapped	BR, Derby Works, 1977
08075	D3090	13090	·	·	Scrapped	BR, Swindon Works, 1982
08076	D3091	13091	·	·	Scrapped	BR, Swindon Works, 1982
08077	D3102	13102	·	·	Scrapped	Wards, Barton-u-Needwood 2014
08078	D3103	13103	·	·	Scrapped	BR, Swindon Works, 1986
08079	D3104	13104	·	·	Scrapped	BR, Swindon Works, 1986
08080	D3105	13105	·	·	Scrapped	BR, Swindon Works, 1981
08081	D3106	13106	·	·	Scrapped	BR, Swindon Works, 1980
08082	D3107	13107	·	·	Scrapped	BR, Swindon Works, 1982
08083	D3108	13108	·	·	Scrapped	BR, Doncaster Works, 1985
08084	D3109	13109	·	·	Scrapped	BR, Swindon Works, 1982
08085	D3110	13110	·	·	Scrapped	C F Booth, Rotherham, 1993
08086	D3111	13111		·	Scrapped	BR, Swindon Works, 1981
08087	D3112	13112	·	·	Scrapped	BR, Swindon Works, 1980
08088	D3113	13113	·	·	Scrapped	BR, Swindon Works, 1986
08089	D3114	13114	·	·	Scrapped	BR, Swindon Works, 1980
08090	D3115	13115	·	·	Scrapped	BR, Swindon Works, 1978
08091	D3116	13116	·	·	Scrapped	BR, Doncaster Works, 1984
08092	D3127	13127	·	·	Scrapped	BR, Doncaster Works, 1979
08093	D3128	13128	·	·	Scrapped	BR, Swindon Works, 1982
08094	D3129	13129	·	·	Scrapped	BR, Doncaster Works, 1985
08095	D3130	13130	·	·	Scrapped	BR, Swindon Works, 1986
08096	D3131	13131	·	·	Scrapped	BR, Doncaster Works, 1985
08097	D3132	13132	·	·	Scrapped	BR, Swindon Works, 1981
08098	D3133	13133	·	·	Scrapped	BR, Swindon Works, 1981
08099	D3134	13134	·	·	Scrapped	BR, Swindon Works, 1983
08100	D3135	13135	·	·	Scrapped	BR, Doncaster Works, 1985
08101	D3136	13136	·	·	Scrapped	BR, Doncaster Works, 1984
08102	D3167	13167	·	·	Preserved	Lincolnshire Wolds Railway
08103	D3168	13168	·	·	Scrapped	BR, Swindon Works, 1985
08104	D3169	13169	·	·	Scrapped	BR, Doncaster Works, 1984
08105	D3170	13170	·	·	Scrapped	BR, Doncaster Works, 1984
08106	D3171	13171	·	·	Scrapped	BR, Swindon Works, 1983
08107	D3173	13173	·	·	Scrapped	BR, Doncaster Works, 1984
08108	D3174	13174	·	·	Preserved	Kent & East Sussex Railway
08109	D3175	13175	·	·	Scrapped	BR, Swindon Works, 1981
08110	D3176	13176	·	·	Scrapped	BR, Swindon Works, 1981
08111	D3177	13177	966512+	968012+	Scrapped	BR, Doncaster Works, 1979
08112	D3178	13178	·	·	Scrapped	BR, Swindon Works, 1984
08113	D3179	13179	·	·	Scrapped	Morley Waste, Leeds, 2007
08114	D3180	13180	·	·	Preserved	Great Central Railway

08115	D3181	13181	·	·	Scrapped	BR, Doncaster Works, 1985
08116	D3182	13182	·	·	Scrapped	BR, Doncaster Works, 1983
08117	D3184	13184	966513+	968013+	Scrapped	BR, Doncaster Works, 1979
08118	D3185	13185	·	·	Scrapped	BR, Swindon Works, 1981
08119	D3186	13186	966511+	968011+	Scrapped	BR, Doncaster Works, 1980
08120	D3187	13187	·	·	Scrapped	BR, Swindon Works, 1982
08121	D3188	13188	·	·	Scrapped	BR, Swindon Works, 1985
08122	D3189	13189	·	·	Scrapped	BR, Doncaster Works, 1977
08123	D3190	13190	·	·	Preserved	Cholsey & Wallingford Railway
08124	D3191	13191	·	·	Scrapped	BR, Swindon Works, 1983
08125	D3192	13192	·	·	Scrapped	BR, Swindon Works, 1984
08126	D3194	13194	·	·	Scrapped	BR, Swindon Works, 1981
08127	D3195	13195	·	·	Scrapped	BR, Swindon Works, 1980
08128	D3196	13196	·	·	Scrapped	BR, Swindon Works, 1984
08129	D3197	13197	·	·	Scrapped	BR, Doncaster Works, 1984
08130	D3198	13198	·	·	Scrapped	BR, Swindon Works, 1985
08131	D3199	13199	·	·	Scrapped	BR, Swindon Works, 1981
08132	D3200	13200	·	·	Scrapped	Birds, Long Marston, 1988
08133	D3201	13201	·	·	Preserved	Severn Valley Railway
08134	D3202	13202	·	·	Scrapped	BR, Swindon Works, 1986
08135	D3203	13203	·	·	Scrapped	BR, Swindon Works, 1977
08136	D3204	13204	·	·	Scrapped	BR, Doncaster Works, 1984
08137	D3205	13205	·	·	Scrapped	BR, Doncaster Works, 1985
08138	D3206	13206	·	·	Scrapped	BR, Swindon Works, 1978
08139	D3207	13207	·	·	Scrapped	BR, Swindon Works, 1982
08140	D3208	13208	·	·	Scrapped	BR, Swindon Works, 1977
08141	D3209	13209	·	·	Scrapped	C F Booth, Rotherham, 1994
08142	D3210	13210	·	·	Scrapped	BR, Swindon Works, 1987
08143	D3211	13211	·	·	Scrapped	BR, Swindon Works, 1977
08144	D3212	13212	·	·	Scrapped	BR, Glasgow Works, 1979
08145	D3213	13213	·	·	Scrapped	BR, Glasgow Works, 1978
08146	D3214	13214	·	·	Scrapped	BR, Swindon Works, 1981
08147	D3215	13215	·	·	Scrapped	BR, Doncaster Works, 1984
08148	D3216	13216	·	·	Scrapped	BR, Doncaster Works, 1984
08149	D3217	13217	·	·	Scrapped	BR, Swindon Works, 1984
08150	D3218	13218	·	·	Scrapped	BR, Swindon Works, 1986
08151	D3219	13219	·	·	Scrapped	BR, Eastleigh Works, 1980
08152	D3220	13220	·	·	Scrapped	BR, Swindon Works, 1980
08153	D3221	13221	·	·	Scrapped	BR, Swindon Works, 1986
08154	D3222	13222	·	·	Scrapped	BR, Swindon Works, 1980
08155	D3223	13223	·	·	Scrapped	BR, Swindon Works, 1980
08156	D3224	13224	·	·	Scrapped	BR, Swindon Works, 1980
08157	D3225	13225	·	·	Scrapped	EMR, Attercliffe, 1996
08158	D3226	13226	·	·	Scrapped	BR, Swindon Works, 1979
08159	D3227	13227	·	·	Scrapped	BR, Doncaster Works, 1986
08160	D3228	13228	·	·	Scrapped	BR, Doncaster Works, 1986
08161	D3229	13229	·	·	Scrapped	BR, Doncaster Works, 1986
08162	D3230	13230	·	·	Scrapped	BR, Swindon Works, 1981
08163	D3231	13231	·	·	Scrapped	BR, Doncaster Works, 1984
08164	D3232	13232	·	·	Preserved	East Lancashire Railway
08165	D3233	13233	·	·	Scrapped	BR, Swindon Works, 1980
08166	D3234	13234	·	·	Scrapped	BR, Doncaster Works, 1983
08167	D3235	13235	·	·	Scrapped	BR, Glasgow Works, 1979
08168	D3236	13236	·	·	Stored	Nemesis Rail, Burton-upon-Trent

08169	D3237	13237	·	·	Scrapped	BR, Swindon Works, 1981
08170	D3238	13238	·	·	Scrapped	C F Booth, Rotherham, 1994
08171	D3239	13239	·	·	Scrapped	BR, Doncaster Works, 1983
08172	D3240	13240	·	·	Scrapped	BR, Doncaster Works, 1985
08173	D3241	13241	PO1	·	Scrapped	Vic Berry, Thornton Yard, 1987
08174	D3242	13242	·	·	Scrapped	BR, Swindon Works, 1982
08175	D3243	13243	·	·	Scrapped	J R Adams, Glasgow, 1985
08176	D3244	13244	·	·	Scrapped	BR, Doncaster Works, 1986
08177	D3245	13245	·	·	Scrapped	MRJ Phillips, Crewe Works, 1996
08178	D3246	13246	·	·	Scrapped	BR, Swindon Works, 1984
08179	D3247	13247	·	·	Scrapped	BR, Swindon Works, 1976
08180	D3248	13248	·	·	Scrapped	BR, Swindon Works, 1981
08181	D3249	13249	·	·	Scrapped	BR, Swindon Works, 1984
08182	D3250	13250	·	·	Scrapped	BR, Swindon Works, 1982
08183	D3251	13251	·	·	Scrapped	BR, Doncaster Works, 1984
08184	D3252	13252	·	·	Scrapped	BR, Swindon Works, 1982
08185	D3253	13253	·	·	Scrapped	BR, Swindon Works, 1982
08186	D3254	13254	·	·	Scrapped	BR, Swindon Works, 1986
08187	D3256	13256	·	·	Scrapped	BR, Swindon Works, 1986
08188	D3257	13257	·	·	Scrapped	BR, Swindon Works, 1986
08189	D3258	13258	·	·	Scrapped	BR, Swindon Works, 1984
08190	D3259	13259	·	·	Scrapped	BR, Swindon Works, 1980
08191	D3260	13260	·	·	Scrapped	Vic Berry, Leicester, 1990
08192	D3262	13262	·	·	Scrapped	BR, Swindon Works, 1985
08193	D3263	13263	·	·	Scrapped	BR, Swindon Works, 1986
08194	D3264	13264	·	·	Scrapped	BR, Swindon Works, 1983
08195	D3265	13265	·	·	Preserved	Llangollen Railway
08196	D3266	13266	·	·	Scrapped	J R Adams, Glasgow, 1985
08197	D3267	13267	·	·	Scrapped	BR, Doncaster Works, 1984
08198	D3268	13268	·	·	Scrapped	BR, Swindon Works, 1981
08199	D3269	13269	·	·	Scrapped	BR, Doncaster Works, 1984
08200	D3270	13270	·	·	Scrapped	C F Booth, Rotherham, 1992
08201	D3271	13271	·	·	Scrapped	BR, Doncaster Works, 1984
08202	D3272	13272	·	·	Preserved	Avon Valley Railway
08203	D3273	13273	08991*	·	Scrapped	Vic Berry, Swansea, 1989
08204	D3274	13274	·	·	Scrapped	BR, Swindon Works, 1984
08205	D3275	13275	·	·	Scrapped	BR, Doncaster Works, 1984
08206	D3276	13276	·	·	Scrapped	Vic Berry, Leicester, 1989
08207	D3277	13277	·	·	Scrapped	BR, Swindon Works, 1983
08208	D3278	13278	·	·	Scrapped	BR, Doncaster Works, 1985
08209	D3279	13279	·	·	Scrapped	BR, Doncaster Works, 1983
08210	D3280	13280	·	·	Scrapped	C F Booth, Rotherham, 1989
08211	D3281	13281	·	·	Scrapped	BR, Doncaster Works, 1986
08212	D3282	13282	·	·	Scrapped	BR, Swindon Works, 1982
08213	D3283	13283	·	·	Scrapped	BR, Swindon Works, 1981
08214	D3284	13284	·	·	Scrapped	BR, Doncaster Works, 1985
08215	D3285	13285	·	·	Scrapped	BR, Doncaster Works, 1983
08216	D3286	13286	·	·	Scrapped	HNRC, Barrow Hill, 2002
08217	D3287	13287	·	·	Scrapped	BR, Doncaster Works, 1983
08218	D3288	13288	·	·	Scrapped	BR, Swindon Works, 1981
08219	D3289	13289	·	·	Scrapped	BR, Doncaster Works, 1983
08220	D3290	13290	·	·	Operational	EMD, Longport Works, Stoke
08221	D3291	13291	·	·	Scrapped	BR, Swindon Works, 1981
08222	D3292	13292	·	·	Scrapped	MRJ Phillips, OOC, 1997

CLASS 08 (Continued)

08223	D3293	13293	·	·	Scrapped	BR, Swindon Works, 1980
08224	D3294	13294	·	·	Scrapped	Gwent Demolition, Margam, 1993
08225	D3295	13295	·	·	Scrapped	BR, Doncaster Works, 1986
08226	D3296	13296	·	·	Scrapped	BR, Doncaster Works, 1986
08227	D3297	13297	·	·	Scrapped	J R Adams, Glasgow, 1985
08228	D3298	13298	·	·	Scrapped	BR, Doncaster Works, 1986
08229	D3299	13299	·	·	Scrapped	BR, Doncaster Works, 1978
08230	D3300	13300	·	·	Scrapped	BR, Swindon Works, 1983
08231	D3301	13301	·	·	Scrapped	BR, Swindon Works, 1981
08232	D3302	13302	·	·	Scrapped	BR, Doncaster Works, 1983
08233	D3303	13303	·	·	Scrapped	G Morris, Stratford, 1982
08234	D3304	13304	·	·	Scrapped	BR, Swindon Works, 1983
08235	D3305	13305	·	·	Scrapped	BR, Doncaster Works, 1984
08236	D3306	13306	·	·	Scrapped	BR, Swindon Works, 1976
08237	D3307	13307	·	·	Scrapped	BR, Doncaster Works, 1986
08238	D3308	13308	·	·	Preserved	Dean Forest Railway
08239	D3309	13309	·	·	Scrapped	HNRC, Kingsbury, 1996
08240	D3310	13310	·	·	Scrapped	BR, Swindon Works, 1985
08241	D3311	13311	·	·	Scrapped	BR, Swindon Works, 1982
08242	D3312	13312	·	·	Scrapped	Vic Berry, Lincoln, 1990
08243	D3313	13313	·	·	Scrapped	Birds, Long Marston, 1988
08244	D3314	13314	·	·	Scrapped	C F Booth, Rotherham, 1989
08245	D3315	13315	·	·	Scrapped	BR, Doncaster Works, 1986
08246	D3316	13316	·	·	Scrapped	D Christie, Camlackie, 1986
08247	D3317	13317	PO1	·	Scrapped	BR, Swindon Works, 1981
08248	D3318	13318	·	·	Scrapped	BR, Doncaster Works, 1985
08249	D3319	13319	·	·	Scrapped	BR, Swindon Works, 1987
08250	D3320	13320	·	·	Scrapped	MC Metals, Springburn, 1991
08251	D3321	13321	·	·	Scrapped	BR, Swindon Works, 1981
08252	D3322	13322	·	·	Scrapped	BR, Swindon Works, 1982
08253	D3323	13323	·	·	Scrapped	Vic Berry, Leicester, 1988
08254	D3324	13324	·	·	Scrapped	C F Booth, Rotherham, 1994
08255	D3325	13325	·	·	Scrapped	BR, Doncaster Works, 1986
08256	D3326	13326	·	·	Scrapped	BR, Doncaster Works, 1985
08257	D3327	13327	·	·	Scrapped	Vic Berry, Leicester, 1989
08258	D3328	13328	·	·	Scrapped	Vic Berry, Leicester, 1989
08259	D3329	13329	08992*	·	Scrapped	Vic Berry, Swansea, 1989
08260	D3330	13330	·	·	Scrapped	BR, Doncaster Works, 1983
08261	D3331	13331	·	·	Scrapped	BR, Doncaster Works, 1984
08262	D3332	13332	·	·	Scrapped	BR, Swindon Works, 1984
08263	D3333	13333	·	·	Scrapped	BR, Doncaster Works, 1984
08264	D3334	13334	·	·	Scrapped	BR, Doncaster Works, 1984
08265	D3335	13335	·	·	Scrapped	BR, Swindon Works, 1987
08266	D3336	13336	·	·	Preserved	Keighley & Worth Valley Railway
08267	D3337	13337	968020~	97801-	Scrapped	Vic Berry, Leicester, 1985
08268	D3338	13338	·	·	Scrapped	BR, Doncaster Works, 1986
08269	D3339	13339	·	·	Scrapped	BR, Doncaster Works, 1985
08270	D3340	13340	·	·	Scrapped	BR, Doncaster Works, 1984
08271	D3341	13341	·	·	Scrapped	BR, Swindon Works, 1983
08272	D3342	13342	·	·	Scrapped	BR, Doncaster Works, 1991
08273	D3343	13343	·	·	Scrapped	BR, Doncaster Works, 1984
08274	D3344	13344	·	·	Scrapped	BR, Doncaster Works, 1985
08275	D3345	13345	·	·	Scrapped	BR, Doncaster Works, 1984
08276	D3346	13346	·	·	Scrapped	BR, Doncaster Works, 1977

CLASS 08 (Continued)

08277	D3347	13347	·	·	Scrapped	BR, Doncaster Works, 1983
08278	D3348	13348	·	·	Scrapped	BR, Glasgow Works, 1977
08279	D3349	13349	·	·	Scrapped	BR, Swindon Works, 1983
08280	D3350	13350	·	·	Scrapped	BR, Swindon Works, 1982
08281	D3351	13351	·	·	Scrapped	BR, Swindon Works, 1985
08282	D3352	13352	·	·	Scrapped	BR, Swindon Works, 1981
08283	D3353	13353	·	·	Scrapped	C F Booth, Rotherham, 1987
08284	D3354	13354	·	·	Scrapped	C F Booth, Rotherham, 1987
08285	D3355	13355	·	·	Scrapped	Gwent Demolition, Margam, 1993
08286	D3356	13356	·	·	Scrapped	H Ralston, Polmadie, 1986
08287	D3357	13357	·	·	Scrapped	BR, Doncaster Works, 1983
08288	D3358	13358	·	·	Preserved	Mid-Hants Railway
08289	D3359	13359	·	·	Scrapped	Birds, Long Marston, 1987
08290	D3360	13360	·	·	Scrapped	BR, Swindon Works, 1984
08291	D3361	13361	·	·	Scrapped	BR, Doncaster Works, 1983
08292	D3362	13362	·	·	Scrapped	Deanside Transit, Glasgow, 1994
08293	D3363	13363	·	·	Scrapped	C F Booth, Rotherham, 1987
08294	D3364	13364	·	·	Scrapped	BR, Swindon Works, 1981
08295	D3365	13365	·	·	Scrapped	Gwent Demolition, Margam, 1993
08296	D3366	13366	·	·	Scrapped	C F Booth, Rotherham, 1994
08297	D3367	·	·	·	Scrapped	Vic Berry, Leicester, 1990
08298	D3368	·	·	·	Scrapped	BR, Swindon Works, 1981
08299	D3369	·	·	·	Scrapped	BR, Swindon Works, 1982
08300	D3370	·	·	·	Scrapped	BR, Doncaster Works, 1984
08301	D3371	·	·	·	Scrapped	BR, Swindon Works, 1985
08302	D3372	·	·	·	Scrapped	BR, Swindon Works, 1902
08303	D3373	·	·	·	Scrapped	BR, Swindon Works, 1987
08304	D3374	·	·	·	Scrapped	BR, Swindon Works, 1987
08305	D3375	·	·	·	Scrapped	Gwent Demolition, Margam, 1995
08306	D3376	·	·	·	Scrapped	BR, Swindon Works, 1978
08307	D3377	·	·	·	Scrapped	BR, Swindon Works, 1978
08308	D3378	23	·	·	Operational	PD Ports, Teesport, Grangetown
08309	D3379	·	·	·	Scrapped	Gwent Demolition, Margam, 1995
08310	D3380	·	·	·	Scrapped	BR, Doncaster Works, 1978
08311	D3381	·	·	·	Scrapped	BR, Doncaster Works, 1984
08312	D3382	·	·	·	Scrapped	J R Adams, Glasgow, 1985
08313	D3383	·	·	·	Scrapped	BR, Doncaster Works, 1983
08314	D3384	·	·	·	Scrapped	BR, Glasgow Works, 1981
08315	D3385	·	·	·	Scrapped	BR, Doncaster Works, 1980
08316	D3386	·	·	·	Scrapped	BR, Swindon Works, 1977
08317	D3387	·	·	·	Scrapped	BR, Doncaster Works, 1983
08318	D3388	·	·	·	Scrapped	BR, Eastleigh Works, 1977
08319	D3389	·	·	·	Scrapped	J R Adams, Glasgow, 1985
08320	D3390	400D	·	·	Scrapped	EMR, Kingsbury, 2010
08321	D3391	·	·	·	Scrapped	J R Adams, Glasgow, 1985
08322	D3392	·	·	·	Scrapped	BR, Swindon Works, 1986
08323	D3393	·	·	·	Scrapped	BR, Swindon Works, 1982
08324	D3394	·	·	·	Scrapped	BR, Doncaster Works, 1985
08325	D3395	·	·	·	Scrapped	BR, Swindon Works, 1985
08326	D3396	·	·	·	Scrapped	J R Adams, Glasgow, 1985
08327	D3397	·	·	·	Scrapped	BR, Swindon Works, 1987
08328	D3398	·	·	·	Scrapped	BR, Swindon Works, 1987
08329	D3399	·	·	·	Scrapped	BR, Swindon Works, 1986
08330	D3400	·	·	·	Scrapped	BR, Doncaster Works, 1985

08331	D3401	·	·	·	Operational	Midland Railway Centre
08332	D3402	·	·	·	Scrapped	BR, Doncaster Works, 1985
08333	D3403	·	·	·	Scrapped	BR, Swindon Works, 1986
08334	D3404	·	·	·	Scrapped	C F Booth, Rotherham, 1994
08335	D3405	·	·	·	Scrapped	Thomas Hill Ltd, Kilnhurst
08336	D3406	·	·	·	Scrapped	BR, Swindon Works, 1982
08337	D3407	·	·	·	Scrapped	BR, Doncaster Works, 1989
08338	D3408	·	·	·	Scrapped	Vic Berry, Swansea, 1990
08339	D3409	·	·	·	Scrapped	BR, Doncaster Works, 1985
08340	D3410	·	·	·	Scrapped	BR, Swindon Works, 1982
08341	D3411	·	·	·	Scrapped	J R Adams, Glasgow, 1985
08342	D3412	·	·	·	Scrapped	BR, Swindon Works, 1983
08343	D3413	·	·	·	Scrapped	H Ralston, Eastfield, 1986
08344	D3414	·	·	·	Scrapped	J R Adams, Glasgow, 1985
08345	D3415	·	·	·	Scrapped	C F Booth, Rotherham, 1985
08346	D3416	·	·	·	Scrapped	J R Adams, Glasgow, 1985
08347	D3417	·	·	·	Scrapped	J R Adams, Glasgow, 1985
08348	D3418	·	·	·	Scrapped	H Ralston, Eastfield, 1986
08349	D3419	·	·	·	Scrapped	BR, Swindon Works, 1986
08350	D3420	·	·	·	Scrapped	C F Booth, Rotherham, 2009
08351	D3421	·	·	·	Scrapped	BR, Swindon Works, 1986
08352	D3422	·	·	·	Scrapped	BR, Swindon Works, 1986
08353	D3423	·	·	·	Scrapped	BR, Swindon Works, 1982
08354	D3424	·	·	·	Scrapped	MC Metals, Springburn, 1991
08355	D3425	·	·	·	Scrapped	BR, Doncaster Works, 1984
08356	D3426	·	·	·	Scrapped	BR, Swindon Works, 1983
08357	D3427	·	·	·	Scrapped	BR, Swindon Works, 1979
08358	D3428	·	·	·	Scrapped	BR, Doncaster Works, 1977
08359	D3429	·	·	·	Preserved	Chasewater Railway
08360	D3430	·	·	·	Scrapped	BR, Swindon Works, 1987
08361	D3431	·	·	·	Scrapped	MC Metals, Springburn, 1991
08362	D3432	·	·	·	Scrapped	BR, Swindon Works, 1983
08363	D3433	·	·	·	Scrapped	BR, Swindon Works, 1983
08364	D3434	·	·	·	Scrapped	BR, Swindon Works, 1983
08365	D3435	·	·	·	Scrapped	BR, Swindon Works, 1981
08366	D3436	·	·	·	Scrapped	BR, Swindon Works, 1982
08367	D3437	·	·	·	Scrapped	Gwent Demolition, Margam, 1994
08368	D3438	·	·	·	Scrapped	BR, Swindon Works, 1984
08369	D3454	·	·	·	Scrapped	BR, Doncaster Works, 1985
08370	D3455	·	·	·	Scrapped	BR, Doncaster Works, 1986
08371	D3456	·	·	·	Scrapped	BR, Doncaster Works, 1985
08372	D3457	·	·	·	Scrapped	BR, Doncaster Works, 1985
08373	D3458	·	·	·	Scrapped	BR, Doncaster Works, 1986
08374	D3459	·	·	·	Scrapped	BR, Doncaster Works, 1984
08375	D3460	21	·	·	Operational	Hanson Cement, Ketton
08376	D3461	·	·	·	Scrapped	BR, Doncaster Works, 1984
08377	D3462	·	·	·	Preserved	Watercress Line
08378	D3463	·	·	·	Scrapped	BR, Swindon Works, 1982
08379	D3464	·	·	·	Scrapped	BR, Swindon Works, 1981
08380	D3465	·	·	·	Scrapped	BR, Swindon Works, 1983
08381	D3466	·	·	·	Scrapped	BR, Doncaster Works, 1984
08382	D3467	·	·	·	Scrapped	BR, Doncaster Works, 1986
08383	D3468	·	·	·	Scrapped	BR, Doncaster Works, 1986
08384	D3469	·	·	·	Scrapped	BR, Doncaster Works, 1986

08385	D3470	·	·	·	Scrapped	Gwent Demolition, Margam, 1994
08386	D3471	·	·	·	Scrapped	Vic Berry, Lincoln, 1990
08387	D3472	·	·	·	Scrapped	BR, Swindon Works, 1986
08388	D3503	·	·	·	Preserved	Private Site
08389	D3504	·	·	·	Operational	HNRC, Celsa Steel UK, Cardiff
08390	D3505	·	·	·	Scrapped	HNRC, Barrow Hill, 2004
08391	D3506	·	·	·	Scrapped	BR, Doncaster Works, 1986
08392	D3507	·	·	·	Scrapped	BR, Doncaster Works, 1985
08393	D3508	·	·	·	Stored	LH Group, Barton-u-Needwood
08394	D3509	·	·	·	Scrapped	Vic Berry, Leicester, 1990
08395	D3510	·	·	·	Scrapped	C F Booth, Rotherham, 1989
08396	D3511	·	·	·	Scrapped	C F Booth, Rotherham, 1987
08397	D3512	·	·	·	Scrapped	Ron Hull, Rotherham, 2010
08398	D3513	402D	·	·	Scrapped	EMR, Kingsbury, 1985
08399	D3514	·	·	·	Scrapped	MC Metals, Springburn, 1993
08400	D3515	·	·	·	Scrapped	Vic Berry, Leicester, 1990
08401	D3516	·	·	·	Operational	Hams Hall Distribution Park
08402	D3517	·	·	·	Scrapped	T J Thomson, Stockton, 2010
08403	D3518	·	·	·	Scrapped	BR, Swindon Works, 1986
08404	D3519	·	·	·	Scrapped	BR, Doncaster Works, 1979
08405	D3520	·	·	·	Operational	EMT, Neville Hill, Leeds
08406	D3521	·	·	·	Scrapped	C F Booth, Rotherham, 1992
08407	D3522	·	·	·	Scrapped	Gwent Demolition, Margam, 1993
08408	D3523	·	·	·	Scrapped	MC Metals, Springburn, 1991
08409	D3524	·	·	·	Scrapped	BR, Doncaster Works, 1986
08410	D3525	·	·	·	Operational	CWR, Long Rock, Penzance
08411	D3526	·	·	·	Stored	RSS, Rye Farm, Sutton Coldfield
08412	D3527	·	·	·	Scrapped	C F Booth, Rotherham, 1992
08413	D3528	·	·	·	Scrapped	Morley Waste, Leeds, 2007
08414	D3529	·	·	·	Scrapped	EMR, Kingsbury, 2007
08415	D3530	·	·	·	Scrapped	EMR, Sheffield, 1995
08416	D3531	·	·	·	Scrapped	C F Booth, Kilnhurst, 1993
08417	D3532	·	·	·	Operational	Loram UK, Derby
08418	D3533	·	·	·	Operational	WCRC, Carnforth
08419	D3534	·	·	·	Scrapped	C F Booth, Rotherham, 2004
08420	D3535	·	·	·	Scrapped	Gwent Demolition, Margam, 1995
08421	D3536	09201	·	·	Operational	HNRR, Hope Cement Works
08422	D3537	·	·	·	Scrapped	Birds, Long Marston, 1992
08423	D3538	H011	14	·	Operational	PD Ports, Teesport, Grangetown
08424	D3539	·	·	·	Scrapped	J R Adams, Glasgow, 1985
08425	D3540	·	·	·	Scrapped	BR, Swindon Works, 1986
08426	D3541	·	·	·	Scrapped	BR, Doncaster Works, 1977
08427	D3542	·	·	·	Scrapped	Gwent Demolition, Margam, 1995
08428	D3543	·	·	·	Stored	HNRC, Barrow Hill
08429	D3544	·	·	·	Scrapped	BR, Doncaster Works, 1983
08430	D3545	·	·	·	Scrapped	J McWilliams, Shettleston, 1986
08431	D3546	·	·	·	Scrapped	Texas Metals, Allerton, 1987
08432	D3547	·	·	·	Scrapped	BR, Doncaster Works, 1984
08433	D3548	·	·	·	Scrapped	J McWilliams, Shettleston, 1986
08434	D3549	·	·	·	Preserved	Gwent Demolition, Margam, 1994
08435	D3550	·	·	·	Scrapped	BR, Swindon Works, 1983
08436	D3551	·	·	·	Preserved	Swanage Railway
08437	D3552	·	·	·	Scrapped	J R Adams, Glasgow, 1985
08438	D3553	·	·	·	Scrapped	C F Booth, Rotherham, 1992

CLASS 08 (Continued)

08439	D3554		·	·	Scrapped	Gwent Demolition, Margam, 1994
08440	D3555		·	·	Scrapped	MC Metals, Springburn, 1991
08441	D3556		·	·	Operational	LNER, Bounds Green, London
08442	D3557		·	·	Stored	Arriva TrainCare, Eastleigh
08443	D3558		·	·	Preserved	Bo'ness & Kinneil Railway
08444	D3559		·	·	Preserved	Bodmin & Wenford Railway
08445	D3560		·	·	Operational	Daventry Freight Terminal
08446	D3561		·	·	Scrapped	J McWilliams, Shettleston, 1986
08447	D3562		·	·	Operational	J G Russell Transport, Glasgow
08448	D3563		·	·	Scrapped	HNRC, Kingsbury, 2007
08449	D3564		·	·	Scrapped	HNRC, Kingsbury, 2007
08450	D3565		·	·	Scrapped	Birds, Long Marston, 1988
08451	D3566		·	·	Operational	Alstom, Longsight, Manchester
08452	D3567		·	·	Scrapped	BR, Swindon Works, 1987
08453	D3568		·	·	Scrapped	BR, Swindon Works, 1982
08454	D3569		·	·	Operational	Alstom, Widnes Tech Centre
08455	D3570		·	·	Scrapped	BR, Swindon Works, 1987
08456	D3571		·	·	Scrapped	C F Booth, Rotherham, 1989
08457	D3572		·	·	Scrapped	BR, Swindon Works, 1986
08458	D3573		·	·	Scrapped	MC Metals, Springburn, 1991
08459	D3574		·	·	Scrapped	Vic Berry, Leicester, 1989
08460	D3575		·	·	Operational	Axiom Rail, Stoke-on-Trent
08461	D3576	·	·	·	Scrapped	MC Metals, Springburn, 1991
08462	D3577	08994*	·	·	Stored	Nemesis Rail, Burton-upon-Trent
08463	D3578		·	·	Scrapped	C F Booth, Rotherham, 1992
08464	D3579		·	·	Scrapped	BR, Swindon Works, 1987
08465	D3580		·	·	Scrapped	BR, Doncaster Works, 1986
08466	D3581		·	·	Scrapped	C F Booth, Rotherham, 2011
08467	D3582		·	·	Scrapped	BR, Swindon Works, 1983
08468	D3583		·	·	Scrapped	Gwent Demolition, Margam, 1995
08469	D3584		·	·	Scrapped	BR, Swindon Works, 1986
08470	D3585		·	·	Scrapped	MRJ Phillips, Crewe Works, 1996
08471	D3586		·	·	Preserved	Severn Valley Railway
08472	D3587		·	·	Operational	LNER, Craigentinny, Edinburgh
08473	D3588		·	·	Preserved	Dean Forest Railway
08474	D3589		·	·	Scrapped	Vic Berry, Leicester, 1988
08475	D3590		·	·	Scrapped	C F Booth, Rotherham, 1987
08476	D3591		·	·	Preserved	Swanage Railway
08477	D3592		·	·	Scrapped	Vic Berry, Allerton, 1990
08478	D3593		·	·	Scrapped	Gwent Demolition, Margam, 1994
08479	D3594		·	·	Preserved	East Lancashire Railway
08480	D3595	TOTON No1	·	·	Operational	GA, Crown Point, Norwich
08481	D3596		·	·	Preserved	Vale of Glamorgan Railway
08482	D3597		·	·	Scrapped	C F Booth, Rotherham, 2011
08483	D3598		·	·	Operational	GWR, St Philip's Marsh, Bristol
08484	D3599		·	·	Operational	Cemex UK, Washwood Heath
08485	D3600		·	·	Operational	WCRC, Carnforth
08486	D3601		·	·	Scrapped	MC Metals, Springburn, 1991
08487	D3602		·	·	Scrapped	MC Metals, Springburn, 1991
08488	D3603		·	·	Scrapped	MC Metals, Springburn, 1991
08489	D3604		·	·	Scrapped	T J Thomson, Stockton, 2009
08490	D3605		·	·	Preserved	Strathspey Railway
08491	D3606		·	·	Scrapped	MC Metals, Springburn, 1991
08492	D3607		·	·	Scrapped	EMR, Kingsbury, 2012

08493	D3608		·	·	Scrapped	C F Booth, Rotherham, 2008
08494	D3609		·	·	Scrapped	MC Metals, Springburn, 1991
08495	D3610		·	·	Preserved	North Yorkshire Moors Railway
08496	D3611		·	·	Scrapped	Birds, Long Marston, 1994
08497	D3652		·	·	Scrapped	BR, Doncaster Works, 1986
08498	D3653		·	·	Scrapped	Birds, Stratford, 1994
08499	D3654		·	·	Operational	Colas Rail, Cardiff Canton
08500	D3655		·	·	Stored	Nemesis Rail, Burton-upon-Trent
08501	D3656		·	·	Scrapped	MC Metals, Springburn, 1991
08502	D3657		·	·	Operational	GBRF, Garston Car Terminal
08503	D3658		·	·	Operational	Barry Rail Centre
08504	D3659		·	·	Scrapped	C F Booth, Rotherham, 1992
08505	D3660		·	·	Scrapped	BR, Swindon Works, 1983
08506	D3661		·	·	Scrapped	T J Thomson, Stockton, 2007
08507	D3662		·	·	Operational	Nemesis Rail, Burton-upon-Trent
08508	D3663		·	·	Scrapped	Gwent Demolition, Margam, 1994
08509	D3664		·	·	Scrapped	C F Booth, Rotherham, 2009
08510	D3672		·	·	Scrapped	C F Booth, Rotherham, 2009
08511	D3673		·	·	Operational	Arriva TrainCare, Cambridge
08512	D3674		·	·	Scrapped	C F Booth, Rotherham, 2009
08513	D3675		·	·	Scrapped	BR, Doncaster Works, 1978
08514	D3676		·	·	Scrapped	EMR, Kingsbury, 2011
08515	D3677		·	·	Scrapped	T J Thomson, Gateshead, 2011
08516	D3678		·	·	Operational	Arriva TrainCare, Bristol
08517	D3679		·	·	Scrapped	C F Booth, Rotherham, 2011
08518	D3680		·	·	Scrapped	Gwent Demolition, Margam, 1994
08519	D3681		·	·	Scrapped	C F Booth, Rotherham, 2000
08520	D3682		·	·	Scrapped	BR, Doncaster Works, 1986
08521	D3683		·	·	Scrapped	Cooper's Metals, Allerton, 1994
08522	D3684		·	·	Scrapped	BR, Doncaster Works, 1985
08523	D3685	H061	·	·	Operational	ScotRail, Inverness
08524	D3686		·	·	Scrapped	C F Booth, Rotherham, 1987
08525	D3687		·	·	Operational	EMT, Neville Hill, Leeds
08526	D3688		·	·	Scrapped	T J Thomson, Stockton, 2008
08527	D3689		·	·	Operational	GBRF, Immingham East Dock
08528	D3690		·	·	Preserved	Battlefield Line
08529	D3691		·	·	Scrapped	C F Booth, Rotherham, 2008
08530	D3692		·	·	Operational	Freightliner, Southampton FLT
08531	D3693		·	·	Operational	Freightliner, Felixtowe FLT
08532	D3694		·	·	Scrapped	Cooper's Metals, Allerton, 1994
08533	D3695		·	·	Scrapped	Gwent Demolition, Margam, 1994
08534	D3696		·	·	Scrapped	T J Thomson, Stockton, 2007
08535	D3699		·	·	Scrapped	C F Booth, Rotherham, 2009
08536	D3700		·	·	Stored	Loram UK, Derby
08537	D3701		·	·	Scrapped	Cooper's Metals, Bescot, 1994
08538	D3702		·	·	Scrapped	EMR, Kingsbury, 2011
08539	D3703		·	·	Scrapped	MC Metals, Springburn, 1993
08540	D3704		·	·	Scrapped	EMR, Kingsbury, 2010
08541	D3705		·	·	Scrapped	EMR, Kingsbury, 2008
08542	D3706		·	·	Scrapped	HNRC, Kingsbury, 2006
08543	D3707		·	·	Scrapped	EMR, Kingsbury, 2010
08544	D3708		·	·	Scrapped	Gwent Demolition, Margam, 1994
08545	D3709		·	·	Scrapped	BR, Swindon Works, 1983
08546	D3710		·	·	Scrapped	BR, Doncaster Works, 1986

08547	D3711	·	·	·	Scrapped	BR, Swindon Works, 1983
08548	D3712	·	·	·	Scrapped	BR, Doncaster Works, 1986
08549	D3713	·	·	·	Scrapped	C F Booth, Rotherham, 1992
08550	D3714	·	·	·	Scrapped	BR, Swindon Works, 1983
08551	D3715	·	·	·	Scrapped	BR, Doncaster Works, 1983
08552	D3716	·	·	·	Scrapped	BR, Doncaster Works, 1983
08553	D3717	·	·	·	Scrapped	BR, Swindon Works, 1983
08554	D3718	·	·	·	Scrapped	BR, Doncaster Works, 1983
08555	D3722	·	·	·	Scrapped	BR, Doncaster Works, 1983
08556	D3723	·	·	·	Preserved	North Yorkshire Moors Railway
08557	D3724	·	·	·	Scrapped	BR, Doncaster Works, 1983
08558	D3725	·	·	·	Scrapped	Vic Berry, Leicester, 1989
08559	D3726	·	·	·	Scrapped	BR, Swindon Works, 1983
08560	D3727	·	·	·	Scrapped	BR, Swindon Works, 1982
08561	D3728	·	·	·	Scrapped	C F Booth, Rotherham, 2011
08562	D3729	·	·	·	Scrapped	MRJ Phillips, OOC, 1997
08563	D3730	·	·	·	Scrapped	D Christie, Camlackie, 1987
08564	D3731	·	·	·	Scrapped	J McWilliams, Shettleston, 1986
08565	D3732	·	·	·	Scrapped	MC Metals, Motherwell, 1997
08566	D3733	·	·	·	Scrapped	BR, Glasgow Works, 1977
08567	D3734	·	·	·	Operational	AFS, Eastleigh
08568	D3735	·	·	·	Stored	RSS, Rye Farm, Sutton Coldfield
08569	D3736	·	·	·	Scrapped	C F Booth, Rotherham, 2011
08570	D3737	·	·	·	Scrapped	MC Metals, Motherwell, 1993
08571	D3738	·	·	·	Operational	Daventry Freight Terminal
08572	D3739	·	·	·	Scrapped	J W Ransome, Frome, 1983
08573	D3740	·	·	·	Operational	Bombardier Transportation, Ilford
08574	D3741	·	·	·	Scrapped	BR, Swindon Works, 1982
08575	D3742	·	·	·	Stored	Nemesis Rail, Burton-upon-Trent
08576	D3743	·	·	·	Scrapped	T J Thomson, Stockton, 2007
08577	D3744	·	·	·	Scrapped	EMR, Kingsbury, 2011
08578	D3745	·	·	·	Stored	Quinton Rail, Long Marston
08579	D3746	·	·	·	Scrapped	Gwent Demolition, Margam, 1995
08580	D3747	·	·	·	Stored	RSS, Rye Farm, Sutton Coldfield
08581	D3748	·	·	·	Scrapped	C F Booth, Rotherham, 2000
08582	D3749	·	·	·	Scrapped	C F Booth, Rotherham, 2009
08583	D3750	·	·	·	Scrapped	C F Booth, Rotherham, 1995
08584	D3751	·	·	·	Scrapped	MC Metals, Springburn, 1993
08585	D3752	·	·	·	Operational	Freightliner, Southampton FLT
08586	D3753	·	·	·	Scrapped	EMR, Ayr, 2000
08587	D3754	·	·	·	Scrapped	T J Thomson, Stockton, 2009
08588	D3755	17	H047	·	Operational	Loram UK, Derby
08589	D3756	·	·	·	Scrapped	Gwent Demolition, Margam, 1995
08590	D3757	·	·	·	Preserved	Midland Railway Centre
08591	D3758	·	·	·	Scrapped	MC Metals, Springburn, 1993
08592	D3759	08993*	·	·	Preserved	Keighley & Worth Valley Railway
08593	D3760	·	·	·	Stored	RSS, Rye Farm, Sutton Coldfield
08594	D3761	·	·	·	Preserved	Private Site
08595	D3762	·	·	·	Scrapped	C F Booth, Rotherham, 1995
08596	D3763	·	·	·	Operational	LNER, Craigentinny, Edinburgh
08597	D3764	·	·	·	Scrapped	C F Booth, Rotherham, 2011
08598	D3765	H016	·	·	Operational	A V Dawson, Ayrton Rail Terminal
08599	D3766	·	·	·	Scrapped	T J Thomson, Stockton, 2009
08600	D3767	97800-	·	·	Operational	A V Dawson, Ayrton Rail Terminal

08601	D3768	601	·	·	Scrapped	HNRC, Wigan, 2005
08602	D3769	004	·	·	Operational	Bombardier Transportation, Derby
08603	D3770	·	·	·	Scrapped	Birds, Long Marston, 1994
08604	D3771	604	·	·	Preserved	Didcot Railway Centre
08605	D3772	WIGAN2	·	·	Operational	DB Cargo UK, Springs Branch
08606	D3773	·	·	·	Scrapped	Vic Berry, Leicester, 1989
08607	D3774	·	·	·	Scrapped	HNRC, Kingsbury, 2007
08608	D3775	·	·	·	Scrapped	C F Booth, Rotherham, 1994
08609	D3776	·	·	·	Scrapped	C F Booth, Rotherham, 2000
08610	D3777	·	·	·	Scrapped	C F Booth, Rotherham, 2004
08611	D3778	·	·	·	Operational	Alstom, Wembley, London
08612	D3779	·	·	·	Scrapped	MC Metals, Springburn, 1991
08613	D3780	H064	·	·	Operational	Weardale Railway
08614	D3781	·	·	·	Scrapped	Gwent Demolition, Margam, 1994
08615	D3782	·	·	·	Operational	LH Group, Barton-u-Needwood
08616	D3783	3783	·	·	Operational	WMT, Tyseley, Birmingham
08617	D3784	·	·	·	Operational	Alstom, Oxley, Wolverhampton
08618	D3785	·	·	·	Scrapped	T J Thomson, Gateshead, 2001
08619	D3786	·	·	·	Scrapped	C F Booth, Rotherham, 2001
08620	D3787	09205	·	·	Scrapped	T J Thomson, Stockton, 2012
08621	D3788	·	·	·	Scrapped	Vic Berry, Leicester, 1990
08622	D3789	H028	19	·	Operational	Weardale Railway
08623	D3790	·	·	·	Stored	HNRC, Hope Cement Works
08624	D3791	·	·	·	Operational	LH Group, Barton-u-Needwood
08625	D3792	·	·	·	Scrapped	HNRC, Kingsbury, 2004
08626	D3793	·	·	·	Scrapped	Cooper's Metals, Allerton, 1994
08627	D3794	·	·	·	Scrapped	Birds, Ipswich, 1997
08628	D3795	·	·	·	Preserved	Private Site
08629	D3796	·	·	·	Operational	Knorr-Bremse Rail UK, Wolverton
08630	D3797	CELSA 3	·	·	Operational	HNRC, Celsa Steel UK, Cardiff
08631	D3798	·	·	·	Operational	Locomotive Services, Crewe
08632	D3799	·	·	·	Operational	EMT, Neville Hill, Leeds
08633	D3800	·	·	·	Preserved	Churnet Valley Railway
08634	D3801	·	·	·	Scrapped	HNRC, Carnforth, 2005
08635	D3802	·	·	·	Preserved	Severn Valley Railway
08636	D3803	·	·	·	Scrapped	BR, Swindon Works, 1983
08637	D3804	·	·	·	Scrapped	MC Metals, Springburn, 1993
08638	D3805	·	·	·	Scrapped	Gwent Demolition, Margam, 1994
08639	D3806	·	·	·	Scrapped	Vic Berry, Leicester, 1989
08640	D3807	·	·	·	Scrapped	MC Metals, Springburn, 1991
08641	D3808	·	·	·	Operational	GWR, Laira, Plymouth
08642	D3809	·	·	·	Scrapped	C F Booth, Rotherham, 2006
08643	D3810	·	·	·	Operational	Aggregate Industries, Merehead
08644	D3811	·	·	·	Operational	GWR, Laira, Plymouth
08645	D3812	·	·	·	Operational	GWR, Landore, Swansea
08646	D3813	·	·	·	Scrapped	EMR, Kingsbury, 2015
08647	D3814	·	·	·	Scrapped	SYPS, Meadowhall, 1997
08648	D3815	·	·	·	Operational	Northern, Heaton, Newcastle
08649	D3816	·	·	·	Operational	Knorr-Bremse Rail UK, Wolverton
08650	D3817	·	·	·	Operational	Hanson Aggregates, Whatley
08651	D3818	·	·	·	Scrapped	EMR, Kingsbury, 2011
08652	D3819	·	·	·	Operational	Aggregate Industries, Merehead
08653	D3820	·	·	·	Stored	Quinton Rail, Long Marston
08654	D3821	·	·	·	Scrapped	C F Booth, Rotherham, 1994

08655	D3822	·	·	·	Scrapped	Wards, Barton-u-Needwood 2007
08656	D3823	·	·	·	Scrapped	Gwent Demolition, Margam, 1994
08657	D3824	·	·	·	Scrapped	Gwent Demolition, Margam, 1994
08658	D3825	·	·	·	Scrapped	Gwent Demolition, Margam, 1994
08659	D3826	·	·	·	Scrapped	Gwent Demolition, Margam, 1995
08660	D3827	·	·	·	Scrapped	Gwent Demolition, Margam, 1994
08661	D3828	·	·	·	Scrapped	EWS, Wigan, 2003
08662	D3829	·	·	·	Scrapped	T J Thomson, Stockton, 2012
08663	D3830	·	·	·	Operational	GWR, St Philip's Marsh, Bristol
08664	D3831	·	·	·	Scrapped	EMR, Kingsbury, 2012
08665	D3832	·	·	·	Scrapped	EMR, Kingsbury, 2011
08666	D3833	·	·	·	Scrapped	HNRC, Kingsbury, 2006
08667	D3834	·	·	·	Scrapped	Gwent Demolition, Margam, 1995
08668	D3835	·	·	·	Scrapped	EMR, Kingsbury, 2011
08669	D3836	·	·	·	Operational	Wabtec Rail, Doncaster Works
08670	D3837	·	·	·	Operational	LNER, Bounds Green, London
08671	D3838	·	·	·	Scrapped	C F Booth, Rotherham, 1994
08672	D3839	·	·	·	Scrapped	Gwent Demolition, Margam, 1994
08673	D3840	·	·	·	Scrapped	S Norton, Liverpool, 2003
08674	D3841	·	·	·	Scrapped	BR, Swindon Works, 1983
08675	D3842	·	·	·	Scrapped	T J Thomson, Stockton, 2007
08676	D3843	·	·	·	Stored	HNRC, East Kent Railway
08677	D3844	·	·	·	Scrapped	C F Booth, Rotherham, 2000
08678	D3845	·	·	·	Operational	WCRC, Carnforth
08679	D3846	·	·	·	Scrapped	C F Booth, Rotherham, 1986
08680	D3847	·	·	·	Scrapped	MC Metals, Motherwell, 1993
08681	D3848	·	·	·	Scrapped	BR, Doncaster Works, 1986
08682	D3849	·	·	·	Operational	Bombardier Transportation, Derby
08683	D3850	·	·	·	Operational	GA, Crown Point, Norwich
08684	D3851	·	·	·	Scrapped	MRJ Phillips, Bicester, 1995
08685	D3852	·	·	·	Stored	HNRC, East Kent Railway
08686	D3853	·	·	·	Scrapped	Cooper's Metals, Allerton, 1994
08687	D3854	08995*	·	·	Preserved	Shillingstone Railway Project
08688	D3855	·	·	·	Scrapped	Cooper's Metals, Allerton, 1994
08689	D3856	·	·	·	Scrapped	EMR, Kingsbury, 2010
08690	D3857	·	·	·	Stored	EMT, Neville Hill, Leeds
08691	D3858	·	·	·	Operational	Freightliner, Felixtowe FLT
08692	D3859	·	·	·	Scrapped	HNRC, Carnforth, 2005
08693	D3860	·	·	·	Scrapped	EWS, Wigan, 2000
08694	D3861	·	·	·	Preserved	Great Central Railway
08695	D3862	·	·	·	Scrapped	C F Booth, Rotherham, 2009
08696	D3863	·	·	·	Operational	Alstom, Wembley, London
08697	D3864	·	·	·	Scrapped	Wards, Ilkeston, 2014
08698	D3865	·	·	·	Scrapped	C F Booth, Rotherham, 2011
08699	D3866	·	·	·	Stored	Weardale Railway
08700	D3867	·	·	·	Operational	Bombardier Transportation, Ilford
08701	D3868	·	·	·	Stored	Quinton Rail, Long Marston
08702	D3869	·	·	·	Scrapped	C F Booth, Rotherham, 2004
08703	D3870	·	·	·	Operational	DB Cargo UK, Springs Branch
08704	D3871	·	·	·	Stored	Nemesis Rail, Burton-upon-Trent
08705	D3872	·	·	·	Scrapped	Birds, Stratford, 1994
08706	D3873	·	·	·	Stored	RSS, Rye Farm, Sutton Coldfield
08707	D3874	·	·	·	Scrapped	HNRC, Carnforth, 2005
08708	D3875	·	·	·	Scrapped	Gwent Demolition, Margam, 1994

CLASS 08 (Continued)

08709	D3876	·	·	·	Stored	RSS, Rye Farm, Sutton Coldfield
08710	D3877	·	·	·	Scrapped	MC Metals, Motherwell, 1993
08711	D3878	·	·	·	Stored	Nemesis Rail, Burton-upon-Trent
08712	D3879	·	·	·	Scrapped	MC Metals, Motherwell, 1993
08713	D3880	·	·	·	Scrapped	C F Booth, Rotherham, 2000
08714	D3881	·	·	·	Stored	HNRC, Hope Cement Works
08715	D3882	·	·	·	Scrapped	T J Thomson, Stockton, 2009
08716	D3883	·	·	·	Scrapped	Vic Berry, Leicester, 1990
08717	D3884	09204	·	·	Operational	Arriva TrainCare, Crewe
08718	D3886	·	·	·	Scrapped	EMR, Ayr, 2000
08719	D3887	·	·	·	Scrapped	Gwent Demolition, Margam, 1994
08720	D3888	·	·	·	Scrapped	T J Thomson, Stockton, 2007
08721	D3889	·	·	·	Operational	Alstom, Widnes Tech Centre
08722	D3890	·	·	·	Scrapped	Vic Berry, Leicester, 1988
08723	D3891	·	·	·	Scrapped	HNRC, Kingsbury, 2002
08724	D3892	·	·	·	Operational	Wabtec Rail, Doncaster Works
08725	D3893	·	·	·	Scrapped	MC Metals, Motherwell, 1993
08726	D3894	·	·	·	Scrapped	Vic Berry, Thornton Yard, 1987
08727	D3895	·	·	·	Scrapped	MC Metals, Motherwell, 1993
08728	D3896	·	·	·	Scrapped	C F Booth, Rotherham, 2009
08729	D3897	·	·	·	Scrapped	Gwent Demolition, Margam, 1994
08730	D3898	·	·	·	Operational	Knorr-Bremse Rail, Springburn
08731	D3899	·	·	·	Scrapped	T J Thomson, Stockton, 2002
08732	D3900	09202	·	·	Scrapped	C F Booth, Rotherham, 2011
08733	D3901	·	·	·	Scrapped	EWS, Wigan, 2000
08734	D3902	·	·	·	Preserved	Dean Forest Railway
08735	D3903	·	·	·	Stored	Arriva TrainCare, Eastleigh
08736	D3904	·	·	·	Scrapped	C F Booth, Rotherham, 2009
08737	D3905	·	·	·	Operational	Locomotive Services, Crewe
08738	D3906	·	·	·	Stored	RSS, Rye Farm, Sutton Coldfield
08739	D3907	·	·	·	Scrapped	S Norton, Liverpool, 2005
08740	D3908	·	·	·	Scrapped	Wards, Barton-u-Needwood 2007
08741	D3909	·	·	·	Scrapped	C F Booth, Rotherham, 1994
08742	D3910	·	·	·	Stored	HNRC, Didcot Railway Centre
08743	D3911	·	·	·	Operational	SembCorp Utilities UK, Wilton
08744	D3912	·	·	·	Scrapped	MC Metals, Springburn, 1993
08745	D3913	·	·	·	Scrapped	C F Booth, Rotherham, 2012
08746	D3914	·	·	·	Scrapped	C F Booth, Rotherham, 2004
08747	D3915	·	·	·	Scrapped	Gwent Demolition, Margam, 1993
08748	D3916	·	·	·	Scrapped	Birds, Ipswich, 1997
08749	D3917	09104	·	·	Scrapped	EMR, Hartlepool, 2011
08750	D3918	·	·	·	Stored	Weardale Railway
08751	D3919	·	·	·	Scrapped	C F Booth, Rotherham, 2004
08752	D3920	·	·	·	Stored	RSS, Rye Farm, Sutton Coldfield
08753	D3921	·	·	·	Scrapped	MC Metals, Motherwell, 1993
08754	D3922	·	·	·	Operational	Mid-Norfolk Railway
08755	D3923	·	·	·	Scrapped	C F Booth, Rotherham, 2000
08756	D3924	·	·	·	Operational	Weardale Railway
08757	D3925	·	·	·	Preserved	Telford Steam Railway
08758	D3926	·	·	·	Scrapped	Ron Hull, Rotherham, 2005
08759	D3927	09106	·	·	Stored	HNRC, Barrow Hill
08760	D3928	·	·	·	Scrapped	MRJ Phillips, Eastleigh, 1996
08761	D3929	·	·	·	Scrapped	MC Metals, Springburn, 1993
08762	D3930	·	·	·	Operational	Weardale Railway

CLASS 08 (Continued)

08763	D3931	·	·	·	Scrapped	MC Metals, Eastfield, 1990
08764	D3932	003	·	·	Operational	Alstom, Polmadie, Glasgow
08765	D3933	·	·	·	Stored	HNRC, Barrow Hill
08766	D3934	09103	·	·	Scrapped	EMR, Ayr, 2010
08767	D3935	·	·	·	Preserved	North Norfolk Railway
08768	D3936	·	·	·	Scrapped	T J Thomson, Stockton, 2007
08769	D3937	968034^	·	·	Preserved	Dean Forest Railway
08770	D3938	·	·	·	Scrapped	T J Thomson, Stockton, 2011
08771	D3939	·	·	·	Scrapped	Gwent Demolition, Margam, 1994
08772	D3940	·	·	·	Preserved	North Norfolk Railway
08773	D3941	·	·	·	Preserved	Embsay & Bolton Abbey Railway
08774	D3942	·	·	·	Operational	A V Dawson, Ayrton Rail Terminal
08775	D3943	·	·	·	Scrapped	C F Booth, Rotherham, 2009
08776	D3944	·	·	·	Scrapped	C F Booth, Rotherham, 2011
08777	D3945	·	·	·	Scrapped	C F Booth, Rotherham, 1997
08778	D3946	·	·	·	Scrapped	Gwent Demolition, Margam, 1994
08779	D3947	·	·	·	Scrapped	MC Metals, Springburn, 1991
08780	D3948	·	·	·	Preserved	Jeremy Hosking, Private Site
08781	D3949	09203	·	·	Scrapped	C F Booth, Rotherham, 2012
08782	D3950	·	·	·	Stored	HNRC, Barrow Hill
08783	D3951	·	·	·	Stored	EMR, Kingsbury
08784	D3952	·	·	·	Preserved	Great Central Railway
08785	D3953	·	·	·	Operational	Freightliner, Trafford Park FLT
08786	D3954	·	·	·	Stored	HNRC, Barrow Hill
08787	D3955	08296	·	·	Operational	Hanson Aggregates, Machen
08788	D3956	·	·	·	Operational	Tata Steel, Shotton Works
08789	D3957	·	·	·	Scrapped	MRJ Phillips, Bicester, 1995
08790	D3958	·	·	·	Operational	AFS, Eastleigh
08791	D3959	·	·	·	Scrapped	MC Metals, Springburn, 1993
08792	D3960	·	·	·	Scrapped	T J Thomson, Stockton, 2007
08793	D3961	·	·	·	Scrapped	C F Booth, Rotherham, 2000
08794	D3962	·	·	·	Scrapped	Gwent Demolition, Margam, 1995
08795	D3963	·	·	·	Operational	GWR, Landore, Swansea
08796	D3964	·	·	·	Scrapped	MC Metals, Springburn, 1993
08797	D3965	·	·	·	Scrapped	Gwent Demolition, Margam, 1994
08798	D3966	·	·	·	Stored	EMR, Attercliffe
08799	D3967	·	·	·	Stored	HNRC, East Kent Railway
08800	D3968	·	·	·	Scrapped	Gwent Demolition, Margam, 1994
08801	D3969	·	·	·	Scrapped	C F Booth, Rotherham, 2004
08802	D3970	·	·	·	Stored	RSS, Rye Farm, Sutton Coldfield
08803	D3971	·	·	·	Scrapped	Gwent Demolition, Margam, 1994
08804	D3972	·	·	·	Stored	HNRC, East Kent Railway
08805	D3973	·	·	·	Operational	WMT, Soho, Birmingham
08806	D3974	·	·	·	Scrapped	T J Thomson, Stockton, 2007
08807	D3975	·	·	·	Scrapped	C F Booth, Rotherham, 2004
08808	D3976	·	·	·	Scrapped	C F Booth, Rotherham, 1992
08809	D3977	24	·	·	Operational	Weardale Railway
08810	D3978	·	·	·	Operational	Arriva TrainCare, Eastleigh
08811	D3979	·	·	·	Scrapped	MRJ Phillips, OOC, 1997
08812	D3980	·	·	·	Scrapped	BR, Swindon Works, 1978
08813	D3981	·	·	·	Scrapped	T J Thomson, Stockton, 2011
08814	D3982	·	·	·	Scrapped	Gwent Demolition, Margam, 1994
08815	D3983	·	·	·	Scrapped	C F Booth, Rotherham, 2005
08816	D3984	·	·	·	Scrapped	Doncaster Works, 1999

08817	D3985	·	·	·	Scrapped	HNRC, Wigan, 2005
08818	D3986	·	·	·	Operational	GBRF, Garston Car Terminal
08819	D3987	·	·	·	Scrapped	C F Booth, Rotherham, 2008
08820	D3988	·	·	·	Scrapped	MC Metals, Springburn, 1991
08821	D3989	·	·	·	Scrapped	Gwent Demolition, Margam, 1993
08822	D3990	·	·	·	Operational	GWR, St Philip's Marsh, Bristol
08823	D3991	·	·	·	Operational	LH Group, Barton-u-Needwood
08824	D3992	IEMD 01	·	·	Stored	HNRC, Barrow Hill
08825	D3993	·	·	·	Preserved	C & PRR
08826	D3994	·	·	·	Scrapped	T J Thomson, Stockton, 2002
08827	D3995	·	·	·	Scrapped	EMR, Kingsbury, 2011
08828	D3996	·	·	·	Scrapped	T J Thomson, Stockton, 2011
08829	D3997	·	·	·	Scrapped	HNRC, Carnforth, 2005
08830	D3998	·	·	·	Preserved	Peak Rail
08831	D3999	·	·	·	Scrapped	Gwent Demolition, Margam, 1994
08832	D4000	09102	·	·	Scrapped	T J Thomson, Stockton, 2011
08833	D4001	09101	·	·	Scrapped	C F Booth, Rotherham, 2011
08834	D4002	·	·	·	Operational	Northern, Allerton, Liverpool
08835	D4003	09105	·	·	Scrapped	C F Booth, Rotherham, 2011
08836	D4004	·	·	·	Operational	GWR, Reading
08837	D4005	·	·	·	Scrapped	S Norton, Liverpool, 2005
08838	D4006	·	·	·	Scrapped	Gwent Demolition, Margam, 1994
08839	D4007	·	·	·	Scrapped	Gwent Demolition, Margam, 1993
08840	D4008	·	·	·	Scrapped	Cooper's Metals, Allerton, 1994
08841	D4009	·	·	·	Scrapped	MC Metals, Springburn, 1993
08842	D4010	·	·	·	Scrapped	EMR, Kingsbury, 2012
08843	D4011	·	·	·	Scrapped	MC Metals, Springburn, 1991
08844	D4012	·	·	·	Scrapped	EMR, Kingsbury, 2012
08845	D4013	09107	·	·	Scrapped	EMR, Kingsbury, 2011
08846	D4014	003	·	·	Operational	RSS, Rye Farm, Sutton Coldfield
08847	D4015	·	·	·	Operational	Mid-Norfolk Railway
08848	D4016	·	·	·	Scrapped	Gwent Demolition, Margam, 1994
08849	D4017	·	·	·	Scrapped	MRJ Phillips, Crewe Works, 1997
08850	D4018	4018	·	·	Operational	North Yorkshire Moors Railway
08851	D4019	·	·	·	Scrapped	MC Metals, Springburn, 1991
08852	D4020	·	·	·	Scrapped	MC Metals, Springburn, 1989
08853	D4021	·	·	·	Operational	Wabtec Rail, Doncaster Works
08854	D4022	·	·	·	Scrapped	EMR, Kingsbury, 2012
08855	D4023	·	·	·	Scrapped	Doncaster Works, 1999
08856	D4024	·	·	·	Scrapped	T J Thomson, Stockton, 2011
08857	D4025	·	·	·	Scrapped	MC Metals, Springburn, 1993
08858	D4026	·	·	·	Scrapped	Cooper's Metals, Allerton, 1994
08859	D4027	·	·	·	Scrapped	Gwent Demolition, Margam, 1994
08860	D4028	·	·	·	Scrapped	BR, Swindon Works, 1981
08861	D4029	·	·	·	Scrapped	BR, Swindon Works, 1982
08862	D4030	·	·	·	Scrapped	BR, Swindon Works, 1981
08863	D4031	·	·	·	Scrapped	BR, Swindon Works, 1981
08864	D4032	·	·	·	Scrapped	BR, Swindon Works, 1982
08865	D4033	·	·	·	Stored	HNRC, Hope Cement Works
08866	D4034	·	·	·	Scrapped	EMR, Kingsbury, 2012
08867	D4035	·	·	·	Scrapped	T J Thomson, Stockton, 2007
08868	D4036	·	·	·	Operational	Arriva TrainCare, Crewe
08869	D4037	·	·	·	Scrapped	EMR, Kingsbury, 2011
08870	D4038	H024	·	·	Operational	Hanson Cement, Ketton

CLASS 08 (Continued)

08871	D4039	H074	22	·	Operational	Tata Steel, Llanelli
08872	D4040	·	·	·	Stored	EMR, Attercliffe
08873	D4041	·	·	·	Operational	LH Group, Barton-u-Needwood
08874	D4042	·	·	·	Operational	Tata Steel, Shotton Works
08875	D4043	·	·	·	Scrapped	C F Booth, Kilnhurst, 1993
08876	D4044	·	·	·	Scrapped	Hudsons, Doncaster, 1991
08877	D4045	·	·	·	Stored	HNRC, Barrow Hill
08878	D4046	·	·	·	Scrapped	MRJ Phillips, OOC, 1997
08879	D4047	·	·	·	Operational	AFS, Eastleigh
08880	D4048	·	·	·	Scrapped	S Norton, Liverpool, 2005
08881	D4095	·	·	·	Preserved	Somerset & Dorset Railway
08882	D4096	·	·	·	Scrapped	Ron Hull, Rotherham, 2005
08883	D4097	·	·	·	Scrapped	T J Thomson, Stockton, 2007
08884	D4098	·	·	·	Scrapped	EMR, Kingsbury, 2010
08885	D4115	H042	18	·	Stored	Weardale Railway
08886	D4116	·	·	·	Scrapped	EMR, Kingsbury, 2012
08887	D4117	·	·	·	Operational	Alstom, Wembley, London
08888	D4118	·	·	·	Preserved	Kent & East Sussex Railway
08889	D4119	·	·	·	Scrapped	Gwent Demolition, Margam, 1994
08890	D4120	·	·	·	Scrapped	C F Booth, Rotherham, 2009
08891	D4121	·	·	·	Stored	Nemesis Rail, Burton-upon-Trent
08892	D4122	·	·	·	Operational	Bombardier, Ashfordby
08893	D4123	·	·	·	Scrapped	Ron Hull, Rotherham, 2005
08894	D4124	·	·	·	Scrapped	T J Thomson, Stockton, 2007
08895	D4125	·	·	·	Scrapped	Gwent Demolition, Margam, 2000
08896	D4126	·	·	·	Preserved	Severn Valley Railway
08897	D4127	·	·	·	Scrapped	C F Booth, Rotherham, 2011
08898	D4128	·	·	·	Scrapped	C F Booth, Doncaster, 1998
08899	D4129	·	·	·	Operational	EMT, Etches Park, Derby
08900	D4130	·	·	·	Scrapped	T J Thomson, Stockton, 2009
08901	D4131	·	·	·	Scrapped	Ron Hull, Rotherham, 2005
08902	D4132	·	·	·	Scrapped	T J Thomson, Stockton, 2007
08903	D4133	·	·	·	Operational	SembCorp Utilities UK, Wilton
08904	D4134	·	·	·	Operational	HNRC, Celsa Steel UK, Cardiff
08905	D4135	·	·	·	Stored	HNRC, Hope Cement Works
08906	D4136	·	·	·	Scrapped	T J Thomson, Stockton, 2006
08907	D4137	·	·	·	Preserved	Great Central Railway
08908	D4138	·	·	·	Stored	EMT, Neville Hill, Leeds
08909	D4139	·	·	·	Scrapped	C F Booth, Rotherham, 2012
08910	D4140	·	·	·	Scrapped	T J Thomson, Stockton, 2007
08911	D4141	·	·	·	Preserved	National Railway Museum Shildon
08912	D4142	·	·	·	Stored	A V Dawson, Ayrton Rail Terminal
08913	D4143	·	·	·	Stored	LH Group, Barton-u-Needwood
08914	D4144	·	·	·	Scrapped	C F Booth, Rotherham, 2005
08915	D4145	·	·	·	Preserved	North Tyneside Steam Railway
08916	D4146	·	·	·	Scrapped	Cooper's Metals, Allerton, 1994
08917	D4147	·	·	·	Scrapped	Cooper's Metals, Allerton, 1994
08918	D4148	·	·	·	Stored	Nemesis Rail, Burton-upon-Trent
08919	D4149	·	·	·	Scrapped	C F Booth, Rotherham, 2009
08920	D4150	·	·	·	Scrapped	EMR, Kingsbury, 2011
08921	D4151	·	·	·	Stored	EMR, Kingsbury
08922	D4152	·	·	·	Preserved	Great Central Railway North
08923	D4153	·	·	·	Scrapped	Birds, Stratford, 1994
08924	D4154	1	CELSA 2	·	Operational	HNRC, Celsa Steel UK, Cardiff

CLASS 08 (Continued)

08925	D4155	·	·	·	Operational	GBRF,Whitemoor Yard, March
08926	D4156	·	·	·	Scrapped	EMR, Kingsbury, 2007
08927	D4157	·	·	·	Operational	EMD, Roberts Road, Doncaster
08928	D4158	·	·	·	Scrapped	EMR, Kingsbury, 2010
08929	D4159	·	·	·	Scrapped	Gwent Demolition, Margam, 1994
08930	D4160	·	·	·	Scrapped	MC Metals, Springburn, 1991
08931	D4161	·	·	·	Scrapped	Ron Hull, Rotherham, 2005
08932	D4162	·	·	·	Scrapped	HNRC, Crewe, 2005
08933	D4163	·	·	·	Operational	Aggregate Industries, Merehead
08934	D4164	·	·	·	Operational	GBRF, Dagenham Car Terminal
08935	D4165	·	·	·	Scrapped	Gwent Demolition, Margam, 1994
08936	D4166	·	·	·	Operational	Weardale Railway
08937	D4167	·	·	·	Operational	Dartmoor Railway
08938	D4168	·	·	·	Scrapped	EWS, Wigan, 2000
08939	D4169	·	·	·	Stored	RSS, Rye Farm, Sutton Coldfield
08940	D4170	·	·	·	Scrapped	S Norton, Liverpool, 2003
08941	D4171	·	·	·	Scrapped	C F Booth, Rotherham, 2011
08942	D4172	·	·	·	Scrapped	T J Thomson, Stockton, 2007
08943	D4173	PET 2	·	·	Operational	Bombardier, Central Rivers
08944	D4174	·	·	·	Preserved	East Lancashire Railway
08945	D4175	·	·	·	Scrapped	Gwent Demolition, Margam, 1993
08946	D4176	·	·	·	Scrapped	Goodmans Sutton Coldfield, 2007
08947	D4177	·	·	·	Operational	Hanson Aggregates, Whatley
08948	D4178	·	·	·	Operational	Eurostar, Temple Mills, London
08949	D4179	·	·	·	Scrapped	Gwent Demolition, Margam, 1994
08950	D4180	·	·	·	Stored	EMT, Neville Hill, Leeds
08951	D4181	·	·	·	Scrapped	C F Booth, Rotherham, 2011
08952	D4182	·	·	·	Scrapped	EWS, Wigan, 2000
08953	D4183	·	·	·	Scrapped	EMR, Attercliffe, 2012
08954	D4184	·	·	·	Operational	Alstom, Polmadie, Glasgow
08955	D4185	·	·	·	Scrapped	C F Booth, Rotherham, 2009
08956	D4186	·	·	·	Operational	Bombardier, Ashfordby
08957	D4191	·	·	·	Scrapped	HNRC, Kingsbury, 2004
08958	D4192	·	·	·	Scrapped	EWS, Wigan, 2001
·	D3000	13000	·	·	Preserved	Peak Rail
·	D3001	13001	·	·	Scrapped	BR, Doncaster Works, 1975
·	D3002	13002	·	·	Preserved	Plym Valley Railway
·	D3003	13003	·	·	Scrapped	Merehead, 1974
·	D3006	13006	966507+	·	Scrapped	BR, Doncaster Works, 1979
·	D3011	13011	·	·	Scrapped	Marple & Gillott, Sheffield, 1985
·	D3012	13012	·	·	Scrapped	BR, Swindon Works, 1973
·	D3013	13013	·	·	Scrapped	Cashmore's, Newport, 1973
·	D3014	13014	·	·	Preserved	Dartmouth Steam Railway
·	D3014	13019	·	·	Preserved	Cambrian Heritage Railways
·	D3020	13020	·	·	Scrapped	BR, Derby Works, 1975
·	D3024	13024	·	·	Scrapped	BR, Doncaster Works, 1974
·	D3026	13026	·	·	Scrapped	BR, Swindon Works, 1973
·	D3028	13028	·	·	Scrapped	BR, Doncaster Works, 1975
·	D3034	13034	·	·	Scrapped	BR, Derby Works, 1973
·	D3035	13035	966508+	·	Scrapped	BR, Doncaster Works, 1980
·	D3037	13037	966510+	·	Scrapped	BR, Doncaster Works, 1979
·	D3038	13038	·	·	Scrapped	NCB Bates Colliery, 1980
·	D3045	13045	·	·	Scrapped	BR, Glasgow Works, 1976
·	D3047	13047	·	·	Operational	LAMCO, Liberia

·	D3051	13051	·	·	Scrapped	BR, Derby Works, 1973
·	D3052	13052	·	·	Scrapped	Cashmore's, Newport, 1974
·	D3053	13053	·	·	Scrapped	BR, Doncaster Works, 1975
·	D3069	13069	966509+	·	Scrapped	BR, Thornaby, 1980
·	D3078	13078	966506+	·	Scrapped	BR, Doncaster Works, 1979
·	D3087	13087	·	·	Scrapped	Wards, Walsall PS, 1983
·	D3088	13088	·	·	Scrapped	NCB Bates Colliery, 1985
·	D3092	13092	·	·	Operational	LAMCO, Liberia
·	D3093	13093	·	·	Scrapped	Cohen's, Kettering, 1974
·	D3094	13094	·	·	Operational	LAMCO, Liberia
·	D3095	13095	·	·	Scrapped	BR, Swindon Works, 1973
·	D3096	13096	·	·	Scrapped	BR, Selhurst, 1972
·	D3097	13097	·	·	Scrapped	BR, Swindon Works, 1973
·	D3098	13098	·	·	Operational	LAMCO, Liberia
·	D3099	13099	·	·	Scrapped	P Woods, Queenborough, 1973
·	D3100	13100	·	·	Operational	LAMCO, Liberia
·	D3101	13101	·	·	Preserved	Great Central Railway
·	D3172	13172	·	·	Scrapped	BR, Derby Works, 1972
·	D3183	13183	·	·	Scrapped	NCB Merthyr Vale Colliery, 1987
·	D3193	13193	·	·	Scrapped	BR, Derby Works, 1967
·	D3255	13255	·	·	Preserved	Private Site
·	D3261	13261	·	·	Preserved	Swindon & Cricklade Railway
·	D3697	13002(S)	·	·	Scrapped	BR, Swindon Works, 1982
·	D3698	13003(S)	·	·	Scrapped	BR, Doncaster Works, 1986
·	D3885		·	·	Scrapped	BR, Glasgow Works, 1972
·	D4187	13002(M)	·	·	Scrapped	BR, Swindon Works, 1982
·	D4188	13003(M)	·	·	Scrapped	BR, Doncaster Works, 1986
·	D4189	13001(S)	·	·	Scrapped	BR, Swindon Works, 1985
·	D4190	13001(M)	·	·	Scrapped	BR, Swindon Works, 1985

(M) Rebuilt as master unit for Class 13   (S) Rebuilt as slave unit for Class 13

* Rebuilt with cut-down cabs for use on the Burry Port & Gwendraeth valley line
+ Converted to snowplough carrying ADB prefix
~ Used for research-departmental purposes and renumbered with RDB prefix
^ Used for static training purposes and renumbered with ADB prefix
- Renumbered for departmental use

Class 08 Names:

08238	Charlie	08575	The Doncaster Postman
08389	NOEL KIRTON OBE	08578	Lybert Dickinson
08442	Richard J Wenham Eastleigh 1989 - 1999	08585	Vicky
08451	M.A. SMITH	LONGSIGHT TMD	08590	RED LION
08460	SPIRIT OF THE OAK	08593	Colchester TMD
08480	TOTON No.1	08600	Ivor
08482	DON GATES 1952 - 2000	08602	BOMBARDIER
08483	DUSTY Driver David Miller	08604	PHANTOM
08484	CAPTAIN NATHANIEL DARELL	08611	DOWNHILL CS	MA Smith
08495	NOEL KIRTON OBE	08616	Cookie	TYSELEY 100
08502	Lybert Dickinson	08617	Steve Purser
08525	DUNCAN BEDFORD	08624	Rambo Paul Ramsey
08561	EWS	08629	BRML Wolverton Level 5
08562	The Doncaster Postman	08630	Bob Brown
08568	St. Rollox	08631	EAGLE C.U.R.C.

CLASS 08 (Continued)

08633	The Sorter	08799	Andy Bower | FRED
08644	Laira Diesel Depot 50 Years 1962-2012	08804	RICHARD J. WENHAM
08645	Mike Baggott	08805	Concorde
08647	CRIMPSALL	08818	Molly
08649	G.H. Stratton | Bradwell	08822	John | Dave Mills
08650	ISLE OF GRAIN	08833	Liverpool St Pilot
08661	Europa	08844	Chris Wren 1955-2002
08663	Jack | St. Silas	08846	Bombardier Transportation
08664	DON GATES 1952-2000	08869	The Canary
08669	Bob Machin	08872	Tony Long, Stratford 1971-2002
08678	Artila	08874	Catherine
08682	Lionheart	08879	Sheffield Children's Hospital
08690	DAVID THIRKILL	08888	Postman's Pride
08691	Terri	08891	JR 1951 - 2005
08694	PAT BARR	08896	STEPHEN DENT
08696	Longsight TMD	08899	Midland Counties Railway 175
08701	Gateshead TMD 1852-1991 | The Sorter	08903	John W Antill
	TYNE 100	08905	DANNY DANIELS
08709	MOLLY'S DAY	08907	MOLLY'S DAY
08711	EAGLE C.U.R.C.	08908	IVAN STEPHENSON
08714	Cambridge	08911	MATEY
08721	STARLET | M A SMITH | DOWNHILL CS	08919	Steep Holm
	Longsight TMD	08928	BILL
08730	The Caley	08943	PET II
08736	Deanside Transit	08950	Neville Hill 1st | David Lightfoot
08738	SILVER FOX	08951	FRED
08743	Angie | Bryan Turner	08958	Serco Railnet
08752	BRIAN	08991	KIDWELLY
08757	EAGLE C.U.R.C.	08992	GWENDRAETH
08772	CAMULODUNUM	08993	ASHBURNHAM
08774	ARTHUR VERNON DAWSON	08994	GWENDRAETH
08782	CASTLETON WORKS		Spirit of Innovation
08790	M.A. SMITH | STARLET | Steve Purser	08995	KIDWELLY

CLASS 09

Total Built	38 (26 & 12*)	Formation	0-6-0	Max T.E.	25,000 lbf
Date Built	1959-61 & 1992-93*	Max Speed	27.5 mph	P.A.R.	269 hp
Builder	BR Darlington & Horwich	Weight	49 t	R.A.	5
Engine	English Electric 6KT, 400 hp	Brakes	Vacuum / Air & Vac	Supply	N/A

09001	D3665	·	·	·	Preserved	Peak Rail
09002	D3666	·	·	·	Operational	GBRF,Whitemoor Yard, March
09003	D3667	·	·	·	Scrapped	EMR, Kingsbury, 2011
09004	D3668	·	·	·	Preserved	Swindon & Cricklade Railway
09005	D3669	·	·	·	Scrapped	C F Booth, Rotherham, 2011
09006	D3670	·	·	·	Stored	Nemesis Rail, Burton-upon-Trent
09007	D3671	·	·	·	Operational	London Overground, Willesden
09008	D3719	·	·	·	Scrapped	EMR, Kingsbury, 2011
09009	D3720	·	·	·	Operational	GBRF, Miles Platting, Manchester
09010	D3721	·	·	·	Preserved	South Devon Railway
09011	D4099	·	·	·	Scrapped	EMR, Kingsbury, 2011
09012	D4100	·	·	·	Preserved	Severn Valley Railway
09013	D4101	·	·	·	Scrapped	C F Booth, Rotherham, 2011

09014	D4102	·	·	·	Stored	Nemesis Rail, Burton-upon-Trent
09015	D4103	·	·	·	Stored	RSS, Rye Farm, Sutton Coldfield
09016	D4104	·	·	·	Preserved	National Railway Museum, York
09017	D4105	97806+	·	·	Preserved	National Railway Museum, York
09018	D4106	·	·	·	Preserved	Bluebell Railway
09019	D4107	·	·	·	Preserved	West Somerset Railway
09020	D4108	·	·	·	Scrapped	EMR, Kingsbury, 2012
09021	D4109	·	·	·	Scrapped	C F Booth, Rotherham, 2008
09022	D4110	·	·	·	Operational	Victoria Group, Port of Boston
09023	D4111	·	·	·	Stored	EMR, Attercliffe
09024	D4112	·	·	·	Preserved	East Lancashire Railway
09025	D4113	·	·	·	Preserved	Lavender Line
09026	D4114	·	·	·	Preserved	Spa Valley Railway
09101*	08833	·	·	·	Scrapped	C F Booth, Rotherham, 2011
09102*	08832	·	·	·	Scrapped	T J Thomson, Stockton, 2011
09103*	08766	·	·	·	Scrapped	EMR, Ayr, 2010
09104*	08749	·	·	·	Scrapped	EMR, Hartlepool, 2011
09105*	08835	·	·	·	Scrapped	C F Booth, Rotherham, 2011
09106*	08759	·	·	·	Stored	HNRC, Barrow Hill
09107*	08845	·	·	·	Preserved	Severn Valley Railway
09201*	08421	·	·	·	Stored	HNRC, Hope Cement Works
09202*	08732	·	·	·	Scrapped	C F Booth, Rotherham, 2011
09203*	08781	·	·	·	Scrapped	C F Booth, Rotherham, 2012
09204*	08717	·	·	·	Operational	Arriva TrainCare, Crewe
09205*	08620	·	·	·	Scrapped	T J Thomson, Stockton, 2012

Class 09/1 fitted with 110V equipment   Class 09/2 fitted with 90V equipment

* Rebuilt from Class 08s to become sub-class 09/1 & 09/2 in 1992/93
\+ Renumbered for departmental use

Class 09 Names:

09008	Sheffield Children's Hospital		09012	Dick Hardy
09009	Three Bridges CED		09026	William Pearson | Cedric Wares

CLASS 10

Total Built	161	Formation	0-6-0	Max T.E.	35,000 lbf
Date Built	1953-62	Max Speed	15 mph	P.A.R.	194 hp
Builder	BR Darlington & Doncaster	Weight	49 t	R.A.	5
Engine	Blackstone ER6T, 400 hp	Brakes	Vacuum	Supply	N/A

·	D3137	13137	·	·	Scrapped	C F Booth, Doncaster, 1970
·	D3138	13138	·	·	Scrapped	C F Booth, Rotherham, 1973
·	D3139	13139	·	·	Scrapped	C F Booth, Rotherham, 1969
·	D3140	13140	·	·	Scrapped	C F Booth, Rotherham, 1969
·	D3141	13141	·	·	Scrapped	C F Booth, Rotherham, 1972
·	D3142	13142	·	·	Scrapped	C F Booth, Rotherham, 1969
·	D3143	13143	·	·	Scrapped	Cohen's, Kettering, 1970
·	D3144	13144	·	·	Scrapped	Hughes Bolckows, Blyth, 1969
·	D3145	13145	·	·	Scrapped	C F Booth, Rotherham, 1973
·	D3146	13146	·	·	Scrapped	Hughes Bolckows, Blyth, 1968
·	D3147	13147	·	·	Scrapped	C F Booth, Rotherham, 1969
·	D3148	13148	·	·	Scrapped	C F Booth, Rotherham, 1969

·	D3149	13149	·	·	Scrapped	C F Booth, Rotherham, 1970
·	D3150	13150	·	·	Scrapped	C F Booth, Rotherham, 1969
·	D3151	13151	·	·	Scrapped	Hughes Bolckows, Blyth, 1968
·	D3439	·	·	·	Scrapped	Steelbreaking, Chesterfield, 1969
·	D3440	·	·	·	Scrapped	Cohen's, Kettering, 1969
·	D3441	·	·	·	Scrapped	Cohen's, Kettering, 1969
·	D3442	·	·	·	Scrapped	C F Booth, Rotherham, 1969
·	D3443	·	·	·	Scrapped	C F Booth, Rotherham, 1969
·	D3444	·	·	·	Scrapped	Cohen's, Kettering, 1969
·	D3445	·	·	·	Scrapped	Cox & Danks, North Acton, 1969
·	D3446	·	·	·	Scrapped	Steelbreaking, Chesterfield, 1969
·	D3447	·	·	·	Scrapped	C F Booth, Rotherham, 1969
·	D3448	·	·	·	Scrapped	Steelbreaking, Chesterfield, 1969
·	D3449	·	·	·	Scrapped	C F Booth, Rotherham, 1968
·	D3450	·	·	·	Scrapped	C F Booth, Rotherham, 1969
·	D3451	·	·	·	Scrapped	C F Booth, Rotherham, 1969
·	D3452	·	·	·	Preserved	Bodmin & Wenford Railway
·	D3453	·	·	·	Scrapped	C F Booth, Rotherham, 1969
·	D3473	·	·	·	Scrapped	C F Booth, Rotherham, 1969
·	D3474	·	·	·	Scrapped	C F Booth, Rotherham, 1969
·	D3475	·	·	·	Scrapped	C F Booth, Rotherham, 1969
·	D3476	·	·	·	Scrapped	T J Thomson, Stockton, 2009
·	D3477	·	·	·	Scrapped	Cohen's, Kettering, 1969
·	D3478	·	·	·	Scrapped	C F Booth, Rotherham, 1969
·	D3479	·	·	·	Scrapped	Cohen's, Kettering, 1969
·	D3480	·	·	·	Scrapped	Steelbreaking, Chesterfield, 1969
·	D3481	·	·	·	Scrapped	C F Booth, Rotherham, 1968
·	D3482	·	·	·	Scrapped	C F Booth, Rotherham, 1969
·	D3483	·	·	·	Scrapped	Cohen's, Kettering, 1969
·	D3484	·	·	·	Scrapped	Steelbreaking, Chesterfield, 1969
·	D3485	·	·	·	Scrapped	Cohen's, Kettering, 1969
·	D3486	·	·	·	Scrapped	C F Booth, Rotherham, 1971
·	D3487	·	·	·	Scrapped	C F Booth, Rotherham, 1969
·	D3488	·	·	·	Scrapped	Cohen's, Kettering, 1969
·	D3489	·	·	·	Preserved	Spa Valley Railway
·	D3490	·	·	·	Scrapped	C F Booth, Rotherham, 1969
·	D3491	·	·	·	Scrapped	Cohen's, Kettering, 1969
·	D3492	·	·	·	Scrapped	Cohen's, Kettering, 1969
·	D3493	·	·	·	Scrapped	C F Booth, Rotherham, 1969
·	D3494	·	·	·	Scrapped	Cohen's, Kettering, 1969
·	D3495	·	·	·	Scrapped	C F Booth, Rotherham, 1969
·	D3496	·	·	·	Scrapped	BR, Doncaster Works, 1968
·	D3497	·	·	·	Scrapped	ECC Ports Ltd, Fowey, 1970
·	D3498	·	·	·	Scrapped	C F Booth, Rotherham, 1969
·	D3499	·	·	·	Scrapped	C F Booth, Rotherham, 1968
·	D3500	·	·	·	Scrapped	Cashmore's, Great Bridge, 1968
·	D3501	·	·	·	Scrapped	C F Booth, Rotherham, 1969
·	D3502	·	·	·	Scrapped	Cashmore's, Great Bridge, 1968
·	D3612	·	·	·	Scrapped	Cohen's, Kettering, 1969
·	D3613	·	·	·	Scrapped	NCB Moor Green Colliery, 1985
·	D3614	·	·	·	Scrapped	Steelbreaking, Chesterfield, 1969
·	D3615	·	·	·	Scrapped	Cohen's, Kettering, 1969
·	D3616	·	·	·	Scrapped	Steelbreaking, Chesterfield, 1969
·	D3617	·	·	·	Scrapped	Steelbreaking, Chesterfield, 1969

CLASS 10 (Continued)

·	D3618	·	·	·	Scrapped	NCB Moor Green Colliery, 1985
·	D3619	·	·	·	Scrapped	NCB Moor Green Colliery, 1985
·	D3620	·	·	·	Scrapped	Slag Reduction Co, Ickles, 1967
·	D3621	·	·	·	Scrapped	C F Booth, Rotherham, 1969
·	D3622	·	·	·	Scrapped	C F Booth, Rotherham, 1969
·	D3623	·	·	·	Scrapped	C F Booth, Rotherham, 1969
·	D3624	·	·	·	Scrapped	C F Booth, Rotherham, 1969
·	D3625	·	·	·	Scrapped	C F Booth, Rotherham, 1969
·	D3626	·	·	·	Scrapped	C F Booth, Rotherham, 1969
·	D3627	·	·	·	Scrapped	C F Booth, Rotherham, 1969
·	D3628	·	·	·	Scrapped	C F Booth, Rotherham, 1968
·	D3629	·	·	·	Scrapped	Cohen's, Kettering, 1969
·	D3630	·	·	·	Scrapped	Cox & Danks, Park Royal, 1969
·	D3631	·	·	·	Scrapped	BR, Stratford, 1967
·	D3632	·	·	·	Scrapped	C F Booth, Rotherham, 1969
·	D3633	·	·	·	Scrapped	Cohen's, Kettering, 1969
·	D3634	·	·	·	Scrapped	C F Booth, Rotherham, 1972
·	D3635	·	·	·	Scrapped	Cohen's, Kettering, 1969
·	D3636	·	·	·	Scrapped	BR, Stratford, 1969
·	D3637	·	·	·	Scrapped	Cohen's, Kettering, 1969
·	D3638	·	·	·	Scrapped	NCB Ashington, 1975
·	D3639	·	·	·	Scrapped	Conakry, Guinea, 1970
·	D3640	·	·	·	Scrapped	Cohen's, Kettering, 1969
·	D3641	·	·	·	Scrapped	C F Booth, Rotherham, 1972
·	D3642	·	·	·	Scrapped	BSC, Appleby Frodingham, 1978
·	D3643	·	·	·	Scrapped	Cohen's, Kettering, 1969
·	D3644	·	·	·	Scrapped	C F Booth, Rotherham, 1971
·	D3645	·	·	·	Scrapped	C F Booth, Rotherham, 1969
·	D3646	·	·	·	Scrapped	C F Booth, Rotherham, 1971
·	D3647	·	·	·	Scrapped	C F Booth, Rotherham, 1970
·	D3648	·	·	·	Scrapped	NCB Bates Colliery, 1977
·	D3649	·	·	·	Scrapped	Conakry, Guinea, 1970
·	D3650	·	·	·	Scrapped	C F Booth, Rotherham, 1972
·	D3651	·	·	·	Scrapped	C F Booth, Rotherham, 1972
·	D4049	·	·	·	Scrapped	Cohen's, Kettering, 1972
·	D4050	·	·	·	Scrapped	C F Booth, Rotherham, 1972
·	D4051	·	·	·	Scrapped	C F Booth, Rotherham, 1972
·	D4052	·	·	·	Scrapped	C F Booth, Rotherham, 1971
·	D4053	·	·	·	Scrapped	C F Booth, Rotherham, 1972
·	D4054	·	·	·	Scrapped	Cohen's, Kettering, 1973
·	D4055	·	·	·	Scrapped	C F Booth, Rotherham, 1972
·	D4056	·	·	·	Scrapped	NCB Shilbottle Colliery, 1983
·	D4057	·	·	·	Scrapped	C F Booth, Rotherham, 1972
·	D4058	·	·	·	Scrapped	Cohen's, Kettering, 1972
·	D4059	·	·	·	Scrapped	Cohen's, Kettering, 1972
·	D4060	·	·	·	Scrapped	C F Booth, Rotherham, 1972
·	D4061	·	·	·	Scrapped	C F Booth, Rotherham, 1972
·	D4062	·	·	·	Scrapped	C F Booth, Rotherham, 1972
·	D4063	·	·	·	Scrapped	Cohen's, Kettering, 1973
·	D4064	·	·	·	Scrapped	C F Booth, Rotherham, 1969
·	D4065	·	·	·	Scrapped	C F Booth, Rotherham, 1972
·	D4066	·	·	·	Scrapped	Cohen's, Kettering, 1973
·	D4067	10119	·	·	Preserved	Great Central Railway
·	D4068	·	·	·	Scrapped	NCB Whittle Colliery, 1985

CLASS 10 (Continued)

·	D4069	·	·	·	Scrapped	NCB Whittle Colliery, 1985
·	D4070	·	·	·	Scrapped	NCB Whittle Colliery, 1985
·	D4071	·	·	·	Scrapped	Cohen's, Kettering, 1969
·	D4072	·	·	·	Scrapped	NCB Lambton Works, 1985
·	D4073	·	·	·	Scrapped	Cohen's, Kettering, 1973
·	D4074	·	·	·	Scrapped	NCB Lambton Works, 1978
·	D4075	·	·	·	Scrapped	Cohen's, Kettering, 1973
·	D4076	·	·	·	Scrapped	C F Booth, Rotherham, 1969
·	D4077	·	·	·	Scrapped	C F Booth, Rotherham, 1971
·	D4078	·	·	·	Scrapped	Cohen's, Kettering, 1973
·	D4079	·	·	·	Scrapped	Cohen's, Kettering, 1973
·	D4080	·	·	·	Scrapped	C F Booth, Rotherham, 1968
·	D4081	·	·	·	Scrapped	C F Booth, Rotherham, 1968
·	D4082	·	·	·	Scrapped	C F Booth, Rotherham, 1968
·	D4083	·	·	·	Scrapped	C F Booth, Rotherham, 1969
·	D4084	·	·	·	Scrapped	C F Booth, Rotherham, 1969
·	D4085	·	·	·	Scrapped	C F Booth, Rotherham, 1969
·	D4086	·	·	·	Scrapped	Cohen's, Kettering, 1969
·	D4087	·	·	·	Scrapped	Cohen's, Kettering, 1969
·	D4088	·	·	·	Scrapped	C F Booth, Rotherham, 1969
·	D4089	·	·	·	Scrapped	C F Booth, Rotherham, 1969
·	D4090	·	·	·	Scrapped	Cohen's, Kettering, 1969
·	D4091	·	·	·	Scrapped	C F Booth, Rotherham, 1969
·	D4092	·	·	·	Preserved	Barrow Hill
·	D4093	·	·	·	Scrapped	Cohen's, Kettering, 1969
·	D4094	·	·	·	Scrapped	Cohen's, Kettering, 1060

CLASS 11

Total Built	106	Formation	0-6-0	Max T.E.	35,000 lbf
Date Built	1945-52	Max Speed	20 mph	P.A.R.	194 hp
Builder	LMS & BR Derby & Darlington	Weight	48 t	R.A.	5
Engine	English Electric 6KT, 350 hp	Brakes	Vacuum	Supply	N/A

·	12033	7120	·	·	Scrapped	Cashmore's, Great Bridge, 1970
·	12034	7121	·	·	Scrapped	J McWilliams, Shettleston, 1969
·	12035	7122	·	·	Scrapped	J McWilliams, Shettleston, 1969
·	12036	7123	·	·	Scrapped	Cashmore's, Great Bridge, 1970
·	12037	7124	·	·	Scrapped	Cashmore's, Great Bridge, 1970
·	12038	7125	·	·	Scrapped	Cohen's, Kettering, 1971
·	12039	7126	·	·	Scrapped	Cashmore's, Great Bridge, 1970
·	12040	7127	·	·	Scrapped	Cashmore's, Great Bridge, 1970
·	12041	7128	·	·	Scrapped	BR, Swindon Works, 1969
·	12042	7129	·	·	Scrapped	Cashmore's, Newport, 1969
·	12043	7130	·	·	Scrapped	Cashmore's, Great Bridge, 1969
·	12044	7131	·	·	Scrapped	Cashmore's, Great Bridge, 1969
·	12045	·	·	·	Scrapped	Cashmore's, Great Bridge, 1969
·	12046	·	·	·	Scrapped	Cohen's, Bletchley, 1969
·	12047	·	·	·	Scrapped	Cashmore's, Great Bridge, 1970
·	12048	·	·	·	Scrapped	Cashmore's, Great Bridge, 1970
·	12049	·	·	·	Scrapped	Mid-Hants Railway, 2010
·	12050	·	·	·	Scrapped	NCB Philadelphia, 1971
·	12051	·	·	·	Scrapped	Cashmore's, Great Bridge, 1973
·	12052	·	·	·	Preserved	Caledonian Railway

·	12053	·	·	·	Scrapped	Birds, Long Marston, 1971
·	12054	·	·	·	Scrapped	A R Adams, Newport, 1984
·	12055	·	·	·	Scrapped	C F Booth, Rotherham, 1972
·	12056	·	·	·	Scrapped	Cohen's, Kettering, 1973
·	12057	·	·	·	Scrapped	Cashmore's, Great Bridge, 1970
·	12058	·	·	·	Scrapped	Cashmore's, Newport, 1973
·	12059	·	·	·	Scrapped	Cashmore's, Great Bridge, 1969
·	12060	·	·	·	Scrapped	NCB Philadelphia, 1985
·	12061	·	·	·	Preserved	Peak Rail
·	12062	·	·	·	Scrapped	BR, Derby Works, 1971
·	12063	·	·	·	Scrapped	NCB Nantgarw Coking Plant 1987
·	12064	·	·	·	Scrapped	Cashmore's, Great Bridge, 1969
·	12065	·	·	·	Scrapped	C F Booth, Rotherham, 1972
·	12066	·	·	·	Scrapped	Cashmore's, Great Bridge, 1970
·	12067	·	·	·	Scrapped	Cohen's, Kettering, 1969
·	12068	·	·	·	Scrapped	Cohen's, Kettering, 1968
·	12069	·	·	·	Scrapped	Birds, Long Marston, 1972
·	12070	·	·	·	Scrapped	C F Booth, Rotherham, 1972
·	12071	·	·	·	Scrapped	Cooper's Metals Meadowhall, 95
·	12072	·	·	·	Scrapped	Cohen's, Kettering, 1969
·	12073	·	·	·	Scrapped	C F Booth, Rotherham, 1972
·	12074	·	·	·	Scrapped	HNRC, Kingsbury, 2002
·	12075	·	·	·	Scrapped	Cohen's, Kettering, 1973
·	12076	·	·	·	Scrapped	Cohen's, Kettering, 1973
·	12077	·	·	·	Preserved	Midland Railway Centre
·	12078	·	·	·	Scrapped	Cohen's, Kettering, 1971
·	12079	·	·	·	Scrapped	C F Booth, Rotherham, 1972
·	12080	·	·	·	Scrapped	BR, Doncaster Works, 1972
·	12081	·	·	·	Scrapped	C F Booth, Rotherham, 1972
·	12082	01553	12049*	·	Preserved	Watercress Line
·	12083	·	·	·	Preserved	Battlefield Line
·	12084	·	·	·	Scrapped	NCB Philadelphia, 1985
·	12085	·	·	·	Scrapped	T W Ward, Barrow, 1973
·	12086	·	·	·	Scrapped	Cashmore's, Great Bridge, 1970
·	12087	·	·	·	Scrapped	Cohen's, Kettering, 1973
·	12088	·	·	·	Preserved	Aln Valley Railway
·	12089	·	·	·	Scrapped	BR, Derby Works, 1971
·	12090	·	·	·	Scrapped	C F Booth, Rotherham, 1972
·	12091	·	·	·	Scrapped	BR, Derby Works, 1971
·	12092	·	·	·	Scrapped	Cashmore's, Great Bridge, 1969
·	12093	·	·	·	Preserved	Caledonian Railway
·	12094	·	·	·	Scrapped	C F Booth, Rotherham, 1972
·	12095	·	·	·	Scrapped	Cashmore's, Great Bridge, 1970
·	12096	·	·	·	Scrapped	Cohen's, Kettering, 1969
·	12097	·	·	·	Scrapped	BR, Doncaster Works, 1972
·	12098	·	·	·	Scrapped	HNRC, Kingsbury, 2006
·	12099	·	·	·	Preserved	Severn Valley Railway
·	12100	·	·	·	Scrapped	Cashmore's, Great Bridge, 1969
·	12101	·	·	·	Scrapped	Cohen's, Kettering, 1971
·	12102	·	·	·	Scrapped	Cohen's, Kettering, 1971
·	12103	·	·	·	Scrapped	Cashmore's, Newport, 1973
·	12104	·	·	·	Scrapped	Cohen's, Stratford, 1967
·	12105	·	·	·	Scrapped	BR, Stratford, 1972
·	12106	·	·	·	Scrapped	C F Booth, Rotherham, 1971

CLASS 11 (Continued)

·	12107	· · ·	Scrapped	J McWilliams, Shettleston, 1968
·	12108	· · ·	Scrapped	Wards, Beighton, 1977
·	12109	· · ·	Scrapped	Marple & Gillott, Sheffield, 1973
·	12110	· · ·	Scrapped	Marple & Gillott, Sheffield, 1973
·	12111	· · ·	Scrapped	BR, Stratford, 1972
·	12112	· · ·	Scrapped	C F Booth, Rotherham, 1970
·	12113	· · ·	Scrapped	Cohen's, Kettering, 1971
·	12114	· · ·	Scrapped	BR, Stratford, 1972
·	12115	· · ·	Scrapped	BR, Stratford, 1972
·	12116	· · ·	Scrapped	Cohen's, Kettering, 1969
·	12117	· · ·	Scrapped	Arnott Young, Parkgate, 1969
·	12118	· · ·	Scrapped	Cohen's, Kettering, 1971
·	12119	· · ·	Scrapped	NCB Philadelphia, 1985
·	12120	· · ·	Scrapped	NCB Philadelphia, 1980
·	12121	· · ·	Scrapped	C F Booth, Rotherham, 1972
·	12122	· · ·	Scrapped	British Oak, Wakefield, 1985
·	12123	· · ·	Scrapped	Wards, Beighton, 1967
·	12124	· · ·	Scrapped	Cohen's, Kettering, 1969
·	12125	· · ·	Scrapped	J McWilliams, Shettleston, 1969
·	12126	· · ·	Scrapped	Arnott Young, Parkgate, 1969
·	12127	· · ·	Scrapped	BR, Doncaster Works, 1975
·	12128	· · ·	Scrapped	C F Booth, Rotherham, 1971
·	12129	· · ·	Scrapped	Steelbreaking, Chesterfield, 1968
·	12130	· · ·	Scrapped	Cashmore's, Newport, 1973
·	12131	· · ·	Preserved	North Norfolk Railway
·	12132	· · ·	Scrapped	Cashmore's, Newport, 1073
·	12133	· · ·	Scrapped	NCB Philadelphia, 1985
·	12134	· · ·	Scrapped	Cohen's, Kettering, 1973
·	12135	· · ·	Scrapped	J McWilliams, Shettleston, 1969
·	12136	· · ·	Scrapped	Wards, Beighton, 1977
·	12137	· · ·	Scrapped	J McMurray, Stratford, 1969
·	12138	· · ·	Scrapped	Cohen's, Kettering, 1969

* Renumbered from 12082 after the original loco was scrapped due to fire damage in 2010

CLASS 12

Total Built	26	Formation	0-6-0	Max T.E.	24,600 lbf
Date Built	1949-52	Max Speed	27.5 mph	P.A.R.	194 hp
Builder	BR Ashford	Weight	48 t	R.A.	5
Engine	English Electric 6KT, 350 hp	Brakes	Vacuum	Supply	N/A

·	15211	· · ·	Scrapped	Cashmore's, Newport, 1972
·	15212	· · ·	Scrapped	Cashmore's, Newport, 1972
·	15213	· · ·	Scrapped	BR, Hither Green, 1972
·	15214	· · ·	Scrapped	Cashmore's, Newport, 1972
·	15215	· · ·	Scrapped	BR, Swindon Works, 1968
·	15216	· · ·	Scrapped	BR, Swindon Works, 1970
·	15217	· · ·	Scrapped	BR, Selhurst, 1971
·	15218	· · ·	Scrapped	C F Booth, Rotherham, 1970
·	15219	· · ·	Scrapped	Cashmore's, Newport, 1972
·	15220	· · ·	Scrapped	Cashmore's, Newport, 1972
·	15221	· · ·	Scrapped	Cashmore's, Newport, 1972
·	15222	· · ·	Scrapped	John Williams Ltd, Kidwelly, 1978

CLASS 12 (Continued)

·	15223	·	·	·	Scrapped	C F Booth, Rotherham, 1970
·	15224	·	·	·	Preserved	Spa Valley Railway
·	15225	·	·	·	Scrapped	Cashmore's, Newport, 1972
·	15226	·	·	·	Scrapped	Cashmore's, Newport, 1969
·	15227	·	·	·	Scrapped	BR, Eastleigh Works, 1970
·	15228	·	·	·	Scrapped	BR, Swindon Works, 1969
·	15229	·	·	·	Scrapped	Cashmore's, Newport, 1972
·	15230	·	·	·	Scrapped	Cashmore's, Newport, 1972
·	15231	·	·	·	Scrapped	Tilcon, Grassington, 1984
·	15232	·	·	·	Scrapped	BR, Swindon Works, 1972
·	15233	·	·	·	Scrapped	Cashmore's, Newport, 1969
·	15234	·	·	·	Scrapped	BR, Swindon Works, 1970
·	15235	·	·	·	Scrapped	Cashmore's, Newport, 1972
·	15236	·	·	·	Scrapped	BR, Swindon Works, 1972

CLASS 13

Total Built	3	Formation	0-6-0 + 0-6-0	Max T.E.	70,000 lbf
Date Built	1965	Max Speed	20 mph	P.A.R.	320 hp
Builder	BR Darlington	Weight	122 t	R.A.	8
Engine	2xEnglish Electric 6KT, 700 hp	Brakes	Vacuum	Supply	N/A

13001	D4501	D4190(M)	D4189(S)	·	Scrapped	BR, Swindon Works, 1985
13002	D4502	D4187(M)	D3697(S)	·	Scrapped	BR, Swindon Works, 1982
13003	D4500	D4188(M)	D3698(S)	·	Scrapped	BR, Doncaster Works, 1986

Rebuilt from Class 08s as master and slave units for Tinsley Marshalling Yard

CLASS 14

Total Built	56	Formation	0-6-0	Max T.E.	30,910 lbf
Date Built	1964-65	Max Speed	40 mph	P.A.R.	480 hp
Builder	BR Swindon Works	Weight	50 t	R.A.	4
Engine	Paxman Ventura 6YJXL, 650hp	Brakes	Vacuum	Supply	N/A

·	D9500	·	·	·	Preserved	Peak Rail
·	D9501	·	·	·	Scrapped	C F Booth, Rotherham, 1968
·	D9502	·	·	·	Preserved	East Lancashire Railway
·	D9503	·	·	·	Scrapped	BSC, Corby, 1980
·	D9504	·	·	·	Preserved	Kent & East Sussex Railway
·	D9505	·	·	·	Scrapped	Gent, Belgium, 1999
·	D9506	·	·	·	Scrapped	Arnott Young, Parkgate, 1968
·	D9507	·	·	·	Scrapped	BSC, Corby, 1982
·	D9508	·	·	·	Scrapped	NCB Ashington, 1984
·	D9509	·	·	·	Scrapped	Cohen's, Kettering, 1970
·	D9510	·	·	·	Scrapped	BSC, Corby, 1982
·	D9511	·	·	·	Scrapped	NCB Ashington, 1979
·	D9512	·	·	·	Scrapped	BSC, Corby, 1982
·	D9513	NCB 8	38	·	Preserved	Embsay & Bolton Abbey Railway
·	D9514	·	·	·	Scrapped	NCB Ashington, 1985
·	D9515	·	·	·	Scrapped	Zarragossa, Spain, 2002
·	D9516	·	·	·	Preserved	Didcot Railway Centre
·	D9517	·	·	·	Scrapped	NCB Ashington, 1984
·	D9518	45	·	·	Preserved	West Somerset Railway
·	D9519	·	·	·	Scrapped	Cohen's, Kettering, 1970

CLASS 14 (Continued)

·	D9520	·	·	·	Preserved	Nene Valley Railway
·	D9521	NCB 3	·	·	Preserved	Dean Forest Railway
·	D9522	·	·	·	Scrapped	Arnott Young, Parkgate, 1968
·	D9523	·	·	·	Preserved	Derwent Valley Light Railway
·	D9524	14901	·	·	Preserved	Peak Rail
·	D9525	·	·	·	Preserved	Peak Rail
·	D9526	·	·	·	Preserved	West Somerset Railway
·	D9527	·	·	·	Scrapped	NCB Ashington, 1984
·	D9528	·	·	·	Scrapped	NCB Ashington, 1981
·	D9529	14029	·	·	Preserved	Nene Valley Railway
·	D9530	·	·	·	Scrapped	NCB Tower Colliery, 1982
·	D9531	·	·	·	Preserved	East Lancashire Railway
·	D9532	·	·	·	Scrapped	BSC, Corby, 1982
·	D9533	·	·	·	Scrapped	BSC, Corby, 1982
·	D9534	·	·	·	Scrapped	Bruges, Belgium ,2002
·	D9535	NCB 37	·	·	Scrapped	NCB Ashington, 1984
·	D9536	·	·	·	Scrapped	NCB Ashington, 1985
·	D9537	·	·	·	Preserved	East Lancashire Railway
·	D9538	·	·	·	Scrapped	BSC, Corby, 1982
·	D9539	·	·	·	Preserved	Ribble Steam Railway
·	D9540	NCB 36	·	·	Scrapped	NCB Ashington, 1984
·	D9541	·	·	·	Scrapped	BSC, Corby, 1982
·	D9542	·	·	·	Scrapped	BSC, Corby, 1982
·	D9543	·	·	·	Scrapped	C F Booth, Rotherham, 1968
·	D9544	·	·	·	Scrapped	BSC, Corby, 1980
·	D9545	·	·	·	Scrapped	NCB Ashington, 1979
·	D9546	·	·	·	Scrapped	C F Booth, Rotherham, 1968
·	D9547	·	·	·	Scrapped	BSC, Corby, 1982
·	D9548	·	·	·	Scrapped	Zarragossa, Spain, 2002
·	D9549	·	·	·	Scrapped	Zarragossa, Spain, 2002
·	D9550	·	·	·	Scrapped	C F Booth, Rotherham, 1968
·	D9551	·	·	·	Preserved	Severn Valley Railway
·	D9552	·	·	·	Scrapped	BSC, Corby, 1980
·	D9553	·	·	·	Preserved	Severn Valley Railway
·	D9554	·	·	·	Scrapped	BSC, Corby, 1982
·	D9555	·	·	·	Preserved	Dean Forest Railway

CLASS 15

Total Built	44	Formation	Bo-Bo	Max T.E.	37,500 lbf
Date Built	1957-61	Max Speed	60 mph	P.A.R.	627 hp
Builder	BTH/Clayton, Sheffield & Derby	Weight	68 t	R.A.	4
Engine	Paxman 16YHXL, 800 hp	Brakes	Vacuum	Supply	Steam

·	D8200	·	·	·	Scrapped	BR, Crewe Works, 1972
·	D8201	·	·	·	Scrapped	BR, Crewe Works, 1972
·	D8202	·	·	·	Scrapped	Cohen's, Kettering, 1969
·	D8203	968003*	·	·	Scrapped	Vic Berry, Colchester, 1981
·	D8204	·	·	·	Scrapped	BR, Crewe Works, 1972
·	D8205	·	·	·	Scrapped	Cohen's, Kettering, 1969
·	D8206	·	·	·	Scrapped	Woodham Brothers, Barry, 1970
·	D8207	·	·	·	Scrapped	BR, Crewe Works, 1972
·	D8208	·	·	·	Scrapped	Cohen's, Kettering, 1969
·	D8209	·	·	·	Scrapped	BR, Crewe Works, 1972

CLASS 15 (Continued)

·	D8210	·	·	·	Scrapped	BR, Crewe Works, 1972
·	D8211	·	·	·	Scrapped	BR, Crewe Works, 1971
·	D8212	·	·	·	Scrapped	Cohen's, Kettering, 1969
·	D8213	·	·	·	Scrapped	Cohen's, Kettering, 1969
·	D8214	·	·	·	Scrapped	BR, Crewe Works, 1971
·	D8215	·	·	·	Scrapped	BR, Crewe Works, 1971
·	D8216	·	·	·	Scrapped	BR, Crewe Works, 1972
·	D8217	·	·	·	Scrapped	Cohen's, Kettering, 1969
·	D8218	·	·	·	Scrapped	BR, Crewe Works, 1971
·	D8219	·	·	·	Scrapped	Cohen's, Kettering, 1969
·	D8220	·	·	·	Scrapped	BR, Crewe Works, 1971
·	D8221	·	·	·	Scrapped	BR, Crewe Works, 1971
·	D8222	·	·	·	Scrapped	BR, Crewe Works, 1971
·	D8223	·	·	·	Scrapped	Cohen's, Kettering, 1969
·	D8224	·	·	·	Scrapped	BR, Crewe Works, 1971
·	D8225	·	·	·	Scrapped	BR, Crewe Works, 1971
·	D8226	·	·	·	Scrapped	BR, Crewe Works, 1971
·	D8227	·	·	·	Scrapped	Cohen's, Kettering, 1969
·	D8228	·	·	·	Scrapped	BR, Crewe Works, 1971
·	D8229	·	·	·	Scrapped	BR, Crewe Works, 1972
·	D8230	·	·	·	Scrapped	BR, Crewe Works, 1971
·	D8231	·	·	·	Scrapped	BR, Crewe Works, 1972
·	D8232	·	·	·	Scrapped	BR, Crewe Works, 1971
·	D8233	968001*	·	·	Preserved	East Lancashire Railway
·	D8234	·	·	·	Scrapped	BR, Crewe Works, 1971
·	D8235	·	·	·	Scrapped	Cohen's, Kettering, 1969
·	D8236	·	·	·	Scrapped	Cohen's, Kettering, 1969
·	D8237	968002*	·	·	Scrapped	Marple & Gillott, Sheffield, 1985
·	D8238	·	·	·	Scrapped	Cohen's, Kettering, 1969
·	D8239	·	·	·	Scrapped	BR, Crewe Works, 1972
·	D8240	·	·	·	Scrapped	Cohen's, Kettering, 1969
·	D8241	·	·	·	Scrapped	Cashmore's, Great Bridge 1968
·	D8242	·	·	·	Scrapped	BR, Crewe Works, 1971
·	D8243	968000*	·	·	Scrapped	Vic Berry, Leicester, 1991

* Converted to static train pre-heating units and renumbered with TDB prefix

CLASS 16

Total Built	10	Formation	Bo-Bo	Max T.E.	42,000 lbf
Date Built	1958	Max Speed	60 mph	P.A.R.	627 hp
Builder	North British Loco Co, Glasgow	Weight	68 t	R.A.	4
Engine	Paxman 16YHXL, 800 hp	Brakes	Vacuum	Supply	Steam

·	D8400	·	·	·	Scrapped	Cohen's, Kettering, 1969
·	D8401	·	·	·	Scrapped	Cohen's, Kettering, 1969
·	D8402	·	·	·	Scrapped	Cohen's, Kettering, 1969
·	D8403	·	·	·	Scrapped	Cohen's, Kettering, 1969
·	D8404	·	·	·	Scrapped	Cox & Danks, North Acton, 1968
·	D8405	·	·	·	Scrapped	Cohen's, Kettering, 1969
·	D8406	·	·	·	Scrapped	Birds, Long Marston, 1969
·	D8407	·	·	·	Scrapped	Cohen's, Kettering, 1969
·	D8408	·	·	·	Scrapped	Cohen's, Kettering, 1969
·	D8409	·	·	·	Scrapped	Cohen's, Kettering, 1969

CLASS 17

Total Built	117	Formation	Bo-Bo	Max T.E.	40,000 lbf
Date Built	1962-65	Max Speed	60 mph	P.A.R.	602 hp
Builder	Clayton and Beyer Peacock	Weight	68 t	R.A.	4
Engine	2xPaxman 6ZHXL, 900 hp	Brakes	Vacuum	Supply	N/A

·	D8500	·	·	·	Scrapped	BR, Glasgow Works, 1971
·	D8501	·	·	·	Scrapped	BR, Glasgow Works, 1971
·	D8502	·	·	·	Scrapped	BR, Glasgow Works, 1973
·	D8503	·	·	·	Scrapped	BR, Glasgow Works, 1972
·	D8504	·	·	·	Scrapped	Cashmore's, Great Bridge 1975
·	D8505	·	·	·	Scrapped	BR, Glasgow Works, 1974
·	D8506	·	·	·	Scrapped	BR, Glasgow Works, 1971
·	D8507	·	·	·	Scrapped	R A Kings, Norwich, 1975
·	D8508	·	·	·	Scrapped	R A Kings, Norwich, 1975
·	D8509	·	·	·	Scrapped	BR, Glasgow Works, 1972
·	D8510	·	·	·	Scrapped	BR, Glasgow Works, 1971
·	D8511	·	·	·	Scrapped	J McWilliams, Shettleston, 1970
·	D8512	·	·	·	Scrapped	BR, Glasgow Works, 1973
·	D8513	·	·	·	Scrapped	BR, Glasgow Works, 1971
·	D8514	·	·	·	Scrapped	BR, Glasgow Works, 1971
·	D8515	·	·	·	Scrapped	BR, Glasgow Works, 1972
·	D8516	·	·	·	Scrapped	R A Kings, Norwich, 1975
·	D8517	·	·	·	Scrapped	J McWilliams, Shettleston, 1970
·	D8518	·	·	·	Scrapped	BR, Glasgow Works, 1972
·	D8519	·	·	·	Scrapped	BR, Glasgow Works, 1972
·	D8520	·	·	·	Scrapped	BR, Glasgow Works, 1972
·	D8521	18521*	·	·	Scrapped	BR, Glasgow Works, 1978
·	D8522	·	·	·	Scrapped	BR, Glasgow Works, 1972
·	D8523	·	·	·	Scrapped	BR, Glasgow Works, 1972
·	D8524	·	·	·	Scrapped	J McWilliams, Shettleston, 1970
·	D8525	·	·	·	Scrapped	R A Kings, Norwich, 1975
·	D8526	·	·	·	Scrapped	BR, Glasgow Works, 1972
·	D8527	·	·	·	Scrapped	BR, Glasgow Works, 1972
·	D8528	·	·	·	Scrapped	BR, Glasgow Works, 1973
·	D8529	·	·	·	Scrapped	R A Kings, Norwich, 1975
·	D8530	·	·	·	Scrapped	BR, Glasgow Works, 1971
·	D8531	·	·	·	Scrapped	R A Kings, Norwich, 1975
·	D8532	·	·	·	Scrapped	BR, Glasgow Works, 1972
·	D8533	·	·	·	Scrapped	J McWilliams, Shettleston, 1972
·	D8534	·	·	·	Scrapped	BR, Glasgow Works, 1973
·	D8535	·	·	·	Scrapped	BR, Glasgow Works, 1971
·	D8536	·	·	·	Scrapped	R A Kings, Norwich, 1975
·	D8537	·	·	·	Scrapped	J McWilliams, Shettleston, 1968
·	D8538	·	·	·	Scrapped	BR, Glasgow Works, 1972
·	D8539	·	·	·	Scrapped	R A Kings, Norwich, 1975
·	D8540	·	·	·	Scrapped	BR, Glasgow Works, 1973
·	D8541	·	·	·	Scrapped	BR, Glasgow Works, 1973
·	D8542	·	·	·	Scrapped	Cashmore's, Great Bridge 1975
·	D8543	·	·	·	Scrapped	BR, Glasgow Works, 1972
·	D8544	·	·	·	Scrapped	J McWilliams, Shettleston, 1971
·	D8545	·	·	·	Scrapped	BR, Glasgow Works, 1973
·	D8546	·	·	·	Scrapped	Cashmore's, Great Bridge 1975
·	D8547	·	·	·	Scrapped	Birds, Long Marston, 1969
·	D8548	·	·	·	Scrapped	Cashmore's, Great Bridge 1975
·	D8549	·	·	·	Scrapped	BR, Glasgow Works, 1972

·	D8550	·	·	·	Scrapped	Cashmore's, Great Bridge 1975
·	D8551	·	·	·	Scrapped	Cashmore's, Great Bridge 1975
·	D8552	·	·	·	Scrapped	R A Kings, Norwich, 1975
·	D8553	·	·	·	Scrapped	J McWilliams, Shettleston, 1969
·	D8554	·	·	·	Scrapped	J McWilliams, Shettleston, 1971
·	D8555	·	·	·	Scrapped	BR, Glasgow Works, 1972
·	D8556	·	·	·	Scrapped	Birds, Long Marston, 1969
·	D8557	·	·	·	Scrapped	J McWilliams, Shettleston, 1975
·	D8558	·	·	·	Scrapped	BR, Glasgow Works, 1973
·	D8559	·	·	·	Scrapped	BR, Glasgow Works, 1974
·	D8560	·	·	·	Scrapped	Birds, Long Marston, 1969
·	D8561	·	·	·	Scrapped	BR, Glasgow Works, 1973
·	D8562	·	·	·	Scrapped	BR, Glasgow Works, 1973
·	D8563	·	·	·	Scrapped	Cashmore's, Great Bridge 1975
·	D8564	·	·	·	Scrapped	Birds, Long Marston, 1969
·	D8565	·	·	·	Scrapped	BR, Glasgow Works, 1973
·	D8566	·	·	·	Scrapped	J McWilliams, Shettleston, 1969
·	D8567	·	·	·	Scrapped	BR, Glasgow Works, 1973
·	D8568	·	·	·	Preserved	C & PRR
·	D8569	·	·	·	Scrapped	J McWilliams, Shettleston, 1969
·	D8570	·	·	·	Scrapped	Birds, Long Marston, 1969
·	D8571	·	·	·	Scrapped	J McWilliams, Shettleston, 1971
·	D8572	·	·	·	Scrapped	Cashmore's, Great Bridge 1970
·	D8573	·	·	·	Scrapped	J McWilliams, Shettleston, 1975
·	D8574	·	·	·	Scrapped	R A Kings, Norwich, 1975
·	D8575	·	·	·	Scrapped	J McWilliams, Shettleston, 1969
·	D8576	·	·	·	Scrapped	Birds, Long Marston, 1969
·	D8577	·	·	·	Scrapped	Birds, Long Marston, 1969
·	D8578	·	·	·	Scrapped	J McWilliams, Shettleston, 1971
·	D8579	·	·	·	Scrapped	BR, Glasgow Works, 1973
·	D8580	·	·	·	Scrapped	R A Kings, Norwich, 1975
·	D8581	·	·	·	Scrapped	BR, Glasgow Works, 1974
·	D8582	·	·	·	Scrapped	J McWilliams, Shettleston, 1969
·	D8583	·	·	·	Scrapped	BR, Glasgow Works, 1973
·	D8584	·	·	·	Scrapped	J McWilliams, Shettleston, 1969
·	D8585	·	·	·	Scrapped	J McWilliams, Shettleston, 1969
·	D8586	·	·	·	Scrapped	BR, Glasgow Works, 1973
·	D8587	·	·	·	Scrapped	BR, Glasgow Works, 1974
·	D8588	·	·	·	Scrapped	BR, Glasgow Works, 1973
·	D8589	·	·	·	Scrapped	W Willoughby, Gateshead, 1971
·	D8590	·	·	·	Scrapped	BR, Glasgow Works, 1971
·	D8591	·	·	·	Scrapped	J McWilliams, Shettleston, 1969
·	D8592	·	·	·	Scrapped	BR, Glasgow Works, 1972
·	D8593	·	·	·	Scrapped	BR, Glasgow Works, 1973
·	D8594	·	·	·	Scrapped	BR, Glasgow Works, 1972
·	D8595	·	·	·	Scrapped	J McWilliams, Shettleston, 1969
·	D8596	·	·	·	Scrapped	J McWilliams, Shettleston, 1969
·	D8597	·	·	·	Scrapped	BR, Glasgow Works, 1973
·	D8598	·	·	·	Scrapped	BR, Glasgow Works, 1979
·	D8599	·	·	·	Scrapped	BR, Glasgow Works, 1971
·	D8600	·	·	·	Scrapped	BR, Glasgow Works, 1973
·	D8601	·	·	·	Scrapped	BR, Glasgow Works, 1973
·	D8602	·	·	·	Scrapped	BR, Glasgow Works, 1972
·	D8603	·	·	·	Scrapped	BR, Glasgow Works, 1972

CLASS 17 (Continued)

·	D8604	·	·	·	Scrapped	BR, Glasgow Works, 1972
·	D8605	·	·	·	Scrapped	Drapers, Hull, 1969
·	D8606	·	·	·	Scrapped	BR, Glasgow Works, 1972
·	D8607	·	·	·	Scrapped	J McWilliams, Shettleston, 1975
·	D8608	·	·	·	Scrapped	J McWilliams, Shettleston, 1975
·	D8609	·	·	·	Scrapped	J McWilliams, Shettleston, 1969
·	D8610	·	·	·	Scrapped	BR, Glasgow Works, 1973
·	D8611	·	·	·	Scrapped	J McWilliams, Shettleston, 1969
·	D8612	·	·	·	Scrapped	J McWilliams, Shettleston, 1975
·	D8613	·	·	·	Scrapped	J McWilliams, Shettleston, 1975
·	D8614	·	·	·	Scrapped	BR, Glasgow Works, 1972
·	D8615	·	·	·	Scrapped	BR, Glasgow Works, 1973
·	D8616	·	·	·	Scrapped	J McWilliams, Shettleston, 1975

* Used for testing as a mobile generator and renumbered with S prefix

CLASS 20

Total Built	228	Formation	Bo-Bo	Max T.E.	42,000 lbf
Date Built	1957-68	Max Speed	75 mph	P.A.R.	770 hp
Builder	English Electric Co, Vulcan	Weight	73 t	R.A.	5
Engine	E.E. 8SVT, 1000 hp	Brakes	Vacuum / Air & Vac	Supply	N/A

20001	D8001	968029^	2011	·	Preserved	Midland Railway Centre
20002	D8002	·	·	·	Scrapped	MC Metals, Springburn, 1990
20003	D8003	·	·	·	Scrapped	BR, Crewe Works, 1984
20004	D0004	·	·	·	Scrapped	MC Metals, Springburn, 1991
20005	D8005	·	·	·	Scrapped	MC Metals, Springburn, 1990
20006	D8006	·	·	·	Scrapped	MC Metals, Springburn, 1991
20007	D8007	·	·	·	Operational	Midland Railway Centre
20008	D8008	·	·	·	Scrapped	MC Metals, Springburn, 1993
20009	D8009	·	·	·	Scrapped	MC Metals, Springburn, 1993
20010	D8010	·	·	·	Scrapped	MC Metals, Springburn, 1994
20011	D8011	968032~	·	·	Scrapped	MC Metals, Springburn, 1994
20012	D8012	·	·	·	Scrapped	BR, Glasgow Works, 1977
20013	D8013	·	·	·	Scrapped	MC Metals, Springburn, 1993
20014	D8014	·	·	·	Scrapped	BR, Glasgow Works, 1977
20015	D8015	·	·	·	Scrapped	Vic Berry, Thornaby, 1988
20016	D8016	·	·	·	Stored	HNRC, Long Marston
20017	D8017	·	·	·	Scrapped	BR, Crewe Works, 1984
20018	D8018	·	·	·	Scrapped	BR, Glasgow Works, 1978
20019	D8019	·	·	·	Scrapped	MC Metals, Springburn, 1994
20020	D8020	·	·	·	Preserved	Bo'ness & Kinneil Railway
20021	D8021	·	·	·	Scrapped	MC Metals, Springburn, 1992
20022	D8022	·	·	·	Scrapped	Vic Berry, Leicester, 1990
20023	D8023	20301*	·	·	Scrapped	MC Metals, Springburn, 1992
20024	D8024	·	·	·	Scrapped	BR, Glasgow Works, 1978
20025	D8025	·	·	·	Scrapped	MC Metals, Springburn, 1995
20026	D8026	·	·	·	Scrapped	MC Metals, Springburn, 1991
20027	D8027	·	·	·	Scrapped	BR, Glasgow Works, 1986
20028	D8028	·	·	·	Scrapped	MC Metals, Springburn, 1995
20029	D8029	·	·	·	Scrapped	MC Metals, Springburn, 1993
20030	D8030	·	·	·	Scrapped	MC Metals, Springburn, 1991
20031	D8031	·	·	·	Preserved	Keighley & Worth Valley Railway

20032	D8032	·	·	·	Scrapped	EMR, Kingsbury, 2012
20033	D8033	·	·	·	Scrapped	BR, Crewe Works, 1980
20034	D8034	·	·	·	Scrapped	MC Metals, Springburn, 1991
20035	D8035	2001	·	·	Preserved	G & WR
20036	D8036	·	·	·	Scrapped	BR, Glasgow Works, 1986
20037	D8037	·	·	·	Scrapped	Vic Berry, Leicester, 1988
20038	D8038	·	·	·	Scrapped	BR, Glasgow Works, 1977
20039	D8039	·	·	·	Scrapped	Vic Berry, Leicester, 1988
20040	D8040	·	·	·	Scrapped	MC Metals, Springburn, 1992
20041	D8041	20904	·	·	Stored	HNRC, Burton-upon-Trent
20042	D8042	20312+	·	·	Stored	DRS, Barrow Hill
20043	D8043	·	·	·	Scrapped	MC Metals, Springburn, 1995
20044	D8044	·	·	·	Scrapped	MC Metals, Springburn, 1991
20045	D8045	·	·	·	Scrapped	MC Metals, Springburn, 1991
20046	D8046	·	·	·	Scrapped	MC Metals, Springburn, 1993
20047	D8047	20301+	2004	04	Stored	DRS, Barrow Hill
20048	D8048	2014	34	·	Preserved	Midland Railway Centre
20049	D8049	·	·	·	Scrapped	Vic Berry, Leicester, 1988
20050	D8000	·	·	·	Preserved	National Railway Museum, York
20051	D8051	·	·	·	Scrapped	C F Booth, Kilnhurst, 1993
20052	D8052	·	·	·	Scrapped	MC Metals, Springburn, 1991
20053	D8053	·	·	·	Scrapped	MC Metals, Springburn, 1991
20054	D8054	·	·	·	Scrapped	MC Metals, Springburn, 1991
20055	D8055	·	·	·	Scrapped	MC Metals, Springburn, 1995
20056	D8056	2012	12	81	Operational	HNRC, Scunthorpe Steelworks
20057	D8057	·	·	·	Preserved	Churnet Valley Railway
20058	D8058	·	·	·	Scrapped	MC Metals, Springburn, 1994
20059	D8059	20302*	·	·	Preserved	C & PRR
20060	D8060	20902	·	·	Scrapped	EMR, Kingsbury, 2011
20061	D8061	·	·	·	Scrapped	MC Metals, Springburn, 1994
20062	D8062	·	·	·	Scrapped	BR, Derby Works, 1979
20063	D8063	2002	·	·	Preserved	Colne Valley Railway
20064	D8064	·	·	·	Scrapped	MC Metals, Springburn, 1991
20065	D8065	·	·	·	Scrapped	MC Metals, Springburn, 1991
20066	D8066	201	33	82	Operational	HNRC, Hope Cement Works
20067	D8067	·	·	·	Scrapped	Vic Berry, Leicester, 1988
20068	D8068	·	·	·	Scrapped	MC Metals, Springburn, 1993
20069	D8069	·	·	·	Preserved	Mid-Norfolk Railway
20070	D8070	·	·	·	Scrapped	MC Metals, Springburn, 1992
20071	D8071	·	·	·	Scrapped	MC Metals, Springburn, 1995
20072	D8072	·	·	·	Scrapped	EMR, Kingsbury, 2012
20073	D8073	·	·	·	Scrapped	C F Booth, Rotherham, 2006
20074	D8074	·	·	·	Scrapped	BR, Glasgow Works, 1976
20075	D8075	20309+	·	·	Stored	DRS, Barrow Hill
20076	D8076	·	·	·	Scrapped	Vic Berry, Thornaby, 1988
20077	D8077	·	·	·	Scrapped	Vic Berry, Leicester, 1990
20078	D8078	·	·	·	Scrapped	MC Metals, Springburn, 1993
20079	D8079	·	·	·	Scrapped	BR, Derby Works, 1978
20080	D8080	·	·	·	Scrapped	MC Metals, Springburn, 1993
20081	D8081	·	·	·	Stored	HNRC, Long Marston
20082	D8082	·	·	·	Scrapped	MC Metals, Springburn, 1995
20083	D8083	20903	·	·	Stored	HNRC, Burton-upon-Trent
20084	D8084	20302+	2002	31	Stored	DRS, Barrow Hill
20085	D8085	·	·	·	Scrapped	CEGB, Castle Donington, 1994

CLASS 20 (Continued)

20086	D8086	·	·	·	Scrapped	MC Metals, Springburn, 1991
20087	D8087	29	35	·	Preserved	East Lancashire Railway
20088	D8088	2017	37	·	Stored	HNRC, Long Marston
20089	D8089	·	·	·	Scrapped	MC Metals, Springburn, 1993
20090	D8090	·	·	·	Scrapped	MC Metals, Springburn, 1995
20091	D8091	·	·	·	Scrapped	BR, Glasgow Works, 1978
20092	D8092	·	·	·	Scrapped	MC Metals, Springburn, 1995
20093	D8093	·	·	·	Scrapped	MC Metals, Springburn, 1992
20094	D8094	·	·	·	Scrapped	Cymru Metals, Llanelli, 2004
20095	D8095	20305+	2020	29	Stored	DRS, Barrow Hill
20096	D8096	·	·	·	Operational	GBRF, Barrow Hill
20097	D8097	·	·	·	Scrapped	MC Metals, Springburn, 1991
20098	D8098	·	·	·	Preserved	Great Central Railway
20099	D8099	·	·	·	Scrapped	MC Metals, Springburn, 1993
20100	D8100	·	·	·	Scrapped	MC Metals, Springburn, 1991
20101	D8101	20901	·	·	Operational	GBRF, Barrow Hill
20102	D8102	20311+	2008	08	Operational	GBRF, Barrow Hill
20103	D8103	·	·	·	Scrapped	MC Metals, Springburn, 1992
20104	D8104	20315+	·	·	Scrapped	C F Booth, Rotherham, 2013
20105	D8105	2016	36	·	Scrapped	T J Thomson, Stockton, 2010
20106	D8106	·	·	·	Scrapped	MC Metals, Springburn, 1994
20107	D8107	2013	33	·	Operational	GBRF, Barrow Hill
20108	D8108	2001	01	·	Scrapped	HNRC, Kingsbury, 2005
20109	D8109	·	·	·	Scrapped	BR, Glasgow Works, 1983
20110	D8110	·	·	·	Stored	HNRC, East Lancashire Railway
20111	D8111	·	·	·	Scrapped	Vic Berry, Leicester, 1988
20112	D8112	·	·	·	Scrapped	MC Metals, Springburn, 1993
20113	D8113	2003	32	·	Scrapped	HNRC, Carlisle Kingmoor, 2003
20114	D8114	·	·	·	Scrapped	MC Metals, Springburn, 1991
20115	D8115	·	·	·	Scrapped	Vic Berry, Leicester, 1988
20116	D8116	·	·	·	Scrapped	Vic Berry, Leicester, 1988
20117	D8117	20314+	·	·	Operational	GBRF, Barrow Hill
20118	D8118	·	·	·	Operational	GBRF, Barrow Hill
20119	D8119	32	34	·	Scrapped	C F Booth, Rotherham, 2009
20120	D8120	20304+	2009	·	Stored	DRS, Barrow Hill
20121	D8121	·	·	·	Stored	HNRC, Barrow Hill
20122	D8122	·	·	·	Scrapped	MC Metals, Springburn, 1993
20123	D8123	·	·	·	Scrapped	Vic Berry, Leicester, 1988
20124	D8124	·	·	·	Scrapped	MC Metals, Springburn, 1993
20125	D8125	·	·	·	Scrapped	Vic Berry, Leicester, 1988
20126	D8126	·	·	·	Scrapped	MC Metals, Springburn, 1992
20127	D8127	20303+	2018	·	Stored	DRS, Barrow Hill
20128	D8050	20307+	·	·	Scrapped	C F Booth, Rotherham, 2013
20129	D8129	·	·	·	Scrapped	MC Metals, Springburn, 1991
20130	D8130	·	·	·	Scrapped	MC Metals, Springburn, 1991
20131	D8131	20306+	·	·	Scrapped	C F Booth, Rotherham, 2013
20132	D8132	·	·	·	Operational	GBRF, Barrow Hill
20133	D8133	2005	5	·	Scrapped	C F Booth, Rotherham, 2002
20134	D8134	20303*	·	·	Scrapped	MC Metals, Springburn, 1991
20135	D8135	·	·	·	Scrapped	J T Landscapes, Caerwent, 2004
20136	D8136	·	·	·	Scrapped	MC Metals, Springburn, 1991
20137	D8137	·	·	·	Preserved	G & WR
20138	D8138	30	·	·	Scrapped	C F Booth, Rotherham, 2010
20139	D8139	·	·	·	Scrapped	EMR, Kingsbury, 2010

20140	D8140	·	·	·	Scrapped	MC Metals, Springburn, 1994
20141	D8141	·	·	·	Scrapped	MC Metals, Springburn, 1993
20142	D8142	·	·	·	Operational	Midland Railway Centre
20143	D8143	·	·	·	Scrapped	MC Metals, Springburn, 1993
20144	D8144	·	·	·	Scrapped	MC Metals, Springburn, 1993
20145	D8145	2019	39	·	Scrapped	EMR, Kingsbury, 2009
20146	D8146	·	·	·	Scrapped	MC Metals, Springburn, 1989
20147	D8147	·	·	·	Scrapped	MC Metals, Springburn, 1991
20148	D8148	·	·	·	Scrapped	MC Metals, Springburn, 1994
20149	D8149	·	·	·	Scrapped	Vic Berry, Leicester, 1988
20150	D8150	·	·	·	Scrapped	Vic Berry, Leicester, 1990
20151	D8151	·	·	·	Scrapped	MC Metals, Springburn, 1995
20152	D8152	·	·	·	Scrapped	MC Metals, Springburn, 1988
20153	D8153	·	·	·	Scrapped	Vic Berry, Leicester, 1988
20154	D8154	·	·	·	Preserved	Great Central Railway North
20155	D8155	·	·	·	Scrapped	Vic Berry, Leicester, 1987
20156	D8156	·	·	·	Scrapped	MC Metals, Springburn, 1993
20157	D8157	·	·	·	Scrapped	MC Metals, Springburn, 1992
20158	D8158	·	·	·	Scrapped	MC Metals, Springburn, 1991
20159	D8159	2010	10	·	Scrapped	HNRC, Kingsbury, 2005
20160	D8160	·	·	·	Scrapped	MC Metals, Springburn, 1994
20161	D8161	·	·	·	Scrapped	Vic Berry, Leicester, 1990
20162	D8162	·	·	·	Scrapped	Vic Berry, Leicester, 1987
20163	D8163	·	·	·	Scrapped	MC Metals, Springburn, 1994
20164	D8164	·	·	·	Scrapped	Vic Berry, Leicester, 1988
20165	D8165	·	·	·	Scrapped	Michael Douglas, Carlisle, 2001
20166	D8166	2015	35	·	Operational	HNRC, Wensleydale Railway
20167	D8167	·	·	·	Scrapped	Vic Berry, Leicester, 1988
20168	D8168	20304*	2	·	Operational	HNRC, Hope Cement Works
20169	D8169	·	·	·	Preserved	Stainmore Railway
20170	D8170	·	·	·	Scrapped	MC Metals, Springburn, 1993
20171	D8171	·	·	·	Scrapped	MC Metals, Springburn, 1991
20172	D8172	20305*	·	·	Scrapped	MC Metals, Springburn, 1995
20173	D8173	20306*	·	·	Scrapped	MC Metals, Springburn, 1992
20174	D8174	·	·	·	Scrapped	MC Metals, Springburn, 1993
20175	D8175	2007	7	·	Scrapped	HNRC, Carlisle Kingmoor, 2003
20176	D8176	·	·	·	Scrapped	MC Metals, Springburn, 1994
20177	D8177	·	·	·	Preserved	Somerset & Dorset Railway
20178	D8178	·	·	·	Scrapped	MC Metals, Springburn, 1992
20179	D8179	·	·	·	Scrapped	MC Metals, Springburn, 1991
20180	D8180	·	·	·	Scrapped	Vic Berry, Leicester, 1990
20181	D8181	·	·	·	Scrapped	MC Metals, Springburn, 1994
20182	D8182	·	·	·	Scrapped	MC Metals, Springburn, 1993
20183	D8183	·	·	·	Scrapped	Vic Berry, Leicester, 1990
20184	D8184	·	·	·	Scrapped	Vic Berry, Leicester, 1988
20185	D8185	·	·	·	Scrapped	MC Metals, Springburn, 1994
20186	D8186	·	·	·	Scrapped	MC Metals, Springburn, 1995
20187	D8187	20308+	·	·	Stored	DRS, Barrow Hill
20188	D8188	·	·	·	Preserved	C & PRR
20189	D8189	L189	·	·	Operational	Midland Railway Centre
20190	D8190	20310+	·	·	Scrapped	C F Booth, Rotherham, 2013
20191	D8191	·	·	·	Scrapped	Vic Berry, Leicester, 1987
20192	D8192	·	·	·	Scrapped	MC Metals, Springburn, 1991
20193	D8193	·	·	·	Scrapped	MC Metals, Springburn, 1991

20194	D8194	20307*	2006	20313+	Scrapped	C F Booth, Rotherham, 2013
20195	D8195	·	·	·	Scrapped	MC Metals, Springburn, 1995
20196	D8196	20308*	·	·	Scrapped	MC Metals, Springburn, 1993
20197	D8197	·	·	·	Scrapped	EMR, Kingsbury, 2011
20198	D8198	·	·	·	Scrapped	MC Metals, Springburn, 1993
20199	D8199	·	·	·	Scrapped	MC Metals, Springburn, 1993
20200	D8300	·	·	·	Scrapped	BR, Glasgow Works, 1979
20201	D8301	·	·	·	Scrapped	Vic Berry, Leicester, 1990
20202	D8302	·	·	·	Scrapped	MC Metals, Springburn, 1993
20203	D8303	·	·	·	Scrapped	MC Metals, Springburn, 1992
20204	D8304	·	·	·	Scrapped	MC Metals, Springburn, 1989
20205	D8305	20907	·	·	Operational	Midland Railway Centre
20206	D8306	·	·	·	Scrapped	C F Booth, Rotherham, 2002
20207	D8307	·	·	·	Scrapped	BR, Glasgow Works, 1986
20208	D8308	·	·	·	Scrapped	CEGB, Castle Donington, 1994
20209	D8309	·	·	·	Scrapped	Michael Douglas, Carlisle, 2001
20210	D8310	·	·	·	Scrapped	MC Metals, Springburn, 1993
20211	D8311	·	·	·	Scrapped	MC Metals, Springburn, 1993
20212	D8312	·	·	·	Scrapped	MC Metals, Springburn, 1993
20213	D8313	·	·	·	Scrapped	MC Metals, Springburn, 1992
20214	D8314	·	·	·	Preserved	Lakeside & Haverthwaite Railway
20215	D8315	·	·	·	Scrapped	C F Booth, Rotherham, 2009
20216	D8316	·	·	·	Scrapped	Vic Berry, Leicester, 1988
20217	D8317	·	·	·	Scrapped	MC Metals, Springburn, 1991
20218	D8318	·	·	·	Scrapped	MC Metals, Springburn, 1991
20219	D8319	20906	3	·	Operational	HNRC, Hope Cement Works
20220	D8320	·	·	·	Scrapped	MC Metals, Springburn, 1994
20221	D8321	·	·	·	Scrapped	MC Metals, Springburn, 1994
20222	D8322	·	·	·	Scrapped	MC Metals, Springburn, 1988
20223	D8323	·	·	·	Scrapped	MC Metals, Springburn, 1993
20224	D8324	·	·	·	Scrapped	MC Metals, Springburn, 1991
20225	D8325	20905	·	·	Operational	GBRF, Barrow Hill
20226	D8326	·	·	·	Scrapped	MC Metals, Springburn, 1992
20227	D8327	·	·	·	Operational	Midland Railway Centre
20228	D8128	2004	·	·	Preserved	Vale of Glamorgan Railway

Class 20/3* (20301 - 20308) Modified brakes for Tunstead aggregate workings
Class 20/3+ (20301 - 20315) Refurbished DRS locos fitted with modified cab equipment
Class 20/9 (20901 - 20906) Refurbished Hunslet Barclay locos for weed killing trains

~ Converted to power unit transporter and renumbered with ADB prefix
^ Converted to static train pre-heating units and renumbered with ADB prefix

Class 20 Names:

20001	VULCAN PIONEER	20142	SIR JOHN BETJEMAN
20075	Sir William Cooke	20165	Henry Pease
20096	Ian Goddard 1938-2016	20168	SIR GEORGE EARLE
20110	RIVER DART	20187	Sir Charles Wheatstone
20118	Saltburn by the Sea | RIVER DON	20214	AUSTIN MAHER L&HR 1970-2006
20122	Cleveland Potash	20227	SIR JOHN BETJEMAN
20128	Guglielmo Marconi	20301	Furness Railway 150 | Max Joule 1958-1999
20131	Almon B. Strowger	20303	Max Joule 1958-1999
20132	Barrow Hill Depot	20305	Gresty Bridge
20137	Murray B Hofmeyr	20311	Class 20 'Fifty'

CLASS 20 (Continued)

20901	NANCY		20904	JANIS
20902	NANCY | LORNA		20905	IONA
20903	ALISON		20906	GEORGINA | KILMARNOCK 400

CLASS 21

Total Built	58	Formation	Bo-Bo	Max T.E.	45,000 lbf
Date Built	1958-60	Max Speed	75 mph	P.A.R.	890 hp
Builder	North British Loco Co, Glasgow	Weight	73 t	R.A.	5
Engine	MANL12V18/21, 1100 hp	Brakes	Vacuum	Supply	Steam

·	D6100*	·	·	·	Scrapped	BR, Glasgow Works, 1972
·	D6101*	·	·	·	Scrapped	BR, Glasgow Works, 1972
·	D6102*	·	·	·	Scrapped	BR, Glasgow Works, 1972
·	D6103*	·	·	·	Scrapped	BR, Glasgow Works, 1972
·	D6104	·	·	·	Scrapped	Barnes & Bell, Coatbridge, 1968
·	D6105	·	·	·	Scrapped	J McWilliams, Shettleston, 1968
·	D6106*	·	·	·	Scrapped	BR, Glasgow Works, 1972
·	D6107*	·	·	·	Scrapped	BR, Glasgow Works, 1972
·	D6108*	·	·	·	Scrapped	J McWilliams, Shettleston, 1971
·	D6109	·	·	·	Scrapped	J McWilliams, Shettleston, 1969
·	D6110	·	·	·	Scrapped	J McWilliams, Shettleston, 1969
·	D6111	·	·	·	Scrapped	J McWilliams, Shettleston, 1969
·	D6112*	·	·	·	Scrapped	BR, Glasgow Works, 1972
·	D6113*	·	·	·	Scrapped	BR, Glasgow Works, 1972
·	D6114*	·	·	·	Scrapped	BR, Glasgow Works, 1972
·	D6115	·	·	·	Scrapped	J McWilliams, Shettleston, 1968
·	D6116*	·	·	·	Scrapped	BR, Glasgow Works, 1972
·	D6117	·	·	·	Scrapped	J McWilliams, Shettleston, 1968
·	D6118	·	·	·	Scrapped	J McWilliams, Shettleston, 1968
·	D6119*	·	·	·	Scrapped	BR, Glasgow Works, 1972
·	D6120	·	·	·	Scrapped	J McWilliams, Shettleston, 1968
·	D6121*	·	·	·	Scrapped	BR, Glasgow Works, 1972
·	D6122	·	·	·	Scrapped	Woodham Brothers, Barry, 1980
·	D6123*	·	·	·	Scrapped	BR, Glasgow Works, 1972
·	D6124*	·	·	·	Scrapped	BR, Glasgow Works, 1972
·	D6125	·	·	·	Scrapped	Barnes & Bell, Coatbridge, 1968
·	D6126	·	·	·	Scrapped	J McWilliams, Shettleston, 1969
·	D6127	·	·	·	Scrapped	Barnes & Bell, Coatbridge, 1968
·	D6128	·	·	·	Scrapped	J McWilliams, Shettleston, 1968
·	D6129*	·	·	·	Scrapped	BR, Glasgow Works, 1972
·	D6130*	·	·	·	Scrapped	BR, Glasgow Works, 1972
·	D6131	·	·	·	Scrapped	J McWilliams, Shettleston, 1968
·	D6132*	·	·	·	Scrapped	BR, Glasgow Works, 1972
·	D6133*	·	·	·	Scrapped	BR, Glasgow Works, 1972
·	D6134	·	·	·	Scrapped	Barnes & Bell, Coatbridge, 1968
·	D6135	·	·	·	Scrapped	J McWilliams, Shettleston, 1968
·	D6136	·	·	·	Scrapped	Barnes & Bell, Coatbridge, 1968
·	D6137*	·	·	·	Scrapped	BR, Glasgow Works, 1972
·	D6138	·	·	·	Scrapped	J McWilliams, Shettleston, 1968
·	D6139	·	·	·	Scrapped	J McWilliams, Shettleston, 1968
·	D6140	·	·	·	Scrapped	J McWilliams, Shettleston, 1968
·	D6141	·	·	·	Scrapped	J McWilliams, Shettleston, 1968
·	D6142	·	·	·	Scrapped	J McWilliams, Shettleston, 1968

CLASS 21 (Continued)

·	D6143	·	·	·	Scrapped	Barnes & Bell, Coatbridge, 1968
·	D6144	·	·	·	Scrapped	J McWilliams, Shettleston, 1968
·	D6145	·	·	·	Scrapped	J McWilliams, Shettleston, 1968
·	D6146	·	·	·	Scrapped	J McWilliams, Shettleston, 1968
·	D6147	·	·	·	Scrapped	J McWilliams, Shettleston, 1968
·	D6148	·	·	·	Scrapped	J McWilliams, Shettleston, 1968
·	D6149	·	·	·	Scrapped	J McWilliams, Shettleston, 1968
·	D6150	·	·	·	Scrapped	J McWilliams, Shettleston, 1968
·	D6151	·	·	·	Scrapped	J McWilliams, Shettleston, 1968
·	D6152	·	·	·	Scrapped	J McWilliams, Shettleston, 1969
·	D6153	·	·	·	Scrapped	J McWilliams, Shettleston, 1968
·	D6154	·	·	·	Scrapped	J McWilliams, Shettleston, 1968
·	D6155	·	·	·	Scrapped	J McWilliams, Shettleston, 1968
·	D6156	·	·	·	Scrapped	J McWilliams, Shettleston, 1968
·	D6157	·	·	·	Scrapped	J McWilliams, Shettleston, 1968

* Re-engined with a Paxman Ventura power unit to become Class 29

CLASS 22

Total Built	58	Formation	B-B	Max T.E.	40,000 lbf
Date Built	1959-62	Max Speed	75 mph	P.A.R.	810 hp
Builder	North British Loco Co, Glasgow	Weight	65-68 t	R.A.	4
Engine	MAN L12V1821B, 1100hp	Brakes	Vacuum	Supply	Steam

·	D6300*	·	·	·	Scrapped	Cashmore's, Newport, 1968
·	D6301*	·	·	·	Scrapped	Cohen's, Morriston, 1968
·	D6302*	·	·	·	Scrapped	Cashmore's, Newport, 1968
·	D6303*	·	·	·	Scrapped	Cashmore's, Newport, 1968
·	D6304*	·	·	·	Scrapped	Cashmore's, Newport, 1968
·	D6305*	·	·	·	Scrapped	Cashmore's, Newport, 1968
·	D6306	·	·	·	Scrapped	Cashmore's, Newport, 1969
·	D6307	·	·	·	Scrapped	BR, Swindon Works, 1971
·	D6308	·	·	·	Scrapped	BR, Swindon Works, 1972
·	D6309	·	·	·	Scrapped	BR, Swindon Works, 1971
·	D6310	·	·	·	Scrapped	BR, Swindon Works, 1972
·	D6311	·	·	·	Scrapped	Cashmore's, Newport, 1969
·	D6312	·	·	·	Scrapped	BR, Swindon Works, 1972
·	D6313	·	·	·	Scrapped	Cashmore's, Newport, 1968
·	D6314	·	·	·	Scrapped	Cashmore's, Newport, 1969
·	D6315	·	·	·	Scrapped	BR, Swindon Works, 1972
·	D6316	·	·	·	Scrapped	Cashmore's, Newport, 1968
·	D6317	·	·	·	Scrapped	Cashmore's, Newport, 1969
·	D6318	·	·	·	Scrapped	BR, Swindon Works, 1972
·	D6319	·	·	·	Scrapped	BR, Swindon Works, 1972
·	D6320	·	·	·	Scrapped	BR, Swindon Works, 1972
·	D6321	·	·	·	Scrapped	Cashmore's, Newport, 1969
·	D6322	·	·	·	Scrapped	BR, Swindon Works, 1972
·	D6323	·	·	·	Scrapped	BR, Swindon Works, 1972
·	D6324	·	·	·	Scrapped	Cashmore's, Newport, 1969
·	D6325	·	·	·	Scrapped	Cashmore's, Newport, 1969
·	D6326	·	·	·	Scrapped	BR, Swindon Works, 1972
·	D6327	·	·	·	Scrapped	BR, Swindon Works, 1972
·	D6328	·	·	·	Scrapped	BR, Swindon Works, 1972

CLASS 22 (Continued)

·	D6329	·	·	·	Scrapped	Cashmore's, Newport, 1969
·	D6330	·	·	·	Scrapped	BR, Swindon Works, 1972
·	D6331	·	·	·	Scrapped	BR, Swindon Works, 1972
·	D6332	·	·	·	Scrapped	BR, Swindon Works, 1971
·	D6333	·	·	·	Scrapped	BR, Swindon Works, 1972
·	D6334	·	·	·	Scrapped	BR, Swindon Works, 1972
·	D6335	·	·	·	Scrapped	Cashmore's, Newport, 1969
·	D6336	·	·	·	Scrapped	BR, Swindon Works, 1972
·	D6337	·	·	·	Scrapped	BR, Swindon Works, 1972
·	D6338	·	·	·	Scrapped	BR, Swindon Works, 1972
·	D6339	·	·	·	Scrapped	BR, Swindon Works, 1972
·	D6340	·	·	·	Scrapped	BR, Swindon Works, 1972
·	D6341	·	·	·	Scrapped	Cashmore's, Newport, 1969
·	D6342	·	·	·	Scrapped	Cashmore's, Newport, 1969
·	D6343	·	·	·	Scrapped	BR, Swindon Works, 1972
·	D6344	·	·	·	Scrapped	Cashmore's, Newport, 1969
·	D6345	·	·	·	Scrapped	Cashmore's, Newport, 1969
·	D6346	·	·	·	Scrapped	Cashmore's, Newport, 1969
·	D6347	·	·	·	Scrapped	Cashmore's, Newport, 1968
·	D6348	·	·	·	Scrapped	BR, Swindon Works, 1972
·	D6349	·	·	·	Scrapped	BR, Swindon Works, 1971
·	D6350	·	·	·	Scrapped	Cashmore's, Newport, 1969
·	D6351	·	·	·	Scrapped	Cashmore's, Newport, 1969
·	D6352	·	·	·	Scrapped	BR, Swindon Works, 1971
·	D6353	·	·	·	Scrapped	Cashmore's, Newport, 1969
·	D6354	·	·	·	Scrapped	BR, Swindon Works, 1972
·	D6355	·	·	·	Scrapped	Cashmore's, Newport, 1969
·	D6356	·	·	·	Scrapped	BR, Swindon Works, 1972
·	D6357	·	·	·	Scrapped	Cashmore's, Newport, 1969

* Fitted with MAN L12V18 21A, 1000 hp Power Unit

CLASS 23

Total Built	11 (10 + 1*)	Formation	Bo-Bo	Max T.E.	47,000 lbf
Date Built	1959	Max Speed	75 mph	P.A.R.	768 hp
Builder	English Electric Co, Vulcan	Weight	75 t	R.A.	5
Engine	Napier T9-29 Deltic, 1100 hp	Brakes	Vacuum	Supply	Steam

·	D5900	·	·	·	Scrapped	Cohen's, Kettering, 1969
·	D5901	·	·	·	Scrapped	BR, Doncaster Works, 1977
·	D5902	·	·	·	Scrapped	Cohen's, Kettering, 1970
·	D5903	·	·	·	Scrapped	Cohen's, Kettering, 1969
·	D5904	·	·	·	Scrapped	Cohen's, Kettering, 1969
·	D5905	·	·	·	Scrapped	Cohen's, Kettering, 1973
·	D5906	·	·	·	Scrapped	Cohen's, Kettering, 1971
·	D5907	·	·	·	Scrapped	Cohen's, Kettering, 1969
·	D5908	·	·	·	Scrapped	Cashmore's, Great Bridge, 1970
·	D5909	·	·	·	Scrapped	Cohen's, Kettering, 1973
·	D5910*	·	·	·	Preserved	Barrow Hill

* Currently undergoing re-build from Class 37 chassis

CLASS 24

Total Built	151	Formation	Bo-Bo	Max T.E.	40,000 lbf
Date Built	1958-61	Max Speed	75 mph	P.A.R.	843 hp
Builder	BR Derby, Darlington & Crewe	Weight	71 - 79 t	R.A.	5 & 6
Engine	Sulzer 6LDA28, 1160 hp	Brakes	Vacuum	Supply	Steam

24001	D5001	·	·	·	Scrapped	BR, Doncaster Works, 1977
24002	D5002	·	·	·	Scrapped	BR, Glasgow Works, 1977
24003	D5003	·	·	·	Scrapped	BR, Doncaster Works, 1976
24004	D5004	·	·	·	Scrapped	BR, Glasgow Works, 1977
24005	D5000	·	·	·	Scrapped	BR, Swindon Works, 1977
24006	D5006	·	·	·	Scrapped	BR, Glasgow Works, 1980
24007	D5007	·	·	·	Scrapped	BR, Doncaster Works, 1978
24008	D5008	·	·	·	Scrapped	BR, Doncaster Works, 1976
24009	D5009	·	·	·	Scrapped	BR, Doncaster Works, 1977
24010	D5010	·	·	·	Scrapped	BR, Doncaster Works, 1977
24011	D5011	·	·	·	Scrapped	BR, Glasgow Works, 1977
24012	D5012	·	·	·	Scrapped	BR, Doncaster Works, 1976
24013	D5013	·	·	·	Scrapped	BR, Doncaster Works, 1978
24014	D5014	·	·	·	Scrapped	BR, Doncaster Works, 1978
24015	D5015	·	·	·	Scrapped	BR, Doncaster Works, 1977
24016	D5016	·	·	·	Scrapped	BR, Doncaster Works, 1977
24017	D5017	·	·	·	Scrapped	BR, Doncaster Works, 1977
24018	D5018	·	·	·	Scrapped	BR, Doncaster Works, 1976
24019	D5019	·	·	·	Scrapped	BR, Doncaster Works, 1978
24020	D5020	·	·	·	Scrapped	BR, Doncaster Works, 1977
24021	D5021	·	·	·	Scrapped	BR, Doncaster Works, 1977
24022	D5022	·	·	·	Scrapped	BR, Doncaster Works, 1978
24023	D5023	·	·	·	Scrapped	BR, Doncaster Works, 1978
24024	D5024	·	·	·	Scrapped	BR, Swindon Works, 1977
24025	D5025	·	·	·	Scrapped	BR, Swindon Works, 1977
24026	D5026	·	·	·	Scrapped	BR, Swindon Works, 1977
24027	D5027	·	·	·	Scrapped	BR, Swindon Works, 1977
24029	D5029	·	·	·	Scrapped	BR, Swindon Works, 1977
24030	D5030	·	·	·	Scrapped	BR, Swindon Works, 1977
24031	D5031	·	·	·	Scrapped	BR, Swindon Works, 1976
24032	D5032	·	·	·	Preserved	North Yorkshire Moors Railway
24033	D5033	·	·	·	Scrapped	BR, Swindon Works, 1977
24034	D5034	·	·	·	Scrapped	BR, Swindon Works, 1977
24035	D5035	·	·	·	Scrapped	BR, Doncaster Works, 1979
24036	D5036	·	·	·	Scrapped	BR, Doncaster Works, 1978
24037	D5037	·	·	·	Scrapped	BR, Swindon Works, 1977
24038	D5038	·	·	·	Scrapped	BR, Swindon Works, 1977
24039	D5039	·	·	·	Scrapped	BR, Swindon Works, 1978
24040	D5040	·	·	·	Scrapped	BR, Swindon Works, 1977
24041	D5041	·	·	·	Scrapped	BR, Swindon Works, 1978
24042	D5042	·	·	·	Scrapped	BR, Swindon Works, 1976
24044	D5044	·	·	·	Scrapped	BR, Swindon Works, 1977
24045	D5045	·	·	·	Scrapped	BR, Swindon Works, 1976
24046	D5046	·	·	·	Scrapped	BR, Swindon Works, 1977
24047	D5047	·	·	·	Scrapped	BR, Doncaster Works, 1979
24048	D5048	·	·	·	Scrapped	BR, Swindon Works, 1976
24049	D5049	·	·	·	Scrapped	BR, Swindon Works, 1976
24050	D5050	·	·	·	Scrapped	BR, Swindon Works, 1976
24052	D5052	·	·	·	Scrapped	BR, Swindon Works, 1978
24053	D5053	·	·	·	Scrapped	BR, Swindon Works, 1976

24054	D5054	968008*	·	·	Preserved	East Lancashire Railway
24055	D5055	·	·	·	Scrapped	BR, Swindon Works, 1976
24056	D5056	·	·	·	Scrapped	BR, Swindon Works, 1976
24057	D5057	·	·	·	Scrapped	BR, Doncaster Works, 1978
24058	D5058	·	·	·	Scrapped	BR, Swindon Works, 1976
24059	D5059	·	·	·	Scrapped	BR, Swindon Works, 1977
24060	D5060	·	·	·	Scrapped	BR, Swindon Works, 1977
24061	D5061	968007+	97201	·	Preserved	North Yorkshire Moors Railway
24062	D5062	·	·	·	Scrapped	BR, Swindon Works, 1976
24063	D5063	·	·	·	Scrapped	BR, Doncaster Works, 1979
24064	D5064	·	·	·	Scrapped	BR, Swindon Works, 1976
24065	D5065	·	·	·	Scrapped	BR, Swindon Works, 1977
24066	D5066	·	·	·	Scrapped	BR, Doncaster Works, 1978
24069	D5069	·	·	·	Scrapped	BR, Doncaster Works, 1977
24070	D5070	·	·	·	Scrapped	BR, Doncaster Works, 1976
24071	D5071	·	·	·	Scrapped	BR, Doncaster Works, 1977
24072	D5072	·	·	·	Scrapped	BR, Doncaster Works, 1977
24073	D5073	·	·	·	Scrapped	BR, Doncaster Works, 1978
24074	D5074	·	·	·	Scrapped	Cashmore's, Great Bridge, 1976
24075	D5075	·	·	·	Scrapped	BR, Swindon Works, 1976
24076	D5076	·	·	·	Scrapped	BR, Swindon Works, 1977
24077	D5077	·	·	·	Scrapped	BR, Swindon Works, 1978
24078	D5078	·	·	·	Scrapped	BR, Swindon Works, 1978
24079	D5079	·	·	·	Scrapped	BR, Swindon Works, 1978
24080	D5080	·	·	·	Scrapped	BR, Doncaster Works, 1978
24081	D5081		·	·	Preserved	G & WR
24082	D5082	·	·	·	Scrapped	BR, Doncaster Works, 1979
24083	D5083	·	·	·	Scrapped	BR, Swindon Works, 1977
24084	D5084	·	·	·	Scrapped	BR, Swindon Works, 1978
24085	D5085	·	·	·	Scrapped	BR, Swindon Works, 1978
24086	D5086	·	·	·	Scrapped	BR, Doncaster Works, 1977
24087	D5087	·	·	·	Scrapped	BR, Doncaster Works, 1978
24089	D5089	·	·	·	Scrapped	BR, Swindon Works, 1977
24090	D5090	·	·	·	Scrapped	BR, Doncaster Works, 1978
24091	D5091	·	·	·	Scrapped	BR, Doncaster Works, 1978
24092	D5092	·	·	·	Scrapped	BR, Swindon Works, 1976
24094	D5094	·	·	·	Scrapped	BR, Doncaster Works, 1977
24095	D5095	·	·	·	Scrapped	BR, Doncaster Works, 1976
24096	D5096	·	·	·	Scrapped	BR, Doncaster Works, 1976
24097	D5097	·	·	·	Scrapped	BR, Doncaster Works, 1977
24098	D5098	·	·	·	Scrapped	BR, Doncaster Works, 1976
24099	D5099	·	·	·	Scrapped	BR, Doncaster Works, 1977
24100	D5100	·	·	·	Scrapped	BR, Doncaster Works, 1976
24101	D5101	·	·	·	Scrapped	BR, Doncaster Works, 1976
24102	D5102	·	·	·	Scrapped	BR, Doncaster Works, 1978
24103	D5103	·	·	·	Scrapped	BR, Doncaster Works, 1977
24104	D5104	·	·	·	Scrapped	BR, Doncaster Works, 1977
24105	D5105	·	·	·	Scrapped	BR, Doncaster Works, 1978
24106	D5106	·	·	·	Scrapped	BR, Doncaster Works, 1977
24107	D5107	·	·	·	Scrapped	BR, Swindon Works, 1977
24108	D5108	·	·	·	Scrapped	BR, Doncaster Works, 1978
24109	D5109	·	·	·	Scrapped	BR, Doncaster Works, 1978
24110	D5110	·	·	·	Scrapped	BR, Doncaster Works, 1977
24111	D5111	·	·	·	Scrapped	BR, Doncaster Works, 1978

24112	D5112	·	·	·	Scrapped	BR, Doncaster Works, 1977
24113	D5113	·	·	·	Scrapped	BR, Doncaster Works, 1977
24115	D5115	·	·	·	Scrapped	BR, Swindon Works, 1977
24116	D5116	·	·	·	Scrapped	BR, Doncaster Works, 1977
24117	D5117	·	·	·	Scrapped	BR, Doncaster Works, 1977
24118	D5118	·	·	·	Scrapped	BR, Doncaster Works, 1977
24119	D5119	·	·	·	Scrapped	BR, Doncaster Works, 1977
24120	D5120	·	·	·	Scrapped	BR, Doncaster Works, 1977
24121	D5121	·	·	·	Scrapped	BR, Doncaster Works, 1978
24123	D5123	·	·	·	Scrapped	BR, Doncaster Works, 1977
24124	D5124	·	·	·	Scrapped	BR, Swindon Works, 1977
24125	D5125	·	·	·	Scrapped	BR, Doncaster Works, 1977
24126	D5126	·	·	·	Scrapped	BR, Doncaster Works, 1977
24127	D5127	·	·	·	Scrapped	BR, Doncaster Works, 1977
24128	D5128	·	·	·	Scrapped	BR, Doncaster Works, 1977
24129	D5129	·	·	·	Scrapped	BR, Doncaster Works, 1977
24130	D5130	·	·	·	Scrapped	BR, Doncaster Works, 1977
24132	D5132	·	·	·	Scrapped	BR, Doncaster Works, 1976
24133	D5133	·	·	·	Scrapped	BR, Doncaster Works, 1978
24134	D5134	·	·	·	Scrapped	BR, Swindon Works, 1978
24135	D5135	·	·	·	Scrapped	BR, Swindon Works, 1977
24136	D5136	·	·	·	Scrapped	BR, Swindon Works, 1977
24137	D5137	·	·	·	Scrapped	BR, Doncaster Works, 1978
24140	D5140	·	·	·	Scrapped	BR, Swindon Works, 1976
24141	D5141	·	·	·	Scrapped	BR, Swindon Works, 1978
24142	D5142	968009*	·	·	Scrapped	Coopor'c Motolo, Shoffiold, 1984
24143	D5143	·	·	·	Scrapped	BR, Swindon Works, 1976
24144	D5144	·	·	·	Scrapped	BR, Swindon Works, 1976
24145	D5145	·	·	·	Scrapped	BR, Swindon Works, 1976
24146	D5146	·	·	·	Scrapped	BR, Swindon Works, 1976
24147	D5147	·	·	·	Scrapped	BR, Doncaster Works, 1977
24148	D5148	·	·	·	Scrapped	BR, Doncaster Works, 1977
24149	D5149	·	·	·	Scrapped	BR, Glasgow Works, 1973
24150	D5150	·	·	·	Scrapped	BR, Doncaster Works, 1977
·	D5005	·	·	·	Scrapped	BR, Derby Works, 1969
·	D5028	·	·	·	Scrapped	BR, Crewe Works, 1972
·	D5043	·	·	·	Scrapped	Cashmore's, Great Bridge, 1970
·	D5051	·	·	·	Scrapped	BR, Inverurie Works, 1968
·	D5067	·	·	·	Scrapped	BR, Glasgow Works, 1973
·	D5068	·	·	·	Scrapped	BR, Glasgow Works, 1973
·	D5088	·	·	·	Scrapped	Cohen's, Kettering, 1972
·	D5093	·	·	·	Scrapped	Cashmore's, Great Bridge, 1970
·	D5114	·	·	·	Scrapped	BR, Glasgow Works, 1973
·	D5122	·	·	·	Scrapped	BR, Glasgow Works, 1971
·	D5131	·	·	·	Scrapped	BR, Glasgow Works, 1971
·	D5138	·	·	·	Scrapped	Cashmore's, Great Bridge, 1970
·	D5139	·	·	·	Scrapped	Cashmore's, Great Bridge, 1970

Class 24/0 (24001 - 24049) Weight 77-79 t   Class 24/1 (24050 - 24150) Weight 71-73 t

* Converted to static train pre-heating units and renumbered with TDB prefix
+ Used for research-departmental purposes and renumbered with RDB prefix

Class 24 Names: | D5054   PHIL SOUTHERN | 97201   Experiment

CLASS 25

Total Built	327	Formation	Bo-Bo	Max T.E.	45,000 lbf
Date Built	1961-67	Max Speed	90 mph	P.A.R.	949 hp
Builder	BR Derby, Darlington & Gorton	Weight	72 - 76 t	R.A.	5
Engine	Sulzer 6LDA28B, 1250 hp	Brakes	Vacuum / Air & Vac	Supply	Steam

25001	D5151	·	·	·	Scrapped	BR, Swindon Works, 1980
25002	D5152	·	·	·	Scrapped	BR, Swindon Works, 1981
25003	D5153	·	·	·	Scrapped	BR, Glasgow Works, 1978
25004	D5154	·	·	·	Scrapped	BR, Glasgow Works, 1977
25005	D5155	·	·	·	Scrapped	BR, Swindon Works, 1981
25006	D5156	·	·	·	Scrapped	BR, Swindon Works, 1983
25007	D5157	·	·	·	Scrapped	BR, Swindon Works, 1982
25008	D5158	·	·	·	Scrapped	BR, Glasgow Works, 1980
25009	D5159	·	·	·	Scrapped	BR, Glasgow Works, 1980
25010	D5160	·	·	·	Scrapped	BR, Swindon Works, 1981
25011	D5161	·	·	·	Scrapped	BR, Swindon Works, 1981
25012	D5162	·	·	·	Scrapped	BR, Glasgow Works, 1977
25013	D5163	·	·	·	Scrapped	BR, Swindon Works, 1983
25014	D5164	·	·	·	Scrapped	BR, Glasgow Works, 1977
25015	D5165	·	·	·	Scrapped	BR, Doncaster Works, 1977
25016	D5166	·	·	·	Scrapped	BR, Swindon Works, 1976
25017	D5167	·	·	·	Scrapped	BR, Swindon Works, 1976
25018	D5168	·	·	·	Scrapped	BR, Glasgow Works, 1978
25019	D5169	·	·	·	Scrapped	BR, Swindon Works, 1983
25020	D5170	·	·	·	Scrapped	BR, Swindon Works, 1976
25021	D5171	·	·	·	Scrapped	BR, Swindon Works, 1980
25022	D5172	·	·	·	Scrapped	BR, Glasgow Works, 1978
25023	D5173	·	·	·	Scrapped	BR, Swindon Works, 1983
25024	D5174	·	·	·	Scrapped	BR, Glasgow Works, 1976
25025	D5175	·	·	·	Scrapped	BR, Glasgow Works, 1978
25026	D5176	·	·	·	Scrapped	BR, Swindon Works, 1981
25027	D5177	·	·	·	Scrapped	Vic Berry, Leicester, 1987
25028	D5178	·	·	·	Scrapped	Vic Berry, Leicester, 1987
25029	D5179	·	·	·	Scrapped	BR, Glasgow Works, 1978
25030	D5180	·	·	·	Scrapped	BR, Derby Works, 1980
25031	D5181	·	·	·	Scrapped	BR, Glasgow Works, 1978
25032	D5182	·	·	·	Scrapped	Vic Berry, Leicester, 1988
25033	D5183	·	·	·	Scrapped	Vic Berry, Derby, 1986
25034	D5184	·	·	·	Scrapped	Vic Berry, Leicester, 1988
25035	D5185	·	·	·	Preserved	Great Central Railway
25036	D5186	·	·	·	Scrapped	BR, Swindon Works, 1985
25037	D5187	·	·	·	Scrapped	Vic Berry, Leicester, 1987
25038	D5188	·	·	·	Scrapped	BR, Derby Works, 1982
25039	D5189	·	·	·	Scrapped	BR, Swindon Works, 1981
25040	D5190	·	·	·	Scrapped	BR, Swindon Works, 1982
25041	D5191	·	·	·	Scrapped	BR, Swindon Works, 1983
25042	D5192	·	·	·	Scrapped	Vic Berry, Leicester, 1987
25043	D5193	·	·	·	Scrapped	BR, Derby Works, 1981
25044	D5194	·	·	·	Scrapped	BR, Doncaster Works, 1986
25045	D5195	·	·	·	Scrapped	BR, Derby Works, 1979
25046	D5196	·	·	·	Scrapped	Vic Berry, Leicester, 1987
25047	D5197	·	·	·	Scrapped	BR, Swindon Works, 1983
25048	D5198	·	·	·	Scrapped	Vic Berry, Leicester, 1987
25049	D5199	·	·	·	Scrapped	BR, Swindon Works, 1985
25050	D5200	·	·	·	Scrapped	BR, Swindon Works, 1985

25051	D5201	·	·	·	Scrapped	Vic Berry, Leicester, 1987
25052	D5202	·	·	·	Scrapped	BR, Swindon Works, 1980
25053	D5203	·	·	·	Scrapped	BR, Swindon Works, 1981
25054	D5204	·	·	·	Scrapped	BR, Doncaster Works, 1986
25055	D5205	·	·	·	Scrapped	BR, Swindon Works, 1981
25056	D5206	·	·	·	Scrapped	BR, Swindon Works, 1985
25057	D5207	·	·	·	Preserved	North Norfolk Railway
25058	D5208	·	·	·	Scrapped	Vic Berry, Leicester, 1988
25059	D5209	·	·	·	Preserved	Keighley & Worth Valley Railway
25060	D5210	·	·	·	Scrapped	Vic Berry, Leicester, 1987
25061	D5211	·	·	·	Scrapped	BR, Swindon Works, 1983
25062	D5212	·	·	·	Scrapped	BR, Swindon Works, 1985
25063	D5213	·	·	·	Scrapped	BR, Swindon Works, 1983
25064	D5214	·	·	·	Scrapped	Vic Berry, Leicester, 1987
25065	D5215	·	·	·	Scrapped	BR, Swindon Works, 1982
25066	D5216	·	·	·	Scrapped	BR, Derby Works, 1983
25067	D5217	·	·	·	Preserved	Nemesis Rail, Burton-upon-Trent
25068	D5218	·	·	·	Scrapped	BR, Glasgow Works, 1981
25069	D5219	·	·	·	Scrapped	BR, Swindon Works, 1986
25070	D5220	·	·	·	Scrapped	BR, Swindon Works, 1983
25071	D5221	·	·	·	Scrapped	BR, Swindon Works, 1983
25072	D5222	·	·	·	Preserved	Caledonian Railway
25073	D5223	·	·	·	Scrapped	BR, Swindon Works, 1982
25074	D5224	·	·	·	Scrapped	BR, Swindon Works, 1982
25075	D5225	·	·	·	Scrapped	Vic Berry, Leicester, 1987
25076	D5226	·	·	·	Scrapped	BR, Swindon Works, 1986
25077	D5227	·	·	·	Scrapped	BR, Glasgow Works, 1978
25078	D5228	·	·	·	Scrapped	Vic Berry, Leicester, 1987
25079	D5229	·	·	·	Scrapped	BR, Swindon Works, 1984
25080	D5230	·	·	·	Scrapped	MC Metals, Springburn, 1993
25081	D5231	·	·	·	Scrapped	BR, Swindon Works, 1982
25082	D5232	·	·	·	Scrapped	BR, Swindon Works, 1982
25083	D5233	·	·	·	Preserved	Caledonian Railway
25084	D5234	·	·	·	Scrapped	BR, Swindon Works, 1986
25085	D5235	·	·	·	Scrapped	BR, Derby Works, 1983
25086	D5236	·	·	·	Scrapped	BR, Swindon Works, 1986
25087	D5237	·	·	·	Scrapped	BR, Swindon Works, 1981
25088	D5238	·	·	·	Scrapped	Vic Berry, Derby, 1986
25089	D5239	·	·	·	Scrapped	Vic Berry, Leicester, 1987
25090	D5240	·	·	·	Scrapped	BR, Swindon Works, 1985
25091	D5241	·	·	·	Scrapped	BR, Glasgow Works, 1979
25092	D5242	·	·	·	Scrapped	BR, Derby Works, 1982
25093	D5243	·	·	·	Scrapped	Vic Berry, Leicester, 1988
25094	D5244	·	·	·	Scrapped	BR, Derby Works, 1982
25095	D5245	·	·	·	Scrapped	Vic Berry, Leicester, 1987
25096	D5246	·	·	·	Scrapped	BR, Glasgow Works, 1978
25097	D5247	·	·	·	Scrapped	BR, Swindon Works, 1985
25098	D5248	·	·	·	Scrapped	BR, Glasgow Works, 1979
25099	D5249	·	·	·	Scrapped	BR, Swindon Works, 1981
25100	D5250	·	·	·	Scrapped	BR, Swindon Works, 1985
25101	D5251	·	·	·	Scrapped	BR, Swindon Works, 1983
25102	D5252	·	·	·	Scrapped	BR, Swindon Works, 1980
25103	D5253	·	·	·	Scrapped	BR, Swindon Works, 1983
25104	D5254	·	·	·	Scrapped	BR, Swindon Works, 1986

CLASS 25 (Continued)

25105	D5255	·	·	·	Scrapped	BR, Swindon Works, 1985
25106	D5256	·	·	·	Scrapped	BR, Swindon Works, 1984
25107	D5257	·	·	·	Scrapped	BR, Swindon Works, 1981
25108	D5258	·	·	·	Scrapped	BR, Glasgow Works, 1981
25109	D5259	·	·	·	Scrapped	Vic Berry, Leicester, 1987
25110	D5260	·	·	·	Scrapped	BR, Swindon Works, 1982
25111	D5261	·	·	·	Scrapped	BR, Swindon Works, 1980
25112	D5262	·	·	·	Scrapped	BR, Swindon Works, 1982
25113	D5263	·	·	·	Scrapped	BR, Swindon Works, 1983
25114	D5264	·	·	·	Scrapped	BR, Swindon Works, 1981
25115	D5265	·	·	·	Scrapped	BR, Swindon Works, 1985
25116	D5266	·	·	·	Scrapped	BR, Swindon Works, 1982
25117	D5267	·	·	·	Scrapped	BR, Swindon Works, 1984
25118	D5268	·	·	·	Scrapped	BR, Swindon Works, 1983
25119	D5269	·	·	·	Scrapped	BR, Doncaster Works, 1986
25120	D5270	·	·	·	Scrapped	BR, Swindon Works, 1984
25121	D5271	·	·	·	Scrapped	BR, Swindon Works, 1982
25122	D5272	·	·	·	Scrapped	BR, Swindon Works, 1983
25123	D5273	·	·	·	Scrapped	Vic Berry, Leicester, 1987
25124	D5274	·	·	·	Scrapped	BR, Swindon Works, 1986
25125	D5275	·	·	·	Scrapped	BR, Swindon Works, 1983
25126	D5276	·	·	·	Scrapped	Vic Berry, Leicester, 1983
25127	D5277	·	·	·	Scrapped	BR, Swindon Works, 1983
25129	D5279	·	·	·	Scrapped	BR, Swindon Works, 1985
25130	D5280	·	·	·	Scrapped	BR, Swindon Works, 1987
25131	D5281	97202~	·	·	Scrapped	Vic Berry, Leicester, 1987
25132	D5282	·	·	·	Scrapped	BR, Swindon Works, 1984
25133	D5283	·	·	·	Scrapped	Vic Berry, Leicester, 1987
25134	D5284	·	·	·	Scrapped	Vic Berry, Leicester, 1988
25135	D5285	·	·	·	Scrapped	BR, Swindon Works, 1986
25136	D5286	·	·	·	Scrapped	BR, Swindon Works, 1986
25137	D5287	·	·	·	Scrapped	BR, Swindon Works, 1983
25138	D5288	·	·	·	Scrapped	BR, Swindon Works, 1986
25139	D5289	·	·	·	Scrapped	BR, Swindon Works, 1986
25140	D5290	·	·	·	Scrapped	BR, Swindon Works, 1986
25141	D5291	·	·	·	Scrapped	BR, Swindon Works, 1987
25142	D5292	·	·	·	Scrapped	BR, Swindon Works, 1982
25143	D5293	·	·	·	Scrapped	BR, Swindon Works, 1984
25144	D5294	·	·	·	Scrapped	Vic Berry, Leicester, 1986
25145	D5295	·	·	·	Scrapped	Vic Berry, Leicester, 1987
25146	D5296	·	·	·	Scrapped	BR, Swindon Works, 1985
25147	D5297	·	·	·	Scrapped	BR, Swindon Works, 1980
25148	D5298	·	·	·	Scrapped	BR, Swindon Works, 1983
25149	D5299	·	·	·	Scrapped	BR, Swindon Works, 1983
25150	D7500	·	·	·	Scrapped	BR, Swindon Works, 1985
25151	D7501	·	·	·	Scrapped	Vic Berry, Toton, 1987
25152	D7502	·	·	·	Scrapped	BR, Swindon Works, 1985
25153	D7503	·	·	·	Scrapped	BR, Swindon Works, 1987
25154	D7504	·	·	·	Scrapped	Vic Berry, Leicester, 1987
25155	D7505	·	·	·	Scrapped	BR, Swindon Works, 1981
25156	D7506	·	·	·	Scrapped	BR, Swindon Works, 1982
25157	D7507	·	·	·	Scrapped	BR, Swindon Works, 1987
25158	D7508	·	·	·	Scrapped	Vic Berry, Leicester, 1987
25159	D7509	·	·	·	Scrapped	BR, Swindon Works, 1981

CLASS 25 (Continued)

25160	D7510	·	·	·	Scrapped	Vic Berry, Leicester, 1987
25161	D7511	·	·	·	Scrapped	Vic Berry, Leicester, 1988
25162	D7512	·	·	·	Scrapped	BR, Swindon Works, 1982
25163	D7513	·	·	·	Scrapped	BR, Swindon Works, 1983
25164	D7514	·	·	·	Scrapped	Vic Berry, Leicester, 1987
25165	D7515	·	·	·	Scrapped	BR, Derby Works, 1979
25166	D7516	·	·	·	Scrapped	BR, Swindon Works, 1981
25167	D7517	·	·	·	Scrapped	BR, Swindon Works, 1984
25168	D7518	·	·	·	Scrapped	BR, Swindon Works, 1984
25169	D7519	·	·	·	Scrapped	BR, Swindon Works, 1982
25170	D7520	·	·	·	Scrapped	BR, Derby Works, 1983
25171	D7521	·	·	·	Scrapped	BR, Arbroath, 1979
25172	D7522	·	·	·	Scrapped	BR, Swindon Works, 1983
25173	D7523	·	·	·	Preserved	Epping Ongar Railway
25174	D7524	·	·	·	Scrapped	BR, Derby Works, 1978
25175	D7525	·	·	·	Scrapped	Vic Berry, Leicester, 1987
25176	D7526	·	·	·	Scrapped	Vic Berry, Leicester, 1988
25177	D7527	·	·	·	Scrapped	BR, Swindon Works, 1986
25178	D7528	·	·	·	Scrapped	Vic Berry, Leicester, 1989
25179	D7529	·	·	·	Scrapped	BR, Swindon Works, 1987
25180	D7530	·	·	·	Scrapped	Vic Berry, Leicester, 1988
25181	D7531	·	·	·	Scrapped	Vic Berry, Eastleigh, 1988
25182	D7532	·	·	·	Scrapped	BR, Swindon Works, 1985
25183	D7533	·	·	·	Scrapped	BR, Swindon Works, 1981
25184	D7534	·	·	·	Scrapped	BR, Swindon Works, 1984
25185	D7535	·	·	·	Preserved	Dartmouth Steam Railway
25186	D7536	·	·	·	Scrapped	BR, Swindon Works, 1987
25187	D7537	·	·	·	Scrapped	BR, Swindon Works, 1987
25188	D7538	·	·	·	Scrapped	BR, Swindon Works, 1987
25189	D7539	·	·	·	Scrapped	BR, Doncaster Works, 1986
25190	D7540	·	·	·	Scrapped	Vic Berry, Leicester, 1987
25191	D7541	·	·	·	Preserved	South Devon Railway
25192	D7542	·	·	·	Scrapped	Vic Berry, Leicester, 1987
25193	D7543	·	·	·	Scrapped	Vic Berry, Leicester, 1987
25194	D7544	·	·	·	Scrapped	MC Metals, Springburn, 1994
25195	D7545	·	·	·	Scrapped	Vic Berry, Leicester, 1986
25196	D7546	·	·	·	Scrapped	Vic Berry, Leicester, 1987
25197	D7547	·	·	·	Scrapped	BR, Swindon Works, 1983
25198	D7548	·	·	·	Scrapped	Vic Berry, Leicester, 1987
25199	D7549	·	·	·	Scrapped	Vic Berry, Leicester, 1989
25200	D7550	·	·	·	Scrapped	Vic Berry, Leicester, 1987
25201	D7551	·	·	·	Scrapped	Vic Berry, Leicester, 1988
25202	D7552	·	·	·	Scrapped	Vic Berry, Leicester, 1989
25203	D7553	·	·	·	Scrapped	BR, Swindon Works, 1986
25204	D7554	·	·	·	Scrapped	BR, Swindon Works, 1980
25205	D7555	·	·	·	Scrapped	MC Metals, Springburn, 1995
25206	D7556	·	·	·	Scrapped	MC Metals, Springburn, 1995
25207	D7557	·	·	·	Scrapped	Vic Berry, Leicester, 1988
25208	D7558	·	·	·	Scrapped	Vic Berry, Leicester, 1987
25209	D7559	·	·	·	Scrapped	MC Metals, Springburn, 1992
25210	D7560	·	·	·	Scrapped	BR, Doncaster Works, 1986
25211	D7561	·	·	·	Scrapped	MC Metals, Springburn, 1995
25212	D7562	·	·	·	Scrapped	Vic Berry, Leicester, 1987
25213	D7563	·	·	·	Scrapped	Vic Berry, Leicester, 1990

25214	D7564	·	·	·	Scrapped	BR, Swindon Works, 1986
25215	D7565	·	·	·	Scrapped	BR, Swindon Works, 1983
25216	D7566	·	·	·	Scrapped	BR, Derby Works, 1983
25217	D7567	·	·	·	Scrapped	BR, Derby Works, 1982
25218	D7568	·	·	·	Scrapped	BR, Swindon Works, 1985
25219	D7569	·	·	·	Scrapped	BR, Swindon Works, 1987
25220	D7570	·	·	·	Scrapped	BR, Swindon Works, 1985
25221	D7571	·	·	·	Scrapped	BR, Swindon Works, 1986
25222	D7572	·	·	·	Scrapped	BR, Swindon Works, 1981
25223	D7573	·	·	·	Scrapped	BR, Swindon Works, 1980
25224	D7574	·	·	·	Scrapped	Vic Berry, Leicester, 1987
25225	D7575	·	·	·	Scrapped	BR, Swindon Works, 1980
25226	D7576	·	·	·	Scrapped	BR, Doncaster Works, 1986
25227	D7577	·	·	·	Scrapped	BR, Swindon Works, 1983
25228	D7578	·	·	·	Scrapped	Vic Berry, Leicester, 1987
25229	D7579	·	·	·	Scrapped	BR, Doncaster Works, 1986
25230	D7580	·	·	·	Scrapped	Vic Berry, Leicester, 1987
25231	D7581	·	·	·	Scrapped	Vic Berry, Leicester, 1987
25232	D7582	·	·	·	Scrapped	BR, Swindon Works, 1983
25233	D7583	·	·	·	Scrapped	BR, Swindon Works, 1985
25234	D7584	·	·	·	Scrapped	Vic Berry, Leicester, 1987
25235	D7585	·	·	·	Preserved	Bo'ness & Kinneil Railway
25236	D7586	·	·	·	Scrapped	BR, Swindon Works, 1986
25237	D7587	·	·	·	Scrapped	BR, Doncaster Works, 1986
25238	D7588	·	·	·	Scrapped	BR, Swindon Works, 1983
25239	D7589	·	·	·	Scrapped	BR, Swindon Works, 1986
25240	D7590	·	·	·	Scrapped	BR, Swindon Works, 1983
25241	D7591	·	·	·	Scrapped	BR, Swindon Works, 1981
25242	D7592	·	·	·	Scrapped	BR, Swindon Works, 1984
25243	D7593	·	·	·	Scrapped	BR, Swindon Works, 1984
25244	D7594	·	·	·	Preserved	Kent & East Sussex Railway
25245	D7595	·	·	·	Scrapped	BR, Doncaster Works, 1986
25246	D7596	·	·	·	Scrapped	BR, Swindon Works, 1983
25247	D7597	·	·	·	Scrapped	BR, Swindon Works, 1983
25248	D7598	·	·	·	Scrapped	BR, Swindon Works, 1986
25249	D7599	·	·	·	Scrapped	Vic Berry, Leicester, 1989
25250	D7600	·	·	·	Scrapped	BR, Swindon Works, 1985
25251	D7601	·	·	·	Scrapped	BR, Swindon Works, 1986
25252	D7602	·	·	·	Scrapped	BR, Swindon Works, 1980
25253	D7603	·	·	·	Scrapped	BR, Swindon Works, 1985
25254	D7604	·	·	·	Scrapped	Vic Berry, Leicester, 1989
25256	D7606	·	·	·	Scrapped	BR, Swindon Works, 1986
25257	D7607	·	·	·	Scrapped	Vic Berry, Leicester, 1987
25258	D7608	·	·	·	Scrapped	BR, Swindon Works, 1986
25259	D7609	·	·	·	Scrapped	MC Metals, Springburn, 1995
25260	D7610	·	·	·	Scrapped	Vic Berry, Leicester, 1987
25261	D7611	·	·	·	Scrapped	Vic Berry, Derby, 1985
25262	D7612	25901	·	·	Preserved	South Devon Railway
25263	D7613	·	·	·	Scrapped	BR, Swindon Works, 1983
25264	D7614	·	·	·	Scrapped	BR, Swindon Works, 1983
25265	D7615	·	·	·	Preserved	Nemesis Rail, Burton-upon-Trent
25266	D7616	·	·	·	Scrapped	Vic Berry, Leicester, 1989
25267	D7617	·	·	·	Scrapped	BR, Derby Works, 1982
25268	D7618	25902	·	·	Scrapped	Vic Berry, Leicester, 1987

CLASS 25 (Continued)

25269	D7619	·	·	·	Scrapped	Vic Berry, Leicester, 1987
25270	D7620	·	·	·	Scrapped	BR, Swindon Works, 1986
25271	D7621	·	·	·	Scrapped	BR, Derby Works, 1982
25272	D7622	·	·	·	Scrapped	BR, Derby Works, 1982
25273	D7623	·	·	·	Scrapped	BR, Swindon Works, 1982
25274	D7624	·	·	·	Scrapped	BR, Swindon Works, 1985
25275	D7625	·	·	·	Scrapped	BR, Swindon Works, 1985
25276	D7626	25903	·	·	Scrapped	Vic Berry, Leicester, 1989
25277	D7627	·	·	·	Scrapped	BR, Swindon Works, 1985
25278	D7628	·	·	·	Operational	North Yorkshire Moors Railway
25279	D7629	·	·	·	Preserved	Great Central Railway North
25280	D7630	·	·	·	Scrapped	BR, Swindon Works, 1983
25281	D7631	·	·	·	Scrapped	BR, Swindon Works, 1981
25282	D7632	·	·	·	Scrapped	Vic Berry, Leicester, 1989
25283	D7633	25904	·	·	Preserved	Dean Forest Railway
25284	D7634	·	·	·	Scrapped	BR, Swindon Works, 1986
25285	D7635	·	·	·	Scrapped	Vic Berry, Leicester, 1987
25286	D7636	25905	·	·	Scrapped	MC Metals, Springburn, 1989
25287	D7637	·	·	·	Scrapped	Vic Berry, Leicester, 1987
25288	D7638	·	·	·	Scrapped	Vic Berry, Leicester, 1988
25289	D7639	·	·	·	Scrapped	BR, Swindon Works, 1984
25290	D7640	·	·	·	Scrapped	BR, Derby Works, 1983
25291	D7641	·	·	·	Scrapped	BR, Swindon Works, 1982
25292	D7642	·	·	·	Scrapped	BR, Swindon Works, 1983
25293	D7643	·	·	·	Scrapped	BR, Swindon Works, 1981
25294	D7644	·	·	·	Scrapped	BR, Swindon Works, 1985
25295	D7645	·	·	·	Scrapped	BR, Derby Works, 1981
25296	D7646	25906	·	·	Scrapped	Vic Berry, Leicester, 1987
25297	D7647	25907	·	·	Scrapped	Vic Berry, Leicester, 1989
25298	D7648	·	·	·	Scrapped	BR, Doncaster Works, 1986
25299	D7649	·	·	·	Scrapped	BR, Derby Works, 1982
25300	D7650	·	·	·	Scrapped	BR, Doncaster Works, 1986
25301	D7651	·	·	·	Scrapped	BR, Swindon Works, 1984
25302	D7652	·	·	·	Scrapped	BR, Doncaster Works, 1986
25303	D7653	·	·	·	Scrapped	Vic Berry, Leicester, 1987
25304	D7654	·	·	·	Scrapped	BR, Swindon Works, 1985
25305	D7655	97251	Ethel 2*	·	Scrapped	MC Metals, Springburn, 1994
25306	D7656	·	·	·	Scrapped	Vic Berry, Leicester, 1988
25307	D7657	25908	968026+	·	Scrapped	Vic Berry, Leicester, 1988
25308	D7658	·	·	·	Scrapped	BR, Swindon Works, 1984
25309	D7659	25909	·	·	Preserved	Peak Rail
25310	D7660	97250	Ethel 1*	·	Scrapped	MC Metals, Springburn, 1994
25311	D7661	·	·	·	Scrapped	Vic Berry, Leicester, 1989
25312	D7662	·	·	·	Scrapped	BR, Swindon Works, 1985
25313	D7663	·	·	·	Preserved	Wensleydale Railway
25314	D7664	97252	Ethel 3*	·	Scrapped	MC Metals, Springburn, 1994
25315	D7665	25910	·	·	Scrapped	Vic Berry, Leicester, 1987
25316	D7666	25911	·	·	Scrapped	Vic Berry, Leicester, 1989
25317	D7667	·	·	·	Scrapped	BR, Swindon Works, 1986
25318	D7668	·	·	·	Scrapped	Vic Berry, Leicester, 1987
25319	D7669	·	·	·	Scrapped	BR, Swindon Works, 1985
25320	D7670	·	·	·	Scrapped	BR, Swindon Works, 1985
25321	D7671	·	·	·	Preserved	Midland Railway Centre
25322	D7672	25912	968027+	·	Preserved	Churnet Valley Railway

CLASS 25 (Continued)

25323	D7673	·	·	·	Scrapped	Vic Berry, Leicester, 1987
25324	D7674	·	·	·	Scrapped	Vic Berry, Leicester, 1987
25325	D7675	·	·	·	Scrapped	MC Metals, Springburn, 1990
25326	D7676	·	·	·	Scrapped	BR, Swindon Works, 1986
25327	D7677	·	·	·	Scrapped	Vic Berry, Leicester, 1988
·	D5278	·	·	·	Scrapped	Cohen's, Peak Forest, 1971
·	D7605	·	·	·	Scrapped	BR, Derby Works, 1972

Class 25/0 (25001 - 25025) Original Design
Class 25/1 (25026 - 25082) Modified cab details and GEC Series 1 equipment
Class 25/2 (25083 - 25247) Modified cab details and GEC Series 2 equipment
Class 25/3 (25248 - 25327) Modified cab details and GEC Series 3 equipment
Class 25/9 (25901 - 25912) Modified from 25/3 with reduced max speed of 60 mph

* Converted for use as a mobile generator (Electric Train Heating Ex-Loco)
+ Used for static training purposes and renumbered with ADB prefix
~ Renumbered for departmental use

Class 25 Names:

25322	TAMWORTH CASTLE		D7628	SYBILLA
D5185	CASTELL DINAS BRAN			

CLASS 26

Total Built	47	Formation	Bo-Bo	Max T.E.	42,000 lbf
Date Built	1958/59	Max Speed	75 mph	P.A.R.	900 hp
Builder	BRC & W, Smethwick	Weight	75 - 79 t	R.A.	5 & 6
Engine	Sulzer 6LDA28A, 1160 hp	Brakes	Vacuum / Air & Vac	Supply	Steam

26001	D5301	·	·	·	Preserved	Lakeside & Haverthwaite Railway
26002	D5302	·	·	·	Preserved	Strathspey Railway
26003	D5303	·	·	·	Scrapped	MC Metals, Springburn, 1995
26004	D5304	·	·	·	Preserved	Nemesis Rail, Burton-upon-Trent
26005	D5305	·	·	·	Scrapped	MC Metals, Springburn, 1995
26006	D5306	·	·	·	Scrapped	MC Metals, Springburn, 1995
26007	D5300	·	·	·	Preserved	Barrow Hill
26008	D5308	·	·	·	Scrapped	MC Metals, Springburn, 1994
26009	D5309	·	·	·	Scrapped	BR, Glasgow Works, 1978
26010	D5310	·	·	·	Preserved	Llangollen Railway
26011	D5311	·	·	·	Preserved	Nemesis Rail, Burton-upon-Trent
26012	D5312	·	·	·	Scrapped	BR, Glasgow Works, 1982
26013	D5313	·	·	·	Scrapped	Vic Berry, Leicester, 1987
26014	D5314	·	·	·	Preserved	Caledonian Railway
26015	D5315	·	·	·	Scrapped	MC Metals, Springburn, 1994
26016	D5316	·	·	·	Scrapped	BR, Glasgow Works, 1976
26017	D5317	·	·	·	Scrapped	BR, Glasgow Works, 1978
26018	D5318	·	·	·	Scrapped	BR, Glasgow Works, 1982
26019	D5319	·	·	·	Scrapped	Vic Berry, Thornton Yard, 1987
26020	D5307	·	·	·	Scrapped	BR, Glasgow Works, 1978
26021	D5321	·	·	·	Scrapped	MC Metals, Springburn, 1994
26022	D5322	·	·	·	Scrapped	BR, Glasgow Works, 1981
26023	D5323	·	·	·	Scrapped	MC Metals, Springburn, 1991
26024	D5324	·	·	·	Preserved	Bo'ness & Kinneil Railway
26025	D5325	·	·	·	Preserved	Strathspey Railway

CLASS 26 (Continued)

26026	D5326	·	·	·	Scrapped	MC Metals, Springburn, 1995
26027	D5327	·	·	·	Scrapped	MC Metals, Springburn, 1995
26028	D5320	·	·	·	Scrapped	MC Metals, Springburn, 1992
26029	D5329	·	·	·	Scrapped	MC Metals, Springburn, 1989
26030	D5330	·	·	·	Scrapped	Vic Berry, Thornton Yard, 1987
26031	D5331	·	·	·	Scrapped	MC Metals, Springburn, 1990
26032	D5332	·	·	·	Scrapped	MC Metals, Springburn, 1995
26033	D5333	·	·	·	Scrapped	Vic Berry, Thornton Yard, 1987
26034	D5334	·	·	·	Scrapped	MC Metals, Springburn, 1990
26035	D5335	·	·	·	Preserved	Caledonian Railway
26036	D5336	·	·	·	Scrapped	MC Metals, Springburn, 1995
26037	D5337	·	·	·	Scrapped	MC Metals, Springburn, 1995
26038	D5338	·	·	·	Preserved	North Yorkshire Moors Railway
26039	D5339	·	·	·	Scrapped	MC Metals, Springburn, 1993
26040	D5340	·	·	·	Preserved	Waverley Route Heritage Centre
26041	D5341	·	·	·	Scrapped	MC Metals, Springburn, 1995
26042	D5342	·	·	·	Scrapped	MC Metals, Springburn, 1995
26043	D5343	·	·	·	Preserved	G & WR
26044	D5344	·	·	·	Scrapped	Vic Berry, Thornton Yard, 1987
26045	D5345	·	·	·	Scrapped	Vic Berry, Leicester, 1987
26046	D5346	·	·	·	Scrapped	MC Metals, Springburn, 1993
·	D5328	·	·	·	Scrapped	BR, Glasgow Works, 1972

Class 26/0 (26001 - 26020) CP171-A1 Traction Motors
Class 26/1 (26021 - 26046) CP171-D3 Traction Motors

Class 26 Names: 26001   Eastfield

CLASS 27

Total Built	69	Formation	Bo-Bo	Max T.E.	40,000 lbf
Date Built	1961/62	Max Speed	90 mph	P.A.R.	933 hp
Builder	BRC & W, Smethwick	Weight	74-77 t	R.A.	5
Engine	Sulzer 6LDA28B, 1250 hp	Brakes	Vacuum / Air & Vac	Supply	Steam

27001	D5347	·	·	·	Preserved	Bo'ness & Kinneil Railway
27002	D5348	·	·	·	Scrapped	Vic Berry, Leicester, 1988
27003	D5349	·	·	·	Scrapped	MC Metals, Springburn, 1987
27004	D5350	·	·	·	Scrapped	Vic Berry, Leicester, 1987
27005	D5351	·	·	·	Preserved	Bo'ness & Kinneil Railway
27006	D5352	·	·	·	Scrapped	BR, Glasgow Works, 1977
27007	D5353	·	·	·	Preserved	Mid-Hants Railway
27008	D5354	·	·	·	Scrapped	MC Metals, Springburn, 1987
27009	D5355	·	·	·	Scrapped	BR, Glasgow Works, 1982
27010	D5356	·	·	·	Scrapped	Vic Berry, Leicester, 1987
27011	D5357	·	·	·	Scrapped	BR, Derby Works, 1982
27012	D5358	·	·	·	Scrapped	Vic Berry, Leicester, 1988
27013	D5359	·	·	·	Scrapped	BR, Glasgow Works, 1977
27014	D5360	·	·	·	Scrapped	Vic Berry, Leicester, 1987
27015	D5361	·	·	·	Scrapped	BR, Glasgow Works, 1977
27016	D5362	·	·	·	Scrapped	Vic Berry, Leicester, 1987
27017	D5363	·	·	·	Scrapped	Vic Berry, Leicester, 1988
27018	D5364	·	·	·	Scrapped	MC Metals, Springburn, 1989
27019	D5365	·	·	·	Scrapped	BR, Swindon Works, 1985

27020	D5366	·	·	·	Scrapped	Vic Berry, Thornton Yard, 1987
27021	D5367	·	·	·	Scrapped	Vic Berry, Thornton Yard, 1987
27022	D5368	·	·	·	Scrapped	Vic Berry, Leicester, 1987
27023	D5369	·	·	·	Scrapped	Vic Berry, Leicester, 1989
27024	D5370	968028*	·	·	Preserved	Caledonian Railway
27025	D5371	·	·	·	Scrapped	Vic Berry, Leicester, 1989
27026	D5372	·	·	·	Scrapped	Vic Berry, Leicester, 1988
27027	D5373	·	·	·	Scrapped	Vic Berry, Thornton Yard, 1987
27028	D5375	·	·	·	Scrapped	BR, Swindon Works, 1985
27029	D5376	·	·	·	Scrapped	Vic Berry, Thornton Yard, 1987
27030	D5377	·	·	·	Scrapped	Vic Berry, Leicester, 1987
27031	D5378	·	·	·	Scrapped	BR, Glasgow Works, 1978
27032	D5379	·	·	·	Scrapped	Vic Berry, Thornton Yard, 1987
27033	D5381	·	·	·	Scrapped	Vic Berry, Thornton Yard, 1987
27034	D5382	·	·	·	Scrapped	BR, Swindon Works, 1986
27035	D5384	·	·	·	Scrapped	BR, Glasgow Works, 1977
27036	D5385	·	·	·	Scrapped	Vic Berry, Thornton Yard, 1987
27037	D5389	·	·	·	Scrapped	Vic Berry, Leicester, 1989
27038	D5390	·	·	·	Scrapped	Vic Berry, Leicester, 1987
27039	D5398	·	·	·	Scrapped	BR, Glasgow Works, 1977
27040	D5402	·	·	·	Scrapped	Vic Berry, Thornton Yard, 1987
27041	D5405	·	·	·	Scrapped	Vic Berry, Leicester, 1987
27042	D5406	·	·	·	Scrapped	Vic Berry, Leicester, 1987
27043	D5414	·	·	·	Scrapped	Paterson's, Mount Vernon, 1985
27044	D5415	·	·	·	Scrapped	BR, Glasgow Works, 1982
27101	D5374	27045	·	·	Scrapped	Vic Berry, Leicester, 1989
27102	D5380	27046	·	·	Scrapped	MC Metals, Springburn, 1988
27103	D5386	27212	27066	·	Preserved	Barrow Hill
27104	D5387	27048	·	·	Scrapped	Vic Berry, Leicester, 1987
27105	D5388	27049	·	·	Scrapped	Vic Berry, Leicester, 1988
27106	D5394	27050	·	·	Preserved	Strathspey Railway
27107	D5395	27051	·	·	Scrapped	Vic Berry, Leicester, 1987
27108	D5396	27052	·	·	Scrapped	Vic Berry, Leicester, 1987
27109	D5397	27053	·	·	Scrapped	Vic Berry, Leicester, 1989
27110	D5399	27054	·	·	Scrapped	MC Metals, Springburn, 1988
27111	D5400	27055	·	·	Scrapped	Vic Berry, Leicester, 1988
27112	D5401	27056	·	·	Preserved	Great Central Railway
27201	D5391	27119	·	·	Scrapped	BR, Glasgow Works, 1982
27202	D5392	27120	·	·	Scrapped	BR, Glasgow Works, 1982
27203	D5393	27121	27057	·	Scrapped	Vic Berry, Derby, 1986
27204	D5403	27122	27058	·	Scrapped	Vic Berry, Leicester, 1987
27205	D5410	27123	27059	·	Preserved	Severn Valley Railway
27206	D5412	27124	27060	·	Scrapped	Vic Berry, Leicester, 1987
27207	D5404	27113	27061	968025*	Scrapped	Vic Berry, Leicester, 1988
27208	D5407	27114	27062	·	Scrapped	Vic Berry, Leicester, 1989
27209	D5408	27115	27063	·	Scrapped	Vic Berry, Leicester, 1989
27210	D5409	27116	27064	·	Scrapped	Vic Berry, Leicester, 1987
27211	D5411	27117	27065	·	Scrapped	Vic Berry, Leicester, 1987
27212	D5413	27118	27047	·	Scrapped	Vic Berry, Leicester, 1987
·	D5383	·	·	·	Scrapped	Cashmore's, Great Bridge, 1967

Class 27/0 (27001 - 27044) Standard Design
Class 27/1 (27101 - 27112) Fitted with push-pull equipment
Class 27/2 (27201 - 27212) Fitted with electric train supply and push-pull equipment

CLASS 27 (Continued)

* Used for static training purposes and renumbered with ADB prefix

Class 27 Names: D5386   THE HOLT PIONEER

CLASS 28

Total Built	20	Formation	Co-Bo	Max T.E.	50,000 lbf
Date Built	1958/59	Max Speed	75 mph	P.A.R.	942 hp
Builder	Metropolitan Vickers, Stockton	Weight	97 t	R.A.	8
Engine	Crossley HSTV8, 1200 hp	Brakes	Vacuum	Supply	Steam

·	D5700	·	·	·	Scrapped	J McWilliams, Shettleston, 1968
·	D5701	·	·	·	Scrapped	Cashmore's, Great Bridge, 1969
·	D5702	·	·	·	Scrapped	Cashmore's, Great Bridge, 1969
·	D5703	·	·	·	Scrapped	J McWilliams, Shettleston, 1968
·	D5704	·	·	·	Scrapped	J McWilliams, Shettleston, 1968
·	D5705	S15705	968006*	·	Preserved	East Lancashire Railway
·	D5706	·	·	·	Scrapped	Cashmore's, Great Bridge, 1969
·	D5707	·	·	·	Scrapped	Cashmore's, Great Bridge, 1969
·	D5708	·	·	·	Scrapped	Cashmore's, Great Bridge, 1969
·	D5709	·	·	·	Scrapped	J McWilliams, Shettleston, 1968
·	D5710	·	·	·	Scrapped	J McWilliams, Shettleston, 1968
·	D5711	·	·	·	Scrapped	Cashmore's, Great Bridge, 1969
·	D5712	·	·	·	Scrapped	Cashmore's, Great Bridge, 1969
·	D5713	·	·	·	Scrapped	J McWilliams, Shettleston, 1968
·	D5714	·	·	·	Scrapped	Cashmore's, Great Bridge, 1969
·	D5715	·	·	·	Scrapped	J McWilliams, Shettleston, 1968
·	D5716	·	·	·	Scrapped	Cashmore's, Great Bridge, 1969
·	D5717	·	·	·	Scrapped	Cashmore's, Great Bridge, 1969
·	D5718	·	·	·	Scrapped	J McWilliams, Shettleston, 1968
·	D5719	·	·	·	Scrapped	Cashmore's, Great Bridge, 1969

* Converted to static train pre-heating units and renumbered with TDB prefix

CLASS 29

Total Built	20	Formation	Bo-Bo	Max T.E.	47,000 lbf
Date Built	1965	Max Speed	80 mph	P.A.R.	925 hp
Builder	BR Glasgow Works	Weight	73 t	R.A.	5
Engine	Paxman 12YJXL, 1350 hp	Brakes	Vacuum	Supply	Steam

·	D6100	·	·	·	Scrapped	BR, Glasgow Works, 1972
·	D6101	·	·	·	Scrapped	BR, Glasgow Works, 1972
·	D6102	·	·	·	Scrapped	BR, Glasgow Works, 1972
·	D6103	·	·	·	Scrapped	BR, Glasgow Works, 1972
·	D6106	·	·	·	Scrapped	BR, Glasgow Works, 1972
·	D6107	·	·	·	Scrapped	BR, Glasgow Works, 1972
·	D6108	·	·	·	Scrapped	J McWilliams, Shettleston, 1971
·	D6112	·	·	·	Scrapped	BR, Glasgow Works, 1972
·	D6113	·	·	·	Scrapped	BR, Glasgow Works, 1972
·	D6114	·	·	·	Scrapped	BR, Glasgow Works, 1972
·	D6116	·	·	·	Scrapped	BR, Glasgow Works, 1972
·	D6119	·	·	·	Scrapped	BR, Glasgow Works, 1972
·	D6121	·	·	·	Scrapped	BR, Glasgow Works, 1972
·	D6123	·	·	·	Scrapped	BR, Glasgow Works, 1972

CLASS 29 (Continued)

·	D6124	·	·	·	Scrapped	BR, Glasgow Works, 1972
·	D6129	·	·	·	Scrapped	BR, Glasgow Works, 1972
·	D6130	·	·	·	Scrapped	BR, Glasgow Works, 1972
·	D6132	·	·	·	Scrapped	BR, Glasgow Works, 1972
·	D6133	·	·	·	Scrapped	BR, Glasgow Works, 1972
·	D6137	·	·	·	Scrapped	BR, Glasgow Works, 1972

Re-built from Class 21

CLASS 31

Total Built	263	Formation	A1A-A1A	Max T.E.	35,900 lbf
Date Built	1958-62	Max Speed	90 mph	P.A.R.	1,170 hp
Builder	Brush Traction, Loughborough	Weight	107 - 111 t	R.A.	5 & 6
Engine	English Electric 12SVT, 1470 hp	Brakes	Vacuum / Air & Vac	Supply	As Below

31001	D5501	·	·	·	Scrapped	BR, Doncaster Works, 1977
31002	D5502	968014*	·	·	Scrapped	BR, Crewe Works, 1984
31003	D5503	·	·	·	Scrapped	BR, Doncaster Works, 1980
31004	D5504	·	·	·	Scrapped	BR, Swindon Works, 1981
31005	D5505	·	·	·	Scrapped	BR, Doncaster Works, 1980
31006	D5506	·	·	·	Scrapped	BR, Doncaster Works, 1980
31007	D5507	·	·	·	Scrapped	BR, Doncaster Works, 1978
31008	D5508	968016*	·	·	Scrapped	BR, Crewe Works, 1985
31009	D5509	·	·	·	Scrapped	BR, Doncaster Works, 1977
31010	D5510	·	·	·	Scrapped	BR, Doncaster Works, 1976
31011	D5511	·	·	·	Scrapped	BR, Doncaster Works, 1977
31012	D5512	·	·	·	Scrapped	BR, Doncaster Works, 1978
31013	D5513	968013*	·	·	Scrapped	BR, Doncaster Works, 1983
31014	D5514	968015*	·	·	Scrapped	BR, Doncaster Works, 1983
31015	D5515	·	·	·	Scrapped	BR, Doncaster Works, 1980
31016	D5516	·	·	·	Scrapped	BR, Doncaster Works, 1976
31017	D5517	·	·	·	Scrapped	BR, Swindon Works, 1983
31018	D5500	·	·	·	Preserved	National Railway Museum, York
31019	D5519	·	·	·	Scrapped	BR, Swindon Works, 1981
31101	D5518	·	·	·	Preserved	Avon Valley Railway
31102	D5520	·	·	·	Scrapped	EMR, Kingsbury, 2007
31103	D5521	·	·	·	Scrapped	BR, Swindon Works, 1983
31104	D5522	31418	·	·	Preserved	Midland Railway Centre
31105	D5523	·	·	·	Stored	Network Rail, Derby
31106	D5524	·	·	·	Preserved	Weardale Railway
31107	D5525	·	·	·	Scrapped	Ron Hull, Rotherham, 2009
31108	D5526	·	·	·	Preserved	Midland Railway Centre
31109	D5527	·	·	·	Scrapped	C F Booth, Rotherham, 1989
31110	D5528	·	·	·	Scrapped	T J Thomson, Stockton, 2007
31111	D5529	·	·	·	Scrapped	BR, Swindon Works, 1986
31112	D5530	·	·	·	Scrapped	T J Thomson, Stockton, 2003
31113	D5531	·	·	·	Scrapped	EMR, Kingsbury, 2008
31114	D5532	31453	31553	·	Scrapped	T J Thomson, Stockton, 2001
31115	D5533	31466	·	·	Preserved	Dean Forest Railway
31116	D5534	·	·	·	Scrapped	T J Thomson, Stockton, 2003
31117	D5535	·	·	·	Scrapped	C F Booth, Doncaster, 1988
31118	D5536	·	·	·	Scrapped	MC Metals, Springburn, 1990
31119	D5537	·	·	·	Preserved	Embsay & Bolton Abbey Railway

31120	D5538	·	·	·	Scrapped	C F Booth, Rotherham, 1994
31121	D5539	·	·	·	Scrapped	MC Metals, Springburn, 1989
31122	D5540	·	·	·	Scrapped	BR, Stratford, 1987
31123	D5541	·	·	·	Scrapped	C F Booth, Rotherham, 2006
31124	D5542	·	·	·	Scrapped	MC Metals, Springburn, 1991
31125	D5543	·	·	·	Scrapped	HNRC, Kingsbury, 2001
31126	D5544	·	·	·	Scrapped	EWS, Wigan, 1999
31127	D5545	·	·	·	Scrapped	Vic Berry, Leicester, 1989
31128	D5546	·	·	·	Operational	Nemesis Rail, Burton-upon-Trent
31129	D5547	31461	·	·	Stored	Nemesis Rail, Burton-upon-Trent
31130	D5548	·	·	·	Preserved	Avon Valley Railway
31131	D5549	·	·	·	Scrapped	Vic Berry, Leicester, 1990
31132	D5550	·	·	·	Scrapped	T J Thomson, Stockton, 2003
31133	D5551	31450	·	·	Scrapped	EWS, Wigan, 1999
31134	D5552	·	·	·	Scrapped	EWS, Wigan, 1999
31135	D5553	·	·	·	Scrapped	T J Thomson, Stockton, 2000
31136	D5554	·	·	·	Scrapped	BR, Swindon Works, 1980
31137	D5555	31444	31544	·	Scrapped	EWS, Wigan, 2001
31138	D5556	·	·	·	Scrapped	MC Metals, Springburn, 1989
31139	D5557	31438	31538	·	Preserved	Epping Ongar Railway
31140	D5558	31421	·	·	Scrapped	EMR, Kingsbury, 2007
31141	D5559	·	·	·	Scrapped	MC Metals, Springburn, 1989
31142	D5560	·	·	·	Scrapped	T J Thomson, Stockton, 2003
31143	D5561	·	·	·	Scrapped	C F Booth, Rotherham, 1989
31144	D5562	·	·	·	Scrapped	EMR, Manchester, 2011
31145	D5563	·	·	·	Scrapped	EWS, Wigan, 1999
31146	D5564	·	·	·	Scrapped	C F Booth, Rotherham, 2004
31147	D5565	·	·	·	Scrapped	HNRC, Barrow Hill, 2001
31148	D5566	31448	31548	·	Scrapped	HNRC, Kingsbury, 2001
31149	D5567	·	·	·	Scrapped	T J Thomson, Stockton, 2004
31150	D5568	·	·	·	Scrapped	BR, Doncaster Works, 1976
31151	D5569	31436	·	·	Scrapped	BR, Doncaster Works, 1988
31152	D5570	·	·	·	Scrapped	Vic Berry, Leicester, 1990
31153	D5571	31432	·	·	Scrapped	EWS, Wigan, 2001
31154	D5572	·	·	·	Scrapped	Ron Hull, Rotherham, 2006
31155	D5573	·	·	·	Scrapped	T J Thomson, Stockton, 2004
31156	D5574	·	·	·	Scrapped	MC Metals, Springburn, 1995
31157	D5575	31424	31524	·	Scrapped	C F Booth, Rotherham, 2006
31158	D5576	·	·	·	Scrapped	T J Thomson, Stockton, 2003
31159	D5577	·	·	·	Scrapped	MC Metals, Springburn, 1996
31160	D5578	·	·	·	Scrapped	EWS, Wigan, 1999
31161	D5579	31400	·	·	Scrapped	C F Booth, Rotherham, 1993
31162	D5580	·	·	·	Preserved	Midland Railway Centre
31163	D5581	·	·	·	Preserved	C & PRR
31164	D5582	·	·	·	Scrapped	T J Thomson, Stockton, 2000
31165	D5583	·	·	·	Scrapped	MRJ Phillips, Crewe Works, 1998
31166	D5584	·	·	·	Scrapped	T J Thomson, Stockton, 2009
31167	D5585	·	·	·	Scrapped	Vic Berry, Leicester, 1989
31168	D5586	·	·	·	Scrapped	HNRC, Kingsbury, 2001
31169	D5587	31457	·	·	Scrapped	C F Booth, Rotherham, 1994
31170	D5588	·	·	·	Scrapped	MC Metals, Springburn, 1991
31171	D5590	·	·	·	Scrapped	T J Thomson, Stockton, 2003
31172	D5591	31420	·	·	Scrapped	C F Booth, Rotherham, 2007
31173	D5593	·	·	·	Scrapped	MC Metals, Springburn, 1991

31174	D5594	·	·	·	Scrapped	HNRC, Kingsbury, 2001
31175	D5595	·	·	·	Scrapped	BR, Carlisle, 1988
31176	D5597	·	·	·	Scrapped	Vic Berry, Leicester, 1988
31177	D5598	31443	·	·	Scrapped	Vic Berry, Leicester, 1990
31178	D5599	·	·	·	Scrapped	T J Thomson, Stockton, 2003
31179	D5600	31435	·	·	Preserved	Embsay & Bolton Abbey Railway
31180	D5601	·	·	·	Scrapped	T J Thomson, Stockton, 2003
31181	D5602	·	·	·	Scrapped	T J Thomson, Stockton, 2003
31182	D5603	31437	31537	·	Scrapped	C F Booth, Rotherham, 2011
31183	D5604	·	·	·	Scrapped	C F Booth, Rotherham, 1989
31184	D5607	·	·	·	Scrapped	T J Thomson, Stockton, 2003
31185	D5608	·	·	·	Scrapped	T J Thomson, Stockton, 2001
31186	D5609	31601	·	·	Operational	BARS, Washwood Heath
31187	D5610	·	·	·	Scrapped	T J Thomson, Stockton, 2003
31188	D5611	·	·	·	Scrapped	T J Thomson, Stockton, 2008
31189	D5612	·	·	·	Scrapped	Vic Berry, Leicester, 1990
31190	D5613	·	·	·	Operational	BARS, Washwood Heath
31191	D5614	31602	·	·	Stored	Weardale Railway
31192	D5615	·	·	·	Scrapped	BR, Doncaster Works, 1983
31193	D5617	31426	31526	·	Scrapped	T J Thomson, Stockton, 2006
31194	D5618	31427	·	·	Scrapped	C F Booth, Rotherham, 2007
31195	D5619	·	·	·	Scrapped	C F Booth, Rotherham, 1988
31196	D5620	·	·	·	Scrapped	HNRC, Stratford, 2001
31197	D5621	31423	·	·	Scrapped	T J Thomson, Stockton, 2009
31198	D5622	·	·	·	Scrapped	MC Metals, Springburn, 1991
31199	D5623	·	·	·	Scrapped	T J Thomson, Stockton, 2003
31200	D5624	·	·	·	Scrapped	C F Booth, Rotherham, 2007
31201	D5625	·	·	·	Scrapped	C F Booth, Rotherham, 2004
31202	D5626	·	·	·	Scrapped	Vic Berry, Cricklewood, 1988
31203	D5627	·	·	·	Preserved	Pontypool & Blaenavon Railway
31204	D5628	31440	·	·	Scrapped	Vic Berry, Leicester, 1988
31205	D5629	·	·	·	Scrapped	T J Thomson, Stockton, 2002
31206	D5630	·	·	·	Preserved	Rushden Transport Museum
31207	D5631	·	·	·	Preserved	North Norfolk Railway
31208	D5632	·	·	·	Scrapped	MC Metals, Springburn, 1991
31209	D5633	·	·	·	Scrapped	T J Thomson, Stockton, 2003
31210	D5634	·	·	·	Preserved	Dean Forest Railway
31211	D5635	31428	·	·	Scrapped	HNRC, Kingsbury, 2001
31212	D5636	·	·	·	Scrapped	MC Metals, Springburn, 1995
31213	D5637	31465	31565	·	Stored	HNRC, Weardale Railway
31214	D5638	·	·	·	Scrapped	BR, Doncaster Works, 1983
31215	D5639	·	·	·	Scrapped	MC Metals, Springburn, 1995
31216	D5641	31467	·	·	Scrapped	EMR, Kingsbury, 2008
31217	D5642	·	·	·	Scrapped	Vic Berry, Leicester, 1999
31218	D5643	·	·	·	Scrapped	C F Booth, Rotherham, 1989
31219	D5644	·	·	·	Scrapped	T J Thomson, Stockton, 2003
31220	D5645	31441	31541	·	Scrapped	HNRC, Old Oak Common, 2002
31221	D5647	·	·	·	Scrapped	MC Metals, Springburn, 1995
31222	D5648	·	·	·	Scrapped	Vic Berry, Leicester, 1990
31223	D5649	·	·	·	Scrapped	MC Metals, Springburn, 1995
31224	D5650	·	·	·	Scrapped	T J Thomson, Stockton, 2002
31225	D5651	·	·	·	Scrapped	MC Metals, Springburn, 1991
31226	D5652	·	·	·	Scrapped	MC Metals, Springburn, 1992
31227	D5653	·	·	·	Scrapped	Vic Berry, Leicester, 1989

CLASS 31 (Continued)

31228	D5654	31454	31554	·	Stored	BARS, Washwood Heath
31229	D5655	·	·	·	Scrapped	HNRC, Kingsbury, 2001
31230	D5657	·	·	·	Scrapped	T J Thomson, Stockton, 2000
31231	D5658	·	·	·	Scrapped	MC Metals, Springburn, 1991
31232	D5659	·	·	·	Scrapped	T J Thomson, Stockton, 2003
31233	D5660	·	·	·	Stored	Network Rail, Derby
31234	D5661	·	·	·	Scrapped	MC Metals, Springburn, 1994
31235	D5662	·	·	·	Preserved	Mid-Norfolk Railway
31236	D5663	31433	31533	·	Scrapped	Ron Hull, Rotherham, 2006
31237	D5664	·	·	·	Scrapped	T J Thomson, Stockton, 2004
31238	D5665	·	·	·	Scrapped	EWS, Wigan, 1999
31239	D5666	31439	·	·	Scrapped	C F Booth, Rotherham, 2011
31240	D5667	·	·	·	Scrapped	Birds, Stratford, 1994
31241	D5668	·	·	·	Scrapped	BR, Swindon Works, 1982
31242	D5670	·	·	·	Scrapped	EWS, Wigan, 1999
31243	D5671	·	·	·	Scrapped	Cooper's Metals, Stratford, 1994
31244	D5672	·	·	·	Scrapped	BR, Doncaster Works, 1983
31245	D5673	·	·	·	Scrapped	BR, Stratford, 1988
31246	D5674	31455	31555	·	Scrapped	EWS, Wigan, 2000
31247	D5675	·	·	·	Scrapped	T J Thomson, Stockton, 2003
31248	D5676	·	·	·	Scrapped	T J Thomson, Stockton, 2000
31249	D5677	·	·	·	Scrapped	MC Metals, Springburn, 1995
31250	D5678	·	·	·	Scrapped	T J Thomson, Stockton, 2000
31251	D5679	31442	·	·	Scrapped	C F Booth, Rotherham, 2004
31252	D5680	·	·	·	Scrapped	EMR, Peterborough, 2000
31253	D5681	31431	31531	·	Scrapped	T J Thomson, Stockton, 2003
31254	D5682	·	·	·	Scrapped	BR, Old Oak Common, 1980
31255	D5683	·	·	·	Preserved	Colne Valley Railway
31256	D5684	31459	·	·	Stored	Loram UK, Weardale Railway
31257	D5685	·	·	·	Scrapped	C F Booth, Rotherham, 1992
31258	D5686	31434	·	·	Scrapped	C F Booth, Rotherham, 2003
31259	D5687	·	·	·	Scrapped	Vic Berry, Leicester, 1990
31260	D5688	·	·	·	Scrapped	MC Metals, Springburn, 1991
31261	D5689	·	·	·	Scrapped	BR, Stratford, 1990
31262	D5690	·	·	·	Scrapped	BR, Doncaster Works, 1983
31263	D5693	·	·	·	Scrapped	HNRC, Kingsbury, 2001
31264	D5694	·	·	·	Scrapped	MC Metals, Springburn, 1995
31265	D5695	31430	31530	·	Preserved	Mangapps Farm Railway Museum
31266	D5696	31460	·	·	Scrapped	T J Thomson, Stockton, 2007
31267	D5697	31419	31519	·	Scrapped	EWS, Wigan, 2001
31268	D5698	·	·	·	Scrapped	T J Thomson, Stockton, 2000
31269	D5699	31429	·	·	Scrapped	C F Booth, Rotherham, 1993
31270	D5800	·	·	·	Preserved	Peak Rail
31271	D5801	·	·	·	Preserved	Nene Valley Railway
31272	D5802	·	·	·	Scrapped	MC Metals, Springburn, 1995
31273	D5803	·	·	·	Scrapped	C F Booth, Rotherham, 2004
31274	D5804	31425	·	·	Scrapped	C F Booth, Rotherham, 1994
31275	D5805	·	·	·	Scrapped	HNRC, Carnforth, 2005
31276	D5806	·	·	·	Scrapped	T J Thomson, Stockton, 2000
31277	D5807	31469	31569	·	Scrapped	T J Thomson, Stockton, 2003
31278	D5808	·	·	·	Scrapped	MC Metals, Springburn, 1989
31279	D5809	31452	31552	·	Operational	BARS, Derby
31280	D5810	·	·	·	Scrapped	C F Booth, Rotherham, 1991
31281	D5811	·	·	·	Scrapped	Vic Berry, Leicester, 1990

31282	D5813	·	·	·	Scrapped	HNRC, Kingsbury, 2001
31283	D5815	·	·	·	Scrapped	HNRC, Stratford, 2001
31284	D5816	·	·	·	Scrapped	MC Metals, Springburn, 1991
31285	D5817	·	·	·	Stored	HNRC, Burton-upon-Trent
31286	D5818	·	·	·	Scrapped	HNRC, Kingsbury, 2001
31287	D5819	·	·	·	Scrapped	MC Metals, Springburn, 1989
31288	D5820	·	·	·	Scrapped	C F Booth, Rotherham, 1992
31289	D5821	·	·	·	Preserved	Spa Valley Railway
31290	D5822	·	·	·	Scrapped	T J Thomson, Stockton, 2003
31291	D5823	31456	31556	·	Scrapped	C F Booth, Rotherham, 2010
31292	D5825	·	·	·	Scrapped	MC Metals, Springburn, 1990
31293	D5826	·	·	·	Scrapped	Cooper's Metals, Stratford, 1994
31294	D5827	·	·	·	Scrapped	T J Thomson, Stockton, 2003
31295	D5828	31447	31547	·	Scrapped	T J Thomson, Stockton, 2002
31296	D5829	·	·	·	Scrapped	R Garrett, Crewe, 2004
31297	D5830	31463	31563	·	Preserved	Great Central Railway
31298	D5831	97203+	·	·	Scrapped	C F Booth, Rotherham, 1989
31299	D5832	·	·	·	Scrapped	HNRC, Stratford, 2001
31300	D5833	31445	31545	·	Scrapped	C F Booth, Rotherham, 2002
31301	D5834	·	·	·	Scrapped	C F Booth, Rotherham, 2011
31302	D5835	·	·	·	Scrapped	EWS, Wigan, 1999
31303	D5836	31458	31558	·	Scrapped	C F Booth, Rotherham, 2005
31304	D5837	·	·	·	Scrapped	EWS, Wigan, 1999
31305	D5838	·	·	·	Scrapped	MC Metals, Springburn, 1994
31306	D5839	·	·	·	Scrapped	HNRC, Old Oak Common, 2006
31307	D5840	31449	31549	·	Scrapped	Ron Hull, Rotherham, 2005
31308	D5841	·	·	·	Scrapped	HNRC, Old Oak Common, 2006
31309	D5843	·	·	·	Scrapped	C F Booth, Rotherham, 1992
31310	D5844	31422	31522	·	Scrapped	C F Booth, Rotherham, 2014
31311	D5845	·	·	·	Scrapped	MC Metals, Springburn, 1989
31312	D5846	·	·	·	Scrapped	EWS, Wigan, 1999
31313	D5847	·	·	·	Scrapped	BR, Doncaster Works, 1983
31314	D5848	·	·	·	Scrapped	BR, Doncaster Works, 1983
31315	D5849	31462	·	·	Scrapped	C F Booth, Rotherham, 2006
31316	D5850	31446	31546	·	Scrapped	T J Thomson, Stockton, 2003
31317	D5851	·	·	·	Scrapped	T J Thomson, Stockton, 2000
31318	D5852	31451	31551	·	Scrapped	MRJ Phillips, Crewe Works, 1998
31319	D5853	·	·	·	Scrapped	C F Booth, Rotherham, 2007
31320	D5854	·	·	·	Scrapped	HNRC, Stratford, 2001
31321	D5855	31468	31568	·	Preserved	Weardale Railway
31322	D5857	·	·	·	Scrapped	Vic Berry, Leicester, 1989
31323	D5858	·	·	·	Scrapped	MC Metals, Springburn, 1991
31324	D5859	·	·	·	Scrapped	C F Booth, Rotherham, 1994
31325	D5860	31464	·	·	Scrapped	MC Metals, Springburn, 1991
31326	D5861	31970	97204+	·	Scrapped	MRJ Phillips, Crewe Works, 1997
31327	D5862	·	·	·	Preserved	Strathspey Railway
31401	D5589	·	·	·	Scrapped	BR, Doncaster Works, 1988
31402	D5592	·	·	·	Scrapped	T J Thomson, Stockton, 2002
31403	D5596	·	·	·	Scrapped	T J Thomson, Stockton, 2003
31404	D5605	·	·	·	Scrapped	C F Booth, Rotherham, 1994
31405	D5606	·	·	·	Scrapped	EMR, Doncaster, 2000
31406	D5616	·	·	·	Scrapped	MC Metals, Springburn, 1991
31407	D5640	31507	·	·	Scrapped	Ron Hull, Rotherham, 2006
31408	D5646	·	·	·	Scrapped	EWS, Wigan, 2001

31409	D5656	·	·	·	Scrapped	MC Metals, Springburn, 1992
31410	D5669	·	·	·	Scrapped	C F Booth, Rotherham, 2014
31411	D5691	31511	·	·	Scrapped	Ron Hull, Rotherham, 2005
31412	D5692	31512	·	·	Scrapped	Ron Hull, Rotherham, 2006
31413	D5812	·	·	·	Scrapped	C F Booth, Rotherham, 1998
31414	D5814	31514	·	·	Preserved	Midland Railway Centre
31415	D5824	·	·	·	Scrapped	C F Booth, Rotherham, 2009
31416	D5842	31516	·	·	Scrapped	HNRC, Kingsbury, 2001
31417	D5856	·	·	·	Scrapped	Ron Hull, Rotherham, 2006

Class 30 (D5500-D5862) Originally fitted with Mirrlees JVS12T power unit
Class 31/0 (31001 - 31019) Original design
Class 31/1 (31101 - 31327) Standard design
Class 31/4 (31401 - 31469) Fitted with electric train supply (ETS)
Class 31/5 (31507 - 31569) Class 31/4 with ETS isolated
Class 31/6 (31601 - 31602) Class 31/1 fitted with ETS through wiring and controls

* Converted to static train pre-heating units and renumbered with ADB prefix
+ Renumbered for departmental use

Class 31 Names:

31101	Brush Veteran	31413	Severn Valley Railway
31102	Cricklewood	31418	Boadicea
31105	Bescot TMD Quality Assured	31421	Wigan Pier
31106	The Blackcountryman | SPALDING TOWN	31423	Jerome K. Jerome
31107	John H Carloss VC	31428	North Yorkshire Moors Railway
31110	TRACTION Magazine	31430	Sister Dora
31116	RAIL 1981 - 1991 | RAIL Celebrity	31435	Newton Heath TMD
31128	CHARYBDIS	31439	North Yorkshire Moors Railway
31130	Calder Hall Power Station	31444	Keighley & Worth Valley Railway
31146	Brush Veteran	31452	MINOTAUR
31147	Floreat Salopia	31454	Heart of Wessex
31165	Stratford Major Depot	31455	Our Eli
31190	GRYPHON	31459	CERBERUS
31201	Fina Energy	31468	The Enginemen's Fund | HYDRA
31203	Steve Organ GM	31530	Sister Dora
31233	Phillips-Imperial | Severn Valley Railway	31544	Keighley & Worth Valley Railway
31271	Stratford 1840 - 2001	31558	Nene Valley Railway
31276	Calder Hall Power Station	31568	The Enginemen's Fund
31289	PHOENIX	31601	BLETCHLEY PARK STATION X
31296	Amlwch Freighter/Tren Nwyddau Amlwch		THE MAYOR OF CASTERBRIDGE
31309	Cricklewood		GAUGE 'O' GUILD 1956-2006
31327	Phillips-Imperial		Devon Diesel Society
31405	Mappa Mundi	31602	CHIMAERA
31410	Granada Telethon		DRIVER DAVE GREEN 19B

CLASS 33

Total Built	98	Formation	Bo-Bo	Max T.E.	45,000 lbf
Date Built	1960-62	Max Speed	85 mph	P.A.R.	1,215 hp
Builder	BRC & W, Smethwick	Weight	76-78 t	R.A.	6
Engine	Sulzer 8LDA28, 1550 hp	Brakes	Air & Vacuum	Supply	Electric

33001	D6500		·	·	·	Scrapped	Vic Berry, Eastleigh, 1989
33002	D6501		·	·	·	Preserved	South Devon Railway
33003	D6503		·	·	·	Scrapped	Vic Berry, Eastleigh, 1990
33004	D6504		·	·	·	Scrapped	BR, Eastleigh Works, 1992
33005	D6505		·	·	·	Scrapped	Vic Berry, Leicester, 1990
33006	D6506		·	·	·	Scrapped	C F Booth, Rotherham, 1994
33007	D6507		·	·	·	Scrapped	BR, Eastleigh Works, 1987
33008	D6508		·	·	·	Preserved	Shillingstone
33009	D6509		·	·	·	Scrapped	MRJ Phillips, Eastleigh, 1997
33010	D6510		·	·	·	Scrapped	Vic Berry, Eastleigh, 1989
33011	D6512		·	·	·	Scrapped	Vic Berry, Leicester, 1990
33012	D6515		·	·	·	Operational	Swanage Railway
33013	D6518		·	·	·	Scrapped	MC Metals, Springburn, 1991
33014	D6522		·	·	·	Scrapped	BR, Eastleigh, 1986
33015	D6523		·	·	·	Scrapped	Vic Berry, Leicester, 1990
33016	D6524		·	·	·	Scrapped	MC Metals, Springburn, 1992
33017	D6526	·	·	·	Scrapped	Vic Berry, Leicester, 1990
33018	D6530	968030*	·	·	Preserved	Midland Railway Centre
33019	D6534		·	·	·	Preserved	Battlefield Line
33020	D6537		·	·	·	Scrapped	MRJ Phillips, Stewarts Lane 1997
33021	D6539		·	·	·	Preserved	Churnet Valley Railway
33022	D6540		·	·	·	Scrapped	MC Metals, Springburn, 1991
33023	D6541		·	·	·	Scrapped	HNRC, Kingsbury, 2005
33024	D6542		·	·	·	Scrapped	BR, Eastleigh, 1986
33025	D6543		·	·	·	Operational	WCRC, Carnforth
33026	D6544		·	·	·	Scrapped	Raxstar, Eastleigh, 2003
33027	D6545		·	·	·	Scrapped	Cooper's Metals, Eastleigh, 1992
33028	D6546		·	·	·	Scrapped	BR, Eastleigh Works, 1989
33029	D6547		·	·	·	Stored	WCRC, Carnforth
33030	D6548		·	·	·	Stored	WCRC, Carnforth
33031	D6549		·	·	·	Scrapped	MC Metals, Springburn, 1991
33032	D6550		·	·	·	Scrapped	BR, Eastleigh Works, 1987
33033	D6551		·	·	·	Scrapped	MRJ Phillips, Stewarts Lane 1997
33034	D6552		·	·	·	Preserved	Swanage Railway
33035	D6553		·	·	·	Preserved	Barrow Hill
33036	D6554		·	·	·	Scrapped	BR, Slade Green, 1979
33037	D6555		·	·	·	Scrapped	MC Metals, Springburn, 1991
33038	D6556		·	·	·	Scrapped	HNRC, Kingsbury, 2001
33039	D6557		·	·	·	Scrapped	MC Metals, Springburn, 1991
33040	D6558		·	·	·	Scrapped	MRJ Phillips, Stewarts Lane 1997
33041	D6559		·	·	·	Scrapped	BR, Selhurst, 1976
33042	D6560		·	·	·	Scrapped	MRJ Phillips, Stewarts Lane 1997
33043	D6561		·	·	·	Scrapped	MC Metals, Springburn, 1991
33044	D6562		·	·	·	Scrapped	Vic Berry, Leicester, 1990
33045	D6563		·	·	·	Scrapped	Vic Berry, Leicester, 1990
33046	D6564		·	·	·	Preserved	East Lancashire Railway
33047	D6565		·	·	·	Scrapped	MRJ Phillips, Eastleigh, 1997
33048	D6566		·	·	·	Preserved	West Somerset Railway
33049	D6567		·	·	·	Scrapped	Vic Berry, Eastleigh, 1989
33050	D6568		·	·	·	Scrapped	MRJ Phillips, Stewarts Lane 1997

33051	D6569		·	·	·	Scrapped	Raxstar, Eastleigh, 2003
33052	D6570		·	·	·	Preserved	Kent & East Sussex Railway
33053	D6571		·	·	·	Preserved	Mid-Hants Railway
33054	D6572		·	·	·	Scrapped	BR, Eastleigh Works, 1987
33055	D6573		·	·	·	Scrapped	MC Metals, Springburn, 1991
33056	D6574		·	·	·	Scrapped	C F Booth, Rotherham, 2006
33057	D6575		·	·	·	Preserved	West Somerset Railway
33058	D6577		·	·	·	Scrapped	C F Booth, Rotherham, 1994
33059	D6578		·	·	·	Scrapped	MC Metals, Springburn, 1991
33060	D6579		·	·	·	Scrapped	Cooper's Metals, Eastleigh, 1992
33061	D6581		·	·	·	Scrapped	BR, Eastleigh Works, 1987
33062	D6582		·	·	·	Scrapped	Vic Berry, Leicester, 1990
33063	D6583		·	·	·	Preserved	Spa Valley Railway
33064	D6584		·	·	·	Scrapped	MRJ Phillips, OOC, 1997
33065	D6585		·	·	·	Preserved	Spa Valley Railway
33101	D6511		·	·	·	Scrapped	MRJ Phillips, Eastleigh, 1997
33102	D6513		·	·	·	Preserved	Churnet Valley Railway
33103	D6514		·	·	·	Preserved	Ecclesbourne Valley Railway
33104	D6516		·	·	·	Scrapped	BR, Slade Green, 1986
33105	D6517		·	·	·	Scrapped	Vic Berry, Leicester, 1990
33106	D6519		·	·	·	Scrapped	Cooper's Metals, Eastleigh, 1992
33107	D6520		·	·	·	Scrapped	MC Metals, Springburn, 1991
33108	D6521		·	·	·	Preserved	Severn Valley Railway
33109	D6525		·	·	·	Preserved	East Lancashire Railway
33110	D6527		·	·	·	Preserved	Bodmin & Wenford Railway
33111	D6528		·	·	·	Preserved	Swanage Railway
33112	D6529		·	·	·	Scrapped	Cooper's Metals, Eastleigh, 1992
33113	D6531		·	·	·	Scrapped	MRJ Phillips, Stewarts Lane 1997
33114	D6532		·	·	·	Scrapped	MRJ Phillips, Eastleigh, 1996
33115	D6533	83301+	·	·	Scrapped	St Leonards, 1994
33116	D6535	·	·	·	Preserved	Great Central Railway
33117	D6536		·	·	·	Preserved	East Lancashire Railway
33118	D6538		·	·	·	Scrapped	MRJ Phillips, Eastleigh, 1997
33119	D6580		·	·	·	Scrapped	MC Metals, Springburn, 1992
33201	D6586		·	·	·	Preserved	Swanage Railway
33202	D6587		·	·	·	Preserved	Spa Valley Railway
33203	D6588		·	·	·	Scrapped	Newton Stewart, 2006
33204	D6589		·	·	·	Scrapped	Raxstar, Mid-Hants Railway 2002
33205	D6590	33302	·	·	Scrapped	HNRC, Barrow Hill, 2003
33206	D6591	·	·	·	Scrapped	MRJ Phillips, Eastleigh, 1997
33207	D6592		·	·	·	Operational	WCRC, Carnforth
33208	D6593		·	·	·	Preserved	Battlefield Line
33209	D6594		·	·	·	Scrapped	BR, Eastleigh Works, 1989
33210	D6595		·	·	·	Scrapped	Vic Berry, Leicester, 1990
33211	D6596		·	·	·	Scrapped	MRJ Phillips, Stewarts Lane 1997
33212	D6597		·	·	·	Scrapped	MC Metals, Springburn, 1991
·	D6502		·	·	·	Scrapped	BR, Eastleigh Works, 1964
·	D6576		·	·	·	Scrapped	BR, Eastleigh Works, 1969

Class 33/0 (33001 - 33065) Standard design
Class 33/1 (33101 - 33119) Fitted with push-pull equipment
Class 33/2 (33201 - 33212) Built to Hastings line loading gauge
Class 33/3 (33302) Modified in 1988 for train ferry loading

CLASS 33 (Continued)

* Used for static training purposes and renumbered with TDB prefix
+ Used as a test vehicle for Eurostar bogies and DC equipment

Class 33 Names:

33002	Sea King	33052	Ashford
33008	Eastleigh	33056	The Burma Star
33009	Walrus	33057	Seagull
33012	Stan Symes	33063	RJ Mitchell -
	Lt Jenny Lewis RN		DESIGNER OF THE SPITFIRE
33019	Griffon	33065	Sealion
33021	Eastleigh	33103	SWORDFISH
33025	Sultan | Glen Falloch	33108	VAMPIRE
33026	Seafire	33109	Captain Bill Smith RNR
33027	Earl Mountbatten of Burma	33112	Templecombe
33029	Glen Loy	33114	Sultan | Ashford 150
33035	Spitfire	33116	Hertfordshire Rail Tours
33046	Merlin	33202	The Burma Star | METEOR
33047	Spitfire		Denis G. Robinson
33050	Isle of Grain	33207	Earl Mountbatten of Burma
33051	Shakespeare Cliff		Jim Martin

CLASS 35

Total Built	101	Formation	B-B		Max T.E.	46,600 lbf
Date Built	1961-64	Max Speed	90 mph		P.A.R.	1,320 hp
Builder	Beyer Peacock, Gorton	Weight	74 t		R.A.	6
Engine	Maybach MD870, 1740 hp	Brakes	Vacuum		Supply	Steam

·	D7000	·	·	·	Scrapped	BR, Swindon Works, 1975
·	D7001	·	·	·	Scrapped	Cohen's, Kettering, 1975
·	D7002	·	·	·	Scrapped	BR, Swindon Works, 1972
·	D7003	·	·	·	Scrapped	BR, Swindon Works, 1972
·	D7004	·	·	·	Scrapped	BR, Swindon Works, 1972
·	D7005	·	·	·	Scrapped	BR, Swindon Works, 1972
·	D7006	·	·	·	Scrapped	BR, Swindon Works, 1972
·	D7007	·	·	·	Scrapped	BR, Swindon Works, 1972
·	D7008	·	·	·	Scrapped	BR, Swindon Works, 1972
·	D7009	·	·	·	Scrapped	BR, Swindon Works, 1974
·	D7010	·	·	·	Scrapped	BR, Swindon Works, 1972
·	D7011	·	·	·	Scrapped	Marple & Gillott, Sheffield, 1977
·	D7012	·	·	·	Scrapped	BR, Swindon Works, 1972
·	D7013	·	·	·	Scrapped	BR, Swindon Works, 1972
·	D7014	·	·	·	Scrapped	BR, Swindon Works, 1972
·	D7015	·	·	·	Scrapped	BR, Swindon Works, 1972
·	D7016	·	·	·	Scrapped	BR, Swindon Works, 1975
·	D7017	·	·	·	Preserved	West Somerset Railway
·	D7018	·	·	·	Preserved	West Somerset Railway
·	D7019	·	·	·	Scrapped	BR, Swindon Works, 1972
·	D7020	·	·	·	Scrapped	BR, Swindon Works, 1972
·	D7021	·	·	·	Scrapped	BR, Swindon Works, 1972
·	D7022	·	·	·	Scrapped	Cohen's, Kettering, 1977
·	D7023	·	·	·	Scrapped	BR, Swindon Works, 1975
·	D7024	·	·	·	Scrapped	BR, Swindon Works, 1972
·	D7025	·	·	·	Scrapped	BR, Swindon Works, 1972

CLASS 35 (Continued)

·	D7026	·	·	·	Scrapped	Cohen's, Kettering, 1977
·	D7027	·	·	·	Scrapped	BR, Swindon Works, 1972
·	D7028	·	·	·	Scrapped	Cohen's, Kettering, 1977
·	D7029	·	·	·	Preserved	Severn Valley Railway
·	D7030	·	·	·	Scrapped	Birds, Long Marston, 1974
·	D7031	·	·	·	Scrapped	BR, Swindon Works, 1975
·	D7032	·	·	·	Scrapped	BR, Swindon Works, 1975
·	D7033	·	·	·	Scrapped	BR, Swindon Works, 1972
·	D7034	·	·	·	Scrapped	BR, Swindon Works, 1972
·	D7035	·	·	·	Scrapped	BR, Swindon Works, 1972
·	D7036	·	·	·	Scrapped	BR, Swindon Works, 1972
·	D7037	·	·	·	Scrapped	BR, Swindon Works, 1972
·	D7038	·	·	·	Scrapped	BR, Swindon Works, 1973
·	D7039	·	·	·	Scrapped	BR, Swindon Works, 1972
·	D7040	·	·	·	Scrapped	BR, Swindon Works, 1972
·	D7041	·	·	·	Scrapped	BR, Swindon Works, 1972
·	D7042	·	·	·	Scrapped	BR, Swindon Works, 1972
·	D7043	·	·	·	Scrapped	BR, Swindon Works, 1972
·	D7044	·	·	·	Scrapped	Birds, Long Marston, 1974
·	D7045	·	·	·	Scrapped	BR, Swindon Works, 1973
·	D7046	·	·	·	Scrapped	BR, Swindon Works, 1972
·	D7047	·	·	·	Scrapped	BR, Swindon Works, 1972
·	D7048	·	·	·	Scrapped	BR, Swindon Works, 1972
·	D7049	·	·	·	Scrapped	BR, Swindon Works, 1972
·	D7050	·	·	·	Scrapped	BR, Swindon Works, 1973
·	D7051	·	·	·	Scrapped	BR, Swindon Works, 1972
·	D7052	·	·	·	Scrapped	BR, Swindon Works, 1973
·	D7053	·	·	·	Scrapped	BR, Swindon Works, 1972
·	D7054	·	·	·	Scrapped	BR, Swindon Works, 1975
·	D7055	·	·	·	Scrapped	BR, Swindon Works, 1975
·	D7056	·	·	·	Scrapped	BR, Swindon Works, 1972
·	D7057	·	·	·	Scrapped	BR, Swindon Works, 1972
·	D7058	·	·	·	Scrapped	BR, Swindon Works, 1972
·	D7059	·	·	·	Scrapped	BR, Swindon Works, 1972
·	D7060	·	·	·	Scrapped	BR, Swindon Works, 1972
·	D7061	·	·	·	Scrapped	BR, Swindon Works, 1972
·	D7062	·	·	·	Scrapped	BR, Swindon Works, 1972
·	D7063	·	·	·	Scrapped	BR, Swindon Works, 1972
·	D7064	·	·	·	Scrapped	BR, Swindon Works, 1972
·	D7065	·	·	·	Scrapped	BR, Swindon Works, 1972
·	D7066	·	·	·	Scrapped	BR, Swindon Works, 1972
·	D7067	·	·	·	Scrapped	BR, Swindon Works, 1972
·	D7068	·	·	·	Scrapped	BR, Swindon Works, 1975
·	D7069	·	·	·	Scrapped	BR, Swindon Works, 1972
·	D7070	·	·	·	Scrapped	BR, Swindon Works, 1972
·	D7071	·	·	·	Scrapped	BR, Swindon Works, 1972
·	D7072	·	·	·	Scrapped	BR, Swindon Works, 1972
·	D7073	·	·	·	Scrapped	BR, Swindon Works, 1972
·	D7074	·	·	·	Scrapped	BR, Swindon Works, 1975
·	D7075	·	·	·	Scrapped	Birds, Long Marston, 1974
·	D7076	·	·	·	Preserved	East Lancashire Railway
·	D7077	·	·	·	Scrapped	BR, Swindon Works, 1972
·	D7078	·	·	·	Scrapped	BR, Swindon Works, 1972
·	D7079	·	·	·	Scrapped	BR, Swindon Works, 1972

CLASS 35 (Continued)

·	D7080	·	·	·	Scrapped	BR, Swindon Works, 1973
·	D7081	·	·	·	Scrapped	BR, Swindon Works, 1972
·	D7082	·	·	·	Scrapped	BR, Swindon Works, 1972
·	D7083	·	·	·	Scrapped	BR, Swindon Works, 1972
·	D7084	·	·	·	Scrapped	BR, Swindon Works, 1972
·	D7085	·	·	·	Scrapped	BR, Swindon Works, 1972
·	D7086	·	·	·	Scrapped	BR, Swindon Works, 1972
·	D7087	·	·	·	Scrapped	BR, Swindon Works, 1973
·	D7088	·	·	·	Scrapped	BR, Swindon Works, 1972
·	D7089	968005*	·	·	Scrapped	T J Thomson, Stockton, 1976
·	D7090	·	·	·	Scrapped	BR, Swindon Works, 1972
·	D7091	·	·	·	Scrapped	BR, Swindon Works, 1972
·	D7092	·	·	·	Scrapped	BR, Swindon Works, 1972
·	D7093	·	·	·	Scrapped	Cohen's, Kettering, 1977
·	D7094	·	·	·	Scrapped	BR, Swindon Works, 1973
·	D7095	·	·	·	Scrapped	BR, Swindon Works, 1972
·	D7096	·	·	·	Scrapped	Marple & Gillott, Sheffield, 1986
·	D7097	·	·	·	Scrapped	BR, Swindon Works, 1975
·	D7098	·	·	·	Scrapped	BR, Swindon Works, 1975
·	D7099	·	·	·	Scrapped	BR, Swindon Works, 1972
·	D7100	·	·	·	Scrapped	BR, Swindon Works, 1974

* Converted to static train pre-heating unit and renumbered with TDB prefix

CLASS 37

Total Built	309	Formation	Co-Co	Max T.E.	55,500 -
Date Built	1960-65	Max Speed	90 mph		62,000 lbf
Builder	English Electric Co, Vulcan	Weight	102 - 120 t	P.A.R.	1,250 hp
	and RS&H, Darlington	Brakes	Vacuum / Dual / Air	R.A.	5 & 7
Engine	EE 12CSVT, 1750 hp			Supply	As Below

37001	D6701	37707	·	·	Scrapped	EMR, Kingsbury, 2011
37002	D6702	37351	·	·	Scrapped	T J Thomson, Stockton, 2007
37003	D6703	37360	·	·	Preserved	Mid-Norfolk Railway
37004	D6704	·	·	·	Scrapped	MC Metals, Springburn, 1996
37005	D6705	37501	37601	·	Operational	Rail Operations Group, Leicester
37006	D6706	37798	·	·	Scrapped	C F Booth, Rotherham, 2009
37007	D6707	37506	37604	·	Stored	DRS, Carlisle Kingmoor
37008	D6708	37352	·	·	Scrapped	MRJ Phillips, Crewe Works, 1996
37009	D6709	37340	·	·	Preserved	Great Central Railway North
37010	D6710	·	·	·	Scrapped	C F Booth, Rotherham, 2007
37011	D6711	·	·	·	Scrapped	J Rollason, Wellington, 1989
37012	D6712	·	·	·	Scrapped	Sims Metals, Beeston, 2003
37013	D6713	·	·	·	Scrapped	HNRC, Kingsbury, 2007
37014	D6714	37709	·	·	Scrapped	EMR, Kingsbury, 2011
37015	D6715	37341	·	·	Scrapped	C F Booth, Rotherham, 2003
37016	D6716	37706	·	·	Operational	WCRC, Carnforth
37017	D6717	37503	·	·	Stored	Europhoenix, Leicester
37018	D6718	37517	·	·	Stored	WCRC, Carnforth
37019	D6719	·	·	·	Scrapped	Sims Metals, Beeston, 2004
37020	D6720	37702	L30~	·	Scrapped	Puigverd de Lleida, Spain, 2008
37021	D6721	37715	·	·	Scrapped	EMR, Kingsbury, 2005
37022	D6722	37512	37608	·	Operational	Rail Operations Group, Leicester

37023	D6723	·	·	·	Preserved	Allely's Yard, Studley
37024	D6724	37714	L26~	·	Preserved	Great Central Railway
37025	D6725	·	·	·	Operational	Colas Rail, Barrow Hill
37026	D6726	37320	·	·	Scrapped	EWS, Wigan, 2000
37027	D6727	37519	·	·	Scrapped	C F Booth, Rotherham, 2008
37028	D6728	37505	·	·	Scrapped	EMR, Kingsbury, 2008
37029	D6729	·	·	·	Preserved	Epping Ongar Railway
37030	D6730	37701	·	·	Scrapped	EMR, Kingsbury, 2008
37031	D6731	·	·	·	Scrapped	MRJ Phillips, Cardiff, 1997
37032	D6732	37353	·	·	Preserved	Mid-Norfolk Railway
37033	D6733	37719	·	·	Scrapped	EMR, Kingsbury, 2008
37034	D6734	37704	·	·	Scrapped	T J Thomson, Stockton, 2009
37035	D6735	·	·	·	Scrapped	C F Booth, Rotherham, 2000
37036	D6736	37507	37605	·	Operational	DRS, Carlisle Kingmoor
37037	D6737	37321	·	·	Preserved	South Devon Railway
37038	D6738	·	·	·	Operational	DRS, Carlisle Kingmoor
37039	D6739	37504	37603	·	Stored	DRS, Derby
37040	D6740	·	·	·	Scrapped	C F Booth, Rotherham, 2006
37041	D6741	37520	·	·	Scrapped	T J Thomson, Stockton, 2007
37042	D6742	·	·	·	Preserved	Eden Valley Railway
37043	D6743	37354	·	·	Scrapped	Sims Metals, Beeston, 2003
37044	D6744	37710	·	·	Stored	WCRC, Carnforth
37045	D6745	37355	·	·	Scrapped	HNRC, Toton, 2003
37046	D6746	·	·	·	Scrapped	C F Booth, Rotherham, 2009
37047	D6747	·	·	·	Scrapped	EMR, Kingsbury, 2008
37048	D6748	·	·	·	Scrapped	HNRC, Toton, 2003
37049	D6749	37322	37343	·	Scrapped	HNRC, Toton, 2003
37050	D6750	37717	·	·	Scrapped	C F Booth, Rotherham, 2009
37051	D6751	·	·	·	Scrapped	Sims Metals, Beeston, 2008
37052	D6752	37713	·	·	Scrapped	HNRC, Crewe, 2007
37053	D6753	37344	·	·	Scrapped	C F Booth, Rotherham, 2006
37054	D6754	·	·	·	Scrapped	SCD, Motherwell, 2003
37055	D6755	·	·	·	Scrapped	EMR, Kingsbury, 2008
37056	D6756	37513	·	·	Scrapped	C F Booth, Rotherham, 2008
37057	D6757	·	·	·	Operational	Colas Rail, Barrow Hill
37058	D6758	·	·	·	Scrapped	C F Booth, Rotherham, 2009
37059	D6759	·	·	·	Operational	DRS, Carlisle Kingmoor
37060	D6760	37705	·	·	Scrapped	T J Thomson, Stockton, 2007
37061	D6761	37799	L27~	·	Scrapped	Celsa Group, Spain, 2008
37062	D6762	·	·	·	Scrapped	Vic Berry, Leicester, 1990
37063	D6763	·	·	·	Scrapped	HNRC, Kingsbury, 2001
37064	D6764	37515	·	·	Scrapped	T J Thomson, Stockton, 2010
37065	D6765	·	·	·	Scrapped	EMR, Kingsbury, 2007
37066	D6766	·	·	·	Scrapped	MRJ Phillips, Crewe Works, 1997
37067	D6767	37703	L25~	·	Operational	DRS, Bo'ness & Kinneil Railway
37068	D6768	37356	·	·	Scrapped	C F Booth, Rotherham, 2005
37069	D6769	·	·	·	Operational	DRS, Carlisle Kingmoor
37070	D6770	025031*	·	·	Scrapped	HNRC, Toton, 2004
37071	D6771	·	·	·	Scrapped	C F Booth, Rotherham, 2005
37072	D6772	·	·	·	Scrapped	HNRC, Kingsbury, 2004
37073	D6773	·	·	·	Scrapped	Ian Riley Engineering, Bury, 2004
37074	D6774	·	·	·	Scrapped	C F Booth, Rotherham, 2005
37075	D6775	·	·	·	Preserved	Keighley & Worth Valley Railway
37076	D6776	37518	·	·	Operational	WCRC, Carnforth

CLASS 37 (Continued)

37077	D6777	·	·	·	Scrapped	C F Booth, Rotherham, 2008
37078	D6778	·	·	·	Scrapped	HNRC, Kingsbury, 2004
37079	D6779	37357	·	·	Scrapped	EMR, Kingsbury, 2008
37080	D6780	·	·	·	Scrapped	MRJ Phillips, Cardiff, 1997
37081	D6781	37797	·	·	Scrapped	C F Booth, Rotherham, 2006
37082	D6782	37502	37602	·	Operational	DRS, Carlisle Kingmoor
37083	D6783	·	·	·	Scrapped	Raxstar, Immingham, 2000
37084	D6784	37718	L22~	·	Scrapped	C F Booth, Rotherham, 2015
37085	D6785	37711	·	·	Scrapped	HNRC, Kingsbury, 2006
37086	D6786	37516	·	·	Operational	WCRC, Carnforth
37087	D6787	·	·	·	Scrapped	C F Booth, Rotherham, 2013
37088	D6788	37323	·	·	Scrapped	C F Booth, Rotherham, 2002
37089	D6789	37708	·	·	Scrapped	C F Booth, Rotherham, 2008
37090	D6790	37508	37606	·	Operational	DRS, Carlisle Kingmoor
37091	D6791	37358	·	·	Scrapped	T J Thomson, Stockton, 2007
37092	D6792	·	·	·	Scrapped	T J Thomson, Stockton, 2001
37093	D6793	37509	·	·	Scrapped	MRJ Phillips, Cardiff, 2005
37094	D6794	37716	L23~	·	Operational	DRS, Carlisle Kingmoor
37095	D6795	·	·	·	Scrapped	HNRC, Carnforth, 2005
37096	D6796	·	·	·	Scrapped	MC Metals, Springburn, 1991
37097	D6797	·	·	·	Preserved	Caledonian Railway
37098	D6798	·	·	·	Scrapped	HNRC, Old Oak Common, 2002
37099	D6799	37324	·	·	Operational	Colas Rail, Barrow Hill
37100	D6800	97301+	·	·	Operational	Network Rail, Derby
37101	D6801	37345	·	·	Scrapped	HNRC, Immingham, 2003
37102	D6802	37712	·	·	Stored	WCRC, Carnforth
37103	D6803	37511	37607	·	Operational	HNRC, Barrow Hill
37104	D6804	·	·	·	Scrapped	Raxstar, Immingham, 2000
37105	D6805	37796	·	·	Scrapped	C F Booth, Rotherham, 2009
37106	D6806	·	·	·	Scrapped	EWS, Wigan, 2000
37107	D6807	·	·	·	Scrapped	EWS, Wigan, 1998
37108	D6808	37325	·	·	Preserved	Crewe Heritage Centre
37109	D6809	·	·	·	Preserved	East Lancashire Railway
37110	D6810	·	·	·	Scrapped	Raxstar, Immingham, 2000
37111	D6811	37326	·	·	Scrapped	HNRC, Kingsbury, 2003
37112	D6812	37510	·	·	Stored	Europhoenix, Leicester
37113	D6813	·	·	·	Scrapped	MC Metals, Edinburgh, 1995
37114	D6814	·	·	·	Scrapped	EMR, Kingsbury, 2008
37115	D6815	37514	37609	·	Operational	DRS, Carlisle Kingmoor
37116	D6816	·	·	·	Operational	Colas Rail, Barrow Hill
37117	D6817	37521	·	·	Stored	HNRC, Washwood Heath
37118	D6818	37359	·	·	Scrapped	HNRC, Carnforth, 2005
37119	D6700	37350	·	·	Preserved	National Railway Museum, York
37120	D6820	37887	·	·	Scrapped	C F Booth, Rotherham, 2008
37121	D6821	37677	·	·	Scrapped	C F Booth, Rotherham, 2008
37122	D6822	37692	·	·	Scrapped	C F Booth, Rotherham, 2009
37123	D6823	37679	·	·	Preserved	Northampton & Lamport Railway
37124	D6824	37894	·	·	Scrapped	EMR, Kingsbury, 2008
37125	D6825	37904	·	·	Scrapped	C F Booth, Rotherham, 2004
37126	D6826	37676	·	·	Stored	WCRC, Carnforth
37127	D6827	37370	·	·	Scrapped	C F Booth, Rotherham, 2005
37128	D6828	37330	·	·	Scrapped	T J Thomson, Stockton, 2001
37129	D6829	37669	·	·	Operational	WCRC, Carnforth
37130	D6830	37681	·	·	Scrapped	MRJ Phillips, Crewe Works, 1995

37131	D6831	·	·	·	Scrapped	C F Booth, Rotherham, 2007
37132	D6832	37673	·	·	Scrapped	EMR, Kingsbury, 2008
37133	D6833	·	·	·	Scrapped	HNRC, Carnforth, 2004
37134	D6834	37684	·	·	Scrapped	C F Booth, Rotherham, 2010
37135	D6835	37888	L31~	·	Scrapped	Puigverd de Lleida, Spain, 2008
37136	D6836	37905	·	·	Operational	UK Rail Leasing, Leicester
37137	D6837	37312	·	·	Scrapped	T J Thomson, Stockton, 2006
37138	D6838	025032*	·	·	Scrapped	HNRC, Toton, 2004
37139	D6839	·	·	·	Scrapped	T J Thomson, Stockton, 2004
37140	D6840	·	·	·	Scrapped	EWS, Wigan, 2001
37141	D6841	·	·	·	Scrapped	HNRC, Carnforth, 2005
37142	D6842	·	·	·	Preserved	Bodmin & Wenford Railway
37143	D6843	37800	L33~	·	Operational	Rail Operations Group, Leicester
37144	D6844	·	·	·	Scrapped	Sims Metals, Beeston, 2003
37145	D6845	37313	37382	·	Scrapped	Raxstar, Immingham, 2000
37146	D6846	·	·	·	Stored	Colas Rail, Wensleydale Railway
37147	D6847	37371	·	·	Scrapped	EWS, Wigan, 2001
37148	D6848	37902	·	·	Scrapped	Sims Metals, Beeston, 2005
37149	D6849	37892	·	·	Scrapped	EMR, Kingsbury, 2008
37150	D6850	37901	·	·	Stored	Colas Rail, St Leonards
37151	D6851	37667	·	·	Stored	Crewe Heritage Centre
37152	D6852	37310	·	·	Preserved	Peak Rail
37153	D6853	·	·	·	Scrapped	C F Booth, Rotherham, 2003
37154	D6854	·	·	·	Scrapped	EWS, Wigan, 2000
37155	D6855	37897	·	·	Scrapped	EMR, Kingsbury, 2008
37156	D6856	37311	·	·	Scrapped	EWS, Wigan, 2000
37157	D6857	37695	·	·	Scrapped	Ron Hull, Rotherham, 2008
37158	D6858	·	·	·	Scrapped	HNRC, Carnforth, 2008
37159	D6859	37372^	·	·	Preserved	Barrow Hill
37160	D6860	37373	·	·	Scrapped	MRJ Phillips, OOC, 1997
37161	D6861	37899	L21~	·	Scrapped	Calatayud, Spain, 2003
37162	D6862	·	·	·	Scrapped	C F Booth, Rotherham, 2005
37163	D6863	37802	L32~	·	Scrapped	Calatayud, Spain, 2003
37164	D6864	37675	·	·	Scrapped	EMR, Kingsbury, 2010
37165	D6865	37374	·	·	Stored	WCRC, Carnforth
37166	D6866	37891	·	·	Scrapped	EMR, Attercliffe, 2011
37167	D6867	37383	·	·	Scrapped	HNRC, Crewe, 2008
37168	D6868	37890	·	·	Scrapped	Ron Hull, Rotherham, 2010
37169	D6869	37674	·	·	Preserved	Stainmore Railway
37170	D6870	97302+	·	·	Operational	Network Rail, Derby
37171	D6871	37690	37611	·	Operational	Europhoenix, Leicester
37172	D6872	37686	·	·	Scrapped	C F Booth, Rotherham, 2006
37173	D6873	37801	~L29~	·	Scrapped	Celsa Group, Spain, 2012
37174	D6874	·	·	·	Scrapped	EMR, Kingsbury, 2008
37175	D6875	·	·	·	Operational	Colas Rail, Barrow Hill
37176	D6876	37883	L28~	·	Scrapped	Celsa Group, Spain, 2012
37177	D6877	37885	L24~	·	Scrapped	Yias Y Construction, Spain, 2003
37178	D6878	97303+	·	·	Operational	Network Rail, Derby
37179	D6879	37691	37612	·	Stored	HNRC, Barrow Hill
37180	D6880	37886	·	·	Scrapped	EMR, Kingsbury, 2011
37181	D6881	37687	37610	·	Stored	Crewe Heritage Centre
37182	D6882	37670	·	·	Stored	Europhoenix, Leicester
37183	D6883	37884	L34~	·	Operational	Rail Operations Group, Leicester
37184	D6884	·	·	·	Scrapped	T J Thomson, Stockton, 2001

37185	D6885	·	·	·	Scrapped	C F Booth, Rotherham, 2006
37186	D6886	37898	·	·	Scrapped	EMR, Kingsbury, 2011
37187	D6887	37683	·	·	Scrapped	C F Booth, Rotherham, 2013
37188	D6888	·	·	·	Stored	Colas Rail, Barrow Hill
37189	D6889	37672	·	·	Scrapped	T J Thomson, Stockton, 2010
37190	D6890	37314	·	·	Preserved	Midland Railway Centre
37191	D6891	·	·	·	Scrapped	EWS, Wigan, 2001
37192	D6892	37694	·	·	Scrapped	EMR, Kingsbury, 2008
37193	D6893	37375	·	·	Scrapped	EMR, Kingsbury, 2008
37194	D6894	·	·	·	Scrapped	C F Booth, Rotherham, 2017
37195	D6895	37689	·	·	Scrapped	EMR, Attercliffe, 2011
37196	D6896	·	·	·	Scrapped	C F Booth, Rotherham, 2009
37197	D6897	·	·	·	Scrapped	EMR, Kingsbury, 2012
37198	D6898	·	·	·	Stored	Nemesis Rail, Burton-upon-Trent
37199	D6899	37376	·	·	Scrapped	C F Booth, Rotherham, 2006
37200	D6900	37377	·	·	Scrapped	C F Booth, Rotherham, 2009
37201	D6901	·	·	·	Scrapped	C F Booth, Rotherham, 2009
37202	D6902	37331	·	·	Scrapped	HNRC, Barrow Hill, 2003
37203	D6903	·	·	·	Scrapped	Ron Hull, Rotherham, 2010
37204	D6904	37378	·	·	Scrapped	C F Booth, Rotherham, 1996
37205	D6905	37688	·	·	Operational	DRS, Carlisle Kingmoor
37206	D6906	37906	·	·	Stored	UK Rail Leasing, Leicester
37207	D6907	·	·	·	Stored	Colas Rail, Barrow Hill
37208	D6908	37803	·	·	Scrapped	EMR, Kingsbury, 2007
37209	D6909	·	·	·	Scrapped	HNRC, Doncaster, 2002
37210	D6910	37693	·	·	Scrapped	EMR, Attercliffe, 2011
37211	D6911	·	·	·	Scrapped	EMR, Kingsbury, 2007
37212	D6912	·	·	·	Scrapped	Raxstar, Eastleigh, 2004
37213	D6913	·	·	·	Scrapped	T J Thomson, Stockton, 2003
37214	D6914	·	·	·	Stored	WCRC, Carnforth
37215	D6915	·	·	·	Preserved	G & WR
37216	D6916	·	·	·	Preserved	Pontypool & Blaenavon Railway
37217	D6917	97304+	·	·	Operational	Network Rail, Derby
37218	D6918	·	·	·	Operational	DRS, Carlisle Kingmoor
37219	D6919	·	·	·	Operational	Colas Rail, Barrow Hill
37220	D6920	·	·	·	Scrapped	EMR, Kingsbury, 2007
37221	D6921	·	·	·	Scrapped	C F Booth, Rotherham, 2009
37222	D6922	·	·	·	Scrapped	T J Thomson, Stockton, 2008
37223	D6923	·	·	·	Scrapped	Sims Metals, Beeston, 2003
37224	D6924	37680	·	·	Scrapped	T J Thomson, Stockton, 2010
37225	D6925	·	·	·	Scrapped	C F Booth, Rotherham, 2004
37226	D6926	37379	·	·	Scrapped	C F Booth, Rotherham, 2008
37227	D6927	·	·	·	Preserved	Nemesis Rail, Burton-upon-Trent
37228	D6928	37696	·	·	Scrapped	C F Booth, Rotherham, 2014
37229	D6929	·	·	·	Scrapped	C F Booth, Rotherham, 2013
37230	D6930	·	·	·	Scrapped	C F Booth, Rotherham, 2006
37231	D6931	37896	·	·	Scrapped	Ron Hull, Rotherham, 2010
37232	D6932	·	·	·	Scrapped	EWS, Wigan, 2000
37233	D6933	37889	·	·	Scrapped	HNRC, Crewe, 2007
37234	D6934	37685	·	·	Operational	WCRC, Carnforth
37235	D6935	·	·	·	Scrapped	HNRC, Carnforth, 2008
37236	D6936	37682	·	·	Scrapped	C F Booth, Rotherham, 2016
37237	D6937	37893	·	·	Scrapped	Ron Hull, Rotherham, 2012
37238	D6938	·	·	·	Scrapped	C F Booth, Rotherham, 2009

CLASS 37 (Continued)

37239	D6939	37332	·	·	Scrapped	HNRC, Old Oak Common, 2000
37240	D6940		·	·	Preserved	Llangollen Railway
37241	D6941		·	·	Scrapped	T J Thomson, Stockton, 2001
37242	D6942	·	·	·	Scrapped	C F Booth, Rotherham, 2006
37243	D6943	37697	·	·	Scrapped	C F Booth, Rotherham, 2006
37244	D6944	·	·	·	Scrapped	EWS, Wigan, 2000
37245	D6945	·	·	·	Scrapped	EWS, Wigan, 2000
37246	D6946	37698	·	·	Scrapped	C F Booth, Rotherham, 2010
37247	D6947	37671	·	·	Scrapped	EMR, Attercliffe, 2011
37248	D6948	·	·	·	Preserved	G & WR
37249	D6949	37903	·	·	Scrapped	HNRC, Crewe, 2005
37250	D6950	·	·	·	Preserved	Wensleydale Railway
37251	D6951	·	·	·	Scrapped	C F Booth, Rotherham, 2001
37252	D6952	·	·	·	Scrapped	HNRC, Doncaster, 2002
37253	D6953	37699	·	·	Scrapped	MRJ Phillips, Crewe Works, 1997
37254	D6954	·	·	·	Operational	Colas Rail, Barrow Hill
37255	D6955	·	·	·	Preserved	Nemesis Rail, Burton-upon-Trent
37256	D6956	37678	·	·	Scrapped	EMR, Kingsbury, 2007
37257	D6957	37668	·	·	Operational	WCRC, Carnforth
37258	D6958	37384	·	·	Scrapped	HNRC, Kingsbury, 2005
37259	D6959	37380	·	·	Operational	DRS, Carlisle Kingmoor
37260	D6960	·	·	·	Scrapped	MC Metals, Springburn, 1991
37261	D6961	·	·	·	Preserved	Bo'ness & Kinneil Railway
37262	D6962	·	·	·	Scrapped	Sims Metals, Beeston, 2004
37263	D6963	·	·	·	Preserved	Telford Steam Railway
37264	D6964	·	·	·	Preserved	North Yorkshire Moors Railway
37265	D6965	37430	·	·	Scrapped	EMR, Kingsbury, 2008
37266	D6966	37422	·	·	Operational	DRS, Carlisle Kingmoor
37267	D6967	37421	·	·	Operational	Colas Rail, Barrow Hill
37268	D6968	37401	·	·	Operational	DRS, Carlisle Kingmoor
37269	D6969	37417	·	·	Scrapped	C F Booth, Rotherham, 2013
37270	D6970	37409	·	·	Operational	DRS, Carlisle Kingmoor
37271	D6971	37418	·	·	Stored	HNRC, Washwood Heath
37272	D6972	37431	·	·	Scrapped	EWS, Wigan, 2000
37273	D6973	37410	·	·	Scrapped	C F Booth, Rotherham, 2013
37274	D6974	37402	·	·	Operational	DRS, Carlisle Kingmoor
37275	D6975	·	·	·	Preserved	South Devon Railway
37276	D6976	37413	·	·	Stored	DRS, Barrow Hill
37277	D6977	37415	·	·	Scrapped	C F Booth, Rotherham, 2013
37278	D6978	·	·	·	Scrapped	T J Thomson, Stockton, 2003
37279	D6979	37424	37558	·	Operational	DRS, Carlisle Kingmoor
37280	D6980	·	·	·	Scrapped	MRJ Phillips, OOC, 1997
37281	D6981	37428	·	·	Scrapped	C F Booth, Rotherham, 2013
37282	D6982	37405	·	·	Operational	DRS, Carlisle Kingmoor
37283	D6819	37895	·	·	Scrapped	EMR, Kingsbury, 2011
37284	D6984	37381	·	·	Scrapped	Raxstar, Frodingham, 2000
37285	D6985	37335	·	·	Scrapped	Raxstar, Immingham, 2000
37286	D6986	37404	·	·	Scrapped	C F Booth, Rotherham, 2002
37287	D6987	37414	·	·	Scrapped	T J Thomson, Stockton, 2009
37288	D6988	37427	·	·	Scrapped	C F Booth, Rotherham, 2013
37289	D6989	37408	·	·	Scrapped	EMR, Kingsbury, 2008
37290	D6990	37411	·	·	Scrapped	C F Booth, Rotherham, 2013
37291	D6991	37419	·	·	Operational	DRS, Carlisle Kingmoor
37292	D6992	37425	·	·	Operational	DRS, Carlisle Kingmoor

37293	D6993	·	·	·	Scrapped	C F Booth, Rotherham, 2009
37294	D6994	·	·	·	Preserved	Embsay & Bolton Abbey Railway
37295	D6995	37406	·	·	Scrapped	C F Booth, Rotherham, 2013
37296	D6996	37423	·	·	Operational	DRS, Carlisle Kingmoor
37297	D6997	37420	·	·	Scrapped	Ron Hull, Rotherham, 2008
37298	D6998	·	·	·	Scrapped	C F Booth, Rotherham, 2006
37299	D6999	37426	·	·	Scrapped	C F Booth, Rotherham, 2013
37300	D6600	37429	·	·	Scrapped	EMR, Kingsbury, 2008
37301	D6601	37412	·	·	Scrapped	EMR, Kingsbury, 2012
37302	D6602	37416	·	·	Scrapped	C F Booth, Rotherham, 2013
37303	D6603	37271	37333	·	Scrapped	MRJ Phillips, Crewe Works, 1997
37304	D6604	37272	37334	·	Scrapped	C F Booth, Rotherham, 2005
37305	D6605	37407	·	·	Operational	DRS, Carlisle Kingmoor
37306	D6606	37273	·	·	Scrapped	Gwent Demolition, Margam, 1993
37307	D6607	37403	·	·	Operational	DRS, Carlisle Kingmoor
37308	D6608	37274	·	·	Preserved	Dean Forest Railway
·	D6983	·	·	·	Scrapped	Hayes, Bridgend, 1966

Class 37/0 (37001 - 37308) Standard design originally fitted with steam heating
Class 37/3 (37330 - 37384) Unrefurbished and fitted with regeared CP7 bogies
Class 37/4 (37401 - 37431) Refurbished, rewired and fitted with alternator and electric train supply
Class 37/5 (37503 - 37521 & 37667 - 699) Refurbished, rewired and fitted with alternator
Class 37/6 (37601 - 37612) Refurbished with through ETS wiring and RCH jumper cables
Class 37/7 (37701 - 37719, 37796 - 37803 & 37883 - 37899) Refurbished heavyweight locos
Class 37/9 (37901 - 37906) Refurbished heavyweight locos with Mirrlees or Ruston power units

* Converted to power unit transporter and renumbered with IU prefix
\+ Refurbished for use on the Cambrian line ERTMS signalling project by Network Rail
~ Renumbered when exported to Spain whilst on hire to GIF for infrastructure use
^ Undergoing re-build to become Class 23

Class 37 Names:

37012	Loch Rannoch	37087	Keighley & Worth Valley Railway
37023	Stratford TMD Quality Approved	37088	Clydesdale
37025	Inverness TMD	37095	British Steel Teesside
37026	Loch Awe | Shapfell	37097	Loch Joy | Old Fettercairn
37027	Loch Eil	37099	Clydebridge
37037	Gartcosh		MERL EVANS 1947-2016
37043	Loch Lomond	37108	Lanarkshire Steel
37049	Imperial	37111	Loch Eil Outward Bound
37051	Merehead		Glengarnock
37055	RAIL Celebrity	37113	Radio Highland
37057	Viking	37114	Dunrobin Castle
37059	Port of Tilbury		City of Worcester
37062	British Steel Corby	37116	Sister Dora
37066	British Steel Workington	37137	Clyde Iron
37068	Grainflow	37152	British Steel Ravenscraig
37069	Thornaby TMD	37154	SABRE
37071	British Steel Skinningrove		Johnson Stevens Agencies
37073	Fort William An Gearasdan	37156	British Steel Hunterston
37077	British Steel Shelton	37178	METEOR
37078	Teesside Steelmaster	37188	Sir Dyfed County of Dyfed
37079	Medite	37185	Lea & Perrins
37081	Loch Long	37188	Jimmy Shand

CLASS 37 (Continued)

37190	Dalzell
37191	International Youth Year 1985
37194	British International Freight Association
	NEIL WEBSTER 1957-2001
37196	Tre Pol and Pen
37197	Loch Laidon
37198	CHIEF ENGINEER
37201	Saint Margaret
37207	William Cookworthy
37214	Loch Laidon
37216	Great Eastern
37219	Shirley Ann Smith
	Jonty Jarvis 8-12-98 to 18-03-05
37220	Westerleigh
37229	The Cardiff Rod Mill
	Jonty Jarvis 8-12-98 to 18-03-05
37232	The Institution of Railway Signal Engineers
37235	The Coal Merchants Association of Scotland
37239	The Coal Merchants Association of Scotland
37248	Midland Railway Centre	Loch Arkaig
37251	The Northern Lights
37254	Driver Robin Prince M.B.E	Cardiff Canton
37260	Radio Highland
37261	Caithness	Loch Arkaig
37262	Dounreay
37275	Stainless Pioneer	Oor Wullic
37310	British Steel Ravenscraig
37311	British Steel Hunterston
37312	Clyde Iron
37314	Dalzell
37320	Shapfell
37321	Gartcosh	Loch Treig
37322	Imperial
37323	Clydesdale
37324	Clydebridge
37325	Lanarkshire Steel
37326	Glengarnock
37332	The Coal Merchants Association of Scotland
37343	Imperial
37350	NRM NATIONAL RAILWAY MUSEUM
37356	Grainflow
37358	P & O Containers
37379	Ipswich WRD Quality Approved
37401	Mary Queen of Scots
	THE ROYAL SCOTSMAN
37402	Oor Wullie	Bont Y Bermo
	Stephen Middlemore 1954-2013
37403	Isle of Mull	Glendarroch	Ben Cruachan
37404	Ben Cruachan	Loch Long
37405	Strathclyde Region
37406	The Saltaire Society
37407	Loch Long	Blackpool Tower
37408	Loch Rannoch	Nick Dodson / Sue Dodson
37409	Loch Awe	Lord Hinton

37410	Aluminium 100
37411	The Institution of Railway -
	Signal Engineers	Ty Hafan
	The Scottish Railway -
	Preservation Society
	Caerphilly Castle
37412	Loch Lomond	Driver John Elliot
37413	Loch Eil Outward Bound
	The Scottish Railway -
	Preservation Society
37414	Cathays C & W Works 1846-1993
37416	Sir Robert McAlpine / Concrete Bob
37417	Highland Region	RAIL MAGAZINE
	Richard Trevithick
37418	An Comunn Gaidhealach
	Gordon Grigg	Pectinidae
	East Lancashire Railway
37419	Carl Haviland 1954-2012
37420	The Scottish Hosteller
37421	Strombidae	Star of the East
	The Kingsman
	FORT WILLIAM HOME -
	OF 1Y11/1BO1
37422	Robert F Fairlie Locomotive -
	Engineer	Cardiff Canton
37423	Sir Murray Morrison 1873-1948
	Spirit of the Lakes
37424	Isle of Mull	Glendarroch
	Avro Vulcan XH558
37425	Sir Robert McAlpine /-
	Concrete Bob	Pride of the Valleys
37426	Y Lein Fach Vale of Rheidol
37427	Bont Y Bermo	Highland Enterprise
37428	David Lloyd George
	THE ROYAL SCOTSMAN
	Loch Awe / Loch Long
37429	Sir Dyfed County of Dyfed
	Eisteddfod Genedlaethol
37430	Cwmbran
37431	Sir Powys County of Powis
	Bullidae
37501	Teesside Steelmaster
37502	British Steel Teesside
37503	British Steel Shelton
37504	British Steel Corby
37505	British Steel Workington
37506	British Steel Skinningrove
37507	Hartlepool Pipe Mill
37511	Stockton Haulage
37512	Thornaby Demon
37516	Loch Laidon
37517	St Aidens CE School
37518	Fort William / An Gearasdan
37521	English China Clays

CLASS 37 (Continued)

37601	Class 37 'Fifty' | Perseus	37716	British Steel Corby
37608	Andromeda	37717	Stainless Pioneer
37610	The MALCOLM Group		Maltby Lilly Hall School,-
	TS Ted Cassady 1961-2008		Rotherham 1996
37611	Pegasus		St Margaret's School,-
37667	Wensleydale | Meldon Quarry Centenary		Durham, 1997
37668	Leyburn		Berwick Middle School 1998
37670	St Blazey T&RS Depot	37718	Hartlepool Pipe Mill
37671	Tre Pol and Pen	37719	Lanarkshire Steel
37672	Freight Transport Association	37799	Sir Dyfed County of Dyfed
37674	Saint Blaise Church 1445-1995	37800	Glo Cymru | Cassiopeia
37675	William Cookworthy	37801	Aberddawan Aberthaw
37676	Loch Rannoch	37884	Gartcosh
37682	Hartlepool Pipe Mill	37886	Sir Dyfed County of Dyfed
37684	Peak National Park	37887	Castell Caerffilli / Caephilly Castle
37685	Loch Arkaig	37888	Petrolea
37688	Great Rocks | Kingmoor TMD	37890	The Railway Observer
37692	The Lass O' Ballochmyle	37892	Ripple Lane
37693	Sir William Arrol	37898	Cwmbargoed DP
37694	The Lass O' Ballochmyle	37899	Sir Gorllewin Morgannwg -
37698	Coedbach		County of West Glamorgan
37702	Taff Merthyr	37901	Mirrlees Pioneer | Star of the East
37706	Conidae	37902	British Steel Llanwern
37711	Tremorfa Steelworks	37905	Vulcan Enterprise
37712	The Cardiff Rod Mill	37906	Star of the East
	Teesside Steelmaster	97304	John Tiley
37713	British Steel Workington	D6703	The 1st East Anglian Regiment
37714	Thornaby TMD	D6704	The 2nd East Anglian Regiment
37715	British Steel Teesside | British Petroleum	D6705	The 3rd East Anglian Regiment

CLASS 40

Total Built	200	Formation	1Co-Co1	Max T.E.	52,000 lbf
Date Built	1958-62	Max Speed	90 mph	P.A.R.	1,550 hp
Builder	English Electric, Vulcan and RS&H	Weight	135 t	R.A.	6
Engine	EE 16SVT Mk2 2000 hp	Brakes	Vacuum / Air & Vac	Supply	Steam

40001	D201		·	·	Scrapped	BR, Swindon Works, 1987
40002	D202		·	·	Scrapped	BR, Doncaster Works, 1985
40003	D203		·	·	Scrapped	BR, Doncaster Works, 1984
40004	D204		·	·	Scrapped	BR, Crewe Works, 1986
40005	D205		·	·	Scrapped	BR, Crewe Works, 1977
40006	D206		·	·	Scrapped	BR, Crewe Works, 1984
40007	D207		·	·	Scrapped	BR, Doncaster Works, 1984
40008	D208		·	·	Scrapped	BR, Crewe Works, 1988
40009	D209		·	·	Scrapped	BR, Doncaster Works, 1985
40010	D210		·	·	Scrapped	BR, Swindon Works, 1983
40011	D211		·	·	Scrapped	BR, Swindon Works, 1980
40012	D212	97407*	·	·	Preserved	Midland Railway Centre
40013	D213		·	·	Preserved	Locomotive Services, Crewe
40014	D214		·	·	Scrapped	BR, Swindon Works, 1983
40015	D215		·	·	Scrapped	BR, Swindon Works, 1986
40016	D216		·	·	Scrapped	BR, Swindon Works, 1983
40017	D217		·	·	Scrapped	BR, Swindon Works, 1981

40018	D218	·	·	·	Scrapped	BR, Crewe Works, 1983
40019	D219	·	·	·	Scrapped	BR, Doncaster Works, 1984
40020	D220	·	·	·	Scrapped	BR, Crewe Works, 1987
40021	D221	·	·	·	Scrapped	BR, Crewe Works, 1977
40022	D222	·	·	·	Scrapped	BR, Doncaster Works, 1984
40023	D223	·	·	·	Scrapped	BR, Crewe Works, 1984
40024	D224	·	·	·	Scrapped	BR, Crewe Works, 1985
40025	D225	·	·	·	Scrapped	BR, Doncaster Works, 1985
40026	D226	·	·	·	Scrapped	BR, Swindon Works, 1983
40027	D227	·	·	·	Scrapped	BR, Crewe Works, 1984
40028	D228	·	·	·	Scrapped	BR, Crewe Works, 1988
40029	D229	·	·	·	Scrapped	BR, Doncaster Works, 1984
40030	D230	·	·	·	Scrapped	BR, Crewe Works, 1984
40031	D231	·	·	·	Scrapped	BR, Crewe Works, 1983
40032	D232	·	·	·	Scrapped	BR, Swindon Works, 1983
40033	D233	·	·	·	Scrapped	BR, Doncaster Works, 1985
40034	D234	·	·	·	Scrapped	BR, Doncaster Works, 1984
40035	D235	·	·	·	Scrapped	BR, Crewe Works, 1985
40036	D236	·	·	·	Scrapped	BR, Swindon Works, 1982
40037	D237	·	·	·	Scrapped	BR, Swindon Works, 1983
40038	D238	·	·	·	Scrapped	BR, Swindon Works, 1982
40039	D239	·	·	·	Scrapped	BR, Crewe Works, 1976
40040	D240	·	·	·	Scrapped	BR, Doncaster Works, 1980
40041	D241	·	·	·	Scrapped	BR, Crewe Works, 1978
40042	D242	·	·	·	Scrapped	BR, Derby Works, 1981
40043	D243	·	·	·	Scrapped	BR, Crewe Works, 1977
40044	D244	·	·	·	Scrapped	BR, Crewe Works, 1988
40045	D245	·	·	·	Scrapped	BR, Derby Works, 1977
40046	D246	·	·	·	Scrapped	Vic Berry, Leicester, 1987
40047	D247	·	·	·	Scrapped	BR, Doncaster Works, 1986
40048	D248	·	·	·	Scrapped	BR, Doncaster Works, 1980
40049	D249	·	·	·	Scrapped	BR, Crewe Works, 1985
40050	D250	·	·	·	Scrapped	BR, Doncaster Works, 1983
40051	D251	·	·	·	Scrapped	BR, Doncaster Works, 1978
40052	D252	·	·	·	Scrapped	BR, Crewe Works, 1983
40053	D253	·	·	·	Scrapped	BR, Crewe Works, 1976
40054	D254	·	·	·	Scrapped	BR, Crewe Works, 1978
40055	D255	·	·	·	Scrapped	BR, Doncaster Works, 1983
40056	D256	·	·	·	Scrapped	BR, Doncaster Works, 1985
40057	D257	·	·	·	Scrapped	BR, Crewe Works, 1988
40058	D258	·	·	·	Scrapped	BR, Crewe Works, 1987
40059	D259	·	·	·	Scrapped	BR, Doncaster Works, 1978
40060	D260	97405*	·	·	Scrapped	Vic Berry, Leicester, 1988
40061	D261	·	·	·	Scrapped	BR, Crewe Works, 1985
40062	D262	·	·	·	Scrapped	BR, Swindon Works, 1983
40063	D263	·	·	·	Scrapped	Vic Berry, Leicester, 1987
40064	D264	·	·	·	Scrapped	BR, Crewe Works, 1983
40065	D265	·	·	·	Scrapped	BR, Crewe Works, 1985
40066	D266	·	·	·	Scrapped	BR, Swindon Works, 1981
40067	D267	·	·	·	Scrapped	BR, Doncaster Works, 1982
40068	D268	·	·	·	Scrapped	BR, Doncaster Works, 1983
40069	D269	·	·	·	Scrapped	BR, Doncaster Works, 1984
40070	D270	·	·	·	Scrapped	BR, Doncaster Works, 1982
40071	D271	·	·	·	Scrapped	BR, Swindon Works, 1981

40072	D272	·	·	·	Scrapped	BR, Glasgow Works, 1978
40073	D273	·	·	·	Scrapped	BR, Crewe Works, 1984
40074	D274	·	·	·	Scrapped	BR, Doncaster Works, 1984
40075	D275	·	·	·	Scrapped	Vic Berry, Leicester, 1987
40076	D276	·	·	·	Scrapped	BR, Doncaster Works, 1983
40077	D277	·	·	·	Scrapped	BR, Doncaster Works, 1984
40078	D278	·	·	·	Scrapped	BR, Swindon Works, 1983
40079	D279	·	·	·	Scrapped	BR, Doncaster Works, 1985
40080	D280	·	·	·	Scrapped	BR, Doncaster Works, 1984
40081	D281	·	·	·	Scrapped	BR, Doncaster Works, 1983
40082	D282	·	·	·	Scrapped	BR, Crewe Works, 1986
40083	D283	·	·	·	Scrapped	BR, Swindon Works, 1981
40084	D284	·	·	·	Scrapped	BR, Crewe Works, 1984
40085	D285	·	·	·	Scrapped	BR, Doncaster Works, 1985
40086	D286	·	·	·	Scrapped	BR, Doncaster Works, 1985
40087	D287	·	·	·	Scrapped	BR, Doncaster Works, 1985
40088	D288	·	·	·	Scrapped	BR, Crewe Works, 1988
40089	D289	·	·	·	Scrapped	BR, Crewe Works, 1978
40090	D290	·	·	·	Scrapped	BR, Doncaster Works, 1984
40091	D291	·	·	·	Scrapped	BR, Crewe Works, 1988
40092	D292	·	·	·	Scrapped	BR, Swindon Works, 1986
40093	D293	·	·	·	Scrapped	BR, Doncaster Works, 1984
40094	D294	·	·	·	Scrapped	BR, Doncaster Works, 1985
40095	D295	·	·	·	Scrapped	BR, Swindon Works, 1983
40096	D296	·	·	·	Scrapped	BR, Doncaster Works, 1984
40097	D297	·			Scrapped	BR, Doncaster Works, 1984
40098	D298	·	·	·	Scrapped	BR, Swindon Works, 1983
40099	D299	·	·	·	Scrapped	BR, Doncaster Works, 1985
40100	D300	·	·	·	Scrapped	BR, Swindon Works, 1981
40101	D301	·	·	·	Scrapped	BR, Crewe Works, 1984
40102	D302	·	·	·	Scrapped	BR, Crewe Works, 1987
40103	D303	·	·	·	Scrapped	BR, Crewe Works, 1983
40104	D304	·	·	·	Scrapped	BR, Crewe Works, 1988
40105	D305	·	·	·	Scrapped	BR, Swindon Works, 1981
40106	D306	·	·	·	Preserved	East Lancashire Railway
40107	D307	·	·	·	Scrapped	BR, Crewe Works, 1984
40108	D308	·	·	·	Scrapped	BR, Swindon Works, 1980
40109	D309	·	·	·	Scrapped	BR, Swindon Works, 1984
40110	D310	·	·	·	Scrapped	BR, Swindon Works, 1983
40111	D311	·	·	·	Scrapped	BR, Swindon Works, 1982
40112	D312	·	·	·	Scrapped	BR, Swindon Works, 1985
40113	D313	·	·	·	Scrapped	BR, Swindon Works, 1984
40114	D314	·	·	·	Scrapped	BR, Swindon Works, 1982
40115	D315	·	·	·	Scrapped	BR, Crewe Works, 1988
40116	D316	·	·	·	Scrapped	BR, Swindon Works, 1981
40117	D317	·	·	·	Scrapped	BR, Swindon Works, 1983
40118	D318	97408*	·	·	Preserved	Tyseley Locomotive Works
40119	D319	·	·	·	Scrapped	BR, Swindon Works, 1982
40120	D320	·	·	·	Scrapped	BR, Swindon Works, 1983
40121	D321	·	·	·	Scrapped	BR, Crewe Works, 1983
40122	D200	·	·	·	Preserved	National Railway Museum, York
40123	D323	·	·	·	Scrapped	BR, Crewe Works, 1983
40124	D324	·	·	·	Scrapped	BR, Doncaster Works, 1984
40125	D325	·	·	·	Scrapped	BR, Swindon Works, 1983

CLASS 40 (Continued)

40126	D326	·	·	·	Scrapped	BR, Doncaster Works, 1984
40127	D327	·	·	·	Scrapped	BR, Swindon Works, 1983
40128	D328	·	·	·	Scrapped	BR, Doncaster Works, 1983
40129	D329	·	·	·	Scrapped	BR, Doncaster Works, 1984
40130	D330	·	·	·	Scrapped	BR, Swindon Works, 1983
40131	D331	·	·	·	Scrapped	BR, Crewe Works, 1984
40132	D332	·	·	·	Scrapped	Vic Berry, Leicester, 1987
40133	D333	·	·	·	Scrapped	BR, Doncaster Works, 1984
40134	D334	·	·	·	Scrapped	BR, Swindon Works, 1983
40135	D335	97406*	·	·	Preserved	East Lancashire Railway
40136	D336	·	·	·	Scrapped	BR, Crewe Works, 1983
40137	D337	·	·	·	Scrapped	BR, Swindon Works, 1981
40138	D338	·	·	·	Scrapped	BR, Crewe Works, 1984
40139	D339	·	·	·	Scrapped	BR, Crewe Works, 1988
40140	D340	·	·	·	Scrapped	BR, Crewe Works, 1983
40141	D341	·	·	·	Scrapped	BR, Doncaster Works, 1984
40142	D342	·	·	·	Scrapped	BR, Crewe Works, 1983
40143	D343	·	·	·	Scrapped	BR, Crewe Works, 1986
40144	D344	·	·	·	Scrapped	BR, Swindon Works, 1983
40145	D345	·	·	·	Operational	East Lancashire Railway
40146	D346	·	·	·	Scrapped	BR, Swindon Works, 1983
40147	D347	·	·	·	Scrapped	BR, Swindon Works, 1983
40148	D348	·	·	·	Scrapped	BR, Doncaster Works, 1985
40149	D349	·	·	·	Scrapped	BR, Swindon Works, 1986
40150	D350	·	·	·	Scrapped	BR, Crewe Works, 1987
40151	D351	·	·	·	Scrapped	BR, Swindon Works, 1982
40152	D352	·	·	·	Scrapped	BR, Doncaster Works, 1985
40153	D353	·	·	·	Scrapped	BR, Crewe Works, 1984
40154	D354	·	·	·	Scrapped	BR, Swindon Works, 1985
40155	D355	·	·	·	Scrapped	BR, Crewe Works, 1988
40156	D356	·	·	·	Scrapped	BR, Swindon Works, 1980
40157	D357	·	·	·	Scrapped	BR, Doncaster Works, 1983
40158	D358	·	·	·	Scrapped	BR, Doncaster Works, 1984
40159	D359	·	·	·	Scrapped	BR, Swindon Works, 1984
40160	D360	·	·	·	Scrapped	BR, Crewe Works, 1987
40161	D361	·	·	·	Scrapped	BR, Swindon Works, 1981
40162	D362	·	·	·	Scrapped	J McWilliams, Millerhill, 1986
40163	D363	·	·	·	Scrapped	Vic Berry, Leicester, 1987
40164	D364	·	·	·	Scrapped	BR, Doncaster Works, 1983
40165	D365	·	·	·	Scrapped	BR, Doncaster Works, 1983
40166	D366	·	·	·	Scrapped	BR, Crewe Works, 1983
40167	D367	·	·	·	Scrapped	BR, Doncaster Works, 1984
40168	D368	·	·	·	Scrapped	BR, Crewe Works, 1986
40169	D369	·	·	·	Scrapped	BR, Doncaster Works, 1984
40170	D370	·	·	·	Scrapped	BR, Doncaster Works, 1984
40171	D371	·	·	·	Scrapped	BR, Swindon Works, 1982
40172	D372	·	·	·	Scrapped	BR, Doncaster Works, 1983
40173	D373	·	·	·	Scrapped	James White, Inverkeithing, 1985
40174	D374	·	·	·	Scrapped	BR, Doncaster Works, 1984
40175	D375	·	·	·	Scrapped	BR, Swindon Works, 1983
40176	D376	·	·	·	Scrapped	BR, Swindon Works, 1985
40177	D377	·	·	·	Scrapped	BR, Crewe Works, 1986
40178	D378	·	·	·	Scrapped	BR, Swindon Works, 1983
40179	D379	·	·	·	Scrapped	BR, Swindon Works, 1982

40180	D380	·	·	·	Scrapped	BR, Crewe Works, 1984
40181	D381	·	·	·	Scrapped	BR, Crewe Works, 1986
40182	D382	·	·	·	Scrapped	BR, Crewe Works, 1984
40183	D383	·	·	·	Scrapped	BR, Crewe Works, 1986
40184	D384	·	·	·	Scrapped	BR, Doncaster Works, 1983
40185	D385	·	·	·	Scrapped	BR, Doncaster Works, 1983
40186	D386	·	·	·	Scrapped	BR, Doncaster Works, 1983
40187	D387	·	·	·	Scrapped	BR, Doncaster Works, 1985
40188	D388	·	·	·	Scrapped	BR, Crewe Works, 1984
40189	D389	·	·	·	Scrapped	BR, Crewe Works, 1976
40190	D390	·	·	·	Scrapped	BR, Crewe Works, 1976
40191	D391	·	·	·	Scrapped	BR, Crewe Works, 1984
40192	D392	·	·	·	Scrapped	BR, Doncaster Works, 1985
40193	D393	·	·	·	Scrapped	BR, Swindon Works, 1986
40194	D394	·	·	·	Scrapped	BR, Doncaster Works, 1985
40195	D395	·	·	·	Scrapped	BR, Crewe Works, 1988
40196	D396	·	·	·	Scrapped	BR, Doncaster Works, 1985
40197	D397	·	·	·	Scrapped	BR, Doncaster Works, 1984
40198	D398	·	·	·	Scrapped	BR, Doncaster Works, 1984
40199	D399	·	·	·	Scrapped	BR, Doncaster Works, 1983
·	D322	·	·	·	Scrapped	BR, Crewe Works, 1967

* Renumbered for departmental use

Class 40 Names:

40010	EMPRESS OF BRITAIN		40025	LUSITANIA
40011	MAURETANIA		40026	MEDIA
40012	AUREOL		40027	PARTHIA
40013	ANDANIA		40028	SAMARIA
40014	ANTONIA		40029	SAXONIA
40015	AQUITANIA		40030	SCYTHIA
40016	CAMPANIA		40031	SYLVANIA
40017	CARINTHIA		40032	EMPRESS OF CANADA
40018	CARMANIA		40033	EMPRESS OF ENGLAND
40019	CARONIA		40034	ACCRA
40020	FRANCONIA		40035	APAPA
40021	IVERNIA		40106	ATLANTIC CONVEYOR
40022	LACONIA		40122	CARONIA
40023	LANCASTRIA		40145	East Lancashire Railway
40024	LUCANIA			

CLASS 41 (Warship)

Total Built	5	Formation	A1A-A1A	Max T.E.	50,000 lbf
Date Built	1958/59	Max Speed	90 mph	P.A.R.	1,700 hp
Builder	North British Loco Co, Glasgow	Weight	118 t	R.A.	5
Engine	2 x MAN L12V18/21A, 2000 hp	Brakes	Vacuum	Supply	Steam

·	D600	·	·	·	Scrapped	Woodham Brothers, Barry, 1970
·	D601	·	·	·	Scrapped	Woodham Brothers, Barry, 1980
·	D602	·	·	·	Scrapped	Cashmore's, Newport, 1968
·	D603	·	·	·	Scrapped	Cashmore's, Newport, 1968
·	D604	·	·	·	Scrapped	Cashmore's, Newport, 1968

CLASS 41 (Continued)

Class 41 Names:

D600	ACTIVE	D602	BULLDOG	D604	COSSACK	
D601	ARK ROYAL	D603	CONQUEST			

CLASS 41 (Prototype HST)

Total Built	2	Formation	Bo-Bo	Max T.E.	17,980 lbf
Date Built	1972	Max Speed	125 mph	P.A.R.	1,770 hp
Builder	BREL, Crewe	Weight	68.5 t	R.A.	6
Engine	Paxman 12RP200L, 2250 hp	Brakes	Air	Supply	Electric

41001	43000	252001	975812*	Preserved	Great Central Railway North
41002	43001	252001	975813*	Scrapped	C F Booth, Rotherham, 1990

* Transferred to departmental stock and renumbered with ADB prefix

CLASS 42

Total Built	38	Formation	B-B	Max T.E.	52,400 lbf
Date Built	1958-61	Max Speed	90 mph	P.A.R.	1,750 hp
Builder	BR, Swindon	Weight	79 t	R.A.	6
Engine	2 x Maybach MD650, 2000 hp	Brakes	Vacuum	Supply	Steam

·	D800	·	·	·	Scrapped	Cashmore's, Newport, 1969
·	D801	·	·	·	Scrapped	BR, Swindon Works, 1970
·	D802	·	·	·	Scrapped	BR, Swindon Works, 1970
·	D803	·	·	·	Scrapped	BR, Swindon Works, 1972
·	D804	·	·	·	Scrapped	BR, Swindon Works, 1972
·	D805	·	·	·	Scrapped	BR, Swindon Works, 1973
·	D806	·	·	·	Scrapped	BR, Swindon Works, 1975
·	D807	·	·	·	Scrapped	BR, Swindon Works, 1972
·	D808	·	·	·	Scrapped	BR, Swindon Works, 1972
·	D809	·	·	·	Scrapped	BR, Swindon Works, 1972
·	D810	·	·	·	Scrapped	BR, Swindon Works, 1973
·	D811	·	·	·	Scrapped	BR, Swindon Works, 1972
·	D812	·	·	·	Scrapped	BR, Swindon Works, 1973
·	D813	·	·	·	Scrapped	BR, Swindon Works, 1972
·	D814	·	·	·	Scrapped	BR, Swindon Works, 1974
·	D815	·	·	·	Scrapped	BR, Swindon Works, 1972
·	D816	·	·	·	Scrapped	BR, Swindon Works, 1972
·	D817	·	·	·	Scrapped	BR, Swindon Works, 1972
·	D818	·	·	·	Scrapped	BR, Swindon Works, 1985
·	D819	·	·	·	Scrapped	BR, Swindon Works, 1972
·	D820	·	·	·	Scrapped	BR, Swindon Works, 1973
·	D821	·	·	·	Preserved	Severn Valley Railway
·	D822	·	·	·	Scrapped	BR, Swindon Works, 1972
·	D823	·	·	·	Scrapped	BR, Swindon Works, 1972
·	D824	·	·	·	Scrapped	BR, Swindon Works, 1975
·	D825	·	·	·	Scrapped	BR, Swindon Works, 1972
·	D826	·	·	·	Scrapped	BR, Swindon Works, 1972
·	D827	·	·	·	Scrapped	BR, Swindon Works, 1972
·	D828	·	·	·	Scrapped	BR, Swindon Works, 1972
·	D829	·	·	·	Scrapped	BR, Swindon Works, 1974
·	D830	·	·	·	Scrapped	BR, Swindon Works, 1971
·	D831	·	·	·	Scrapped	BR, Swindon Works, 1972

CLASS 42 (Continued)

·	D832	·	·	·	Preserved	East Lancashire Railway
·	D866	·	·	·	Scrapped	BR, Swindon Works, 1972
·	D867	·	·	·	Scrapped	BR, Swindon Works, 1972
·	D868	·	·	·	Scrapped	BR, Swindon Works, 1972
·	D869	·	·	·	Scrapped	BR, Swindon Works, 1972
·	D870	·	·	·	Scrapped	BR, Swindon Works, 1972

Class 42 Names:

D800	SIR BRIAN ROBERTSON		D819	GOLIATH
D801	VANGUARD		D820	GRENVILLE
D802	FORMIDABLE		D821	GREYHOUND
D803	ALBION		D822	HERCULES
D804	AVENGER		D823	HERMES
D805	BENBOW		D824	HIGHFLYER
D806	CAMBRIAN		D825	INTREPID
D807	CARADOC		D826	JUPITER
D808	CENTAUR		D827	KELLY
D809	CHAMPION		D828	MAGNIFICENT
D810	COCKADE		D829	MAGPIE
D811	DARING		D830	MAJESTIC
D812	ROYAL NAVAL RESERVE		D831	MONARCH
D813	DIADEM		D832	ONSLAUGHT
D814	DRAGON		D866	ZEBRA
D815	DRUID		D867	ZENITH
D816	ECLIPSE		D868	ZEPHYR
D817	FOXHOUND		D869	ZEST
D818	GLORY		D870	ZULU

CLASS 43 (Warship)

Total Built	33	Formation	B-B	Max T.E.	49,030 lbf
Date Built	1960-62	Max Speed	90 mph	P.A.R.	1,800 hp
Builder	North British Loco Co, Glasgow	Weight	79 t	R.A.	6
Engine	2 x MAN L12V18/21, 2200 hp	Brakes	Vacuum	Supply	Steam

·	D833	·	·	·	Scrapped	BR, Swindon Works, 1972
·	D834	·	·	·	Scrapped	BR, Swindon Works, 1972
·	D835	·	·	·	Scrapped	BR, Swindon Works, 1971
·	D836	·	·	·	Scrapped	BR, Swindon Works, 1972
·	D837	·	·	·	Scrapped	BR, Swindon Works, 1972
·	D838	·	·	·	Scrapped	BR, Swindon Works, 1972
·	D839	·	·	·	Scrapped	BR, Swindon Works, 1972
·	D840	·	·	·	Scrapped	BR, Swindon Works, 1971
·	D841	·	·	·	Scrapped	BR, Swindon Works, 1972
·	D842	·	·	·	Scrapped	BR, Swindon Works, 1972
·	D843	·	·	·	Scrapped	BR, Swindon Works, 1972
·	D844	·	·	·	Scrapped	BR, Swindon Works, 1972
·	D845	·	·	·	Scrapped	BR, Swindon Works, 1972
·	D846	·	·	·	Scrapped	BR, Swindon Works, 1971
·	D847	·	·	·	Scrapped	BR, Swindon Works, 1972
·	D848	·	·	·	Scrapped	BR, Swindon Works, 1971
·	D849	·	·	·	Scrapped	BR, Swindon Works, 1972
·	D850	·	·	·	Scrapped	BR, Swindon Works, 1972
·	D851	·	·	·	Scrapped	BR, Swindon Works, 1972

CLASS 43 (Continued)

·	D852	·	·	·	Scrapped	BR, Swindon Works, 1972
·	D853	·	·	·	Scrapped	BR, Swindon Works, 1972
·	D854	·	·	·	Scrapped	BR, Swindon Works, 1972
·	D855	·	·	·	Scrapped	BR, Swindon Works, 1972
·	D856	·	·	·	Scrapped	BR, Swindon Works, 1972
·	D857	·	·	·	Scrapped	BR, Swindon Works, 1972
·	D858	·	·	·	Scrapped	BR, Swindon Works, 1972
·	D859	·	·	·	Scrapped	BR, Swindon Works, 1972
·	D860	·	·	·	Scrapped	BR, Swindon Works, 1971
·	D861	·	·	·	Scrapped	BR, Swindon Works, 1972
·	D862	·	·	·	Scrapped	BR, Swindon Works, 1972
·	D863	·	·	·	Scrapped	Cashmore's, Newport, 1969
·	D864	·	·	·	Scrapped	BR, Swindon Works, 1971
·	D865	·	·	·	Scrapped	BR, Swindon Works, 1972

Class 43 Names:

D833	PANTHER	D844	SPARTAN	D855	TRIUMPH
D834	PATHFINDER	D845	SPRIGHTLY	D856	TROJAN
D835	PEGASUS	D846	STEADFAST	D857	UNDAUNTED
D836	POWERFUL	D847	STRONGBOW	D858	VALOUROUS
D837	RAMILLIES	D848	SULTAN	D859	VANQUISHER
D838	RAPID	D849	SUPERB	D860	VICTORIOUS
D839	RELENTLESS	D850	SWIFT	D861	VIGILANT
D840	RESISTANCE	D851	TEMERAIRE	D862	VIKING
D841	ROEBUCK	D852	TENACIOUS	D863	WARRIOR
D842	ROYAL OAK	D853	THRUSTER	D864	ZAMBESI
D843	SHARPSHOOTER	D854	TIGER	D865	ZEALOUS

CLASS 43 (HST)

Total Built	197	Formation	Bo-Bo	Max T.E.	17,980 lbf
Date Built	1976-82	Max Speed	125 mph	P.A.R.	1,770 hp
Builder	BREL, Crewe	Weight	70 t	R.A.	5
Engine	Built with Paxman 12RP200L	Brakes	Air	Supply	Electric

43002	253001	·	·	·	Operational	GWR, Laira, Plymouth
43003	253001	·	·	·	Operational	GWR, Laira, Plymouth
43004	253002	·	·	·	Operational	GWR, Laira, Plymouth
43005	253002	·	·	·	Operational	GWR, Laira, Plymouth
43006	253003	43206	·	·	Operational	LNER, Craigentinny, Edinburgh
43007	253003	43207	·	·	Operational	XC, Craigentinny, Edinburgh
43008	253004	43208	·	·	Operational	LNER, Craigentinny, Edinburgh
43009	253004	·	·	·	Operational	GWR, Laira, Plymouth
43010	253005	·	·	·	Operational	GWR, Laira, Plymouth
43011	253005	·	·	·	Scrapped	Crewe Works, 2002
43012	253006	·	·	·	Stored	ScotRail, Loughborough Works
43013	253006	·	·	·	Operational	NR, Craigentinny, Edinburgh
43014	253007	·	·	·	Operational	NR, Craigentinny, Edinburgh
43015	253007	·	·	·	Operational	GWR, Laira, Plymouth
43016	253008	·	·	·	Operational	GWR, Laira, Plymouth
43017	253008	·	·	·	Operational	GWR, Laira, Plymouth
43018	253009	·	·	·	Operational	GWR, Laira, Plymouth
43019	253009	·	·	·	Scrapped	Sims Metals, Beeston, 2005
43020	253010	·	·	·	Operational	GWR, Laira, Plymouth

CLASS 43 (Continued)

43021	253010	·	·	·	Operational	ScotRail, Craigentinny, Edinburgh
43022	253011	·	·	·	Operational	GWR, Laira, Plymouth
43023	253011	·	·	·	Operational	GWR, Laira, Plymouth
43024	253012	·	·	·	Operational	GWR, Laira, Plymouth
43025	253012	·	·	·	Operational	GWR, Laira, Plymouth
43026	253013	·	·	·	Operational	GWR, Laira, Plymouth
43027	253013	·	·	·	Operational	GWR, Laira, Plymouth
43028	253014	·	·	·	Operational	GWR, Laira, Plymouth
43029	253014	·	·	·	Operational	GWR, Laira, Plymouth
43030	253015	·	·	·	Operational	GWR, Laira, Plymouth
43031	253015	·	·	·	Operational	GWR, Laira, Plymouth
43032	253016	·	·	·	Operational	GWR, Laira, Plymouth
43033	253016	·	·	·	Stored	ScotRail, Loughborough Works
43034	253017	·	·	·	Operational	GWR, Laira, Plymouth
43035	253017	·	·	·	Operational	GWR, Laira, Plymouth
43036	253018	·	·	·	Stored	ScotRail, Loughborough Works
43037	253018	·	·	·	Operational	ScotRail, Haymarket, Edinburgh
43038	253019	43238	·	·	Operational	LNER, Craigentinny, Edinburgh
43039	253019	43239	·	·	Operational	LNER, Craigentinny, Edinburgh
43040	253020	·	·	·	Operational	GWR, Laira, Plymouth
43041	253020	·	·	·	Operational	GWR, Landore, Swansea
43042	253021	·	·	·	Operational	GWR, Landore, Swansea
43043*	253021	·	·	·	Operational	EMT, Neville Hill, Leeds
43044*	253022	·	·	·	Operational	EMT, Neville Hill, Leeds
43045*	253022	·	·	·	Operational	EMT, Neville Hill, Leeds
43046*	253023	·	·	·	Operational	EMT, Neville Hill, Leeds
43047*	253023	·	·	·	Operational	EMT, Neville Hill, Leeds
43048*	253024	·	·	·	Operational	EMT, Neville Hill, Leeds
43049*	253024	·	·	·	Operational	EMT, Neville Hill, Leeds
43050*	253025	·	·	·	Operational	EMT, Neville Hill, Leeds
43051	253025	43251	·	·	Operational	LNER, Craigentinny, Edinburgh
43052*	253026	·	·	·	Operational	EMT, Neville Hill, Leeds
43053	253026	·	·	·	Operational	GWR, Landore, Swansea
43054*	253027	·	·	·	Operational	EMT, Neville Hill, Leeds
43055*	253027	·	·	·	Operational	EMT, Neville Hill, Leeds
43056	254001	·	·	·	Operational	GWR, Landore, Swansea
43057	254001	43257	·	·	Operational	LNER, Craigentinny, Edinburgh
43058*	254002	·	·	·	Operational	EMT, Neville Hill, Leeds
43059*	254002	·	·	·	Operational	EMT, Neville Hill, Leeds
43060*	254003	·	·	·	Operational	EMT, Neville Hill, Leeds
43061*	254003	·	·	·	Operational	EMT, Neville Hill, Leeds
43062	254004	·	·	·	Operational	NR, Craigentinny, Edinburgh
43063	254004	·	·	·	Operational	GWR, Landore, Swansea
43064*	254005	·	·	·	Operational	EMT, Neville Hill, Leeds
43065	254005	43465	·	·	Operational	EMT, Etches Park, Derby
43066*	254006	·	·	·	Operational	EMT, Neville Hill, Leeds
43067	254006	43467	·	·	Operational	EMT, Etches Park, Derby
43068	254007	43468	·	·	Operational	EMT, Etches Park, Derby
43069	254007	·	·	·	Operational	GWR, Landore, Swansea
43070	254008	·	·	·	Operational	GWR, Landore, Swansea
43071	254008	·	·	·	Operational	GWR, Landore, Swansea
43072	254009	43272	·	·	Operational	LNER, Craigentinny, Edinburgh
43073*	254009	·	·	·	Operational	EMT, Neville Hill, Leeds
43074	254010	43274	·	·	Operational	LNER, Craigentinny, Edinburgh

CLASS 43 (Continued)

43075*	254010	·	·	·	Operational	EMT, Neville Hill, Leeds
43076*	254011	·	·	·	Operational	EMT, Neville Hill, Leeds
43077	254011	43277	·	·	Operational	LNER, Craigentinny, Edinburgh
43078	254012	·	·	·	Operational	GWR, Landore, Swansea
43079	254012	·	·	·	Operational	GWR, Landore, Swansea
43080	254013	43480	·	·	Operational	EMT, Etches Park, Derby
43081*	254013	·	·	·	Operational	EMT, Neville Hill, Leeds
43082*	254014	·	·	·	Operational	EMT, Neville Hill, Leeds
43083*	254014	·	·	·	Operational	EMT, Neville Hill, Leeds
43084	254015	43484	·	·	Operational	EMT, Etches Park, Derby
43085	254015	43285	·	·	Operational	XC, Craigentinny, Edinburgh
43086	254016	·	·	·	Operational	GWR, Landore, Swansea
43087	254016	·	·	·	Operational	GWR, Landore, Swansea
43088	254017	·	·	·	Operational	GWR, Landore, Swansea
43089*	254017	·	·	·	Operational	EMT, Neville Hill, Leeds
43090	254018	43290	·	·	Operational	LNER, Craigentinny, Edinburgh
43091	254018	·	·	·	Operational	GWR, Landore, Swansea
43092	254019	·	·	·	Operational	GWR, Landore, Swansea
43093	254019	·	·	·	Operational	GWR, Landore, Swansea
43094	254020	·	·	·	Operational	GWR, Landore, Swansea
43095	254020	43295	·	·	Operational	LNER, Craigentinny, Edinburgh
43096	254021	43296	·	·	Operational	LNER, Craigentinny, Edinburgh
43097	254021	·	·	·	Operational	GWR, Landore, Swansea
43098	254022	·	·	·	Operational	GWR, Landore, Swansea
43099	254022	43299	·	·	Operational	LNER, Craigentinny, Edinburgh
43100	254023	43300	·	·	Operational	LNER, Craigentinny, Edinburgh
43101	254023	43301	·	·	Operational	XC, Craigentinny, Edinburgh
43102	254024	43302	·	·	Operational	LNER, Craigentinny, Edinburgh
43103	254024	43303	·	·	Operational	XC, Craigentinny, Edinburgh
43104	254025	43304	·	·	Operational	XC, Craigentinny, Edinburgh
43105	254025	43305	·	·	Operational	LNER, Craigentinny, Edinburgh
43106	254026	43306	·	·	Operational	LNER, Craigentinny, Edinburgh
43107	254026	43307	·	·	Operational	LNER, Craigentinny, Edinburgh
43108	254027	43308	·	·	Operational	LNER, Craigentinny, Edinburgh
43109	254027	43309	·	·	Operational	LNER, Craigentinny, Edinburgh
43110	254028	43310	·	·	Operational	LNER, Craigentinny, Edinburgh
43111	254028	43311	·	·	Operational	LNER, Craigentinny, Edinburgh
43112	254029	43312	·	·	Operational	LNER, Craigentinny, Edinburgh
43113	254029	43313	·	·	Operational	LNER, Craigentinny, Edinburgh
43114	254030	43314	·	·	Operational	LNER, Craigentinny, Edinburgh
43115	254030	43315	·	·	Operational	LNER, Craigentinny, Edinburgh
43116	254031	43316	·	·	Operational	LNER, Craigentinny, Edinburgh
43117	254031	43317	·	·	Operational	LNER, Craigentinny, Edinburgh
43118	254032	43318	·	·	Operational	LNER, Craigentinny, Edinburgh
43119	254032	43319	·	·	Operational	LNER, Craigentinny, Edinburgh
43120	43320	·	·	·	Operational	LNER, Craigentinny, Edinburgh
43121	43321	·	·	·	Operational	XC, Craigentinny, Edinburgh
43122	·	·	·	·	Operational	GWR, Landore, Swansea
43123	43423	·	·	·	Operational	EMT, Etches Park, Derby
43124	·	·	·	·	Operational	GWR, Landore, Swansea
43125	253028	·	·	·	Operational	GWR, Landore, Swansea
43126	253028	·	·	·	Operational	ScotRail, Haymarket, Edinburgh
43127	253029	·	·	·	Operational	GWR, Landore, Swansea
43128	253029	·	·	·	Operational	GWR, Landore, Swansea

43129	253030	·	·	·	Operational	GWR, Landore, Swansea
43130	253030	·	·	·	Operational	GWR, Landore, Swansea
43131	253031	·	·	·	Operational	GWR, Landore, Swansea
43132	253031	·	·	·	Operational	ScotRail, Craigentinny, Edinburgh
43133	253032	·	·	·	Operational	GWR, Landore, Swansea
43134	253032	·	·	·	Stored	ScotRail, Loughborough Works
43135	253033	·	·	·	Operational	ScotRail, Haymarket, Edinburgh
43136	253033	·	·	·	Operational	GWR, Landore, Swansea
43137	253034	·	·	·	Operational	GWR, Landore, Swansea
43138	253034	·	·	·	Operational	GWR, Landore, Swansea
43139	253035	·	·	·	Operational	GWR, Landore, Swansea
43140	253035	·	·	·	Operational	GWR, Landore, Swansea
43141	253036	·	·	·	Operational	GWR, Landore, Swansea
43142	253036	·	·	·	Operational	GWR, Landore, Swansea
43143	253037	·	·	·	Stored	ScotRail, Loughborough Works
43144	253037	·	·	·	Operational	GWR, Landore, Swansea
43145	253038	·	·	·	Operational	GWR, Landore, Swansea
43146	253038	·	·	·	Stored	ScotRail, Loughborough Works
43147	253039	·	·	·	Operational	GWR, Landore, Swansea
43148	253039	·	·	·	Stored	ScotRail, Loughborough Works
43149	253040	·	·	·	Operational	GWR, Landore, Swansea
43150	253040	·	·	·	Operational	GWR, Landore, Swansea
43151	253041	·	·	·	Operational	GWR, Landore, Swansea
43152	253041	·	·	·	Operational	GWR, Landore, Swansea
43153	254033	·	·	·	Operational	GWR, Old Oak Common
43154	254033	·	·	·	Operational	CWR, Old Oak Common
43155	254034	·	·	·	Operational	GWR, Old Oak Common
43156	254034	·	·	·	Operational	GWR, Old Oak Common
43157	254035	43357	·	·	Operational	XC, Craigentinny, Edinburgh
43158	254035	·	·	·	Operational	GWR, Old Oak Common
43159	254036	·	·	·	Operational	GWR, Old Oak Common
43160	254036	·	·	·	Operational	GWR, Old Oak Common
43161	254037	·	·	·	Operational	GWR, Old Oak Common
43162	254037	·	·	·	Operational	GWR, Old Oak Common
43163	253042	·	·	·	Stored	ScotRail, Loughborough Works
43164	253042	·	·	·	Operational	GWR, Old Oak Common
43165	253043	·	·	·	Operational	GWR, Old Oak Common
43166	253043	43366	·	·	Operational	XC, Craigentinny, Edinburgh
43167	253044	43367	·	·	Operational	LNER, Craigentinny, Edinburgh
43168	253044	·	·	·	Operational	GWR, Old Oak Common
43169	253045	·	·	·	Operational	GWR, Old Oak Common
43170	253045	·	·	·	Operational	GWR, Old Oak Common
43171	253046	·	·	·	Operational	GWR, Old Oak Common
43172	253046	·	·	·	Operational	GWR, Old Oak Common
43173	253047	·	·	·	Scrapped	Serco, Shoeburyness, 2003
43174	253047	·	·	·	Operational	GWR, Old Oak Common
43175	253048	·	·	·	Operational	GWR, Old Oak Common
43176	253048	·	·	·	Operational	GWR, Old Oak Common
43177	253049	·	·	·	Operational	GWR, Old Oak Common
43178	253049	43378	·	·	Operational	XC, Craigentinny, Edinburgh
43179	253050	·	·	·	Operational	ScotRail, Haymarket, Edinburgh
43180	253050	·	·	·	Operational	GWR, Old Oak Common
43181	253051	·	·	·	Operational	GWR, Old Oak Common
43182	253051	·	·	·	Operational	GWR, Old Oak Common

43183	253052	·	·	·	Operational	GWR, Old Oak Common
43184	253052	43384	·	·	Operational	XC, Craigentinny, Edinburgh
43185	253053	·	·	·	Operational	GWR, Old Oak Common
43186	253053	·	·	·	Operational	GWR, Old Oak Common
43187	253054	·	·	·	Operational	GWR, Old Oak Common
43188	253054	·	·	·	Operational	GWR, Old Oak Common
43189	253055	·	·	·	Operational	GWR, Old Oak Common
43190	253055	·	·	·	Operational	GWR, Old Oak Common
43191	253056	·	·	·	Operational	GWR, Old Oak Common
43192	253056	·	·	·	Operational	GWR, Old Oak Common
43193	253057	·	·	·	Operational	GWR, Old Oak Common
43194	253057	·	·	·	Operational	GWR, Old Oak Common
43195	253058	·	·	·	Operational	GWR, Old Oak Common
43196	253058	·	·	·	Operational	GWR, Old Oak Common
43197	253059	·	·	·	Operational	GWR, Old Oak Common
43198	253059	·	·	·	Operational	GWR, Old Oak Common

Originally classified as multiple units under Classes 253 & 254

* Fitted with Paxman/MAN VP185, 2100 hp engine
All remaining servicable power cars are now fitted with MTU 16V4000 R41, 2250 hp engine

Class 43 Names:

43002	Top of the Pops | TECHNI?UEST
	Sir Kenneth Grange
43003	IEAMBARD KINCDOM BRUNEL
43004	Swan Hunter | Borough of Swindon
	First for the Future
43006	Kingdom of Fife
43008	City of Aberdeen
43009	First Transforming Travel
43010	TSW Today
43011	Reader 125
43012	Exeter Panel Signal Box 21st Anniversary 2009
43013	University of Bristol
	CROSSCOUNTRY VOYAGER
43014	The Railway Observer
43016	Garden Festival Wales 1992
	Peninsula Medical School
43017	HTV WEST | Hannahs discoverhannahs.org
43018	The Red Cross
43019	City of Swansea Dinas Abertawe
43020	John Grooms
	MTU Power. Passion. Partnership
43021	David Austin - Cartoonist
43022	The Duke of Edinburgh's Award 1956-2016 -
	Diamond Anniversary 1956-2016
43023	County of Cornwall
	SQN LDR HAROLD STARR One of the Few
43024	Great Western Society 1961-2011 -
	Didcot Railway Centre
43025	Exeter | IRO The Institution of Railway -
	Operators 2000-2010 TEN YEARS
43026	City of Westminster | Michael Eavis

43027	Westminster Abbey
	Glorious Devon
43030	Christian Lewis Trust
43032	The Royal Regiment of Wales
43033	Driver Brian Cooper 1947-1999
43034	The Black Horse
	TravelWatch SouthWest
43037	PENYDARREN 1804-2004
43038	National Railway Museum -
	The First 10 Years 1975 - 1985
	City of Dundee
43039	The Royal Dragoon Guards
43040	Granite City
	Bristol St Phillips Marsh
43041	City of Discovery
	Meningitis Trust Support for Life
43043	Leicestershire County Cricket Club
	University of Worcester
43044	Borough of Kettering
43045	The Grammar School Doncaster -
	AD 1350
43046	Royal Philharmonic
43047	Rotherham Enterprise
43048	T.C.B. Miller MBE
43049	Neville Hill
43051	The Duke and Duchess of York
43052	City of Peterborough
43053	County of Humberside
	Leeds United
	University of Worcester
43055	The Sheffield Star 125 Years

CLASS 43 (Continued)

43056	University of Bradford | Royal British Legion	43102	City of Wakefield
43057	Bounds Green		HST Silver Jubilee
43058	MIDLAND PRIDE		Diocese of Newcastle
43060	County of Leicestershire	43103	John Wesley
43061	City of Lincoln | The Fearless Foxes		Helston Furry Dance
43062	John Armitt	43104	County of Cleveland
43063	Maiden Voyager | Rio Challenger		City of Edinburgh
43064	City of York | 125 Group	43105	Hartlepool | City of Inverness
43065	City of Edinburgh	43106	Songs of Praise | Fountains Abbey
43066	Nottingham Playhouse	43107	City of Derby | Tayside
43068	The Red Nose | The Red Arrows	43108	BBC Television Railwatch
43069	Rio Enterprise		Old Course St Andrews
43070	Rio Pathfinder	43109	Yorkshire Evening Press
	The Corps of Royal Electrical -		SCONE PALACE
	and Mechanical Engineers		Leeds International Film Festival
43071	Forward Birmingham	43110	Darlington | Stirlingshire
43072	Derby Etches Park	43111	Scone Palace
43074	BBC EAST MIDLANDS TODAY	43112	Doncaster
43076	BBC East Midlands Today	43113	City of Newcastle Upon Tyne
	THE MASTER CUTLER 1947-1997		The Highlands
	In Support of Help for Heroes	43114	National Garden Festival -
43077	County of Nottingham		Gateshead 1990
43078	Shildon, County Durham		East Riding of Yorkshire
	Golowan Festival Penzance | Rio Crusader	43115	Yorkshire Cricket Academy
43079	Rio Venturer		Aberdeenshire
43081	Midland Valenta	43116	City of Kingston Upon Hull
43082	DERBYSHIRE FIRST		The Black Dyke Band
	RAILWAY Children, The Voice For -	43117	Bonnie Prince Charlie
	Street Children Worldwide	43118	Charles Wesley
43084	County of Derbyshire		City of Kingston Upon Hull
43085	City of Bradford	43119	HarRail Operations Groupate Spa
43086	Rio Talisman	43120	National Galleries of Scotland
43087	Rio Invader	43121	West Yorkshire -
	11 Explosive Ordnance Disposal -		Metropolitan County
	Regiment Royal Logistic Corps	43122	South Yorkshire -
43088	XIII Commonwealth Games Scotland 1986		Metropolitan County
	Rio Campaigner	43124	BBC Points West
43089	Rio Thunderer | HAYABUSA	43125	Merchant Venturer
43091	Edinburgh Military Tattoo	43126	City of Bristol
43092	Highland Chieftan	43127	Sir Peter Parker 1924-2002 -
	Institution of Mechanical Engineers 150		Cotswold Line 150
43093	York Festival '88 | Lady in Red	43130	Sulis Minerva
	Old Oak Common HST Depot 1976-2018	43131	Sir Felix Pole
43095	Heaton | Perth	43132	Worship Company of Carmen
43096	The Queens Own Hussars		We Save The Children - Will You?
	The Great Racer | Stirling Castle		Aberdeen Station 150th Anniversary
43097	The Light Infantry | Environment Agency	43134	County of Somerset
43098	Tyne and Wear Metropolitan County	43135	Quaker Enterprise
	Railway Children	43137	Newton Abbot 150
43099	Diocese of Newcastle	43139	Driver Stan Martin 1950-2004
43100	Craigentinny | Blackpool Rock	43140	Landore Diesel Depot 1963 -
43101	Edinburgh International Fastival		Celebrating 50 years 2013
	The Irish Mail Tren Post Gwyddelig	43141	Cardiff Panel Signal Box 1966-2016

CLASS 43 (Continued)

43142	St Mary's Hospital Paddington Reading Panel Signal Box 1965-2010	43186	Sir Francis Drake
43143	Stroud 700	43188	City of Plymouth
43147	The Red Cross | Royal Marines - Celebrating 350 Years	43189	RAILWAY HERITAGE TRUST
43149	BBC Wales Today | University of Plymouth	43191	Seahawk
43150	Bristol Evening Post	43192	City of Truro
43151	Blue Peter II	43193	Yorkshire Post
43152	St Peter's School York AD 627		Plymouth spirit of discovery
43153	University of Durham		Rio Triumph
	THE ENGLISH RIVIERA -	43194	Royal Signals
	TORQUAY PAIGNTON BRIXHAM	43195	British Red Cross | Rio Swift
43154	INTERCITY	43196	The Newspaper Society, 1836
43155	BBC Look North | City of Aberdeen		Rio Prince
	The Red Arrows 50 Seasons of Excellence	43197	Railway Magazine Centenary -
43156	Rio Champion | Dartington -		1897-1997 | Rio Princess
	International Summer School	43198	HMS Penzance | Rio Victorious
43157	Yorkshire Evening Post | HMS Penzance		Oxfordshire 2007
43158	Dartmoor the Pony Express	43206	Kingdom of Fife
43159	Rio Warrior	43208	Lincolnshire Echo
43160	Storm Force | PORTERBROOK	43238	City of Dundee
	Sir Moir Lockhead OBE		National Railway Museum -
43161	Reading Evening Post | Rio Monarch		40 Years 1975-2015
43162	Borough of Stevenage | Project Rio	43257	Bounds Green
43163	Exeter Panel Signal Box 21st Anniversary 2009	43274	Spirit of Sunderland
43166	Prince Michael of Kent	43290	mtu fascination of Power
43167	DELTIC 50 1955-2005	43296	Stirling Castle
43169	THE NATIONAL TRUST	43300	Craigentinny 100 Years 1914-2014
43170	Edward Paxman	43306	Fountains Abbey
43172	Harry Patch The last survivor of the trenches	43308	HIGHLAND CHIEFTAIN
43173	Swansea University	43309	Leeds International Film Festival
43174	Bristol - Bordeaux	43313	The Highlands
43175	GWR 175TH ANNIVERSARY	43314	East Riding of Yorkshire
43177	University of Exeter	43316	The Black Dyke Band
43179	Pride of Laira	43318	City of Kingston Upon Hull
43180	City of Newcastle Upon Tyne | Rio Glory	43320	National Galleries of Scotland
43181	Devonport Royal Dockyard	43367	DELTIC 50 1955-2005
43185	Great Western	43423	VALENTA 1972-2010
		43484	PETER FOX 1942-2011 - PLATFORM 5

CLASS 44

Total Built	10	Formation	1Co-Co1	Max T.E.	70,000 lbf
Date Built	1959/60	Max Speed	90 mph	P.A.R.	1,800 hp
Builder	BR, Derby	Weight	138 t	R.A.	7
Engine	Sulzer 12 LDA28A, 2300 hp	Brakes	Vacuum	Supply	Steam

44001	D1	·	·	·	Scrapped	BR, Derby Works, 1977
44002	D2	·	·	·	Scrapped	BR, Derby Works, 1979
44003	D3	·	·	·	Scrapped	BR, Derby Works, 1976
44004	D4	·	·	·	Preserved	Midland Railway Centre
44005	D5	·	·	·	Scrapped	BR, Derby Works, 1978
44006	D6	·	·	·	Scrapped	BR, Derby Works, 1977
44007	D7	·	·	·	Scrapped	BR, Derby Works, 1981
44008	D8	·	·	·	Preserved	Peak Rail

| 44009 | D9 | · | · | · | Scrapped | BR, Derby Works, 1980 |
| 44010 | D10 | · | · | · | Scrapped | BR, Derby Works, 1978 |

Class 44 Names:

44001	SCAFELL PIKE		44006	WHERNSIDE
44002	HELVELLYN		44007	INGLEBOROUGH
44003	SKIDDAW		44008	PENYGHENT
44004	GREAT GABLE		44009	SNOWDON
44005	CROSS FELL		44010	TRYFAN

CLASS 45

Total Built	127	Formation	1Co-Co1	Max T.E.	55,000 lbf
Date Built	1960- 62	Max Speed	90 mph	P.A.R.	2,000 hp
Builder	BR, Derby & Crewe	Weight	138 t	R.A.	7
Engine	Sulzer 12 LDA28B, 2500 hp	Brakes	Vacuum / Air & Vac	Supply	As Below

45001	D13	·	·	·	Scrapped	MC Metals, Springburn, 1988
45002	D29	·	·	·	Scrapped	MC Metals, Springburn, 1988
45003	D133	·	·	·	Scrapped	Vic Berry, Leicester, 1987
45004	D77	·	·	·	Scrapped	MC Metals, Springburn, 1988
45005	D79	·	·	·	Scrapped	Vic Berry, Leicester, 1988
45006	D89	·	·	·	Scrapped	Vic Berry, Leicester, 1988
45007	D119	·	·	·	Scrapped	MC Metals, Springburn, 1992
45008	D90	·	·	·	Scrapped	BR, Swindon Works, 1983
45009	D37	·	·	·	Scrapped	Vic Berry, Leicester, 1988
45010	D112	·	·	·	Scrapped	MC Metals, Springburn, 1989
45011	D12	·	·	·	Scrapped	BR, Derby Works, 1981
45012	D108	·	·	·	Scrapped	MC Metals, Springburn, 1992
45013	D20	·	·	·	Scrapped	MC Metals, Springburn, 1994
45014	D137	·	·	·	Scrapped	Vic Berry, Ashburys, 1986
45015	D14	·	·	·	Preserved	Battlefield Line
45016	D16	·	·	·	Scrapped	Vic Berry, Leicester, 1986
45017	D23	968024+	·	·	Scrapped	MC Metals, Springburn, 1991
45018	D15	·	·	·	Scrapped	BR, Swindon Works, 1982
45019	D33	·	·	·	Scrapped	Vic Berry, Leicester, 1986
45020	D26	·	·	·	Scrapped	Vic Berry, Leicester, 1988
45021	D25	·	·	·	Scrapped	BR, Swindon Works, 1983
45022	D60	97409~	·	·	Scrapped	MC Metals, Springburn, 1991
45023	D54	·	·	·	Scrapped	Vic Berry, Leicester, 1986
45024	D17	·	·	·	Scrapped	BR, Swindon Works, 1983
45025	D19	·	·	·	Scrapped	BR, Derby Works, 1981
45026	D21	·	·	·	Scrapped	MC Metals, Springburn, 1989
45027	D24	·	·	·	Scrapped	BR, Swindon Works, 1983
45028	D27	·	·	·	Scrapped	BR, Swindon Works, 1983
45029	D30	97410~	·	·	Scrapped	MC Metals, Springburn, 1991
45030	D31	·	·	·	Scrapped	BR, Derby Works, 1981
45031	D36	·	·	·	Scrapped	BR, Derby Works, 1981
45032	D38	·	·	·	Scrapped	BR, Swindon Works, 1983
45033	D39	·	·	·	Scrapped	MC Metals, Springburn, 1992
45034	D42	97411~	·	·	Scrapped	MC Metals, Springburn, 1992
45035	D44	·	·	·	Scrapped	BR, Derby Works, 1981
45036	D45	·	·	·	Scrapped	Vic Berry, Leicester, 1988
45037	D46	·	·	·	Scrapped	MC Metals, Springburn, 1992

45038	D48	·	·	·	Scrapped	Vic Berry, Leicester, 1986
45039	D49	·	·	·	Scrapped	BR, Swindon Works, 1983
45040	D50	97412~	·	·	Scrapped	MC Metals, Springburn, 1991
45041	D53	·	·	·	Preserved	Nene Valley Railway
45042	D57	·	·	·	Scrapped	Vic Berry, Leicester, 1987
45043	D58	·	·	·	Scrapped	Vic Berry, Leicester, 1987
45044	D63	·	·	·	Scrapped	MC Metals, Springburn, 1989
45045	D64	·	·	·	Scrapped	Vic Berry, Leicester, 1986
45046	D68	·	·	·	Scrapped	MC Metals, Springburn, 1992
45047	D69	·	·	·	Scrapped	BR, Derby Works, 1981
45048	D70	·	·	·	Scrapped	MC Metals, Springburn, 1989
45049	D71	·	·	·	Scrapped	MC Metals, Springburn, 1989
45050	D72	·	·	·	Scrapped	Vic Berry, Leicester, 1987
45051	D74	·	·	·	Scrapped	MC Metals, Springburn, 1989
45052	D75	·	·	·	Scrapped	MC Metals, Springburn, 1991
45053	D76	·	·	·	Scrapped	BR, Crewe Works, 1988
45054	D78*	45150	·	·	Scrapped	MC Metals, Springburn, 1991
45054	D95*	·	·	·	Scrapped	Vic Berry, Toton, 1985
45055	D84	·	·	·	Scrapped	Vic Berry, Leicester, 1986
45056	D91	·	·	·	Scrapped	Vic Berry, Leicester, 1987
45057	D93	·	·	·	Scrapped	Vic Berry, Leicester, 1987
45058	D97	·	·	·	Scrapped	MC Metals, Springburn, 1994
45059	D98	·	·	·	Scrapped	Vic Berry, Leicester, 1988
45060	D100	·	·	·	Preserved	Barrow Hill
45061	D101	·	·	·	Scrapped	BR, Swindon Works, 1982
45062	D103	·	·	·	Scrapped	MC Metals, Springburn, 1004
45063	D104	·	·	·	Scrapped	Vic Berry, Leicester, 1988
45064	D105	·	·	·	Scrapped	Vic Berry, Leicester, 1988
45065	D110	·	·	·	Scrapped	Vic Berry, Leicester, 1988
45066	D114	97413~	·	·	Scrapped	MC Metals, Springburn, 1991
45067	D115	·	·	·	Scrapped	BR, Derby Works, 1980
45068	D118	·	·	·	Scrapped	Vic Berry, Allerton, 1986
45069	D121	·	·	·	Scrapped	Vic Berry, Leicester, 1988
45070	D122	·	·	·	Scrapped	MC Metals, Springburn, 1989
45071	D125	·	·	·	Scrapped	BR, Swindon Works, 1983
45072	D127	·	·	·	Scrapped	Vic Berry, Leicester, 1986
45073	D129	·	·	·	Scrapped	BR, Derby Works, 1982
45074	D131	·	·	·	Scrapped	Vic Berry, Leicester, 1988
45075	D132	·	·	·	Scrapped	Vic Berry, Leicester, 1987
45076	D134	·	·	·	Scrapped	MC Metals, Springburn, 1994
45077	D136	·	·	·	Scrapped	Vic Berry, Leicester, 1988
45101	D96	·	·	·	Scrapped	Vic Berry, Leicester, 1988
45102	D51	·	·	·	Scrapped	Vic Berry, Leicester, 1988
45103	D116	·	·	·	Scrapped	MC Metals, Springburn, 1990
45104	D59	·	·	·	Scrapped	MC Metals, Springburn, 1992
45105	D86	·	·	·	Preserved	Barrow Hill
45106	D106	·	·	·	Scrapped	C F Booth, Rotherham, 1971
45107	D43	·	·	·	Scrapped	MC Metals, Springburn, 1990
45108	D120	·	·	·	Preserved	East Lancashire Railway
45109	D85	·	·	·	Scrapped	Vic Berry, Leicester, 1986
45110	D73	·	·	·	Scrapped	MC Metals, Springburn, 1990
45111	D65	·	·	·	Scrapped	MC Metals, Springburn, 1992
45112	D61	·	·	·	Preserved	Nemesis Rail, Burton-upon-Trent
45113	D80	·	·	·	Scrapped	MC Metals, Springburn, 1990

45114	D94	·	·	·	Scrapped	MC Metals, Springburn, 1994
45115	D81	·	·	·	Scrapped	MC Metals, Springburn, 1990
45116	D47	·	·	·	Scrapped	Vic Berry, Leicester, 1988
45117	D35	·	·	·	Scrapped	Vic Berry, Leicester, 1987
45118	D67	·	·	·	Preserved	Locomotive Services, Crewe
45119	D34	·	·	·	Scrapped	MC Metals, Springburn, 1994
45120	D107	·	·	·	Scrapped	MC Metals, Springburn, 1993
45121	D18	·	·	·	Scrapped	BR, Derby Works, 1993
45122	D11	·	·	·	Scrapped	MC Metals, Springburn, 1994
45123	D52	·	·	·	Scrapped	Vic Berry, Leicester, 1988
45124	D28	·	·	·	Scrapped	MC Metals, Springburn, 1992
45125	D123	·	·	·	Preserved	Great Central Railway
45126	D32	·	·	·	Scrapped	MC Metals, Springburn, 1992
45127	D87	·	·	·	Scrapped	BR, Crewe Works, 1994
45128	D113	·	·	·	Scrapped	MC Metals, Springburn, 1992
45129	D111	·	·	·	Scrapped	Vic Berry, Leicester, 1988
45130	D117	·	·	·	Scrapped	MC Metals, Springburn, 1993
45131	D124	·	·	·	Scrapped	Vic Berry, Leicester, 1988
45132	D22	·	·	·	Preserved	Epping Ongar Railway
45133	D40	·	·	·	Preserved	Midland Railway Centre
45134	D126	·	·	·	Scrapped	MC Metals, Springburn, 1994
45135	D99	·	·	·	Preserved	East Lancashire Railway
45136	D88	·	·	·	Scrapped	MC Metals, Springburn, 1992
45137	D56	·	·	·	Scrapped	MC Metals, Springburn, 1994
45138	D92	·	·	·	Scrapped	MC Metals, Springburn, 1994
45139	D109	·	·	·	Scrapped	MC Metals, Springburn, 1994
45140	D102	·	·	·	Scrapped	MC Metals, Springburn, 1991
45141	D82	·	·	·	Scrapped	MC Metals, Springburn, 1992
45142	D83	·	·	·	Scrapped	MC Metals, Springburn, 1994
45143	D62	·	·	·	Scrapped	MC Metals, Springburn, 1994
45144	D55	·	·	·	Scrapped	Vic Berry, Leicester, 1988
45145	D128	·	·	·	Scrapped	MC Metals, Springburn, 1992
45146	D66	·	·	·	Scrapped	MC Metals, Springburn, 1992
45147	D41	·	·	·	Scrapped	Vic Berry, Patricroft, 1985
45148	D130	·	·	·	Scrapped	MC Metals, Springburn, 1992
45149	D135	·	·	·	Preserved	G & WR

Class 45/0 (45001 - 45077) Standard design with steam heating
Class 45/1 (45101 - 45150) Rebuilt with electric train supply (ETS)

* D78 originally became 45054 prior to being fitted with ETS, D95 utilised the vacated number
\+ Used for static training purposes and renumbered with ADB prefix
~ Renumbered for departmental use

Class 45 Names:

45004	ROYAL IRISH FUSILIER	45043	THE KING'S OWN ROYAL -
45006	HONOURABLE ARTILLERY COMPANY		BORDER REGIMENT
45014	THE CHESHIRE REGIMENT	45044	ROYAL INNISKILLING FUSILIER
45022	LYTHAM ST ANNES	45045	COLDSTREAM GUARDSMAN
45023	THE ROYAL PIONEER CORPS	45046	ROYAL FUSILIER
45039	THE MANCHESTER REGIMENT	45048	ROYAL MARINES
45040	KING'S SHROPSHIRE LIGHT INFANTRY	45049	THE STAFFORDSHIRE -
45041	ROYAL TANK REGIMENT		REGIMENT

CLASS 45 (Continued)

45055	ROYAL CORPS OF TRANSPORT		45123	THE LANCASHIRE FUSILIER
45059	ROYAL ENGINEER		45125	LEICESTERSHIRE & -
45060	SHERWOOD FORESTER			DERBYSHIRE YEOMANRY
45104	THE ROYAL WARWICKSHIRE -		45135	3RD CARABINIER
	FUSILIER		45137	THE BEDFORDSHIRE & -
45111	GRENARDIER GUARDSMAN			HERTFORDSHIRE REGIMENT
45112	ROYAL ARMY ORDNANCE -		45143	5TH ROYAL INNISKILLING -
	CORPS			DRAGOON GUARDS 1685-1985
45118	THE ROYAL ARTILLERYMAN		45144	ROYAL SIGNALS

CLASS 46

Total Built	56	Formation	1Co-Co1	Max T.E.	55,000 lbf
Date Built	1961/62	Max Speed	90 mph	P.A.R.	1,960 hp
Builder	BR, Derby	Weight	138 t	R.A.	7
Engine	Sulzer 12 LDA28B, 2500 hp	Brakes	Vacuum / Air & Vac	Supply	Steam

46001	D138	·	·	·	Scrapped	BR, Swindon Works, 1982
46002	D139	·	·	·	Scrapped	BR, Swindon Works, 1984
46003	D140	·	·	·	Scrapped	BR, Derby Works, 1980
46004	D141	·	·	·	Scrapped	BR, Swindon Works, 1985
46005	D142	·	·	·	Scrapped	BR, Derby Works, 1978
46006	D143	·	·	·	Scrapped	BR, Swindon Works, 1985
46007	D144	·	·	·	Scrapped	BR, Swindon Works, 1985
46008	D145	·	·	·	Scrapped	BR, Swindon Works, 1982
46009	D146	97401*	·	·	Scrapped	Vic Berry, Old Dalby, 1984
46010	D147	·	·	·	Preserved	Great Central Railway North
46011	D148	·	·	·	Scrapped	BR, Swindon Works, 1986
46012	D149	·	·	·	Scrapped	BR, Swindon Works, 1980
46013	D150	·	·	·	Scrapped	BR, Swindon Works, 1985
46014	D151	·	·	·	Scrapped	BR, Swindon Works, 1986
46015	D152	·	·	·	Scrapped	BR, Swindon Works, 1985
46016	D153	·	·	·	Scrapped	BR, Swindon Works, 1984
46017	D154	·	·	·	Scrapped	BR, Swindon Works, 1986
46018	D155	·	·	·	Scrapped	BR, Swindon Works, 1985
46019	D156	·	·	·	Scrapped	BR, Swindon Works, 1983
46020	D157	·	·	·	Scrapped	BR, Swindon Works, 1984
46021	D158	·	·	·	Scrapped	BR, Swindon Works, 1985
46022	D159	·	·	·	Scrapped	BR, Swindon Works, 1983
46023	D160	97402*	·	·	Scrapped	J & S Metals, Crewe, 1994
46024	D161	·	·	·	Scrapped	BR, Derby Works, 1978
46025	D162	·	·	·	Scrapped	BR, Doncaster Works, 1985
46026	D163	·	·	·	Scrapped	BR, Doncaster Works, 1985
46027	D164	·	·	·	Scrapped	Vic Berry, Leicester, 1986
46028	D165	·	·	·	Scrapped	BR, Doncaster Works, 1985
46029	D166	·	·	·	Scrapped	BR, Swindon Works, 1986
46030	D167	·	·	·	Scrapped	BR, Swindon Works, 1982
46031	D168	·	·	·	Scrapped	BR, Swindon Works, 1983
46032	D169	·	·	·	Scrapped	BR, Doncaster Works, 1985
46033	D170	·	·	·	Scrapped	BR, Swindon Works, 1984
46034	D171	·	·	·	Scrapped	BR, Swindon Works, 1982
46035	D172	97403*	·	·	Preserved	Peak Rail
46036	D173	·	·	·	Scrapped	BR, Swindon Works, 1983
46037	D174	·	·	·	Scrapped	BR, Doncaster Works, 1985

CLASS 46 (Continued)

46038	D175	·	·	·	Scrapped	BR, Swindon Works, 1985
46039	D176	·	·	·	Scrapped	BR, Swindon Works, 1985
46040	D177	·	·	·	Scrapped	BR, Derby Works, 1982
46041	D178	·	·	·	Scrapped	BR, Swindon Works, 1983
46042	D179	·	·	·	Scrapped	BR, Swindon Works, 1982
46043	D180	·	·	·	Scrapped	BR, Swindon Works, 1984
46044	D181	·	·	·	Scrapped	BR, Swindon Works, 1986
46045	D182	97404*	·	·	Preserved	Midland Railway Centre
46046	D183	·	·	·	Scrapped	BR, Doncaster Works, 1985
46047	D184	·	·	·	Scrapped	BR, Swindon Works, 1986
46048	D185	·	·	·	Scrapped	BR, Swindon Works, 1983
46049	D186	·	·	·	Scrapped	BR, Swindon Works, 1985
46050	D187	·	·	·	Scrapped	BR, Swindon Works, 1985
46051	D188	·	·	·	Scrapped	BR, Swindon Works, 1984
46052	D189	·	·	·	Scrapped	BR, Doncaster Works, 1986
46053	D190	·	·	·	Scrapped	BR, Derby Works, 1981
46054	D191	·	·	·	Scrapped	BR, Swindon Works, 1983
46055	D192	·	·	·	Scrapped	BR, Swindon Works, 1984
46056	D193	·	·	·	Scrapped	BR, Swindon Works, 1985

* Renumbered for departmental use

Class 46 Names:
46026　LEICESTERSHIRE & DERBYSHIRE YEOMANRY　　|　46035　Ixion

CLASS 47

Total Built	512	Formation	Co-Co	Max T.E.	60,000 lbf
Date Built	1962-67	Max Speed	95 mph	P.A.R.	2,080 hp
Builder	Brush Traction, Loughborough & BR, Crewe	Weight	111 - 125 t	R.A.	6 or 7
Engine	Sulzer 12 LDA28C, 2580 hp	Brakes	Dual / Air	Supply	As Below

47001	D1521	·	·	·	Scrapped	C F Booth, Rotherham, 1994
47002	D1522	·	·	·	Scrapped	C F Booth, Rotherham, 1994
47003	D1523	·	·	·	Scrapped	C F Booth, Rotherham, 1992
47004	D1524	·	·	·	Preserved	Embsay & Bolton Abbey Railway
47005	D1526	·	·	·	Scrapped	C F Booth, Rotherham, 1994
47006	D1528	·	·	·	Scrapped	C F Booth, Rotherham, 1993
47007	D1529	·	·	·	Scrapped	C F Booth, Rotherham, 1994
47008	D1530	·	·	·	Scrapped	Birds, Stratford, 1993
47009	D1532	·	·	·	Scrapped	C F Booth, Rotherham, 1992
47010	D1537	·	·	·	Scrapped	C F Booth, Rotherham, 1994
47011	D1538	·	·	·	Scrapped	C F Booth, Rotherham, 1994
47012	D1539	·	·	·	Scrapped	C F Booth, Rotherham, 1992
47013	D1540	·	·	·	Scrapped	C F Booth, Doncaster, 1988
47014	D1543	·	·	·	Scrapped	C F Booth, Rotherham, 1992
47015	D1544	·	·	·	Scrapped	C F Booth, Rotherham, 1994
47016	D1546	·	·	·	Scrapped	EWS, Wigan, 2000
47017	D1570	·	·	·	Scrapped	C F Booth, Rotherham, 1992
47018	D1572	·	·	·	Scrapped	Cooper's Metals, Attercliffe, 1994
47019	D1573	·	·	·	Scrapped	MRJ Phillips, Eastleigh, 1997
47020	D1583	47556	47844	·	Scrapped	HNRC, Crewe, 2004
47021	D1584	47531	47974	47775	Scrapped	HNRC, Crewe, 2006

CLASS 47 (Continued)

47022	D1585	47542	·	·	Scrapped	Birds, Stratford, 1994
47023	D1588	47543	·	·	Scrapped	C F Booth, Rotherham, 1998
47024	D1591	47557	47721	·	Scrapped	EMR, Kingsbury, 2007
47025	D1592	47544	·	·	Scrapped	MC Metals, Springburn, 1991
47026	D1597	47597	47741	·	Scrapped	EMR, Kingsbury, 2008
47027	D1599	47558	47722	·	Scrapped	EMR, Kingsbury, 2007
47028	D1605	47559	47759	·	Scrapped	Ron Hull, Rotherham, 2008
47029	D1606	47635	·	·	Preserved	Epping Ongar Railway
47030	D1609	47618	47836	47780	Scrapped	EMR, Kingsbury, 2007
47031	D1610	47560	47832	·	Operational	WCRC, Carnforth
47032	D1611	47662	47817	57311	Operational	DRS, Carlisle Kingmoor
47033	D1613	·	·	·	Scrapped	T J Thomson, Stockton, 2008
47034	D1614	47561	97561~	47973	Scrapped	MRJ Phillips, Crewe Works, 1997
47035	D1615	47594	47739	·	Operational	AFS, Eastleigh
47036	D1617	47562	47672	47760	Operational	WCRC, Carnforth
47037	D1618	47563	47831	57310	Operational	DRS, Carlisle Kingmoor
47038	D1619	47564	47761	·	Preserved	Midland Railway Centre
47039	D1620	47565	·	·	Scrapped	C F Booth, Rotherham, 2004
47040	D1621	47642	47766	·	Scrapped	HNRC, Toton, 2004
47041	D1622	47630	47764	·	Scrapped	HNRC, Kingsbury, 2005
47042	D1623	47586	47676	·	Scrapped	C F Booth, Rotherham, 1998
47043	D1624	47566	·	·	Scrapped	C F Booth, Rotherham, 2006
47044	D1625	47567	47725	·	Scrapped	C F Booth, Rotherham, 2006
47045	D1626	47568	47726	·	Scrapped	EMR, Kingsbury, 2007
47046	D1628	47601	47901	·	Scrapped	MC Metals, Springburn, 1992
47047	D1620	47560	47727	·	Operational	AFS, Eastleigh
47048	D1630	47570	47849	·	Scrapped	C F Booth, Rotherham, 2002
47049	D1631	·	·	·	Scrapped	EWS, Wigan, 2000
47050	D1632	·	·	·	Scrapped	C F Booth, Tinsley, 1996
47051	D1633	·	·	·	Scrapped	EWS, Wigan, 2000
47052	D1634	·	·	·	Scrapped	R Garrett, Crewe, 2003
47053	D1635	·	·	·	Scrapped	EMR, Kingsbury, 2007
47054	D1638	·	·	·	Scrapped	C F Booth, Rotherham, 1993
47055	D1639	47652	47807	57304	Operational	DRS, Carlisle Kingmoor
47056	D1640	47654	47809	47783	Scrapped	Ron Hull, Rotherham, 2007
47057	D1641	47532	·	·	Scrapped	EWS, Wigan, 2001
47058	D1642	47547	·	·	Scrapped	Ron Hull, Rotherham, 2005
47059	D1643	47631	47765	·	Preserved	Great Central Railway North
47060	D1644	57008	·	·	Stored	DRS, MOD Longtown
47061	D1645	47649	47830	·	Operational	Freightliner, Crewe Basford Hall
47062	D1646	47545	97545~	47972	Scrapped	C F Booth, Rotherham, 2010
47063	D1647	·	·	·	Scrapped	MRJ Phillips, Crewe Works, 1996
47064	D1648	47639	47851	·	Operational	WCRC, Carnforth
47065	D1649	47535	·	·	Scrapped	HNRC, Old Oak Common, 2004
47066	D1650	47661	47816	·	Stored	Locomotive Services, Crewe
47067	D1651	47533	·	·	Scrapped	MRJ Phillips, OOC, 1995
47068	D1652	47632	47848	·	Operational	Rail Operations Group, Leicester
47069	D1653	47638	47845	57301	Operational	DRS, Carlisle Kingmoor
47070	D1654	47620	47835	47799	Preserved	Eden Valley Railway
47071	D1655	47536	·	·	Scrapped	C F Booth, Rotherham, 2005
47072	D1656	47609	47834	47798	Operational	National Railway Museum, York
47073	D1657	47537	47772	·	Operational	WCRC, Carnforth
47074	D1658	47646	47852	·	Scrapped	C F Booth, Rotherham, 1993
47075	D1659	47645	·	·	Scrapped	MC Metals, Springburn, 1992

CLASS 47 (Continued)

47076	D1660	47625	47749	·	Operational	AFS, Eastleigh
47077	D1661	47613	47840	·	Preserved	West Somerset Railway
47078	D1663	47628	·	·	Scrapped	Ron Hull, Rotherham, 2006
47079	D1664	57009	·	·	Stored	DRS, MOD Longtown
47080	D1665	47612	47838	47779	Scrapped	HNRC, Kingsbury, 2006
47081	D1666	47606	47842	47778	Scrapped	HNRC, Kingsbury, 2006
47082	D1667	47626	47750	·	Scrapped	EMR, Kingsbury, 2008
47083	D1668	47633	·	·	Scrapped	MC Metals, Springburn, 1994
47084	D1669	47538	968035+	·	Scrapped	MRJ Phillips, Crewe Works, 1997
47085	D1670	·	·	·	Scrapped	EWS, Wigan, 1999
47086	D1672	47641	47767	·	Scrapped	C F Booth, Rotherham, 2009
47087	D1673	47624	·	·	Scrapped	C F Booth, Rotherham, 2006
47088	D1674	47653	47808	47781	Scrapped	EMR, Kingsbury, 2007
47089	D1675	·	·	·	Scrapped	Cooper's Metals, Attercliffe, 1989
47090	D1676	47623	47843	·	Stored	Rail Operations Group, Leicester
47091	D1677	47647	47846	57308	Operational	DRS, Carlisle Kingmoor
47092	D1678	47534	·	·	Scrapped	MRJ Phillips, Crewe Works, 1995
47093	D1679	·	·	·	Scrapped	MC Metals, Springburn, 1990
47094	D1680	·	·	·	Scrapped	MC Metals, Springburn, 1994
47095	D1681	·	·	·	Scrapped	HNRC, Carnforth, 2004
47096	D1682	·	·	·	Scrapped	C F Booth, Rotherham, 2000
47097	D1684	·	·	·	Scrapped	C F Booth, Rotherham, 1992
47098	D1685	·	·	·	Scrapped	Gwent Demolition, Cardiff, 1994
47099	D1686	·	·	·	Scrapped	C F Booth, Rotherham, 1994
47100	D1687	·	·	·	Scrapped	C F Booth, Rotherham, 1994
47101	D1688	·	·	·	Scrapped	C F Booth, Rotherham, 1994
47102	D1690	·	·	·	Scrapped	C F Booth, Rotherham, 1998
47103	D1691	·	·	·	Scrapped	Vic Berry, Leicester, 1989
47104	D1692	·	·	·	Scrapped	MC Metals, Springburn, 1990
47105	D1693	·	·	·	Preserved	G & WR
47106	D1694	·	·	·	Scrapped	Vic Berry, Leicester, 1989
47107	D1695	·	·	·	Scrapped	Cooper's Metals, Attercliffe, 1994
47108	D1696	·	·	·	Scrapped	MRJ Phillips, OOC, 1997
47109	D1697	·	·	·	Scrapped	MC Metals, Springburn, 1989
47110	D1698	·	·	·	Scrapped	Gwent Demolition, Eastleigh, 1993
47111	D1699	·	·	·	Scrapped	BR, Cardiff Canton, 1987
47112	D1700	·	·	·	Scrapped	MRJ Phillips, OOC, 1997
47113	D1701	·	·	·	Scrapped	Vic Berry, Leicester, 1990
47114	D1702	·	·	·	Scrapped	C F Booth, Rotherham, 2005
47115	D1703	·	·	·	Scrapped	MRJ Phillips, Frodingham, 1995
47116	D1704	·	·	·	Scrapped	C F Booth, Rotherham, 1994
47117	D1705	·	·	·	Preserved	Great Central Railway
47118	D1706	·	·	·	Scrapped	MRJ Phillips, Doncaster, 1995
47119	D1708	·	·	·	Scrapped	MRJ Phillips, Frodingham, 1995
47120	D1709	·	·	·	Scrapped	C F Booth, Rotherham, 1994
47121	D1710	·	·	·	Scrapped	MRJ Phillips, OOC 1997
47122	D1711	·	·	·	Scrapped	MC Metals, Springburn, 1989
47123	D1712	·	·	·	Scrapped	Cooper's Metals, Attercliffe, 1994
47124	D1714	·	·	·	Scrapped	MC Metals, Springburn, 1990
47125	D1715	47548	·	·	Scrapped	HNRC, Kingsbury, 2002
47126	D1717	47555	·	·	Scrapped	EWS, Wigan, 1999
47127	D1718	47539	·	·	Scrapped	HNRC, Kingsbury, 2002
47128	D1719	47656	47811	·	Stored	Locomotive Services, Crewe
47129	D1720	47658	47813	·	Operational	Rail Operations Group, Leicester

47130	D1721	·	·	·	Scrapped	MC Metals, Springburn, 1990
47131	D1722	·	·	·	Scrapped	Vic Berry, Leicester, 1988
47132	D1723	47540	47975	·	Preserved	Wensleydale Railway
47133	D1724	47549	·	·	Scrapped	MRJ Phillips, Crewe Works, 1995
47134	D1726	47622	47841	·	Stored	Locomotive Services, Crewe
47135	D1727	47664	47819	47784	Scrapped	Ron Hull, Rotherham, 2007
47136	D1728	47621	47839	·	Scrapped	Raxstar, Eastleigh, 2013
47137	D1729	·	·	·	Scrapped	MC Metals, Springburn, 1992
47138	D1730	47607	47821	47786	Operational	WCRC, Carnforth
47139	D1731	47550	·	·	Scrapped	EMR, Kingsbury, 2010
47140	D1732	·	·	·	Scrapped	Vic Berry, Leicester, 1989
47141	D1733	47614	47853	·	Stored	HNRC, Barrow Hill
47142	D1735	·	·	·	Scrapped	Vic Berry, Leicester, 1999
47143	D1736	·	·	·	Scrapped	D Higgs, Doncaster, 1994
47144	D1737	·	·	·	Scrapped	C F Booth, Rotherham, 1998
47145	D1738	·	·	·	Scrapped	T J Thomson, Stockton, 2009
47146	D1739	·	·	·	Scrapped	C F Booth, Rotherham, 2006
47147	D1740	·	·	·	Scrapped	Vic Berry, Leicester, 1999
47148	D1741	·	·	·	Scrapped	MC Metals, Springburn, 1989
47149	D1742	47617	47677	·	Scrapped	C F Booth, Rotherham, 1998
47150	D1743	47399	·	·	Scrapped	T J Thomson, Stockton, 2010
47151	D1744	47648	47850	·	Scrapped	MRJ Phillips, Crewe Works, 1997
47152	D1745	47398	·	·	Scrapped	Southampton Steel, 2003
47153	D1746	47551	47801	47774	Scrapped	HNRC, Crewe, 2006
47154	D1747	47546	47976	·	Scrapped	EWS, Wigan, 2000
47155	D1748	47660	47815	·	Operational	Rail Operations Group, Leicester
47156	D1749	·	·	·	Scrapped	C F Booth, Rotherham, 2005
47157	D1750	·	·	·	Scrapped	C F Booth, Rotherham, 2004
47158	D1751	47634	·	·	Scrapped	HNRC, Kingsbury, 2004
47159	D1752	·	·	·	Scrapped	Gwent Demolition, Eastleigh,1993
47160	D1754	47605	47746	·	Operational	WCRC, Carnforth
47161	D1755	47541	47773	·	Operational	Tyseley Locomotive Works
47162	D1756	·	·	·	Scrapped	BR, Crewe Works, 1987
47163	D1757	47610	47823	47787	Stored	WCRC, Carnforth
47164	D1758	47571	47822	57305	Operational	DRS, Carlisle Kingmoor
47165	D1759	47590	47825	57601	Operational	WCRC, Carnforth
47166	D1761	47611	47837	·	Scrapped	C F Booth, Rotherham, 1993
47167	D1762	47580	47732	·	Operational	Tyseley Locomotive Works
47168	D1763	47572	·	·	Scrapped	EWS, Wigan, 1999
47169	D1764	47581	47763	·	Scrapped	SCD, Motherwell, 2003
47170	D1765	47582	47733	·	Scrapped	EMR, Kingsbury, 2008
47171	D1766	47592	47738	·	Scrapped	S Norton, Liverpool, 2003
47172	D1767	47583	47734	·	Scrapped	EMR, Kingsbury, 2008
47173	D1768	47573	47762	·	Scrapped	C F Booth, Rotherham, 2005
47174	D1769	47574	·	·	Scrapped	Ron Hull, Rotherham, 2005
47175	D1770	47575	·	·	Scrapped	C F Booth, Rotherham, 2010
47176	D1771	47576	·	·	Scrapped	C F Booth, Rotherham, 2005
47177	D1772	47599	47743	·	Scrapped	BR, Skelton Junction, 1995
47178	D1773	47588	47737	·	Scrapped	EMR, Kingsbury, 2008
47179	D1774	47577	47847	·	Stored	Rail Operations Group, Leicester
47180	D1775	47584	47735	·	Scrapped	C F Booth, Rotherham, 2002
47181	D1776	47578	47776	·	Stored	WCRC, Carnforth
47182	D1777	47598	47742	·	Scrapped	EMR, Kingsbury, 2007
47183	D1778	47579	47793	·	Preserved	Mangapps Farm Railway Museum

47184	D1779	47585	47757	·	Scrapped	T J Thomson, Stockton, 2006
47185	D1780	47602	47824	47782	Scrapped	T J Thomson, Stockton, 2007
47186	D1781	·	·	·	Scrapped	EMR, Kingsbury, 2007
47187	D1837	57006	·	·	Stored	WCRC, Carnforth
47188	D1838	·	·	·	Scrapped	HNRC, Crewe, 2005
47189	D1839	·	·	·	Scrapped	MC Metals, Springburn, 1992
47190	D1840	·	·	·	Scrapped	C F Booth, Rotherham, 1998
47191	D1841	·	·	·	Scrapped	Gwent Demolition, Thornaby, 93
47192	D1842	·	·	·	Preserved	Crewe Heritage Centre
47193	D1843	·	·	·	Scrapped	C F Booth, Rotherham, 2004
47194	D1844	·	·	·	Stored	WCRC, Carnforth
47195	D1845	·	·	·	Scrapped	Cooper's Metals, Attercliffe, 1994
47196	D1846	·	·	·	Scrapped	Cooper's Metals, Attercliffe, 1994
47197	D1847	·	·	·	Scrapped	T J Thomson, Stockton, 2008
47198	D1848	·	·	·	Scrapped	Cooper's Metals, Cardiff, 1994
47199	D1849	·	·	·	Scrapped	MC Metals, Springburn, 1993
47200	D1850	·	·	·	Scrapped	T J Thomson, Stockton, 2008
47201	D1851	·	·	·	Scrapped	EMR, Kingsbury, 2007
47202	D1852	·	·	·	Scrapped	Maize Metals, Bristol, 1991
47203	D1853	·	·	·	Scrapped	Vic Berry, Leicester, 1990
47204	D1854	47388	57012	·	Stored	DRS, MOD Longtown
47205	D1855	47395	·	·	Preserved	Northampton & Lamport Railway
47206	D1856	57605	·	·	Operational	GWR, Old Oak Common
47207	D1857	·	·	·	Scrapped	C F Booth, Rotherham, 2005
47208	D1858	·	·	·	Scrapped	Kennedy & Co, Dundee, 1980
47209	D1859	47393	57604	·	Operational	GWR, Old Oak Common
47210	D1860	·	·	·	Scrapped	EWS, Wigan, 2000
47211	D1861	47394	·	·	Scrapped	Raxstar, Eastleigh, 2003
47212	D1862	·	·	·	Scrapped	R Garrett, Crewe, 2004
47213	D1863	·	·	·	Scrapped	HNRC, Crewe, 2005
47214	D1864	·	·	·	Scrapped	C F Booth, Rotherham, 1998
47215	D1865	·	·	·	Scrapped	Gwent Demolition, Cardiff, 1994
47216	D1866	47299	·	·	Scrapped	EWS, Wigan, 2000
47217	D1867	·	·	·	Scrapped	C F Booth, Rotherham, 2005
47218	D1868	·	·	·	Scrapped	HNRC, Kingsbury, 2002
47219	D1869	·	·	·	Scrapped	EMR, Kingsbury, 2007
47220	D1870	·	·	·	Scrapped	Cooper's Metals, Attercliffe, 1994
47221	D1871	·	·	·	Scrapped	HNRC, Kingsbury, 2002
47222	D1872	·	·	·	Scrapped	C F Booth, Rotherham, 1998
47223	D1873	·	·	·	Scrapped	C F Booth, Rotherham, 2005
47224	D1874	·	·	·	Scrapped	HNRC, Crewe, 2007
47225	D1901	57307	·	·	Operational	DRS, Carlisle Kingmoor
47226	D1902	47384	·	·	Scrapped	EMR, Kingsbury, 2008
47227	D1903	·	·	·	Scrapped	Cooper's Metals, Attercliffe, 1994
47228	D1904	·	·	·	Scrapped	EMR, Kingsbury, 2007
47229	D1905	·	·	·	Scrapped	T J Thomson, Stockton, 2007
47230	D1906	·	·	·	Scrapped	C F Booth, Rotherham, 1989
47231	D1907	57010	·	·	Stored	DRS, MOD Longtown
47232	D1909	47665	47820	47785	Preserved	Wensleydale Railway
47233	D1910	·	·	·	Scrapped	MRJ Phillips, Frodingham, 1995
47234	D1911	57315	·	·	Operational	WCRC, Carnforth
47235	D1912	·	·	·	Scrapped	Vic Berry, Leicester, 1990
47236	D1913	·	·	·	Stored	WCRC, Carnforth
47237	D1914	·	·	·	Operational	WCRC, Carnforth

CLASS 47 (Continued)

47238	D1915	·	·	·	Scrapped	HNRC, Kingsbury, 2001
47239	D1916	47657	47812	·	Operational	Rail Operations Group, Leicester
47240	D1917	47663	47818	·	Stored	AFS, Eastleigh
47241	D1918	·	·	·	Scrapped	C F Booth, Rotherham, 2006
47242	D1919	47659	47814	57306	Operational	DRS, Carlisle Kingmoor
47243	D1920	47636	47777	·	Scrapped	HNRC, Toton, 2004
47244	D1921	47640	·	·	Preserved	Battlefield Line
47245	D1922	·	·	·	Operational	WCRC, Carnforth
47246	D1923	47644	47756	·	Scrapped	Ron Hull, Rotherham, 2006
47247	D1924	47655	47810	·	Stored	AFS, Eastleigh
47248	D1925	47616	47671	47789	Scrapped	EMR, Kingsbury, 2007
47249	D1926	·	·	·	Scrapped	C F Booth, Rotherham, 1998
47250	D1927	47600	47744	·	Preserved	Nemesis Rail, Burton-upon-Trent
47251	D1928	47589	47827	57302	Operational	DRS, Carlisle Kingmoor
47252	D1929	47615	47747	·	Scrapped	C F Booth, Rotherham, 2013
47253	D1930	47530	·	·	Scrapped	EWS, Wigan, 2001
47254	D1931	47651	47806	57309	Operational	DRS, Carlisle Kingmoor
47255	D1933	47596	·	·	Preserved	Mid-Norfolk Railway
47256	D1934	·	·	·	Scrapped	HNRC, Doncaster, 2002
47257	D1935	47650	47805	·	Operational	Locomotive Services, Crewe
47258	D1938	·	·	·	Scrapped	C F Booth, Rotherham, 2005
47259	D1950	47552	47802	·	Operational	WCRC, Carnforth
47260	D1956	47553	47803	·	Scrapped	Ron Hull, Rotherham, 2007
47261	D1957	47554	47705	57303	Operational	DRS, Carlisle Kingmoor
47262	D1962	47608	47833	47788	Scrapped	EWS, Wigan, 2000
47263	D1963	47687	47736	·	Scrapped	Ron Hull, Rotherham, 2007
47264	D1964	47619	47829	·	Scrapped	C F Booth, Rotherham, 2013
47265	D1965	47591	47804	47792	Operational	WCRC, Carnforth
47266	D1966	47629	47828	·	Preserved	Great Central Railway North
47267	D1967	47603	47745	·	Scrapped	HNRC, Toton, 2004
47268	D1969	47595	47675	47791	Scrapped	C F Booth, Rotherham, 2013
47269	D1970	47643	·	·	Preserved	Bo'ness & Kinneil Railway
47270	D1971	·	·	·	Operational	WCRC, Carnforth
47271	D1972	47604	47674	47854	Operational	WCRC, Carnforth
47272	D1973	47593	47673	47790	Operational	Locomotive Services, Crewe
47273	D1974	47627	·	·	Scrapped	EWS, Wigan, 2000
47274	D1976	47637	47826	·	Operational	WCRC, Carnforth
47275	D1977	·	·	·	Scrapped	C F Booth, Rotherham, 1989
47276	D1978	·	·	·	Scrapped	EWS, Wigan, 2001
47277	D1979	·	·	·	Scrapped	Raxstar, Immingham, 2000
47278	D1980	·	·	·	Scrapped	EWS, Wigan, 1999
47279	D1981	·	·	·	Scrapped	T J Thomson, Stockton, 2007
47280	D1982	·	·	·	Scrapped	EMR, Kingsbury, 2007
47281	D1983	·	·	·	Scrapped	EWS, Wigan, 2000
47282	D1984	·	·	·	Scrapped	C F Booth, Rotherham, 1989
47283	D1985	·	·	·	Scrapped	HNRC, Kingsbury, 2004
47284	D1986	·	·	·	Scrapped	EWS, Wigan, 1999
47285	D1987	·	·	·	Scrapped	Ron Hull, Rotherham, 2005
47286	D1988	·	·	·	Scrapped	EWS, Wigan, 2000
47287	D1989	·	·	·	Scrapped	C F Booth, Rotherham, 2005
47288	D1990	·	·	·	Scrapped	C F Booth, Tinsley, 1996
47289	D1991	·	·	·	Scrapped	T J Thomson, Stockton, 2010
47290	D1992	57316	·	·	Operational	WCRC, Carnforth
47291	D1993	·	·	·	Scrapped	C F Booth, Rotherham, 2004

CLASS 47 (Continued)

47292	D1994	·	·	·	Preserved	Great Central Railway North
47293	D1995	·	·	·	Scrapped	EMR, Kingsbury, 2007
47294	D1996	·	·	·	Scrapped	HNRC, Toton, 2002
47295	D1997	·	·	·	Scrapped	EMR, Kingsbury, 2011
47296	D1998	·	·	·	Scrapped	Southampton Steel, 2003
47297	D1999	·	·	·	Scrapped	HNRC, Kingsbury, 2002
47298	D1100	·	·	·	Scrapped	C F Booth, Rotherham, 2007
47301	D1782	·	·	·	Scrapped	R Garrett, Crewe, 2003
47302	D1783	·	·	·	Scrapped	EMR, Kingsbury, 2007
47303	D1784	47397	·	·	Scrapped	EMR, Kingsbury, 2007
47304	D1785	47392	·	·	Scrapped	EWS, Wigan, 2000
47305	D1786	·	·	·	Scrapped	R Garrett, Crewe, 2003
47306	D1787	·	·	·	Preserved	Bodmin & Wenford Railway
47307	D1788	·	·	·	Scrapped	EMR, Kingsbury, 2008
47308	D1789	·	·	·	Scrapped	Sims Metals, Beeston, 2004
47309	D1790	47389	·	·	Scrapped	EMR, Kingsbury, 2009
47310	D1791	·	·	·	Scrapped	C F Booth, Rotherham, 2004
47311	D1792	·	·	·	Scrapped	C F Booth, Rotherham, 1993
47312	D1793	·	·	·	Scrapped	EWS, Wigan, 2003
47313	D1794	·	·	·	Scrapped	EMR, Kingsbury, 2007
47314	D1795	47387	·	·	Scrapped	EMR, Kingsbury, 2008
47315	D1796	·	·	·	Scrapped	EWS, Wigan, 2000
47316	D1797	·	·	·	Scrapped	T J Thomson, Stockton, 2008
47317	D1798	57003	·	·	Stored	AFS, Eastleigh
47318	D1799	·	·	·	Scrapped	T J Thomson, Stockton, 2004
47319	D1800	·	·	·	Scrapped	Raxstar, Immingham, 2000
47320	D1801	·	·	·	Scrapped	MRJ Phillips, Crewe Works, 1996
47321	D1802	·	·	·	Scrapped	C F Booth, Rotherham, 1998
47322	D1803	57002	·	·	Operational	DRS, Carlisle Kingmoor
47323	D1804	·	·	·	Scrapped	R Garrett, Crewe, 2003
47324	D1805	·	·	·	Scrapped	C F Booth, Rotherham, 1994
47325	D1806	·	·	·	Scrapped	C F Booth, Rotherham, 1998
47326	D1807	·	·	·	Scrapped	T J Thomson, Stockton, 2006
47327	D1808	·	·	·	Scrapped	C F Booth, Rotherham, 1993
47328	D1809	47396	·	·	Scrapped	C F Booth, Rotherham, 2005
47329	D1810	57011	·	·	Stored	AFS, Eastleigh
47330	D1811	47390	57312	·	Operational	DRS, Carlisle Kingmoor
47331	D1812	·	·	·	Scrapped	HNRC, Kingsbury, 2005
47332	D1813	57007	·	·	Operational	DRS, Carlisle Kingmoor
47333	D1814	·	·	·	Scrapped	C F Booth, Rotherham, 1998
47334	D1815	·	·	·	Scrapped	C F Booth, Rotherham, 2005
47335	D1816	·	·	·	Scrapped	EMR, Kingsbury, 2007
47336	D1817	·	·	·	Scrapped	C F Booth, Rotherham, 1993
47337	D1818	57602	·	·	Operational	GWR, Old Oak Common
47338	D1819	·	·	·	Scrapped	C F Booth, Rotherham, 2006
47339	D1820	·	·	·	Scrapped	C F Booth, Rotherham, 2005
47340	D1821	·	·	·	Scrapped	MRJ Phillips, Crewe Works, 1998
47341	D1822	·	·	·	Scrapped	HNRC, Toton, 2003
47342	D1823	·	·	·	Scrapped	MC Metals, Springburn, 1992
47343	D1824	·	·	·	Scrapped	MC Metals, Springburn, 1992
47344	D1825	·	·	·	Scrapped	HNRC, Kingsbury, 2002
47345	D1826	·	·	·	Scrapped	Ron Hull, Rotherham, 2007
47346	D1827	·	·	·	Scrapped	C F Booth, Rotherham, 1998
47347	D1828	57004	·	·	Stored	DRS, MOD Longtown

47348	D1829	·	·	·	Scrapped	Ron Hull, Rotherham, 2006
47349	D1830	57603	·	·	Operational	GWR, Old Oak Common
47350	D1831	57005	·	·	Stored	WCRC, Carnforth
47351	D1832	·	·	·	Scrapped	EWS, Wigan, 2001
47352	D1833	·	·	·	Scrapped	Raxstar, Frodingham, 2000
47353	D1834	·	·	·	Scrapped	C F Booth, Rotherham, 2005
47354	D1835	·	·	·	Scrapped	R Garrett, Crewe, 2003
47355	D1836	47391	·	·	Stored	WCRC, Carnforth
47356	D1875	57001	·	·	Operational	WCRC, Carnforth
47357	D1876	·	·	·	Scrapped	EWS, Wigan, 2001
47358	D1877	·	·	·	Scrapped	T J Thomson, Stockton, 2009
47359	D1878	·	·	·	Scrapped	C F Booth, Rotherham, 1998
47360	D1879	·	·	·	Scrapped	EMR, Kingsbury, 2007
47361	D1880	·	·	·	Scrapped	HNRC, Kingsbury, 2004
47362	D1881	·	·	·	Scrapped	EWS, Wigan, 2000
47363	D1882	47385	·	·	Scrapped	C F Booth, Rotherham, 2010
47364	D1883	47981	·	·	Scrapped	EWS, Wigan, 2000
47365	D1884	·	·	·	Scrapped	C F Booth, Rotherham, 2007
47366	D1885	·	·	·	Scrapped	EWS, Wigan, 1999
47367	D1886	·	·	·	Preserved	Mid-Norfolk Railway
47368	D1887	·	·	·	Stored	WCRC, Carnforth
47369	D1888	·	·	·	Scrapped	C F Booth, Rotherham, 1998
47370	D1889	·	·	·	Scrapped	T J Thomson, Stockton, 2009
47371	D1890	57313	·	·	Operational	WCRC, Carnforth
47372	D1891	57314	·	·	Operational	WCRC, Carnforth
47373	D1892	·	·	·	Scrapped	MC Metals, Springburn, 1004
47374	D1893	·	·	·	Scrapped	C F Booth, Rotherham, 1994
47375	D1894	47375-5^	·	·	Operational	CRS, Hungary
47376	D1895	·	·	·	Preserved	G & WR
47377	D1896	·	·	·	Scrapped	R Garrett, Crewe, 2003
47378	D1897	47386	·	·	Scrapped	C F Booth, Rotherham, 1998
47379	D1898	·	·	·	Scrapped	EWS, Wigan, 1999
47380	D1899	·	·	·	Scrapped	MC Metals, Springburn, 1994
47381	D1900	·	·	·	Scrapped	MC Metals, Springburn, 1994
47401	D1500	·	·	·	Preserved	Midland Railway Centre
47402	D1501	·	·	·	Preserved	East Lancashire Railway
47403	D1502	968033*	·	·	Preserved	J & S Metals, Crewe, 1993
47404	D1503	·	·	·	Scrapped	Vic Berry, Leicester, 1990
47405	D1504	·	·	·	Scrapped	A Hampton, Crewe, 1988
47406	D1505	·	·	·	Scrapped	MRJ Phillips, Frodingham, 1995
47407	D1506	·	·	·	Scrapped	MRJ Phillips, Frodingham, 1995
47408	D1507	·	·	·	Scrapped	Vic Berry, Leicester, 1989
47409	D1508	·	·	·	Scrapped	Vic Berry, Leicester, 1989
47410	D1509	·	·	·	Scrapped	Vic Berry, Leicester, 1990
47411	D1510	·	·	·	Scrapped	MRJ Phillips, Frodingham, 1994
47412	D1511	·	·	·	Scrapped	C F Booth, Rotherham, 1992
47413	D1512	·	·	·	Scrapped	MRJ Phillips, Frodingham, 1995
47414	D1513	·	·	·	Scrapped	Vic Berry, Leicester, 1989
47415	D1514	·	·	·	Scrapped	Vic Berry, Leicester, 1990
47416	D1515	·	·	·	Scrapped	BR, Crewe Works, 1987
47417	D1516	·	·	·	Preserved	Midland Railway Centre
47418	D1517	·	·	·	Scrapped	MRJ Phillips, Frodingham, 1995
47419	D1518	·	·	·	Scrapped	Vic Berry, Leicester, 1990
47420	D1519	·	·	·	Scrapped	Vic Berry, Leicester, 1989

47421	D1520	·	·	·	Scrapped	MRJ Phillips, Crewe Works, 1997
47422	D1525	·	·	·	Scrapped	C F Booth, Rotherham, 1993
47423	D1527	·	·	·	Scrapped	MRJ Phillips, OOC, 1997
47424	D1531	·	·	·	Scrapped	C F Booth, Rotherham, 1994
47425	D1533	·	·	·	Scrapped	MRJ Phillips, OOC, 1997
47426	D1534	·	·	·	Scrapped	MRJ Phillips, OOC, 1997
47427	D1535	·	·	·	Scrapped	MC Metals, Springburn, 1992
47428	D1536	·	·	·	Scrapped	Vic Berry, Leicester, 1990
47429	D1541	·	·	·	Scrapped	A Hampton, Crewe, 1989
47430	D1542	·	·	·	Scrapped	MRJ Phillips, OOC, 1997
47431	D1545	·	·	·	Scrapped	MRJ Phillips, OOC, 1997
47432	D1547	·	·	·	Scrapped	C F Booth, Bristol, 1995
47433	D1548	·	·	·	Scrapped	MRJ Phillips, Crewe Works, 1996
47434	D1549	·	·	·	Scrapped	C F Booth, Rotherham, 1993
47435	D1550	·	·	·	Scrapped	C F Booth, Rotherham, 1993
47436	D1552	·	·	·	Scrapped	MC Metals, Springburn, 1993
47437	D1553	·	·	·	Scrapped	C F Booth, Bristol, 1989
47438	D1554	·	·	·	Scrapped	MRJ Phillips, OOC, 1997
47439	D1555	·	·	·	Scrapped	MRJ Phillips, Crewe Works, 1997
47440	D1556	·	·	·	Scrapped	MRJ Phillips, OOC, 1997
47441	D1557	·	·	·	Scrapped	MRJ Phillips, OOC, 1997
47442	D1558	·	·	·	Scrapped	MRJ Phillips, Crewe Works, 1997
47443	D1559	·	·	·	Scrapped	MRJ Phillips, Crewe Works, 1996
47444	D1560	·	·	·	Scrapped	MRJ Phillips, Crewe Works, 1995
47445	D1561	·	·	·	Scrapped	C F Booth, Rotherham, 1994
47446	D1563	·	·	·	Scrapped	MRJ Phillips, OOC, 1997
47447	D1564	·	·	·	Scrapped	C F Booth, Rotherham, 1994
47448	D1565	·	·	·	Scrapped	C F Booth, Rotherham, 1996
47449	D1566	·	·	·	Preserved	Llangollen Railway
47450	D1567	·	·	·	Scrapped	C F Booth, Rotherham, 1993
47451	D1568	·	·	·	Scrapped	C F Booth, Rotherham, 1994
47452	D1569	·	·	·	Scrapped	MRJ Phillips, OOC, 1997
47453	D1571	·	·	·	Scrapped	MRJ Phillips, OOC, 1997
47454	D1574	·	·	·	Scrapped	C F Booth, Rotherham, 1994
47455	D1575	·	·	·	Scrapped	MRJ Phillips, Crewe Works, 1995
47456	D1576	·	·	·	Scrapped	C F Booth, Rotherham, 1993
47457	D1577	·	·	·	Scrapped	MRJ Phillips, OOC, 1997
47458	D1578	·	·	·	Scrapped	C F Booth, Rotherham, 1996
47459	D1579	·	·	·	Scrapped	C F Booth, Rotherham, 1993
47460	D1580	·	·	·	Scrapped	C F Booth, Rotherham, 1994
47461	D1581	·	·	·	Scrapped	C F Booth, Rotherham, 1993
47462	D1582	·	·	·	Scrapped	HNRC, Toton, 2003
47463	D1586	·	·	·	Scrapped	MRJ Phillips, Crewe Works, 1996
47464	D1587	·	·	·	Scrapped	BR, Crewe Works, 1987
47465	D1589	·	·	·	Scrapped	MRJ Phillips, OOC, 1997
47466	D1590	·	·	·	Scrapped	MRJ Phillips, Crewe Works, 1997
47467	D1593	·	·	·	Scrapped	EWS, Wigan, 2000
47468	D1594	47300	·	·	Scrapped	HNRC, Kingsbury, 2002
47469	D1595	·	·	·	Scrapped	MC Metals, Springburn, 1989
47470	D1596	·	·	·	Scrapped	MRJ Phillips, Crewe Works, 1995
47471	D1598	·	·	·	Scrapped	Ron Hull, Rotherham, 2005
47472	D1600	97472~	·	·	Scrapped	MRJ Phillips, OOC, 1997
47473	D1601	·	·	·	Scrapped	MRJ Phillips, Crewe Works, 1998
47474	D1602	·	·	·	Scrapped	T J Thomson, Stockton, 2005

47475	D1603	·	·	·	Scrapped	T J Thomson, Stockton, 2008
47476	D1604	·	·	·	Scrapped	C F Booth, Rotherham, 2004
47477	D1607	·	·	·	Scrapped	C F Booth, Rotherham, 1993
47478	D1608	·	·	·	Scrapped	HNRC, Kingsbury, 2006
47479	D1612	·	·	·	Scrapped	C F Booth, Rotherham, 1993
47480	D1616	97480~	47971	·	Scrapped	HNRC, Kingsbury, 2001
47481	D1627	·	·	·	Scrapped	Sims Metals, Beeston, 2003
47482	D1636	·	·	·	Scrapped	MRJ Phillips, Crewe Works, 1995
47483	D1637	·	·	·	Scrapped	MRJ Phillips, Crewe Works, 1996
47484	D1662	·	·	·	Preserved	Sutton Coldfield
47485	D1683	·	·	·	Scrapped	MRJ Phillips, Crewe Works, 1997
47486	D1689	·	·	·	Scrapped	Vic Berry, Leicester, 1989
47487	D1707	·	·	·	Scrapped	MC Metals, Springburn, 1989
47488	D1713	·	·	·	Preserved	Nemesis Rail, Burton-upon-Trent
47489	D1716	·	·	·	Scrapped	C F Booth, Rotherham, 2010
47490	D1725	47768	·	·	Stored	WCRC, Carnforth
47491	D1753	47769	·	·	Stored	HNRC, Barrow Hill
47492	D1760	·	·	·	Stored	WCRC, Carnforth
47493	D1932	47701	·	·	Preserved	Nemesis Rail, Burton-upon-Trent
47494	D1936	47706	·	·	Scrapped	MRJ Phillips, Crewe Works, 1995
47495	D1937	47704	·	·	Scrapped	Ron Hull, Rotherham, 2006
47496	D1939	47710	·	·	Scrapped	EMR, Kingsbury, 2007
47497	D1940	47717	·	·	Scrapped	EMR, Kingsbury, 2007
47498	D1941	47711	·	·	Scrapped	HNRC, Toton, 2004
47499	D1942	47709	·	·	Scrapped	Eastleigh Works, 2012
47500	D1943	47770	·	·	Storod	WCRC, Carnforth
47501	D1944	·	·	·	Operational	Locomotive Services, Crewe
47502	D1945	47715	·	·	Preserved	Wensleydale Railway
47503	D1946	47771	·	·	Preserved	Colne Valley Railway
47504	D1947	47702	·	·	Scrapped	HNRC, Toton, 2005
47505	D1948	47712	·	·	Preserved	Crewe Heritage Centre
47506	D1949	47707	·	·	Scrapped	C F Booth, Rotherham, 2010
47507	D1951	47716	·	·	Scrapped	C F Booth, Rotherham, 2010
47508	D1952	·	·	·	Scrapped	MRJ Phillips, Bristol, 1995
47509	D1953	·	·	·	Scrapped	MRJ Phillips, Bristol, 1995
47510	D1954	47713	·	·	Scrapped	Vic Berry, Leicester, 1990
47511	D1955	47714	·	·	Operational	HNRC, Old Dalby Test Centre
47512	D1958	·	·	·	Scrapped	C F Booth, Rotherham, 1994
47513	D1959	·	·	·	Scrapped	C F Booth, Rotherham, 2004
47514	D1960	47703	·	·	Operational	HNRC, Doncaster Works
47515	D1961	·	·	·	Scrapped	HNRC, Crewe, 2006
47516	D1968	47708	·	·	Scrapped	MRJ Phillips, Crewe Works, 1995
47517	D1975	47758	·	·	Scrapped	EMR, Kingsbury, 2008
47518	D1101	·	·	·	Scrapped	MC Metals, Springburn, 1994
47519	D1102	·	·	·	Scrapped	T J Thomson, Stockton, 2005
47520	D1103	·	·	·	Scrapped	C F Booth, Rotherham, 1998
47521	D1104	·	·	·	Scrapped	MRJ Phillips, Crewe Works, 1995
47522	D1105	·	·	·	Scrapped	EWS, Wigan, 2000
47523	D1106	·	·	·	Scrapped	EWS, Wigan, 2000
47524	D1107	·	·	·	Preserved	Churnet Valley Railway
47525	D1108	·	·	·	Scrapped	EMR, Kingsbury, 2010
47526	D1109	·	·	·	Stored	WCRC, Carnforth
47527	D1110	·	·	·	Scrapped	MRJ Phillips, Bristol, 1995
47528	D1111	·	·	·	Scrapped	Ron Hull, Rotherham, 2008

47529	D1551	·	·	·	Scrapped	BR, Crewe Works, 1987
·	D1562	·	·	·	Scrapped	BR, Crewe Works, 1971
·	D1671	·	·	·	Scrapped	Hayes, Bridgend, 1966
·	D1734	·	·	·	Scrapped	BR, Crewe Works, 1965
·	D1908	·	·	·	Scrapped	BR, Crewe Works, 1969

Class 47/0 (47001 - 47299) Standard design originally fitted with steam heating
Class 47/3 (47300 - 47381) Standard design without steam heating
Class 47/4 (47401 - 47854) Fitted with dual or electric heating
Class 47/6 (47601) Fitted with Ruston-Paxman 16RK3CT engine for Class 56 development
Class 47/6 (47671 - 47677) Fitted with high phosphorus brake blocks
Class 47/7 (47701 - 47717) Fitted with push-pull equipment
Class 47/7 (47721 - 47799) Modified RES dedicated locos
Class 47/9 (47901) Fitted with Ruston-Paxman 12RK3ACT engine for Class 58 development
Class 48 (D1702 - D1706) Originally fitted with Sulzer 12LVA24, 2650 hp power unit

* Used for static training purposes and renumbered with TDB prefix
+ Converted to power unit transporter and renumbered with ADB prefix
~ Renumbered for departmental use
^ Renumbered when exported to the Hungary whilst on hire to Continental Railway Solution

Class 47 Names:

47004	Old Oak Common Traction & Rolling - Stock Depot	47121	Pochard
47007	Stratford	47125	Tonnidae
47010	Xancidae	47142	The Sapper
47016	The Toleman Group | ATLAS	47145	MERDDIN EMRYS
47033	The Royal Logistics Corps	47146	Loughborough Grammar School
47049	GEFCO	47157	Johnson Stevens Agencies
47053	Cory Brothers1842 - 1992 Dollands Moor International	47158	Henry Ford
		47167	County of Essex
47054	Xancidae	47169	Great Eastern
47060	Halewood Silver Jubilee 1988	47170	County of Norfolk
47076	CITY OF TRURO	47172	County of Hertfordshire
47077	NORTH STAR	47180	County of Suffolk
47078	SIR DANIEL GOOCH	47184	County of Cambridshire
47079	GEORGE JACKSON CHURCHWARD	47186	Catcliffe Demon
47080	TITAN	47190	Pectinidae
47081	ODIN	47193	Lucinidae
47082	ATLAS	47194	Bullidae
47083	ORION		Carlisle Currock Quality Approved
47085	MAMMOTH | Conidae | REPTA 1893-1993	47195	Muricidae
47086	COLOSSUS	47196	Haliotadae
47087	CYCLOPS	47200	Herbert Austin | The Fosse Way
47088	SAMSON	47206	The Morris Dancer
47089	AMAZON	47207	Bulmers of Hereford The Felixstowe Partnership
47090	VULCAN		
47091	THOR	47209	Herbert Austin
47095	Southampton WRD Quality Approved	47210	Blue Circle Cement
47114	Freightlinerbulk	47211	Johnson Stevens Agencies
47117	SPARROW HAWK	47213	Marchwood Military Port
47119	Arcidae	47214	Tinsley Traction Depot Distillers MG
47120	R.A.F. Kinloss		
		47218	United Transport Europe

47219	Arnold Kunzler
47222	Appleby - Frodingham | W.A. Camwell
47223	British Petroleum
47224	Arcidae
47228	axial
47231	The Silcock Express
47233	Stomibidae | Strombidae
47236	ROVER GROUP QUALITY ASSURED
47238	Bescot Yard
47241	The Silcock Express
	Halewood Silver Jubilee 1988
47245	The Institute of Export
47258	Forth Ports Tilbury
47270	Cory Brothers 1842-1992 | SWIFT
47278	Vasidae
47280	Pedigree
47283	Johnnie Walker
47286	Port of Liverpool
47291	The Port of Felixstowe
47293	Transfesa
47297	cobra RAILFREIGHT
47298	PAGASUS
47301	Freightliner Birmingham
47303	Freightliner Cleveland
47304	Cory Brothers 1842-1992
47306	The Sapper
47309	The Halewood Transmission
	European Rail Operator of the Year
47310	Henry Ford
47311	Warrington Yard
47312	Parsec of Europe
47314	Transmark
47315	Templecombe
47316	Cam Peak
47317	Willesden Yard
47319	Norsk Hydro
47323	ROVER GROUP QUALITY ASSURED
47324	Glossidae
47326	Saltley Depot Quality Approved
47330	Amlwch Freighter / Tren Nwyddau Amlwch
47333	Civil Link
47334	P & O Nedlloyd
47337	Herbert Austin
47338	Warrington Yard
47348	St Christopher's Railway Home
47350	British Petroleum
47355	AVOCET
47357	The Permanent Way Institution
47361	Wilton Endeavour
47363	Billingham Enterprise
47365	ICI Diamond Jubilee | Diamond Jubilee
47366	The Institution of Civil Engineers
	Capital Radio's Help a London Child
47368	Neritidae
47370	Andrew A Hodgkinson
47374	Petrolea
47375	Tinsley Traction Depot -
	Quality Approved
47376	Freightliner 1995
47379	Total Energy
47380	Immingham
47387	Transmark
47389	The Halewood Transmission
47390	Amlwch Freighter /
	Tren Nwyddau Amlwch
47392	Cory Brothers 1842-1992
47393	Herbert Austin
47394	Johnson Stevens Agencies
47397	Freightliner Cleveland
47401	North Eastern | Star of the East
47402	Gateshead
47403	The Geordie
47404	Hadrian
47405	Northumbria
47406	Rail Riders
47407	Aycliffe
47408	Finsbury Park
47409	David Lloyd George
47411	The Geordie
47421	The Brontes of Haworth
47424	The Brontes of Haworth
47425	Holbeck
47434	Pride in Huddersfield
47443	North Eastern
47444	University of Nottingham
47448	Gateshead
47449	ORION
47452	Aycliffe
47457	Ben Line
47458	County of Cambridgeshire
47461	Charles Rennie Mackintosh
47462	Cambridge Traction & -
	Rolling Stock Depot
47469	Glasgow Chamber of Commerce
47470	University of Edinburgh
47471	Norman Tuna G.C.
47474	Sir Rowland Hill
47475	Restive
47476	Night Mail
47479	Track 29
47480	Robin Hood
47484	ISAMBARD KINGDOM BRUNEL
47487	VB Menon
47488	Rail Riders | DAVIES THE OCEAN
47489	Crewe Diesel Depot -
	Quality Approved
47490	Bristol Bath Road | Resonant
47491	Horwich Enterprise | Resolve

47492	The Enterprising Scot	47582	County of Norfolk
47500	GREAT WESTERN	47583	County of Hertfordshire
47501	CRAFTSMAN	47584	County of Suffolk
47503	The Geordie | Heaton Traincare Depot		THE LOCOMOTIVE & -
47508	Great Britain | SS Great Britain		CARRIAGE INSTITUTION 1911
47509	Albion	47585	County of Cambridgeshire
47510	Fair Rosamund	47586	Northamptonshire
47511	Thames	47587	Ruskin College Oxford
47513	Severn	47588	Carlisle Currock | Resurgent
47515	Night Mail	47590	Thomas Telford
47517	Andrew Carnegie	47592	County of Avon
47520	Thunderbird	47593	Galloway Princess
47522	Doncaster Enterprise	47594	Resourceful
47524	Res Gestae	47595	Confederation of British Industry
47526	Northumbria	47596	Aldeburgh Festival
47527	Kettering	47597	Resilient
47528	The Queen's Own Mercian Yeomanry	47600	Dewi Sant Saint David
47531	Respite	47602	Glorious Devon
47535	University of Leicester | Saint Aidan	47603	County of Somerset
47537	Sir Gwynedd County of Gwynedd	47604	Women's Royal Voluntary Service
47538	Python	47606	ODIN | Irresistible
47539	Rochdale Pioneers	47607	Royal Worcester
47540	The Institution of Civil Engineers	47609	FIRE FLY
47541	The Queen Mother	47611	Thames
47546	Aviemore Centre	47612	TITAN
47547	University of Oxford	47613	NORTH STAR
47549	Royal Mail	47615	Castell Caerffilli Caerphilly Castle
47550	University of Dundee	47616	Y Ddraig Goch The Red Dragon
47551	Poste Restante	47617	University of Stirling
47555	The Commonwealth Spirit	47618	Fair Rosamund
47558	Mayflower	47620	Windsor Castle
47559	Sir Joshua Reynolds	47621	Royal County of Berkshire
47560	Tamar	47622	The Institution of -
47562	Sir William Burrell | Restless		Mechanical Engineers
47563	Woman's Guild	47623	VULCAN
47564	COLOSSUS	47624	CYCLOPS | Saint Andrew
47565	Responsive	47625	CITY OF TRURO | Resplendent
47567	Red Star	47626	ATLAS
47568	Royal Engineers Postal & Courier Services	47627	City of Oxford
	Royal Logistics Corps Postal & -	47628	SIR DANIEL GOOCH
	Courier Services	47630	Resounding
47569	The Gloucestershire Regiment	47631	Ressaldar
47572	Ely Cathedral	47633	ORION
47573	The LONDON STANDARD	47634	Henry Ford | Holbeck
47574	LLOYDS LIST 250th ANNIVERSARY	47635	Jimmy Milne
	Benjamin Gimbert G.C.		The Lass O' Ballochmyle
47575	City of Hereford	47636	Sir John de Graeme | Restored
47576	Kings Lynn	47637	Springburn
47577	Benjamin Gimbert G.C.	47638	County of Kent
47578	The Royal Society of Edinburgh | Respected	47639	Industry Year 1986
47579	James Nightall G.C.	47640	University of Strathclyde
47580	County of Essex	47641	Fife Region
47581	Great Eastern	47642	Strathisla | Resolute

47644	The Permanent Way Institution	47745	Royal London Society for the Blind
47645	Robert F Fairlie Locomotive Engineer	47746	The Bobby
47647	THOR		Chris Fudge 1970-2010
47654	Finsbury Park	47747	Res Publica | Graham Farish
47671	Y Ddraig Goch The Red Dragon		Florence Nightingale
47672	Sir William Burrell	47749	Atlantic College | Demelza
47673	Galloway Princess | York InterCity Control		CITY OF TRURO
47674	Woman's Royal Voluntary Service	47750	Royal Mail Cheltenham | ATLAS
47675	Confederation of British Industry	47756	The Permanent Way Institution
47676	Northamptonshire		Royal Mail Tyneside
47677	University of Stirling	47757	Restitution | Capability Brown
47701	Saint Andrew | Old Oak Common -	47758	Regency Rail Cruises
	Traction & Rolling Stock Depot | Waverley	47760	Restless | Ribblehead Viaduct
47702	Saint Cuthbert | County of Suffolk	47763	Research
47703	Saint Mungo | The Queen Mother	47764	Resounding
	LEWIS CARROLL | HERMES	47765	Ressaldar
47704	Dunedin	47766	Resolute
47705	Lothian | GUY FAWKES	47767	Saint Columba | Mappa Mundi
47706	Strathclyde	47768	Resonant
47707	Holyrood	47769	Resolve
47708	Waverley | Templecombe	47770	Reserved
47709	The Lord Provost | DIONYSOS	47771	Heaton Traincare Depot
47710	Sir Walter Scott	47772	Carnforth TMD
	Capital Radio's Help a London Child	47773	Reservist | The Queen Mother
	LADY GODIVA | QUASIMODO	47774	Poste Restante
47711	Groyfriars Bobby | County of Hertfordshire	47775	Respite
47712	Lady Diana Spencer | DICK WHITTINGTON	47776	Respected
	ARTEMIS | Pride of Carlisle	47777	Restored
47713	Tayside Region	47778	Irresistible
47714	Grampion Region | Thames		Duke of Edinburgh's Award
47715	Haymarket | POSEIDON	47781	Isle of Iona
47716	Duke of Edinburgh's Award	47783	Finsbury Park | Saint Peter
47717	Tayside Region	47784	Condover Hall
47721	Saint Bede	47785	The Statesman | Fiona Castle
47722	The Queen Mother	47786	Roy Castle OBE
47725	Red Star | The Railway Mission	47787	Victim Support | Windsor Castle
	Bristol Barton Hill	47788	Captain Peter Manisty RN
47726	Manchester Airport Progress	47789	Lindisfarne
47727	Duke of Edinburgh's Award	47790	Saint David Dewi Sant
	Castell Caerffilli / Caerphilly Castle | Rebecca		Galloway Princess
47732	Restormal	47791	VENICE SIMPLON -
47733	Eastern Star		ORIENT-EXPRESS
47734	Crewe Diesel Depot Quality Approved	47792	Saint Cuthbert | Robin Hood
47736	Cambridge Traction & Rolling Stock Depot	47793	Saint Augustine | Christopher Wren
47737	Resurgent	47798	FIRE FLY | Prince William
47738	Bristol Barton Hill	47799	Windsor Castle | Prince Henry
47739	Resourceful	47802	Pride of Cumbria
	Robin of Templecombe 1938-2013	47803	Women's Guild
47741	Resilient	47804	Kettering
47742	The Enterprising Scot	47805	Bristol Bath Road | Pride of Toton
47743	The Bobby		TALISMAN | John Scott 1945-2012
47744	Saint Edwin | The Cornish Experience	47807	The Lion of Vienna
	Royal Mail Cheltenham	47808	SAMSON

CLASS 47 (Continued)

47809	Finsbury Park	47839	Royal County of Berkshire
47810	PORTERBROOK | Captain Sensible		Pride of Saltley | PEGASUS
	Peter Bath MBE 1927-2006	47840	NORTH STAR
47812	Pride of Eastleigh	47841	The Institution of Mechanical -
47813	S.S. Great Britain | John Peel | Solent		Engineers | Spirit of Chester
47814	Totnes Castle	47842	ODIN
47815	Abertawe Landore	47843	VULCAN
	GREAT WESTERN	47844	Derby & Derbyshire Chamber -
47816	Bristol Bath Road Quality Approved		of Commerce & Industry
47817	The Institution of Mechanical Engineers	47845	County of Kent
47818	Strathclyde | Emily	47846	THOR
47821	Royal Worcester	47847	Railway World Magazine /-
47822	Pride of Shrewsbury		Brian Morrison
47823	SS Great Britain	47848	Newton Abbot Festival of Transport
47824	Glorious Devon		TITAN STAR
47825	Thomas Telford	47849	Cadeirlan Bangor Cathedral
47826	Springburn	47851	Traction Magazine
47828	Severn Valley Railway | Joe Strummer	47853	RAIL EXPRESS
47830	BEECHING'S LEGACY	47854	Women's Royal Voluntary Service
47831	Bolton Wanderer		Diamond Jubilee
47832	Tamar | DRIVER TOM CLARK O.B.E.	47971	Robin Hood
	Solway Princess	47972	The Royal Army Ordance Corps
47833	Captain Peter Manisty RN	47973	Midland Counties Railway 150
47834	FIRE FLY		Derby Evening Telegraph
47835	Windsor Castle	47974	The Permanent Way Institution
47836	Fair Rosamund	47975	The Institution of Civil Engineers
47837	Thames	47976	Aviemore Centre

CLASS 50

Total Built	50	Formation	Co-Co	Max T.E.	48,500 lbf
Date Built	1967/68	Max Speed	100 mph	P.A.R.	2,070 hp
Builder	English Electric, Vulcan	Weight	117 t	R.A.	6
Engine	EE 16CVST 2700 hp	Brakes	Dual	Supply	Electric

50001	D401		·	·	Scrapped	C F Booth, Rotherham, 2002
50002	D402		·	·	Preserved	South Devon Railway
50003	D403		·	·	Scrapped	MC Metals, Springburn, 1992
50004	D404		·	·	Scrapped	C F Booth, Rotherham, 1992
50005	D405		·	·	Scrapped	Cooper's Metals, OOC, 1991
50006	D406		·	·	Scrapped	Vic Berry, Leicester, 1988
50007	D407		·	·	Operational	Severn Valley Railway
50008	D408		·	·	Operational	BARS, Derby
50009	D409		·	·	Scrapped	Cooper's Metals, OOC, 1991
50010	D410		·	·	Scrapped	Cooper's Metals, Laira, 1992
50011	D411	968031*	·	·	Scrapped	Texas Metals, Crewe, 1992
50012	D412		·	·	Scrapped	Vic Berry, Leicester, 1989
50013	D413		·	·	Scrapped	Vic Berry, Leicester, 1989
50014	D414		·	·	Scrapped	Vic Berry, Leicester, 1989
50015	D415		·	·	Preserved	East Lancashire Railway
50016	D416		·	·	Scrapped	C F Booth, Rotherham, 1992
50017	D417	50117	·	·	Operational	Washwood Heath
50018	D418		·	·	Scrapped	MC Metals, Springburn, 1992
50019	D419		·	·	Preserved	Mid-Norfolk Railway

50020	D420	·	·	·	Scrapped	C F Booth, Rotherham, 1992
50021	D421	·	·	·	Preserved	Eastleigh
50022	D422	·	·	·	Scrapped	Vic Berry, Leicester, 1989
50023	D423	·	·	·	Scrapped	HNRC, Barrow Hill, 2003
50024	D424	·	·	·	Scrapped	Cooper's Metals, OOC, 1991
50025	D425	·	·	·	Scrapped	Vic Berry, OOC, 1989
50026	D426	·	·	·	Preserved	Severn Valley Railway
50027	D427	·	·	·	Preserved	Mid-Hants Railway
50028	D428	·	·	·	Scrapped	Cooper's Metals, OOC, 1991
50029	D429	·	·	·	Preserved	Peak Rail
50030	D430	·	·	·	Preserved	Peak Rail
50031	D431	·	·	·	Preserved	Severn Valley Railway
50032	D432	·	·	·	Scrapped	Cooper's Metals, OOC, 1991
50033	D433	·	·	·	Preserved	Tyseley Locomotive Works
50034	D434	·	·	·	Scrapped	Cooper's Metals, OOC, 1991
50035	D435	50135	·	·	Preserved	Severn Valley Railway
50036	D436	·	·	·	Scrapped	C F Booth, Rotherham, 1992
50037	D437	·	·	·	Scrapped	MC Metals, Springburn, 1992
50038	D438	·	·	·	Scrapped	Vic Berry, Leicester, 1989
50039	D439	·	·	·	Scrapped	Cooper's Metals, OOC, 1991
50040	D440	·	·	·	Scrapped	Sims Metals, Halesowen, 2008
50041	D441	·	·	·	Scrapped	Cooper's Metals, OOC, 1991
50042	D442	·	·	·	Preserved	Bodmin & Wenford Railway
50043	D443	·	·	·	Scrapped	Raxstar, Blaenavon, 2002
50044	D444	·	·	·	Operational	Severn Valley Railway
50045	D445	·	·	·	Scrapped	C F Booth, Rotherham, 1992
50046	D446	·	·	·	Scrapped	MC Metals, Springburn, 1992
50047	D447	·	·	·	Scrapped	Vic Berry, Leicester, 1989
50048	D448	·	·	·	Scrapped	MC Metals, Springburn, 1992
50049	D449	50149	·	·	Operational	Severn Valley Railway
50050	D400	·	·	·	Operational	Washwood Heath

Class 50/0 (50001 - 50050) Standard design
Class 50/1 (50149) Re-geared for experimental purposes

* Converted to power unit transporter and renumbered with ADB prefix

Class 50 Names:

50001	Dreadnought	50016	Barham	50032	Courageous
50002	Superb	50017	Royal Oak	50033	Glorious
50003	Temeraire	50018	Resolution	50034	Furious
50004	St Vincent	50019	Ramilies	50035	Ark Royal
50005	Collingwood	50020	Revenge	50036	Victorious
50006	Neptune	50021	Rodney	50037	Illustrious
50007	Hercules	50022	Anson	50038	Formidable
	SIR EDWARD ELGAR	50023	Howe	50039	Implacable
50008	Thunderer	50024	Vanguard	50040	Leviathan | Centurion
50009	Conqueror	50025	Invincible	50041	Bulwark
50010	Monarch	50026	Indomitable	50042	Triumph
50011	Centurian	50027	Lion	50043	Eagle
50012	Benbow	50028	Tiger	50044	Exeter | EXETER
50013	Agincourt	50029	Renown	50045	Achilles
50014	Warspite	50030	Repulse	50046	Ajax
50015	Valiant	50031	Hood	50047	Swiftsure

CLASS 50 (Continued)

| 50048 | Dauntless | 50050 | Fearless | 50135 | Ark Royal |
| 50049 | Defiance | 50117 | Royal Oak | 50149 | Defiance |

CLASS 52

Total Built	74	Formation	C-C	Max T.E.	70,000 lbf
Date Built	1961-64	Max Speed	90 mph	P.A.R.	2,350 hp
Builder	BR, Swindon & Crewe	Weight	108 t	R.A.	6
Engine	2 x Maybach MD655, 2700 hp	Brakes	Vacuum / Air & Vac	Supply	Steam

·	D1000	·	·	·	Scrapped	BR, Swindon Works, 1974
·	D1001	·	·	·	Scrapped	BR, Swindon Works, 1977
·	D1002	·	·	·	Scrapped	BR, Swindon Works, 1974
·	D1003	·	·	·	Scrapped	BR, Swindon Works, 1977
·	D1004	·	·	·	Scrapped	BR, Swindon Works, 1974
·	D1005	·	·	·	Scrapped	BR, Swindon Works, 1977
·	D1006	·	·	·	Scrapped	BR, Swindon Works, 1977
·	D1007	·	·	·	Scrapped	BR, Swindon Works, 1975
·	D1008	·	·	·	Scrapped	BR, Swindon Works, 1975
·	D1009	·	·	·	Scrapped	BR, Swindon Works, 1978
·	D1010	·	·	·	Preserved	West Somerset Railway
·	D1011	·	·	·	Scrapped	BR, Swindon Works, 1978
·	D1012	·	·	·	Scrapped	BR, Swindon Works, 1979
·	D1013	·	·	·	Preserved	Severn Valley Railway
·	D1014	·	·	·	Scrapped	BR, Swindon Works, 1975
·	D1015	·	·	·	Operational	Severn Valley Railway
·	D1016	·	·	·	Scrapped	BR, Swindon Works, 1977
·	D1017	·	·	·	Scrapped	BR, Swindon Works, 1975
·	D1018	·	·	·	Scrapped	BR, Swindon Works, 1974
·	D1019	·	·	·	Scrapped	BR, Swindon Works, 1974
·	D1020	·	·	·	Scrapped	BR, Swindon Works, 1974
·	D1021	·	·	·	Scrapped	BR, Swindon Works, 1979
·	D1022	·	·	·	Scrapped	BR, Swindon Works, 1978
·	D1023	·	·	·	Preserved	National Railway Museum, York
·	D1024	·	·	·	Scrapped	BR, Swindon Works, 1974
·	D1025	·	·	·	Scrapped	BR, Swindon Works, 1979
·	D1026	·	·	·	Scrapped	BR, Swindon Works, 1976
·	D1027	·	·	·	Scrapped	BR, Swindon Works, 1976
·	D1028	·	·	·	Scrapped	BR, Swindon Works, 1979
·	D1029	·	·	·	Scrapped	BR, Swindon Works, 1975
·	D1030	·	·	·	Scrapped	BR, Swindon Works, 1976
·	D1031	·	·	·	Scrapped	BR, Swindon Works, 1976
·	D1032	·	·	·	Scrapped	BR, Swindon Works, 1974
·	D1033	·	·	·	Scrapped	BR, Swindon Works, 1979
·	D1034	·	·	·	Scrapped	BR, Swindon Works, 1977
·	D1035	·	·	·	Scrapped	BR, Swindon Works, 1976
·	D1036	·	·	·	Scrapped	BR, Swindon Works, 1977
·	D1037	·	·	·	Scrapped	BR, Swindon Works, 1977
·	D1038	·	·	·	Scrapped	BR, Swindon Works, 1974
·	D1039	·	·	·	Scrapped	BR, Swindon Works, 1974
·	D1040	·	·	·	Scrapped	BR, Swindon Works, 1976
·	D1041	·	·	·	Preserved	East Lancashire Railway
·	D1042	·	·	·	Scrapped	BR, Swindon Works, 1974
·	D1043	·	·	·	Scrapped	BR, Swindon Works, 1977

·	D1044	· · ·	Scrapped	BR, Swindon Works, 1975
·	D1045	· · ·	Scrapped	BR, Swindon Works, 1975
·	D1046	· · ·	Scrapped	BR, Swindon Works, 1976
·	D1047	· · ·	Scrapped	BR, Swindon Works, 1976
·	D1048	· · ·	Preserved	Midland Railway Centre
·	D1049	· · ·	Scrapped	BR, Swindon Works, 1977
·	D1050	· · ·	Scrapped	BR, Swindon Works, 1976
·	D1051	· · ·	Scrapped	BR, Swindon Works, 1977
·	D1052	· · ·	Scrapped	BR, Swindon Works, 1976
·	D1053	· · ·	Scrapped	BR, Swindon Works, 1977
·	D1054	· · ·	Scrapped	BR, Swindon Works, 1977
·	D1055	· · ·	Scrapped	BR, Swindon Works, 1976
·	D1056	· · ·	Scrapped	BR, Swindon Works, 1979
·	D1057	· · ·	Scrapped	BR, Swindon Works, 1977
·	D1058	· · ·	Scrapped	BR, Swindon Works, 1979
·	D1059	· · ·	Scrapped	BR, Swindon Works, 1976
·	D1060	· · ·	Scrapped	BR, Swindon Works, 1974
·	D1061	· · ·	Scrapped	BR, Swindon Works, 1975
·	D1062	· · ·	Preserved	Severn Valley Railway
·	D1063	· · ·	Scrapped	BR, Swindon Works, 1977
·	D1064	· · ·	Scrapped	BR, Swindon Works, 1977
·	D1065	· · ·	Scrapped	BR, Swindon Works, 1977
·	D1066	· · ·	Scrapped	BR, Swindon Works, 1975
·	D1067	· · ·	Scrapped	BR, Swindon Works, 1976
·	D1068	· · ·	Scrapped	BR, Swindon Works, 1977
·	D1069	· · ·	Scrapped	BR, Swindon Works, 1977
·	D1070	· · ·	Scrapped	BR, Swindon Works, 1979
·	D1071	· · ·	Scrapped	BR, Swindon Works, 1978
·	D1072	· · ·	Scrapped	BR, Swindon Works, 1977
·	D1073	· · ·	Scrapped	BR, Swindon Works, 1975

Class 52 Names:

D1000	WESTERN ENTERPRISE		D1022	WESTERN SENTINEL
D1001	WESTERN PATHFINDER		D1023	WESTERN FUSILIER
D1002	WESTERN EXPLORER		D1024	WESTERN HUNTSMAN
D1003	WESTERN PIONEER		D1025	WESTERN GUARDSMAN
D1004	WESTERN CRUSADER		D1026	WESTERN CENTURION
D1005	WESTERN VENTURER		D1027	WESTERN LANCER
D1006	WESTERN STALWART		D1028	WESTERN HUSSAR
D1007	WESTERN TALISMAN		D1029	WESTERN LEGIONNAIRE
D1008	WESTERN HARRIER		D1030	WESTERN MUSKETEER
D1009	WESTERN INVADER		D1031	WESTERN RIFLEMAN
D1010	WESTERN CAMPAIGNER		D1032	WESTERN MARKSMAN
D1011	WESTERN THUNDERER		D1033	WESTERN TROOPER
D1012	WESTERN FIREBRAND		D1034	WESTERN DRAGOON
D1013	WESTERN RANGER		D1035	WESTERN YEOMAN
D1014	WESTERN LEVIATHAN		D1036	WESTERN EMPEROR
D1015	WESTERN CHAMPION		D1037	WESTERN EMPRESS
D1016	WESTERN GLADIATOR		D1038	WESTERN SOVEREIGN
D1017	WESTERN WARRIOR		D1039	WESTERN KING
D1018	WESTERN BUCCANEER		D1040	WESTERN QUEEN
D1019	WESTERN CHALLENGER		D1041	WESTERN PRINCE
D1020	WESTERN HERO		D1042	WESTERN PRINCESS
D1021	WESTERN CAVALIER		D1043	WESTERN DUKE

D1044	WESTERN DUCHESS		D1059	WESTERN EMPIRE
D1045	WESTERN VISCOUNT		D1060	WESTERN DOMINION
D1046	WESTERN MARQUIS		D1061	WESTERN ENVOY
D1047	WESTERN LORD		D1062	WESTERN COURIER
D1048	WESTERN LADY		D1063	WESTERN MONITOR
D1049	WESTERN MONARCH		D1064	WESTERN REGENT
D1050	WESTERN RULER		D1065	WESTERN CONSORT
D1051	WESTERN EMBASSADOR		D1066	WESTERN PREFECT
D1052	WESTERN VICEROY		D1067	WESTERN DRUID
D1053	WESTERN PATRIARCH		D1068	WESTERN RELIANCE
D1054	WESTERN GOVERNOR		D1069	WESTERN VANGUARD
D1055	WESTERN ADVOCATE		D1070	WESTERN GAUNTLET
D1056	WESTERN SULTAN		D1071	WESTERN RENOWN
D1057	WESTERN CHIEFTAN		D1072	WESTERN GLORY
D1058	WESTERN NOBLEMAN		D1073	WESTERN BULWARK

CLASS 53

Total Built	1	Formation	Co-Co	Max T.E.	60,000 lbf
Date Built	1961	Max Speed	100 mph	P.A.R.	2,165 hp
Builder	Brush Traction, Loughborough	Weight	116 t	R.A.	6
Engine	2 x Maybach MD655, 2700 hp	Brakes	Vacuum / Air	Supply	Steam

·	D0280	D1200	·	·	Scrapped	Cashmore's, Newport, 1976

Class 53 Names: D0280   FALCON

CLASS 55

Total Built	22	Formation	Co-Co	Max T.E.	50,000 lbf
Date Built	1961	Max Speed	100 mph	P.A.R.	2,460 hp
Builder	English Electric, Vulcan	Weight	100 t	R.A.	5
Engine	2xNapier-Deltic D18.25, 3300 hp	Brakes	Vacuum / Air & Vac	Supply	Dual

55001	D9001	·	·	·	Scrapped	BR, Doncaster Works, 1980
55002	D9002	·	·	·	Operational	National Railway Museum, York
55003	D9003	·	·	·	Scrapped	BR, Doncaster Works, 1981
55004	D9004	·	·	·	Scrapped	BR, Doncaster Works, 1983
55005	D9005	·	·	·	Scrapped	BR, Doncaster Works, 1983
55006	D9006	·	·	·	Scrapped	BR, Doncaster Works, 1981
55007	D9007	·	·	·	Scrapped	BR, Doncaster Works, 1982
55008	D9008	·	·	·	Scrapped	BR, Doncaster Works, 1982
55009	D9009	·	·	·	Operational	Barrow Hill
55010	D9010	·	·	·	Scrapped	BR, Doncaster Works, 1982
55011	D9011	·	·	·	Scrapped	BR, Doncaster Works, 1982
55012	D9012	·	·	·	Scrapped	BR, Doncaster Works, 1981
55013	D9013	·	·	·	Scrapped	BR, Doncaster Works, 1982
55014	D9014	·	·	·	Scrapped	BR, Doncaster Works, 1982
55015	D9015	·	·	·	Preserved	Barrow Hill
55016	D9016	·	·	·	Preserved	Locomotive Services, Crewe
55017	D9017	·	·	·	Scrapped	BR, Doncaster Works, 1983
55018	D9018	·	·	·	Scrapped	BR, Doncaster Works, 1982
55019	D9019	·	·	·	Preserved	Barrow Hill
55020	D9020	·	·	·	Scrapped	BR, Doncaster Works, 1980
55021	D9021	·	·	·	Scrapped	BR, Doncaster Works, 1982

CLASS 55 (Continued)

55022	D9000	·	·	·	Operational Locomotive Services, Crewe

Class 55 Names:

55001	ST PADDY		55012	CREPELLO
55002	THE KING'S OWN YORKSHIRE -		55013	THE BLACK WATCH
	LIGHT INFANTRY		55014	THE DUKE OF WELLINGTON'S -
55003	MELD			REGIMENT
55004	QUEEN'S OWN HIGHLANDER		55015	TULYAR
55005	THE PRINCE OF WALES'S -		55016	GORDON HIGHLANDER
	OWN REGIMENT OF YORKSHIRE		55017	THE DURHAM LIGHT INFANTRY
55006	THE FIFE AND FORFAR YEOMANRY		55018	BALLYMOSS
55007	PINZA		55019	ROYAL HIGHLAND FUSILIER
55008	THE GREEN HOWARDS		55020	NIMBUS
55009	ALYCIDON		55021	ARGYLL AND SUTHERLAND -
55010	THE KING'S OWN SCOTTISH BORDERER			HIGHLANDER
55011	THE ROYAL NORTHUMBERLAND FUSILIERS		55022	ROYAL SCOTS GREY

CLASS 56

Total Built	135	Formation	Co-Co	Max T.E.	61,800 lbf
Date Built	1976-84	Max Speed	80 mph	P.A.R.	2,400 hp
Builder	Electroputere* and	Weight	126 t	R.A.	7
	BREL, Doncaster & Crewe	Brakes	Air	Supply	N/A
Engine	Paxman 16RK3CT, 3250 hp				

56001	·	·	·	·	Scrapped	MRJ Phillips, Cardiff, 1997
56002	·	·	·	·	Scrapped	Ron Hull, Doncaster, 1994
56003	56312	·	·	·	Stored	BARS, Leicester
56004	·	·	·	·	Scrapped	C F Booth, Rotherham, 2006
56005	·	·	·	·	Scrapped	C F Booth, Rotherham, 1996
56006	·	·	·	·	Stored	UKRL, Leicester
56007	·	·	·	·	Stored	UKRL, Leicester
56008	·	·	·	·	Scrapped	Raxstar, Immingham, 2000
56009	56201+	·	·	·	Stored	UKRL, Battlefield Railway
56010	·	·	·	·	Scrapped	C F Booth, Rotherham, 2004
56011	·	·	·	·	Scrapped	C F Booth, Rotherham, 2009
56012	·	·	·	·	Scrapped	Raxstar, Immingham, 2000
56013	·	·	·	·	Scrapped	T J Thomson, Stockton, 2001
56014	·	·	·	·	Scrapped	Raxstar, Immingham, 2000
56015	·	·	·	·	Scrapped	MRJ Phillips, Doncaster, 1996
56016	·	·	·	·	Scrapped	MRJ Phillips, Cardiff, 1997
56017	·	·	·	·	Scrapped	Birds, Toton, 1994
56018	·	·	·	·	Stored	UKRL, Loughborough Works
56019	·	·	·	·	Scrapped	HNRC, Immingham, 2003
56020	·	·	·	·	Scrapped	C F Booth, Rotherham, 1998
56021	·	·	·	·	Scrapped	T J Thomson, Stockton, 2009
56022	·	·	·	·	Scrapped	EMR, Kingsbury, 2012
56023	·	·	·	·	Scrapped	C F Booth, Rotherham, 2004
56024	·	·	·	·	Scrapped	C F Booth, Rotherham, 1996
56025	·	·	·	·	Scrapped	C F Booth, Rotherham, 2009
56026	·	·	·	·	Scrapped	C F Booth, Rotherham, 1996
56027	·	·	·	·	Scrapped	C F Booth, Rotherham, 2009
56028	·	·	·	·	Scrapped	MRJ Phillips, Crewe, 1998
56029	·	·	·	·	Scrapped	EMR, Kingsbury, 2007

56030		·	·	·	·	Scrapped	MRJ Phillips, Crewe, 1998
56031		·	·	·	·	Stored	UKRL, Leicester
56032		·	·	·	·	Stored	UKRL, Leicester
56033		·	·	·	·	Scrapped	EMR, Kingsbury, 2010
56034		·	·	·	·	Scrapped	C F Booth, Rotherham, 2007
56035		·	·	·	·	Scrapped	EWS, Wigan, 2000
56036		·	·	·	·	Scrapped	C F Booth, Rotherham, 2006
56037		·	·	·	·	Stored	UKRL, Leicester
56038		·	·	·	·	Stored	UKRL, Leicester
56039		·	·	·	·	Scrapped	T J Thomson, Stockton, 2004
56040		·	·	·	·	Scrapped	T J Thomson, Stockton, 2011
56041		·	·	·	·	Scrapped	EMR, Attercliffe, 2011
56042		·	·	·	·	Scrapped	Birds, Toton, 1994
56043		·	·	·	·	Scrapped	C F Booth, Rotherham, 2009
56044		·	·	·	·	Scrapped	C F Booth, Rotherham, 2007
56045	56301	·	·	·	·	Operational	UKRL, Leicester
56046		·	·	·	·	Scrapped	EMR, Kingsbury, 2012
56047		·	·	·	·	Scrapped	HNRC, Immingham, 2003
56048		·	·	·	·	Scrapped	EMR, Kingsbury, 2010
56049		·	·	·	·	Operational	Colas Rail, Washwood Heath
56050		·	·	·	·	Scrapped	C F Booth, Rotherham, 2004
56051		·	·	·	·	Stored	Colas Rail, Washwood Heath
56052		·	·	·	·	Scrapped	C F Booth, Rotherham, 2009
56053		·	·	·	·	Scrapped	EMR, Attercliffe, 2011
56054		·	·	·	·	Scrapped	T J Thomson, Stockton, 2011
56055		·	·	·	·	Scrapped	EMR, Attercliffe, 2011
56056		·	·	·	·	Scrapped	EMR, Kingsbury, 2010
56057	56311	·	·	·	·	Stored	BARS, Leicester
56058		·	·	·	·	Scrapped	EMR, Kingsbury, 2012
56059		·	·	·	·	Scrapped	T J Thomson, Stockton, 2011
56060		·	·	·	·	Stored	UKRL, Leicester
56061		·	·	·	·	Scrapped	T J Thomson, Stockton, 2006
56062		·	·	·	·	Scrapped	EMR, Kingsbury, 2010
56063		·	·	·	·	Scrapped	C F Booth, Rotherham, 2007
56064		·	·	·	·	Scrapped	C F Booth, Rotherham, 2009
56065		·	·	·	·	Stored	UKRL, Leicester
56066		·	·	·	·	Scrapped	Ron Hull, Rotherham, 2005
56067		·	·	·	·	Scrapped	T J Thomson, Stockton, 2011
56068		·	·	·	·	Scrapped	EMR, Kingsbury, 2010
56069		·	·	·	·	Stored	UKRL, Leicester
56070		·	·	·	·	Scrapped	T J Thomson, Stockton, 2011
56071		·	·	·	·	Scrapped	T J Thomson, Stockton, 2011
56072		·	·	·	·	Scrapped	EMR, Attercliffe, 2010
56073		·	·	·	·	Scrapped	EMR, Kingsbury, 2012
56074		·	·	·	·	Scrapped	Ron Hull, Rotherham, 2014
56075		·	·	·	·	Scrapped	C F Booth, Rotherham, 2004
56076		·	·	·	·	Scrapped	C F Booth, Rotherham, 2009
56077		·	·	·	·	Stored	UKRL, Leicester
56078		·	·	·	·	Operational	Colas Rail, Washwood Heath
56079		·	·	·	·	Scrapped	EMR, Kingsbury, 2010
56080		·	·	·	·	Scrapped	Raxstar, Cardiff, 2003
56081		·	·	·	·	Operational	UKRL, Leicester
56082		·	·	·	·	Scrapped	C F Booth, Rotherham, 2009
56083		·	·	·	·	Scrapped	T J Thomson, Stockton, 2011

CLASS 56 (Continued)

56084	·	·	·	·	Scrapped	C F Booth, Rotherham, 2009
56085	·	·	·	·	Scrapped	EMR, Hartlepool, 2011
56086	·	·	·	·	Scrapped	EMR, Kingsbury, 2013
56087	·	·	·	·	Operational	Colas Rail, Washwood Heath
56088	·	·	·	·	Scrapped	EMR, Hartlepool, 2010
56089	·	·	·	·	Scrapped	C F Booth, Rotherham, 2009
56090	·	·	·	·	Stored	Colas Rail, Washwood Heath
56091	·	·	·	·	Stored	BARS, Leicester
56092	·	·	·	·	Scrapped	EWS, Wigan, 2001
56093	·	·	·	·	Scrapped	EMR, Attercliffe, 2010
56094	·	·	·	·	Operational	Colas Rail, Washwood Heath
56095	·	·	·	·	Scrapped	T J Thomson, Stockton, 2011
56096	·	·	·	·	Operational	Colas Rail, Washwood Heath
56097	·	·	·	·	Preserved	Great Central Railway North
56098	·	·	·	·	Operational	UKRL, Leicester
56099	·	·	·	·	Scrapped	EMR, Attercliffe, 2010
56100	·	·	·	·	Scrapped	EMR, Kingsbury, 2010
56101	0659001-5~	·	·	·	Operational	FLOYD, Hungary
56102	·	·	·	·	Scrapped	EMR, Hartlepool, 2010
56103	·	·	·	·	Stored	BARS, Leicester
56104	·	·	·	·	Operational	UKRL, Leicester
56105	·	·	·	·	Operational	Colas Rail, Washwood Heath
56106	·	·	·	·	Stored	UKRL, Leicester
56107	·	·	·	·	Scrapped	T J Thomson, Stockton, 2011
56108	·	·	·	·	Scrapped	EMR, Hartlepool, 2011
56100	·	·	·	·	Scrapped	T J Thomson, Stockton, 2011
56110	·	·	·	·	Scrapped	EMR, Attercliffe, 2011
56111	·	·	·	·	Scrapped	EMR, Hartlepool, 2010
56112	·	·	·	·	Scrapped	EMR, Kingsbury, 2012
56113	·	·	·	·	Operational	Colas Rail, Washwood Heath
56114	·	·	·	·	Scrapped	EMR, Kingsbury, 2012
56115	0659002-3~	·	·	·	Operational	FLOYD, Hungary
56116	·	·	·	·	Scrapped	EMR, Kingsbury, 2010
56117	0659003-1~	·	·	·	Stored	FLOYD, Hungary
56118	·	·	·	·	Scrapped	C F Booth, Rotherham, 2009
56119	·	·	·	·	Scrapped	EMR, Attercliffe, 2011
56120	·	·	·	·	Scrapped	T J Thomson, Stockton, 2011
56121	·	·	·	·	Scrapped	C F Booth, Rotherham, 2005
56122	·	·	·	·	Scrapped	C F Booth, Rotherham, 1998
56123	·	·	·	·	Scrapped	HNRC, Immingham, 2003
56124	56302	·	·	·	Operational	Colas Rail, Washwood Heath
56125	56303	·	·	·	Operational	Rail Operations Group, Leicester
56126	·	·	·	·	Scrapped	EWS, Wigan, 1999
56127	·	·	·	·	Scrapped	EMR, Hartlepool, 2010
56128	·	·	·	·	Scrapped	C F Booth, Rotherham, 2018
56129	·	·	·	·	Scrapped	EMR, Hartlepool, 2011
56130	·	·	·	·	Scrapped	C F Booth, Rotherham, 2004
56131	·	·	·	·	Scrapped	C F Booth, Rotherham, 2007
56132	·	·	·	·	Scrapped	C F Booth, Rotherham, 2006
56133	·	·	·	·	Scrapped	EMR, Kingsbury, 2012
56134	·	·	·	·	Scrapped	C F Booth, Rotherham, 2010
56135	·	·	·	·	Scrapped	HNRC, Immingham, 2003

CLASS 56 (Continued)

* 56001-030 built by Electroputere at Craiova, Romania as sub contractors to Brush
+ Converted to power unit transporter / testbed and unofficially renumbered
~ Renumbered when exported to Hungary for use with FLOYD

Class 56 Names:

56001	Whatley	56080	Selby Coalfield
56006	Ferrybridge 'C' Power Station	56086	The Magistrates Association
56012	Maltby Colliery	56087	ABP Port of Hull
56028	West Burton Power Station	56089	Ferrybridge 'C' Power Station
56030	Eggborough Power Station	56091	Castle Donnington Power Station
56031	Merehead		Stanton
56032	Sir De Morgannwg /	56093	The Institution of Mining Engineers
	County of South Glamorgan	56094	Eggborough Power Station
56033	Shotton Paper Mill	56095	Harworth Colliery
56034	Castell Ogwr Ogmore Castle	56098	Lost Boys 68-88
56035	Taff Merthyr	56099	Fiddlers Ferry Power Station
56037	Richard Trevithick	56101	Mutual Improvement
56038	Western Mail | Pathfinder Tours 1973-2003		Frank Hornby
56039	ABP Port of Hull	56102	Scunthorpe Steel Centenary
56040	Oystermouth	56103	STORA
56044	Cardiff Canton Quality Approved	56110	Croft
56045	British Steel Shelton	56112	Stainless Pioneer
56049	Robin of Templecombe 1938-2013	56114	Maltby Colliery
56050	British Steel Teeside	56115	Bassetlaw | Barry Needham
56051	Isle of Grain	56117	Wilton-Coalpower
56052	The Cardiff Rod Mill	56122	Wilton-Coalpower
56053	Sir Morgannwg Ganol / County of -	56123	Drax Power Station
	Mid Glamorgan	56124	Blue Circle Cement
56054	British Steel Llanwern	56128	West Burton Power Station
56057	British Fuels	56130	Wardley Opencast
56060	The Cardiff Rod Mill	56131	Ellington Colliery
56062	Mountsorrel	56132	Fina Energy
56063	Bardon Hill	56133	Crewe Locomotive Works
56069	Thornaby TMD	56134	Blyth Power
	Wolverhampton Steel Terminal WST	56135	Port of Tyne Authority
56073	Tremorfa Steelworks	56302	Wilson Walshe
56074	Kellingley Colliery		PECO The Railway Modeller -
56075	West Yorkshire Enterprise		2016 40 Years
56076	Blyth Power | British Steel Trostre	56312	ARTEMIS | Jeremiah Dixon -
56077	Thorpe Marsh Power Station		Son of County Durham Surveyor -
56078	Doncaster Enterprise		of the Mason-Dixon Line U.S.A.

CLASS 57

Total Built	33	Formation	Co-Co	Max T.E.	55,000 lbf
Date Built	1997-2004	Max Speed	95 mph	P.A.R.	2,025 hp
Builder	Brush Traction, Loughborough	Weight	117-120.6 t	R.A.	6
Engine	GM 12 645 E3, 2500hp	Brakes	Air	Supply	As Below

57001	47356	·	·	·	Stored	WCRC, Carnforth
57002	47322	·	·	·	Operational	DRS, Carlisle Kingmoor
57003	47317	·	·	·	Operational	DRS, Carlisle Kingmoor
57004	47347	·	·	·	Stored	DRS, MOD Longtown
57005	47350	·	·	·	Stored	WCRC, Carnforth

57006	47187	·	·	·	Stored	WCRC, Carnforth
57007	47332	·	·	·	Operational	DRS, Carlisle Kingmoor
57008	47060	·	·	·	Stored	DRS, MOD Longtown
57009	47079	·	·	·	Stored	DRS, MOD Longtown
57010	47231	·	·	·	Stored	DRS, MOD Longtown
57011	47329	·	·	·	Stored	AFS, Eastleigh
57012	47204	·	·	·	Stored	DRS, MOD Longtown
57301	47845	·	·	·	Operational	DRS, Carlisle Kingmoor
57302	47827	·	·	·	Stored	AFS, Eastleigh
57303	47705	·	·	·	Operational	DRS, Carlisle Kingmoor
57304	47807	·	·	·	Operational	DRS, Carlisle Kingmoor
57305	47822	·	·	·	Operational	Rail Operations Group, Leicester
57306	47814	·	·	·	Operational	DRS, Carlisle Kingmoor
57307	47225	·	·	·	Operational	DRS, Carlisle Kingmoor
57308	47846	·	·	·	Operational	DRS, Carlisle Kingmoor
57309	47806	·	·	·	Operational	DRS, Carlisle Kingmoor
57310	47831	·	·	·	Operational	DRS, Carlisle Kingmoor
57311	47817	·	·	·	Operational	DRS, Carlisle Kingmoor
57312	47330	·	·	·	Operational	DRS, Carlisle Kingmoor
57313	47371	·	·	·	Operational	WCRC, Carnforth
57314	47372	·	·	·	Operational	WCRC, Carnforth
57315	47234	·	·	·	Operational	WCRC, Carnforth
57316	47290	·	·	·	Operational	WCRC, Carnforth
57601	47825	·	·	·	Operational	WCRC, Carnforth
57602	47337	·	·	·	Operational	GWR, Old Oak Common
57603	47349	·	·	·	Operational	GWR, Old Oak Common
57604	47209	·	·	·	Operational	GWR, Old Oak Common
57605	47206	·	·	·	Operational	GWR, Old Oak Common

Class 57/0 (57001 - 57012) Not fitted with electric train supply
Class 57/3 (57301 - 57316) Fitted with electric train supply and retractable Dellner couplers
Class 57/6 (57601 - 57605) Fitted with electric train supply

Re-built from Class 47

Class 57 Names:

57001	Freightliner Pioneer		57306	Jeff Tracy
57002	Freightliner Phoenix | RAIL EXPRESS			Her Majesty's Railway Inspectorate
57003	Freightliner Evolution		57307	LADY PENELOPE
57004	Freightliner Quality		57308	Tin Tin | County of Staffordshire
57005	Freightliner Exellence		57309	Brains | Pride of Crewe
57006	Freightliner Reliance		57310	Kyrano | Pride of Cumbria
57007	Freightliner Bond		57311	Parker | Thunderbird
57008	Freightliner Explorer		57312	The Hood | Peter Henderson
	Telford International Freight Park 2009			Solway Princess
57009	Freightliner Venturer		57313	Tracy Island
57010	Freightliner Crusader		57314	Fire Fly
57011	Freightliner Challenger		57315	The Mole
57012	Freightliner Envoy		57316	Fab 1
57301	Scott Tracy | Goliath		57601	Sheila
57302	Virgil Tracy | Chad Varah		57602	Restormel Castle
57303	Alan Tracy | Pride of Carlisle		57603	Tintagel Castle
57304	Gordon Tracy | Pride of Cheshire		57604	PENDENNIS CASTLE
57305	John Tracy | Northern Princess		57605	Totnes Castle

CLASS 58

Total Built	50		Formation	Co-Co		Max T.E.	61,800 lbf
Date Built	1983-87		Max Speed	80 mph		P.A.R.	2,387 hp
Builder	BREL, Doncaster		Weight	130 t		R.A.	7
Engine	Paxman 12RK3ACT, 3300hp		Brakes	Air		Supply	N/A

Number	Code					Status	Location
58001		·	·	·	·	Stored	DB, Alizay, France
58002		·	·	·	·	Scrapped	EMR, Eastleigh, 2013
58003		·	·	·	·	Scrapped	EMR, Kingsbury, 2010
58004		·	·	·	·	Stored	DB, Alizay, France
58005		·	·	·	·	Stored	DB, Alizay, France
58006		·	·	·	·	Stored	DB, Alizay, France
58007		·	·	·	·	Stored	DB, Alizay, France
58008		·	·	·	·	Scrapped	Ron Hull, Rotherham, 2016
58009		·	·	·	·	Stored	DB, Alizay, France
58010		·	·	·	·	Stored	DB, Alizay, France
58011		·	·	·	·	Stored	DB, Alizay, France
58012		·	·	·	·	Stored	Battlefield Line
58013		·	·	·	·	Stored	DB, Alizay, France
58014		·	·	·	·	Scrapped	EMR, Kingsbury, 2010
58015	L54*	·	·	·	·	Operational	Transfesa, Alicante, Spain
58016		·	·	·	·	Preserved	Leicester
58017		·	·	·	·	Scrapped	EMR, Eastleigh, 2014
58018		·	·	·	·	Stored	DB, Alizay, France
58019		·	·	·	·	Scrapped	EMR, Kingsbury, 2010
58020	L43*	·	·	·	·	Operational	Transfesa, Alicante, Spain
58021		·	·	·	·	Stored	DB, Alizay, France
58022		·	·	·	·	Preserved	Peak Rail
58023		·	·	·	·	Stored	Battlefield Line
58024	L42*	·	·	·	·	Operational	Transfesa, Alicante, Spain
58025	L41*	·	·	·	·	Stored	DB, Albacete, Spain
58026		·	·	·	·	Stored	DB, Alizay, France
58027	L52*	·	·	·	·	Stored	DB, Albacete, Spain
58028		·	·	·	·	Scrapped	EMR, Kingsbury, 2010
58029	L44*	·	·	·	·	Stored	Transfesa, Alicante, Spain
58030	L46*	·	·	·	·	Operational	Transfesa, Alicante, Spain
58031	L45*	·	·	·	·	Operational	Transfesa, Alicante, Spain
58032		·	·	·	·	Stored	DB, Alizay, France
58033		·	·	·	·	Stored	DB, Alizay, France
58034		·	·	·	·	Stored	DB, Alizay, France
58035		·	·	·	·	Stored	DB, Alizay, France
58036		·	·	·	·	Stored	DB, Alizay, France
58037		·	·	·	·	Scrapped	EMR, Eastleigh, 2013
58038	5814+	·	·	·	·	Stored	DB, Alizay, France
58039	5811+	·	·	·	·	Stored	DB, Alizay, France
58040		·	·	·	·	Stored	DB, Alizay, France
58041	L36*	·	·	·	·	Stored	Transfesa, Albacete, Spain
58042		·	·	·	·	Stored	DB, Alizay, France
58043	L37*	·	·	·	·	Operational	Transfesa, Alicante, Spain
58044	5812+	·	·	·	·	Stored	DB, Metz, France
58045		·	·	·	·	Scrapped	EMR, Kingsbury, 2010
58046		·	·	·	·	Stored	DB, Alizay, France
58047	L51*	·	·	·	·	Operational	Transfesa, Alicante, Spain
58048		·	·	·	·	Stored	Battlefield Line
58049		·	·	·	·	Stored	DB, Alizay, France
58050	L53*	·	·	·	·	Stored	DB, Albacete, Spain

CLASS 58 (Continued)

* Renumbered when exported to Spain whilst on hire to GIF
+ Renumbered when exported to the Netherlands whilst on hire to ACTS

Class 58 Names:

58002	Daw Mill Colliery		58007	Drakelow Power Station
58003	Markham Colliery		58011	Worksop Depot
58005	Ironbridge Power Station		58014	Didcot Power Station
58017	Eastleigh Depot		58041	Ratcliffe Power Station
58018	High Marnham Power Station		58042	Ironbridge Power Station
58019	Shirebrook Colliery			Petrolea
58020	Doncaster Works | Caballero Ferroviaio		58043	Knottingley
58021	Hither Green Depot		58044	Oxcroft Opencast
58023	Peterborough Depot		58045	Worksop Depot -
58025	Worksop Depot - Charity Train Committee			Charity Train Committee
58032	Thoresby Colliery		58046	Thoresby Colliery | Ashfordby Mine
58034	Bassetlaw		58047	Manton Colliery
58037	Worksop Depot		58048	Coventry Colliery
58039	Rugeley Power Station		58049	Littleton Colliery
58040	Cottam Power Station		58050	Toton Traction Depot

CLASS 59

Total Built	15	Formation	Co-Co	Max T.E.	113,550 lbf
Date Built	1985-95	Max Speed	75 mph	P.A.R.	2,533 hp
Builder	General Motors, USA & Canada	Weight	121 t	R.A.	7
Engine	GM645E3C, 3300hp	Brakes	Air	Supply	N/A

59001	·	·	·	·	Operational	Mendip Rail, Merehead
59002	·	·	·	·	Operational	Mendip Rail, Merehead
59003	259003-2*	·	·	·	Operational	GBRF, Doncaster Roberts Road
59004	·	·	·	·	Operational	Mendip Rail, Merehead
59005	·	·	·	·	Operational	Mendip Rail, Merehead
59101	·	·	·	·	Operational	Mendip Rail, Merehead
59102	·	·	·	·	Operational	Mendip Rail, Merehead
59103	·	·	·	·	Operational	Mendip Rail, Merehead
59104	·	·	·	·	Operational	Mendip Rail, Merehead
59201	·	·	·	·	Operational	DB Cargo, Merehead
59202	·	·	·	·	Operational	DB Cargo, Merehead
59203	·	·	·	·	Operational	DB Cargo, Merehead
59204	·	·	·	·	Operational	DB Cargo, Merehead
59205	·	·	·	·	Operational	DB Cargo, Merehead
59206	·	·	·	·	Operational	DB Cargo, Merehead

Class 59/0 (59001 - 59005) Originally owned and operated by Foster Yeoman
Class 59/1 (59101 - 59104) Originally owned and operated by ARC
Class 59/2 (59201 - 59206) Originally owned and operated by National Power

* Renumbered when exported to work in Germany

CLASS 59 (Continued)

Class 59 Names:

59001	YEOMAN ENDEAVOUR		59201	Vale of York
59002	YEOMAN ENTERPRISE | ALAN J DAY		59202	Vale of White Horse
59003	YEOMAN HIGHLANDER			Alan Meddows Taylor -
59004	YEOMAN CHALLENGER			MD Mendip Rail Limited
	PAUL A HAMMOND		59203	Vale of Pickering
59005	KENNETH J PAINTER		59204	Vale of Glamorgan
59101	Village of Whatley		59205	Vale of Evesham
59102	Village of Chantry			L. Keith McNair
59103	Village of Mells		59206	Pride of Ferrybride
59104	Village of Great Elm			John F Yeoman Rail Pioneer

CLASS 60

Total Built	100	Formation	Co-Co	Max T.E.	106,500 lbf
Date Built	1989-93	Max Speed	60 mph	P.A.R.	2,415 hp
Builder	Brush Traction, Loughborough	Weight	130 t	R.A.	7
Engine	Mirrlees 8MB275T, 3100hp	Brakes	Air	Supply	N/A

60001	·	·	·	·	Operational	DB Cargo, Toton
60002	·	·	·	·	Operational	Colas Rail, Toton
60003	·	·	·	·	Stored	DB Cargo, Toton
60004	·	·	·	·	Stored	DB Cargo, Toton
60005	·	·	·	·	Stored	DB Cargo, Toton
60006	·	·	·	·	Stored	DB Cargo, Toton
60007	·	·	·	·	Operational	DB Cargo, Toton
60008	·	·	·	·	Stored	DB Cargo, Toton
60009	·	·	·	·	Stored	DB Cargo, Toton
60010	·	·	·	·	Stored	DB Cargo, Toton
60011	·	·	·	·	Operational	DB Cargo, Toton
60012	·	·	·	·	Stored	DB Cargo, Toton
60013	·	·	·	·	Stored	DB Cargo, Toton
60014	·	·	·	·	Stored	DB Cargo, Toton
60015	·	·	·	·	Operational	DB Cargo, Toton
60016	60500	·	·	·	Stored	DB Cargo, Toton
60017	·	·	·	·	Operational	DB Cargo, Toton
60018	·	·	·	·	Stored	DB Cargo, Toton
60019	·	·	·	·	Operational	DB Cargo, Toton
60020	·	·	·	·	Operational	DB Cargo, Toton
60021	·	·	·	·	Operational	Colas Rail, Toton
60022	·	·	·	·	Stored	DB Cargo, Toton
60023	·	·	·	·	Stored	DB Cargo, Toton
60024	·	·	·	·	Stored	DB Cargo, Toton
60025	·	·	·	·	Stored	DB Cargo, Toton
60026	·	·	·	·	Operational	Colas Rail, Toton
60027	·	·	·	·	Stored	DB Cargo, Toton
60028	·	·	·	·	Stored	DB Cargo, Crewe Electric Depot
60029	·	·	·	·	Stored	DB Cargo, Crewe Electric Depot
60030	·	·	·	·	Stored	DB Cargo, Toton
60031	·	·	·	·	Stored	DB Cargo, Toton
60032	·	·	·	·	Stored	DB Cargo, Toton
60033	·	·	·	·	Stored	DB Cargo, Toton
60034	·	·	·	·	Stored	DB Cargo, Toton
60035	·	·	·	·	Stored	DB Cargo, Toton

60036	·	·	·	·	Stored	DB Cargo, Toton
60037	·	·	·	·	Stored	DB Cargo, Toton
60038	·	·	·	·	Stored	DB Cargo, Crewe Electric Depot
60039	·	·	·	·	Operational	DB Cargo, Toton
60040	·	·	·	·	Stored	DB Cargo, Toton
60041	·	·	·	·	Stored	DB Cargo, Toton
60042	·	·	·	·	Stored	DB Cargo, Toton
60043	·	·	·	·	Stored	DB Cargo, Toton
60044	·	·	·	·	Operational	DB Cargo, Toton
60045	·	·	·	·	Stored	DB Cargo, Toton
60046	·	·	·	·	Stored	DB Cargo, Crewe Electric Depot
60047	·	·	·	·	Operational	Colas Rail, Toton
60048	·	·	·	·	Stored	DB Cargo, Toton
60049	·	·	·	·	Stored	DB Cargo, Toton
60050	·	·	·	·	Stored	DB Cargo, Toton
60051	·	·	·	·	Stored	DB Cargo, Toton
60052	·	·	·	·	Stored	DB Cargo, Toton
60053	·	·	·	·	Stored	DB Cargo, Toton
60054	·	·	·	·	Operational	DB Cargo, Toton
60055	·	·	·	·	Stored	DB Cargo, Crewe Electric Depot
60056	·	·	·	·	Operational	Colas Rail, Toton
60057	·	·	·	·	Stored	DB Cargo, Toton
60058	·	·	·	·	Stored	DB Cargo, Toton
60059	·	·	·	·	Operational	DB Cargo, Toton
60060	·	·	·	·	Stored	DB Cargo, Toton
60061	·	·	·	·	Stored	DB Cargo, Toton
60062	·	·	·	·	Stored	DB Cargo, Toton
60063	·	·	·	·	Operational	DB Cargo, Toton
60064	·	·	·	·	Stored	DB Cargo, Toton
60065	·	·	·	·	Operational	DB Cargo, Toton
60066	·	·	·	·	Operational	DB Cargo, Toton
60067	·	·	·	·	Stored	DB Cargo, Toton
60068	·	·	·	·	Stored	DB Cargo, Toton
60069	·	·	·	·	Stored	DB Cargo, Toton
60070	·	·	·	·	Stored	DB Cargo, Toton
60071	·	·	·	·	Stored	DB Cargo, Toton
60072	·	·	·	·	Stored	DB Cargo, Toton
60073	·	·	·	·	Stored	DB Cargo, Toton
60074	·	·	·	·	Operational	DB Cargo, Toton
60075	·	·	·	·	Stored	DB Cargo, Toton
60076	·	·	·	·	Operational	Colas Rail, Toton
60077	·	·	·	·	Stored	DB Cargo, Toton
60078	·	·	·	·	Stored	DB Cargo, Toton
60079	·	·	·	·	Stored	DB Cargo, Toton
60080	·	·	·	·	Stored	DB Cargo, Toton
60081	·	·	·	·	Stored	DB Cargo, Toton
60082	·	·	·	·	Stored	DB Cargo, Crewe Electric Depot
60083	·	·	·	·	Stored	DB Cargo, Toton
60084	·	·	·	·	Stored	DB Cargo, Toton
60085	·	·	·	·	Operational	Colas Rail, Toton
60086	·	·	·	·	Stored	DB Cargo, Toton
60087	·	·	·	·	Operational	Colas Rail, Toton
60088	·	·	·	·	Stored	DB Cargo, Toton
60089	·	·	·	·	Stored	DB Cargo, Toton

60090	·	·	·	·	Stored	DB Cargo, Toton
60091	·	·	·	·	Operational	DB Cargo, Toton
60092	·	·	·	·	Stored	DB Cargo, Toton
60093	·	·	·	·	Stored	DB Cargo, Toton
60094	·	·	·	·	Stored	DB Cargo, Toton
60095	·	·	·	·	Operational	Colas Rail, Toton
60096	·	·	·	·	Operational	Colas Rail, Toton
60097	·	·	·	·	Stored	DB Cargo, Toton
60098	·	·	·	·	Stored	DB Cargo, Toton
60099	·	·	·	·	Stored	DB Cargo, Toton
60100	·	·	·	·	Operational	DB Cargo, Toton

Class 60 Names:

60001	Steadfast | The Railway Observer
60002	Capability Brown | High Peak
60003	Christopher Wren
	FREIGHT TRANSPORT ASSOCIATION
60004	Lochnagar
60005	Skiddaw | BP Gas Avonmouth
60006	Great Gable | Scunthorpe Ironmaster
60007	Robert Adam | The Spirit of Tom Kendell
60008	Moel Fammau | GYPSUM QUEEN II
	Sir William McAlpine
60009	Carnedd Dafydd
60010	Pumlumon / Plynlimon
60011	Cader Idris
60012	Glyder Fawr
60013	Robert Boyle
60014	Alexander Fleming
60015	Bow Fell
60016	Langdale Pikes | RAIL MAGAZINE
60017	Arenig Fawr
	Shotton Works Centenary Year 1996
60018	Moel Siabod
60019	Wild Boar Fell | PATHFINDER TOURS -
	30 Years of Railtouring 1973-2003
	Port of Grimsby & Immingham
60020	Great Whernside | The Willows
60021	Pen Y Ghent | Star of the East
60022	Ingleborough
60023	The Cheviot
60024	Elizabeth Fry | Clitheroe Castle
60025	Joseph Lister | Caledonian Paper
60026	William Caxton
60027	Joseph Banks
60028	John Flamstead
60029	Ben Nevis
	CASTLE CEMENT Clitheroe Castle
60030	Cir Mhor
60031	Ben Lui | ABP Connect
60032	William Booth
60033	Anthony Ashley Cooper
	Tees Steel Express
60034	Carnedd Llewelyn

60035	Florence Nightingale
60036	Sgurr Na Ciche | GEFCO
60037	Helvellyn | Aberddawan Aberthaw
60038	Bidean Nam Bian | Total Oil GB
	Avesta Polarit
60039	Glastonbury Tor | Dove Holes
60040	Brecon Beacons
	The Territorial Army Centenary
60041	High Willhays
60042	Dunkery Beacon
	The Hundred of Hoo
60043	Yes Tor
60044	Aisla Craig | Dowlow
60045	Josephine Butler
	The Permanent Way Institution
60046	William Wilberforce
60047	Robert Owen
60048	Saddleback | EASTERN
60049	Scafell
60050	Roseberry Topping
60051	Mary Sommerville
60052	Goat Fell
	Glofa Twr, Last Deep Mine in -
	Wales,Tower Colliery
60053	John Reith | NORDIC TERMINAL
60054	Charles Babbage
60055	Thomas Barnardo
60056	William Beveridge
60057	Adam Smith
60058	John Howard
60059	Samuel Plimsoll
	Swinden Dalesman
60060	James Watt
60061	Alexander Graham Bell
60062	Samuel Johnson
	Stainless Pioneer
60063	James Murray
60064	Back Tor
60065	Kinder Low | Spirit of JAGUAR
60066	John Logie Baird
60067	Charles Clerk-Maxwell

CLASS 60 (Continued)

60068	Charles Darwin	60084	Cross Fell
60069	Humphry Davy | Slioch	60085	Axe Edge | MINI Pride of Oxford
60070	John Loudon McAdam	60086	Schiehallion
60071	Dorothy Garrod | Ribblehead Viaduct	60087	Slioch | Barry Needham
60072	Cairn Toul		CLIC Sargent
60073	Cairn Gorm	60088	Buachaille Etive Mor
60074	Braeriach | Teenage Spirit	60089	Arcuil | THE RAILWAY HORSE
60075	Liathach	60090	Quinag
60076	Suilven | Dunbar	60091	An Teallach | Barry Needham
60077	Canisp	60092	Reginald Munns
60078	Stac Pollaidh	60093	Jack Stirk
60079	Foinaven		Adrian Harrington 1955-2003 -
60080	Kinder Scout		Royal Navy/Burges Salmon
	Cloudside Junior School 2001	60094	Tryfan | Rugby Flyer
	Little Eaton Primary School 2002	60095	Crib Goch
	Stanley Common Primary School 2003	60096	Ben Macdui
	Bispham Drive Junior School 2004	60097	Pillar
60081	Bleaklow Hill		ABP port of Grimsby & Immingham
	ISAMBARD KINGDOM BRUNEL	60098	Charles Francis Brush
60082	Mam Tor	60099	Ben More Assynt
60083	Shining Tor	60100	Boar of Badenoch | Pride of Acton
	Mountsorrel	60500	RAIL MAGAZINE

CLASS 66

Total Built	485	Formation	Co-Co	Max T.E.	92,000 lbf
Date Built	1998-2016	Max Speed	75 mph	P.A.R.	2,480 hp
Builder	GM/EMD, Ontario, Canada	Weight	126 t	R.A.	7
Engine	GM 12N-710G3B-EC, 3200hp	Brakes	Air	Supply	N/A

66001	·	·	·	·	Operational	DB Cargo, Toton
66002	·	·	·	·	Operational	DB Cargo, Toton
66003	·	·	·	·	Operational	DB Cargo, Toton
66004	·	·	·	·	Operational	DB Cargo, Toton
66005	·	·	·	·	Operational	DB Cargo, Toton
66006	·	·	·	·	Operational	DB Cargo, Toton
66007	·	·	·	·	Operational	DB Cargo, Toton
66008	66780	·	·	·	Operational	GBRF, Doncaster Roberts Road
66009	·	·	·	·	Operational	DB Cargo, Toton
66010	·	·	·	·	Operational	Euro Cargo Rail, France
66011	·	·	·	·	Operational	DB Cargo, Toton
66012	·	·	·	·	Operational	DB Cargo, Toton
66013	·	·	·	·	Operational	DB Cargo, Toton
66014	·	·	·	·	Operational	DB Cargo, Toton
66015	·	·	·	·	Operational	DB Cargo, Toton
66016	66781	·	·	·	Operational	GBRF, Doncaster Roberts Road
66017	·	·	·	·	Operational	DB Cargo, Toton
66018	·	·	·	·	Operational	DB Cargo, Toton
66019	·	·	·	·	Operational	DB Cargo, Toton
66020	·	·	·	·	Operational	DB Cargo, Toton
66021	·	·	·	·	Operational	DB Cargo, Toton
66022	·	·	·	·	Operational	Euro Cargo Rail, France
66023	·	·	·	·	Operational	DB Cargo, Toton
66024	·	·	·	·	Operational	DB Cargo, Toton
66025	·	·	·	·	Operational	DB Cargo, Toton

66026	·	·	·	·	Operational	Euro Cargo Rail, France
66027	·	·	·	·	Operational	DB Cargo, Toton
66028	·	·	·	·	Operational	Euro Cargo Rail, France
66029	·	·	·	·	Operational	Euro Cargo Rail, France
66030	·	·	·	·	Operational	DB Cargo, Toton
66031	·	·	·	·	Operational	DB Cargo, Toton
66032	·	·	·	·	Operational	Euro Cargo Rail, France
66033	·	·	·	·	Operational	Euro Cargo Rail, France
66034	·	·	·	·	Operational	DB Cargo, Toton
66035	·	·	·	·	Operational	DB Cargo, Toton
66036	·	·	·	·	Operational	Euro Cargo Rail, France
66037	·	·	·	·	Operational	DB Cargo, Toton
66038	·	·	·	·	Operational	Euro Cargo Rail, France
66039	·	·	·	·	Operational	DB Cargo, Toton
66040	·	·	·	·	Operational	DB Cargo, Toton
66041	·	·	·	·	Operational	DB Cargo, Toton
66042	·	·	·	·	Operational	Euro Cargo Rail, France
66043	·	·	·	·	Operational	DB Cargo, Toton
66044	·	·	·	·	Operational	DB Cargo, Toton
66045	·	·	·	·	Operational	Euro Cargo Rail, France
66046	66782	·	·	·	Operational	GBRF, Doncaster Roberts Road
66047	·	·	·	·	Operational	DB Cargo, Toton
66048	·	·	·	·	Scrapped	EMD, Longport Works, 2018
66049	·	·	·	·	Operational	Euro Cargo Rail, France
66050	·	·	·	·	Operational	DB Cargo, Toton
66051	·	·	·	·	Operational	DB Cargo, Toton
66052	·	·	·	·	Operational	Euro Cargo Rail, France
66053	·	·	·	·	Operational	DB Cargo, Toton
66054	·	·	·	·	Operational	DB Cargo, Toton
66055	·	·	·	·	Operational	DB Cargo, Toton
66056	·	·	·	·	Operational	DB Cargo, Toton
66057	·	·	·	·	Operational	DB Cargo, Toton
66058	66783	·	·	·	Operational	GBRF, Doncaster Roberts Road
66059	·	·	·	·	Operational	DB Cargo, Toton
66060	·	·	·	·	Operational	DB Cargo, Toton
66061	·	·	·	·	Operational	DB Cargo, Toton
66062	·	·	·	·	Operational	Euro Cargo Rail, France
66063	·	·	·	·	Operational	DB Cargo, Toton
66064	·	·	·	·	Operational	Euro Cargo Rail, France
66065	·	·	·	·	Operational	DB Cargo, Toton
66066	·	·	·	·	Operational	DB Cargo, Toton
66067	·	·	·	·	Operational	DB Cargo, Toton
66068	·	·	·	·	Operational	DB Cargo, Toton
66069	·	·	·	·	Operational	DB Cargo, Toton
66070	·	·	·	·	Operational	DB Cargo, Toton
66071	·	·	·	·	Operational	Euro Cargo Rail, France
66072	·	·	·	·	Operational	Euro Cargo Rail, France
66073	·	·	·	·	Operational	Euro Cargo Rail, France
66074	·	·	·	·	Operational	DB Cargo, Toton
66075	·	·	·	·	Operational	DB Cargo, Toton
66076	·	·	·	·	Operational	DB Cargo, Toton
66077	·	·	·	·	Operational	DB Cargo, Toton
66078	·	·	·	·	Operational	DB Cargo, Toton
66079	·	·	·	·	Operational	DB Cargo, Toton

CLASS 66 (Continued)

66080	·	·	·	·	Operational	DB Cargo, Toton
66081	66784	·	·	·	Operational	GBRF, Doncaster Roberts Road
66082	·	·	·	·	Operational	DB Cargo, Toton
66083	·	·	·	·	Operational	DB Cargo, Toton
66084	·	·	·	·	Operational	DB Cargo, Toton
66085	·	·	·	·	Operational	DB Cargo, Toton
66086	·	·	·	·	Operational	DB Cargo, Toton
66087	·	·	·	·	Operational	DB Cargo, Toton
66088	·	·	·	·	Operational	DB Cargo, Toton
66089	·	·	·	·	Operational	DB Cargo, Toton
66090	·	·	·	·	Operational	DB Cargo, Toton
66091	·	·	·	·	Operational	DB Cargo, Toton
66092	·	·	·	·	Operational	DB Cargo, Toton
66093	·	·	·	·	Operational	DB Cargo, Toton
66094	·	·	·	·	Operational	DB Cargo, Toton
66095	·	·	·	·	Operational	DB Cargo, Toton
66096	·	·	·	·	Operational	DB Cargo, Toton
66097	·	·	·	·	Operational	DB Cargo, Toton
66098	·	·	·	·	Stored	DB Cargo, Toton
66099	·	·	·	·	Operational	DB Cargo, Toton
66100	·	·	·	·	Operational	DB Cargo, Toton
66101	·	·	·	·	Operational	DB Cargo, Toton
66102	·	·	·	·	Operational	DB Cargo, Toton
66103	·	·	·	·	Operational	DB Cargo, Toton
66104	·	·	·	·	Operational	DB Cargo, Toton
66105	·	·	·	·	Operational	DB Cargo, Toton
66106	·	·	·	·	Operational	DB Cargo, Toton
66107	·	·	·	·	Operational	DB Cargo, Toton
66108	·	·	·	·	Operational	DB Cargo, Toton
66109	·	·	·	·	Operational	DB Cargo, Toton
66110	·	·	·	·	Operational	DB Cargo, Toton
66111	·	·	·	·	Operational	DB Cargo, Toton
66112	·	·	·	·	Operational	DB Cargo, Toton
66113	·	·	·	·	Operational	DB Cargo, Toton
66114	·	·	·	·	Operational	DB Cargo, Toton
66115	·	·	·	·	Operational	DB Cargo, Toton
66116	·	·	·	·	Operational	DB Cargo, Toton
66117	·	·	·	·	Operational	DB Cargo, Toton
66118	·	·	·	·	Operational	DB Cargo, Toton
66119	·	·	·	·	Operational	DB Cargo, Toton
66120	·	·	·	·	Operational	DB Cargo, Toton
66121	·	·	·	·	Operational	DB Cargo, Toton
66122	·	·	·	·	Operational	DB Cargo, Toton
66123	·	·	·	·	Operational	Euro Cargo Rail, France
66124	·	·	·	·	Operational	DB Cargo, Toton
66125	·	·	·	·	Operational	DB Cargo, Toton
66126	·	·	·	·	Operational	DB Cargo, Toton
66127	·	·	·	·	Operational	DB Cargo, Toton
66128	·	·	·	·	Operational	DB Cargo, Toton
66129	·	·	·	·	Operational	DB Cargo, Toton
66130	·	·	·	·	Operational	DB Cargo, Toton
66131	·	·	·	·	Operational	DB Cargo, Toton
66132	66785	·	·	·	Operational	GBRF, Doncaster Roberts Road
66133	·	·	·	·	Operational	DB Cargo, Toton

66134	·	·	·	·	Operational	DB Cargo, Toton
66135	·	·	·	·	Operational	DB Cargo, Toton
66136	·	·	·	·	Operational	DB Cargo, Toton
66137	·	·	·	·	Operational	DB Cargo, Toton
66138	·	·	·	·	Operational	DB Cargo, Toton
66139	·	·	·	·	Operational	DB Cargo, Toton
66140	·	·	·	·	Operational	DB Cargo, Toton
66141	66786	·	·	·	Operational	GBRF, Doncaster Roberts Road
66142	·	·	·	·	Operational	DB Cargo, Toton
66143	·	·	·	·	Operational	DB Cargo, Toton
66144	·	·	·	·	Operational	DB Cargo, Toton
66145	·	·	·	·	Operational	DB Cargo, Toton
66146	·	·	·	·	Operational	DB Cargo, Poland
66147	·	·	·	·	Operational	DB Cargo, Toton
66148	·	·	·	·	Operational	DB Cargo, Toton
66149	·	·	·	·	Operational	DB Cargo, Toton
66150	·	·	·	·	Operational	DB Cargo, Toton
66151	·	·	·	·	Operational	DB Cargo, Toton
66152	·	·	·	·	Operational	DB Cargo, Toton
66153	·	·	·	·	Operational	DB Cargo, Poland
66154	·	·	·	·	Operational	DB Cargo, Toton
66155	·	·	·	·	Operational	DB Cargo, Toton
66156	·	·	·	·	Operational	DB Cargo, Toton
66157	·	·	·	·	Operational	DB Cargo, Poland
66158	·	·	·	·	Operational	DB Cargo, Toton
66159	·	·	·	·	Operational	DB Cargo, Poland
66160	·	·	·	·	Operational	DB Cargo, Toton
66161	·	·	·	·	Operational	DB Cargo, Toton
66162	·	·	·	·	Operational	DB Cargo, Toton
66163	·	·	·	·	Operational	DB Cargo, Poland
66164	·	·	·	·	Operational	DB Cargo, Toton
66165	·	·	·	·	Operational	DB Cargo, Toton
66166	·	·	·	·	Operational	DB Cargo, Poland
66167	·	·	·	·	Operational	DB Cargo, Toton
66168	·	·	·	·	Operational	DB Cargo, Toton
66169	·	·	·	·	Operational	DB Cargo, Toton
66170	·	·	·	·	Operational	DB Cargo, Toton
66171	·	·	·	·	Operational	DB Cargo, Toton
66172	·	·	·	·	Operational	DB Cargo, Toton
66173	·	·	·	·	Operational	DB Cargo, Poland
66174	·	·	·	·	Operational	DB Cargo, Toton
66175	·	·	·	·	Operational	DB Cargo, Toton
66176	·	·	·	·	Operational	DB Cargo, Toton
66177	·	·	·	·	Operational	DB Cargo, Toton
66178	·	·	·	·	Operational	DB Cargo, Poland
66179	·	·	·	·	Operational	Euro Cargo Rail, France
66180	·	·	·	·	Operational	DB Cargo, Poland
66181	·	·	·	·	Operational	DB Cargo, Toton
66182	·	·	·	·	Operational	DB Cargo, Toton
66183	·	·	·	·	Operational	DB Cargo, Toton
66184	66787	·	·	·	Operational	GBRF, Doncaster Roberts Road
66185	·	·	·	·	Operational	DB Cargo, Toton
66186	·	·	·	·	Operational	DB Cargo, Toton
66187	·	·	·	·	Operational	DB Cargo, Toton

CLASS 66 (Continued)

66188	·	·	·	·	Operational	DB Cargo, Toton
66189	·	·	·	·	Operational	DB Cargo, Poland
66190	·	·	·	·	Operational	Euro Cargo Rail, France
66191	·	·	·	·	Operational	Euro Cargo Rail, France
66192	·	·	·	·	Operational	DB Cargo, Toton
66193	·	·	·	·	Operational	Euro Cargo Rail, France
66194	·	·	·	·	Operational	DB Cargo, Toton
66195	·	·	·	·	Operational	Euro Cargo Rail, France
66196	·	·	·	·	Operational	DB Cargo, Poland
66197	·	·	·	·	Operational	DB Cargo, Toton
66198	·	·	·	·	Operational	DB Cargo, Toton
66199	·	·	·	·	Operational	DB Cargo, Toton
66200	·	·	·	·	Operational	DB Cargo, Toton
66201	·	·	·	·	Operational	Euro Cargo Rail, France
66202	·	·	·	·	Operational	Euro Cargo Rail, France
66203	·	·	·	·	Operational	Euro Cargo Rail, France
66204	·	·	·	·	Operational	Euro Cargo Rail, France
66205	·	·	·	·	Operational	Euro Cargo Rail, France
66206	·	·	·	·	Operational	DB Cargo, Toton
66207	·	·	·	·	Operational	DB Cargo, Toton
66208	·	·	·	·	Operational	Euro Cargo Rail, France
66209	·	·	·	·	Operational	Euro Cargo Rail, France
66210	·	·	·	·	Operational	Euro Cargo Rail, France
66211	·	·	·	·	Operational	Euro Cargo Rail, France
66212	·	·	·	·	Operational	Euro Cargo Rail, France
66213	·	·	·	·	Operational	Euro Cargo Rail, France
66214	·	·	·	·	Operational	Euro Cargo Rail, France
66215	·	·	·	·	Operational	Euro Cargo Rail, France
66216	·	·	·	·	Operational	Euro Cargo Rail, France
66217	·	·	·	·	Operational	Euro Cargo Rail, France
66218	·	·	·	·	Operational	Euro Cargo Rail, France
66219	·	·	·	·	Operational	Euro Cargo Rail, France
66220	·	·	·	·	Operational	DB Cargo, Poland
66221	·	·	·	·	Operational	DB Cargo, Toton
66222	·	·	·	·	Operational	Euro Cargo Rail, France
66223	·	·	·	·	Operational	Euro Cargo Rail, France
66224	·	·	·	·	Operational	Euro Cargo Rail, France
66225	·	·	·	·	Operational	Euro Cargo Rail, France
66226	·	·	·	·	Operational	Euro Cargo Rail, France
66227	·	·	·	·	Operational	DB Cargo, Poland
66228	·	·	·	·	Operational	Euro Cargo Rail, France
66229	·	·	·	·	Operational	Euro Cargo Rail, France
66230	·	·	·	·	Operational	DB Cargo, Toton
66231	·	·	·	·	Operational	Euro Cargo Rail, France
66232	·	·	·	·	Operational	Euro Cargo Rail, France
66233	·	·	·	·	Operational	Euro Cargo Rail, France
66234	·	·	·	·	Operational	Euro Cargo Rail, France
66235	·	·	·	·	Operational	Euro Cargo Rail, France
66236	·	·	·	·	Operational	Euro Cargo Rail, France
66237	·	·	·	·	Operational	DB Cargo, Poland
66238	66788	·	·	·	Operational	GBRF, Doncaster Roberts Road
66239	·	·	·	·	Operational	Euro Cargo Rail, France
66240	·	·	·	·	Operational	Euro Cargo Rail, France
66241	·	·	·	·	Operational	Euro Cargo Rail, France

66242	·	·	·	·	Operational	Euro Cargo Rail, France
66243	·	·	·	·	Operational	Euro Cargo Rail, France
66244	·	·	·	·	Operational	Euro Cargo Rail, France
66245	·	·	·	·	Operational	Euro Cargo Rail, France
66246	·	·	·	·	Operational	Euro Cargo Rail, France
66247	·	·	·	·	Operational	Euro Cargo Rail, France
66248	·	·	·	·	Operational	DB Cargo, Poland
66249	·	·	·	·	Operational	Euro Cargo Rail, France
66250	66789	·	·	·	Operational	GBRF, Doncaster Roberts Road
66301	·	·	·	·	Operational	DRS, Carlisle Kingmoor
66302	·	·	·	·	Operational	DRS, Carlisle Kingmoor
66303	·	·	·	·	Operational	DRS, Carlisle Kingmoor
66304	·	·	·	·	Operational	DRS, Carlisle Kingmoor
66305	·	·	·	·	Operational	DRS, Carlisle Kingmoor
66401	66733	·	·	·	Operational	GBRF, Doncaster Roberts Road
66402	66734	·	·	·	Scrapped	Loch Treig, 2012
66403	66735	·	·	·	Operational	GBRF, Doncaster Roberts Road
66404	66736	·	·	·	Operational	GBRF, Doncaster Roberts Road
66405	66737	·	·	·	Operational	GBRF, Doncaster Roberts Road
66406	66841	66742	·	·	Operational	GBRF, Doncaster Roberts Road
66407	66842	66743	·	·	Operational	GBRF, Doncaster Roberts Road
66408	66843	66744	·	·	Operational	GBRF, Doncaster Roberts Road
66409	66844	66745	·	·	Operational	GBRF, Doncaster Roberts Road
66410	66845	66746	·	·	Operational	GBRF, Doncaster Roberts Road
66411	66013*	·	·	·	Operational	Freightliner, Poland
66412	66015*	·	·	·	Operational	Freightliner, Poland
66413	·	·	·	·	Operational	Freightliner, Leeds Midland Road
66414	·	·	·	·	Operational	Freightliner, Leeds Midland Road
66415	·	·	·	·	Operational	Freightliner, Leeds Midland Road
66416	·	·	·	·	Operational	Freightliner, Leeds Midland Road
66417	66014*	·	·	·	Operational	Freightliner, Poland
66418	·	·	·	·	Operational	Freightliner, Leeds Midland Road
66419	·	·	·	·	Operational	Freightliner, Leeds Midland Road
66420	·	·	·	·	Operational	Freightliner, Leeds Midland Road
66421	·	·	·	·	Operational	DRS, Carlisle Kingmoor
66422	·	·	·	·	Operational	DRS, Carlisle Kingmoor
66423	·	·	·	·	Operational	DRS, Carlisle Kingmoor
66424	·	·	·	·	Operational	DRS, Carlisle Kingmoor
66425	·	·	·	·	Operational	DRS, Carlisle Kingmoor
66426	·	·	·	·	Operational	DRS, Carlisle Kingmoor
66427	·	·	·	·	Operational	DRS, Carlisle Kingmoor
66428	·	·	·	·	Stored	DRS, Wolverton Works
66429	·	·	·	·	Operational	DRS, Carlisle Kingmoor
66430	·	·	·	·	Operational	DRS, Carlisle Kingmoor
66431	·	·	·	·	Operational	DRS, Carlisle Kingmoor
66432	·	·	·	·	Operational	DRS, Carlisle Kingmoor
66433	·	·	·	·	Operational	DRS, Carlisle Kingmoor
66434	·	·	·	·	Operational	DRS, Carlisle Kingmoor
66501	·	·	·	·	Operational	Freightliner, Leeds Midland Road
66502	·	·	·	·	Operational	Freightliner, Leeds Midland Road
66503	·	·	·	·	Operational	Freightliner, Leeds Midland Road
66504	·	·	·	·	Operational	Freightliner, Leeds Midland Road
66505	·	·	·	·	Operational	Freightliner, Leeds Midland Road
66506	·	·	·	·	Operational	Freightliner, Leeds Midland Road

CLASS 66 (Continued)

66507	·	·	·	·	Operational	Freightliner, Leeds Midland Road
66508	·	·	·	·	Operational	Freightliner, Leeds Midland Road
66509	·	·	·	·	Operational	Freightliner, Leeds Midland Road
66510	·	·	·	·	Operational	Freightliner, Leeds Midland Road
66511	·	·	·	·	Operational	Freightliner, Leeds Midland Road
66512	·	·	·	·	Operational	Freightliner, Leeds Midland Road
66513	·	·	·	·	Operational	Freightliner, Leeds Midland Road
66514	·	·	·	·	Operational	Freightliner, Leeds Midland Road
66515	·	·	·	·	Operational	Freightliner, Leeds Midland Road
66516	·	·	·	·	Operational	Freightliner, Leeds Midland Road
66517	·	·	·	·	Operational	Freightliner, Leeds Midland Road
66518	·	·	·	·	Operational	Freightliner, Leeds Midland Road
66519	·	·	·	·	Operational	Freightliner, Leeds Midland Road
66520	·	·	·	·	Operational	Freightliner, Leeds Midland Road
66521	·	·	·	·	Scrapped	C F Booth, Rotherham, 2006
66522	·	·	·	·	Operational	Freightliner, Leeds Midland Road
66523	·	·	·	·	Operational	Freightliner, Leeds Midland Road
66524	·	·	·	·	Operational	Freightliner, Leeds Midland Road
66525	·	·	·	·	Operational	Freightliner, Leeds Midland Road
66526	·	·	·	·	Operational	Freightliner, Leeds Midland Road
66527	66016*	·	·	·	Operational	Freightliner, Poland
66528	·	·	·	·	Operational	Freightliner, Leeds Midland Road
66529	·	·	·	·	Operational	Freightliner, Leeds Midland Road
66530	66017*	·	·	·	Operational	Freightliner, Poland
66531	·	·	·	·	Operational	Freightliner, Leeds Midland Road
66532	·	·	·	·	Operational	Freightliner, Leeds Midland Road
66533	·	·	·	·	Operational	Freightliner, Leeds Midland Road
66534	·	·	·	·	Operational	Freightliner, Leeds Midland Road
66535	66018*	·	·	·	Operational	Freightliner, Poland
66536	·	·	·	·	Operational	Freightliner, Leeds Midland Road
66537	·	·	·	·	Operational	Freightliner, Leeds Midland Road
66538	·	·	·	·	Operational	Freightliner, Leeds Midland Road
66539	·	·	·	·	Operational	Freightliner, Leeds Midland Road
66540	·	·	·	·	Operational	Freightliner, Leeds Midland Road
66541	·	·	·	·	Operational	Freightliner, Leeds Midland Road
66542	·	·	·	·	Operational	Freightliner, Leeds Midland Road
66543	·	·	·	·	Operational	Freightliner, Leeds Midland Road
66544	·	·	·	·	Operational	Freightliner, Leeds Midland Road
66545	·	·	·	·	Operational	Freightliner, Leeds Midland Road
66546	·	·	·	·	Operational	Freightliner, Leeds Midland Road
66547	·	·	·	·	Operational	Freightliner, Leeds Midland Road
66548	·	·	·	·	Operational	Freightliner, Leeds Midland Road
66549	·	·	·	·	Operational	Freightliner, Leeds Midland Road
66550	·	·	·	·	Operational	Freightliner, Leeds Midland Road
66551	·	·	·	·	Operational	Freightliner, Leeds Midland Road
66552	·	·	·	·	Operational	Freightliner, Leeds Midland Road
66553	·	·	·	·	Operational	Freightliner, Leeds Midland Road
66554	·	·	·	·	Operational	Freightliner, Leeds Midland Road
66555	·	·	·	·	Operational	Freightliner, Leeds Midland Road
66556	·	·	·	·	Operational	Freightliner, Leeds Midland Road
66557	·	·	·	·	Operational	Freightliner, Leeds Midland Road
66558	·	·	·	·	Operational	Freightliner, Leeds Midland Road
66559	·	·	·	·	Operational	Freightliner, Leeds Midland Road
66560	·	·	·	·	Operational	Freightliner, Leeds Midland Road

66561	·	·	·	·	Operational	Freightliner, Leeds Midland Road
66562	·	·	·	·	Operational	Freightliner, Leeds Midland Road
66563	·	·	·	·	Operational	Freightliner, Leeds Midland Road
66564	·	·	·	·	Operational	Freightliner, Leeds Midland Road
66565	·	·	·	·	Operational	Freightliner, Leeds Midland Road
66566	·	·	·	·	Operational	Freightliner, Leeds Midland Road
66567	·	·	·	·	Operational	Freightliner, Leeds Midland Road
66568	·	·	·	·	Operational	Freightliner, Leeds Midland Road
66569	·	·	·	·	Operational	Freightliner, Leeds Midland Road
66570	·	·	·	·	Operational	Freightliner, Leeds Midland Road
66571	·	·	·	·	Operational	Freightliner, Leeds Midland Road
66572	·	·	·	·	Operational	Freightliner, Leeds Midland Road
66573	66846	·	·	·	Operational	Colas Rail, Hoo Junction
66574	66847	·	·	·	Operational	Colas Rail, Hoo Junction
66575	66848	·	·	·	Operational	Colas Rail, Hoo Junction
66576	66849	·	·	·	Operational	Colas Rail, Hoo Junction
66577	66850	·	·	·	Operational	Colas Rail, Hoo Junction
66578	66738	·	·	·	Operational	GBRF, Doncaster Roberts Road
66579	66739	·	·	·	Operational	GBRF, Doncaster Roberts Road
66580	66740	·	·	·	Operational	GBRF, Doncaster Roberts Road
66581	66741	·	·	·	Operational	GBRF, Doncaster Roberts Road
66582	66009*	·	·	·	Operational	Freightliner, Poland
66583	66010*	·	·	·	Operational	Freightliner, Poland
66584	66011*	·	·	·	Operational	Freightliner, Poland
66585	·	·	·	·	Operational	Freightliner, Leeds Midland Road
66586	66008*	·	·	·	Operational	Freightliner, Poland
66587	·	·	·	·	Operational	Freightliner, Leeds Midland Road
66588	·	·	·	·	Operational	Freightliner, Leeds Midland Road
66589	·	·	·	·	Operational	Freightliner, Leeds Midland Road
66590	·	·	·	·	Operational	Freightliner, Leeds Midland Road
66591	·	·	·	·	Operational	Freightliner, Leeds Midland Road
66592	·	·	·	·	Operational	Freightliner, Leeds Midland Road
66593	·	·	·	·	Operational	Freightliner, Leeds Midland Road
66594	·	·	·	·	Operational	Freightliner, Leeds Midland Road
66595	·	·	·	·	Operational	Freightliner, Leeds Midland Road
66596	·	·	·	·	Operational	Freightliner, Leeds Midland Road
66597	·	·	·	·	Operational	Freightliner, Leeds Midland Road
66598	·	·	·	·	Operational	Freightliner, Leeds Midland Road
66599	·	·	·	·	Operational	Freightliner, Leeds Midland Road
66601	·	·	·	·	Operational	Freightliner, Leeds Midland Road
66602	·	·	·	·	Operational	Freightliner, Leeds Midland Road
66603	·	·	·	·	Operational	Freightliner, Leeds Midland Road
66604	·	·	·	·	Operational	Freightliner, Leeds Midland Road
66605	·	·	·	·	Operational	Freightliner, Leeds Midland Road
66606	·	·	·	·	Operational	Freightliner, Leeds Midland Road
66607	·	·	·	·	Operational	Freightliner, Leeds Midland Road
66608	66603*	·	·	·	Operational	Freightliner, Poland
66609	66604*	·	·	·	Operational	Freightliner, Poland
66610	·	·	·	·	Operational	Freightliner, Leeds Midland Road
66611	66605*	·	·	·	Operational	Freightliner, Poland
66612	66606*	·	·	·	Operational	Freightliner, Poland
66613	·	·	·	·	Operational	Freightliner, Leeds Midland Road
66614	·	·	·	·	Operational	Freightliner, Leeds Midland Road
66615	·	·	·	·	Operational	Freightliner, Leeds Midland Road

66616	·	·	·	·	Operational	Freightliner, Leeds Midland Road
66617	·	·	·	·	Operational	Freightliner, Leeds Midland Road
66618	·	·	·	·	Operational	Freightliner, Leeds Midland Road
66619	·	·	·	·	Operational	Freightliner, Leeds Midland Road
66620	·	·	·	·	Operational	Freightliner, Leeds Midland Road
66621	·	·	·	·	Operational	Freightliner, Leeds Midland Road
66622	·	·	·	·	Operational	Freightliner, Leeds Midland Road
66623	·	·	·	·	Operational	Freightliner, Leeds Midland Road
66624	66602*	·	·	·	Operational	Freightliner, Poland
66625	66601*	·	·	·	Operational	Freightliner, Poland
66701	·	·	·	·	Operational	GBRF, Doncaster Roberts Road
66702	·	·	·	·	Operational	GBRF, Doncaster Roberts Road
66703	·	·	·	·	Operational	GBRF, Doncaster Roberts Road
66704	·	·	·	·	Operational	GBRF, Doncaster Roberts Road
66705	·	·	·	·	Operational	GBRF, Doncaster Roberts Road
66706	·	·	·	·	Operational	GBRF, Doncaster Roberts Road
66707	·	·	·	·	Operational	GBRF, Doncaster Roberts Road
66708	·	·	·	·	Operational	GBRF, Doncaster Roberts Road
66709	·	·	·	·	Operational	GBRF, Doncaster Roberts Road
66710	·	·	·	·	Operational	GBRF, Doncaster Roberts Road
66711	·	·	·	·	Operational	GBRF, Doncaster Roberts Road
66712	·	·	·	·	Operational	GBRF, Doncaster Roberts Road
66713	·	·	·	·	Operational	GBRF, Doncaster Roberts Road
66714	·	·	·	·	Operational	GBRF, Doncaster Roberts Road
66715	·	·	·	·	Operational	GBRF, Doncaster Roberts Road
66716	·			·	Operational	GBRF, Doncaster Roberts Road
66717	·	·	·	·	Operational	GBRF, Doncaster Roberts Road
66718	·	·	·	·	Operational	GBRF, Doncaster Roberts Road
66719	·	·	·	·	Operational	GBRF, Doncaster Roberts Road
66720	·	·	·	·	Operational	GBRF, Doncaster Roberts Road
66721	·	·	·	·	Operational	GBRF, Doncaster Roberts Road
66722	·	·	·	·	Operational	GBRF, Doncaster Roberts Road
66723	·	·	·	·	Operational	GBRF, Doncaster Roberts Road
66724	·	·	·	·	Operational	GBRF, Doncaster Roberts Road
66725	·	·	·	·	Operational	GBRF, Doncaster Roberts Road
66726	·	·	·	·	Operational	GBRF, Doncaster Roberts Road
66727	·	·	·	·	Operational	GBRF, Doncaster Roberts Road
66728	·	·	·	·	Operational	GBRF, Doncaster Roberts Road
66729	·	·	·	·	Operational	GBRF, Doncaster Roberts Road
66730	·	·	·	·	Operational	GBRF, Doncaster Roberts Road
66731	·	·	·	·	Operational	GBRF, Doncaster Roberts Road
66732	·	·	·	·	Operational	GBRF, Doncaster Roberts Road
66747	·	·	·	·	Operational	GBRF, Doncaster Roberts Road
66748	·	·	·	·	Operational	GBRF, Doncaster Roberts Road
66749	·	·	·	·	Operational	GBRF, Doncaster Roberts Road
66750	·	·	·	·	Operational	GBRF, Doncaster Roberts Road
66751	·	·	·	·	Operational	GBRF, Doncaster Roberts Road
66752	·	·	·	·	Operational	GBRF, Doncaster Roberts Road
66753	·	·	·	·	Operational	GBRF, Doncaster Roberts Road
66754	·	·	·	·	Operational	GBRF, Doncaster Roberts Road
66755	·	·	·	·	Operational	GBRF, Doncaster Roberts Road
66756	·	·	·	·	Operational	GBRF, Doncaster Roberts Road
66757	·	·	·	·	Operational	GBRF, Doncaster Roberts Road
66758	·	·	·	·	Operational	GBRF, Doncaster Roberts Road

66759	·	·	·	·	Operational	GBRF, Doncaster Roberts Road
66760	·	·	·	·	Operational	GBRF, Doncaster Roberts Road
66761	·	·	·	·	Operational	GBRF, Doncaster Roberts Road
66762	·	·	·	·	Operational	GBRF, Doncaster Roberts Road
66763	·	·	·	·	Operational	GBRF, Doncaster Roberts Road
66764	·	·	·	·	Operational	GBRF, Doncaster Roberts Road
66765	·	·	·	·	Operational	GBRF, Doncaster Roberts Road
66766	·	·	·	·	Operational	GBRF, Doncaster Roberts Road
66767	·	·	·	·	Operational	GBRF, Doncaster Roberts Road
66768	·	·	·	·	Operational	GBRF, Doncaster Roberts Road
66769	·	·	·	·	Operational	GBRF, Doncaster Roberts Road
66770	·	·	·	·	Operational	GBRF, Doncaster Roberts Road
66771	·	·	·	·	Operational	GBRF, Doncaster Roberts Road
66772	·	·	·	·	Operational	GBRF, Doncaster Roberts Road
66773	·	·	·	·	Operational	GBRF, Doncaster Roberts Road
66774	·	·	·	·	Operational	GBRF, Doncaster Roberts Road
66775	·	·	·	·	Operational	GBRF, Doncaster Roberts Road
66776	·	·	·	·	Operational	GBRF, Doncaster Roberts Road
66777	·	·	·	·	Operational	GBRF, Doncaster Roberts Road
66778	·	·	·	·	Operational	GBRF, Doncaster Roberts Road
66779	·	·	·	·	Operational	GBRF, Doncaster Roberts Road
66951	·	·	·	·	Operational	Freightliner, Leeds Midland Road
66952	·	·	·	·	Operational	Freightliner, Leeds Midland Road
66953	·	·	·	·	Operational	Freightliner, Leeds Midland Road
66954	·	·	·	·	Operational	Freightliner, Leeds Midland Road
66955	·	·	·	·	Operational	Freightliner, Leeds Midland Road
66956	·	·	·	·	Operational	Freightliner, Leeds Midland Road
66957	·	·	·	·	Operational	Freightliner, Leeds Midland Road

* Renumbered when exported to Poland

Class 66 Names:

66002	Lafarge Buddon Wood | Lafarge Quorn
66022	Lafarge Charnwood
66035	Resourceful
66042	Lafarge Buddon Wood
66048	James the Engine
66050	EWS Energy
66055	Alain Thauvette
66058	Derek Clark
66066	Geoff Spencer
66077	Benjamin Gimbert G.C.
66079	James Nightall G.C.
66152	Derek Holmes Railway Operator
66172	PAUL MELLENEY
66185	DP WORLD London Gateway
66200	RAILWAY HERITAGE COMMITTEE
66250	In Memory of Robert K Romak
66301	Kingmoor TMD
66411	Eddie the Engine
66414	James the Engine
66418	PATRIOT IN MEMORY OF FALLEN - RAILWAY EMPLOYEES

66501	Japan 2001
66502	Basford Hall Centenary 2001
66503	The RAILWAY MAGAZINE
66506	Crewe Regeneration
66526	Driver Steve Dunn (George)
66527	Don Raider
66528	Madge Elliott MBE - Borders Railway
66532	P&O Nedlloyd Atlas
66533	Hanjin Express / Senator Express
66534	OOCL Express
66540	Ruby
66552	Maltby Raider
66576	Hamburg Sud Advantage
66581	Sophie
66585	The Drax Flyer
66592	Johnson Stevens Agencies
66593	3MG Mersey Multimodal Gateway
66594	NYK Spirit of Kyoto
66597	Viridor
66601	The Hope Valley

CLASS 66 (Continued)

66612	Forth Raider		66730	Whitemoor
66614	1916 POPPY 2016		66731	interhub GB
66618	Railways Illustrated Annual Photographic -		66732	GBRF The First Decade -
	Awards Alan Barnes			1999-2009 John Smith MD
66619	Derek W Johnson MBE		66733	Cambridge PSB
66623	Bill Bolsover		66736	Wolverhampton Wanderers
66701	Railtrack Logistics | Whitemoor		66737	Lesia
66702	Blue Lightning		66738	HUDDERSFIELD TOWN
66703	Doncaster PSB 1981-2002		66739	Bluebell Railway
66704	Colchester Power Signal Box		66740	Sarah
66705	Golden Jubilee		66741	Swanage Railway
66706	Nene Valley		66742	ABP Port of Immingham
66707	Sir Sam Fay GREAT CENTRAL RAILWAY		66744	Crossrail
66708	Jayne		66745	Modern Railways First 50 Years
66709	Joseph Arnold Davies | Sorrento		66748	West Burton 50
66710	Phil Packer BRIT		66750	Bristol Panel Signal Box
66711	Sence		66751	Inspiration Delivered -
66712	Peterborough Power Signalbox			Hitachi Rail Europe
66713	Forest City		66752	The Hoosier State
66714	Cromer Lifeboat		66753	EMD Roberts Road
66715	VALOUR		66754	Northampton Saints
66716	Willesden Traincare Centre		66756	Royal Corps of Signals
	Locomotive & Carriage Institution -		66757	West Somerset Railway
	Centenary 1911-2011		66759	Chippy
66717	Good Old Boy		66760	David Gordon Harris
66718	Gwyneth Dunwoody | Sir Peter Hendy CBE		66761	Wensleydale Railway Association -
66719	METRO-LAND			25 Years 1990-2015
66720	Metronet Pathfinder		66763	Severn Valley Railway
66721	Harry Beck		66775	HMS Argyll
66722	Sir Edward Watkin		66776	Joanne
66723	Chinook		66777	Annette
66724	Drax Power Station		66778	Darius Cheskin
66725	SUNDERLAND		66779	EVENING STAR
66726	SHEFFIELD WEDNESDAY		66849	Wylam Dilly
66727	Andrew Scott CBE | Maritime One		66850	David Maidment OBE
66728	Institution of Railway Operators		66957	Stephenson Locomotive Society -
66729	DERBY COUNTY			1909-2009

CLASS 67

Total Built	30	Formation	Bo-Bo	Max T.E.	31,770 lbf
Date Built	1999-2000	Max Speed	125 mph	P.A.R.	
Builder	Alstom, Valencia, Spain	Weight	90 t	R.A.	8
Engine	GM 12N-710G3B-EC, 3200hp	Brakes	Air	Supply	Electric

67001	·	·	·	·	Stored	DB Cargo, Toton
67002	·	·	·	·	Operational	DB Cargo, Crewe Electric Depot
67003	·	·	·	·	Operational	DB Cargo, Crewe Electric Depot
67004	·	·	·	·	Stored	DB Cargo, Toton
67005	·	·	·	·	Operational	DB Cargo, Crewe Electric Depot
67006	·	·	·	·	Operational	DB Cargo, Crewe Electric Depot
67007	·	·	·	·	Operational	DB Cargo, Crewe Electric Depot
67008	·	·	·	·	Operational	DB Cargo, Crewe Electric Depot
67009	·	·	·	·	Stored	DB Cargo, Crewe Electric Depot

CLASS 67 (Continued)

67010	·	·	·	·	Operational	DB Cargo, Crewe Electric Depot
67011	·	·	·	·	Stored	DB Cargo, Crewe Electric Depot
67012	·	·	·	·	Operational	DB Cargo, Crewe Electric Depot
67013	·	·	·	·	Operational	DB Cargo, Crewe Electric Depot
67014	·	·	·	·	Operational	DB Cargo, Crewe Electric Depot
67015	·	·	·	·	Operational	DB Cargo, Crewe Electric Depot
67016	·	·	·	·	Operational	DB Cargo, Crewe Electric Depot
67017	·	·	·	·	Stored	DB Cargo, Crewe Electric Depot
67018	·	·	·	·	Operational	DB Cargo, Crewe Electric Depot
67019	·	·	·	·	Stored	DB Cargo, Toton
67020	·	·	·	·	Operational	DB Cargo, Crewe Electric Depot
67021	·	·	·	·	Operational	DB Cargo, Crewe Electric Depot
67022	·	·	·	·	Operational	DB Cargo, Crewe Electric Depot
67023	·	·	·	·	Operational	Colas Rail, Rugby
67024	·	·	·	·	Operational	DB Cargo, Crewe Electric Depot
67025	·	·	·	·	Stored	DB Cargo, Crewe Electric Depot
67026	·	·	·	·	Stored	DB Cargo, Crewe Electric Depot
67027	·	·	·	·	Operational	Colas Rail, Rugby
67028	·	·	·	·	Operational	DB Cargo, Crewe Electric Depot
67029	·	·	·	·	Operational	DB Cargo, Crewe Electric Depot
67030	·	·	·	·	Operational	DB Cargo, Crewe Electric Depot

Class 67 Names:

67001	Night Mail	67010	Unicorn	67018	Rapid	Keith Heller
67002	Special Delivery	67012	A Shropshire Lad	67023	Stella
67004	Post Haste	67013	Dyfrbont Pontcysyllte	67025	Western Star
	Cairn Gorm	67014	Thomas Telford	67026	Diamond Jubilee
67005	Queen's Messenger	67015	David J Lloyd	67027	Rising Star	Charlotte
67006	Royal Sovereign	67017	Arrow	67029	Royal Diamond

CLASS 68

Total Built	34	Formation	Bo-Bo		Max T.E.	71,260 lbf
Date Built	2012-2017	Max Speed	100 mph		P.A.R.	
Builder	Vossloh, Valencia, Spain	Weight	86 t		R.A.	7
Engine	Caterpillar C175-16, 3750hp	Brakes	Air		Supply	Electric

68001	·	·	·	·	Operational	DRS, Crewe Gresty Bridge
68002	·	·	·	·	Operational	DRS, Crewe Gresty Bridge
68003	·	·	·	·	Operational	DRS, Crewe Gresty Bridge
68004	·	·	·	·	Operational	DRS, Crewe Gresty Bridge
68005	·	·	·	·	Operational	DRS, Crewe Gresty Bridge
68006	·	·	·	·	Operational	DRS, Crewe Gresty Bridge
68007	·	·	·	·	Operational	DRS, Crewe Gresty Bridge
68008	·	·	·	·	Operational	DRS, Crewe Gresty Bridge
68009	·	·	·	·	Operational	DRS, Crewe Gresty Bridge
68010	·	·	·	·	Operational	DRS, Crewe Gresty Bridge
68011	·	·	·	·	Operational	DRS, Crewe Gresty Bridge
68012	·	·	·	·	Operational	DRS, Crewe Gresty Bridge
68013	·	·	·	·	Operational	DRS, Crewe Gresty Bridge
68014	·	·	·	·	Operational	DRS, Crewe Gresty Bridge
68015	·	·	·	·	Operational	DRS, Crewe Gresty Bridge
68016	·	·	·	·	Operational	DRS, Crewe Gresty Bridge
68017	·	·	·	·	Operational	DRS, Crewe Gresty Bridge

CLASS 68 (Continued)

68018	·	·	·	·	Operational	DRS, Crewe Gresty Bridge
68019	·	·	·	·	Operational	DRS, Crewe Gresty Bridge
68020	·	·	·	·	Operational	DRS, Crewe Gresty Bridge
68021	·	·	·	·	Operational	DRS, Crewe Gresty Bridge
68022	·	·	·	·	Operational	DRS, Crewe Gresty Bridge
68023	·	·	·	·	Operational	DRS, Crewe Gresty Bridge
68024	·	·	·	·	Operational	DRS, Crewe Gresty Bridge
68024	·	·	·	·	Operational	DRS, Crewe Gresty Bridge
68025	·	·	·	·	Operational	DRS, Crewe Gresty Bridge
68026	·	·	·	·	Operational	DRS, Crewe Gresty Bridge
68027	·	·	·	·	Operational	DRS, Crewe Gresty Bridge
68028	·	·	·	·	Operational	DRS, Crewe Gresty Bridge
68029	·	·	·	·	Operational	DRS, Crewe Gresty Bridge
68030	·	·	·	·	Operational	DRS, Crewe Gresty Bridge
68031	·	·	·	·	Operational	DRS, Crewe Gresty Bridge
68032	·	·	·	·	Operational	DRS, Crewe Gresty Bridge
68033	·	·	·	·	Operational	DRS, Crewe Gresty Bridge
68034	·	·	·	·	Operational	DRS, Crewe Gresty Bridge

Class 68 Names:

68001	Evolution	68016	Fearless	68026	Nautilus
68002	Intrepid	68017	Hornet	68027	Endeavour
68003	Astute	68018	Vigilant	68028	Splendid
68004	Rapid	68019	Brutus	68029	Destroyer
68005	Defiant	68020	Reliance	68030	Enterprise
68006	Daring	68021	Tireless	68031	Excelsior
68007	Valiant	68022	Resolution	68032	Patriot
68008	Avenger	68023	Achilles	68033	Courageous
68009	Titan	68024	Centaur	68034	Victorious
68010	Oxford Flyer	68025	Superb		

CLASS 70

Total Built	37	Formation	Co-Co	Max T.E.	122,000 lbf
Date Built	2009-2017	Max Speed	75 mph	P.A.R.	
Builder	GE, USA and Turkey*	Weight	129 t	R.A.	7
Engine	GE P616LDA1, 3820hp	Brakes	Air	Supply	N/A

70001	·	·	·	·	Stored	Freightliner, Leeds Midland Road
70002	·	·	·	·	Stored	Freightliner, Leeds Midland Road
70003	·	·	·	·	Operational	Freightliner, Leeds Midland Road
70004	·	·	·	·	Operational	Freightliner, Leeds Midland Road
70005	·	·	·	·	Operational	Freightliner, Leeds Midland Road
70006	·	·	·	·	Operational	Freightliner, Leeds Midland Road
70007	·	·	·	·	Operational	Freightliner, Leeds Midland Road
70008	·	·	·	·	Operational	Freightliner, Leeds Midland Road
70009	·	·	·	·	Stored	Freightliner, Leeds Midland Road
70010	·	·	·	·	Operational	Freightliner, Leeds Midland Road
70011	·	·	·	·	Operational	Freightliner, Leeds Midland Road
70012	·	·	·	·	Scrapped	GE, Erie, Pennsylvania, 2012
70013	·	·	·	·	Stored	Freightliner, Leeds Midland Road
70014	·	·	·	·	Operational	Freightliner, Leeds Midland Road
70015	·	·	·	·	Operational	Freightliner, Leeds Midland Road
70016	·	·	·	·	Stored	Freightliner, Leeds Midland Road

CLASS 70 (Continued)

70017	·	·	·	·	Operational	Freightliner, Leeds Midland Road
70018	·	·	·	·	Stored	Freightliner, Leeds Midland Road
70019	·	·	·	·	Operational	Freightliner, Leeds Midland Road
70020	·	·	·	·	Operational	Freightliner, Leeds Midland Road
70099	70801	·	·	·	Operational	Colas Rail, Cardiff Canton
70802	·	·	·	·	Operational	Colas Rail, Cardiff Canton
70803	·	·	·	·	Operational	Colas Rail, Cardiff Canton
70804	·	·	·	·	Operational	Colas Rail, Cardiff Canton
70805	·	·	·	·	Operational	Colas Rail, Cardiff Canton
70806	·	·	·	·	Operational	Colas Rail, Cardiff Canton
70807	·	·	·	·	Operational	Colas Rail, Cardiff Canton
70808	·	·	·	·	Operational	Colas Rail, Cardiff Canton
70809	·	·	·	·	Operational	Colas Rail, Cardiff Canton
70810	·	·	·	·	Operational	Colas Rail, Cardiff Canton
70811	·	·	·	·	Operational	Colas Rail, Cardiff Canton
70812	·	·	·	·	Operational	Colas Rail, Cardiff Canton
70813	·	·	·	·	Operational	Colas Rail, Cardiff Canton
70814	·	·	·	·	Operational	Colas Rail, Cardiff Canton
70815	·	·	·	·	Operational	Colas Rail, Cardiff Canton
70816	·	·	·	·	Operational	Colas Rail, Cardiff Canton
70817	·	·	·	·	Operational	Colas Rail, Cardiff Canton

* 70099 built in Turkey as a demonstrator loco and transferred to the UK in 2012

Class 70 Names:

70001	PowerHaul		70004	The Coal Industry Society

NOTES

CLASS 70

Total Built	3	Formation	Co-Co	Max T.E.	49,000 lbf
Date Built	1941-48	Max Speed	75 mph	P.A.R.	
Builder	SR Ashford & BR Brighton	Weight	100-105 t	R.A.	
T.M.s	6 x English Electric 245, 1470hp	Brakes	Vacuum	Supply	Steam

·	20001	CC1	·	·	Scrapped	Cashmore's, Newport, 1969
·	20002	CC2	·	·	Scrapped	Cashmore's, Newport, 1969
·	20003		·	·	Scrapped	Cohen's, Kettering, 1969

CLASS 71

Total Built	24	Formation	Bo-Bo	Max T.E.	43,000 lbf
Date Built	1958-60	Max Speed	90 mph	P.A.R.	2,552 hp
Builder	BR Doncaster Works	Weight	77 t	R.A.	6
T.M.s	4 x EE 532A, 3000hp	Brakes	Dual	Supply	Electric

71001	E5001	·	·	·	Preserved	NRM, Shildon
71002	E5002	·	·	·	Scrapped	Cashmore's, Newport, 1978
71003	E5018	E5003	·	·	Scrapped	Cashmore's, Newport, 1980
71004	E5004	·	·	·	Scrapped	BR, Doncaster Works, 1979
71005	E5020	E5005	·	·	Scrapped	Cashmore's, Newport, 1978
71006	E5022	E5006	·	·	Scrapped	Cashmore's, Newport, 1978
71007	E5007	·	·	·	Scrapped	Cashmore's, Newport, 1978
71008	E5008	·	·	·	Scrapped	Cashmore's, Newport, 1978
71009	E5009	·	·	·	Scrapped	BR, Doncaster Works, 1979
71010	E5010	·	·	·	Scrapped	BR, Doncaster Works, 1979
71011	E5011	·	·	·	Scrapped	BR, Doncaster Works, 1979
71012	E5012	·	·	·	Scrapped	Cashmore's, Newport, 1978
71013	E5013	·	·	·	Scrapped	BR, Doncaster Works, 1979
71014	E5014	·	·	·	Scrapped	BR, Doncaster Works, 1979
·	E5000	E5024*	·	·	Scrapped	Birds, Long Marston, 1978
·	E5003*	·	·	·	Scrapped	Cashmore's, Newport, 1977
·	E5005*	·	·	·	Scrapped	Cashmore's, Newport, 1977
·	E5006*	·	·	·	Scrapped	Birds, Long Marston, 1981
·	E5015*	·	·	·	Scrapped	Pounds, Fratton, 1981
·	E5016*	·	·	·	Scrapped	Cohen's, Kettering, 1977
·	E5017*	·	·	·	Scrapped	Birds, Long Marston, 1978
·	E5019*	·	·	·	Scrapped	Birds, Long Marston, 1978
·	E5021*	·	·	·	Scrapped	Birds, Long Marston, 1978
·	E5023*	·	·	·	Scrapped	BR, Doncaster Works, 1979

*Converted to electro-diesel locos in 1967/68 to become Class 74

CLASS 73

Total Built	49	Formation	Bo-Bo	Max TE(D)	36,000 lbf
Date Built	1962-67	Max Speed	90 mph	Max TE(E)	40,000 lbf
Builder	BR Eastleigh & EE, Vulcan	Weight	77 t	P.A.R.(D)	402 hp
Engine	EE 4SRKT, 600hp	Brakes	Dual	P.A.R.(E)	3,150 hp
T.M.s	EE 546/1B	Supply	Electric	R.A.	6

73001	E6001	73901	·	·	Preserved	East Lancashire Railway
73002	E6002	·	·	·	Preserved	Dean Forest Railway
73003	E6003	·	·	·	Preserved	Swindon & Cricklade Railway
73004	E6004	·	·	·	Scrapped	HNRC, Kingsbury, 2004
73005	E6005	73966	·	·	Operational	GBRF, Edinburgh Craigentinny
73006	E6006	73906	73967	·	Operational	GBRF, Edinburgh Craigentinny
73101	E6007	73100	·	·	Stored	Loram UK, Derby
73102	E6008	73212	·	·	Operational	GBRF, St Leonards Depot
73103	E6009	73970	·	·	Operational	GBRF, Edinburgh Craigentinny
73104	E6010	73951	·	·	Operational	Network Rail, Derby
73105	E6011	73969	·	·	Operational	GBRF, Edinburgh Craigentinny
73106	E6012	·	·	·	Scrapped	C F Booth, Rotherham, 2004
73107	E6013	·	·	·	Operational	GBRF, St Leonards Depot
73108	E6014	·	·	·	Scrapped	C F Booth, Rotherham, 2004
73109	E6015	·	·	·	Operational	GBRF, St Leonards Depot
73110	E6016	·	·	·	Stored	AFS, Eastleigh
73111	E6017	·	·	·	Scrapped	MRJ Phillips, Stewarts Lane 1997
73112	E6018	73213	·	·	Operational	GBRF, St Leonards Depot
73113	E6019	73211	73952	·	Operational	Network Rail, Derby
73114	E6020	·	·	·	Preserved	Battlefield Line
73115	E6021	·	·	·	Scrapped	BR, Slade Green, 1982
73116	E6022	73210	·	·	Preserved	Mid-Norfolk Railway
73117	E6023	73968	·	·	Operational	GBRF, Edinburgh Craigentinny
73118	E6024	·	·	·	Preserved	Barry Rail Centre
73119	E6025	·	·	·	Operational	GBRF, St Leonards Depot
73120	E6026	73209	73961	·	Operational	GBRF, St Leonards Depot
73121	E6028	73208	73965	·	Operational	GBRF, St Leonards Depot
73122	E6029	73207	73971	·	Operational	GBRF, Edinburgh Craigentinny
73123	E6030	73206	73963	·	Operational	GBRF, St Leonards Depot
73124	E6031	73205	73964	·	Operational	GBRF, St Leonards Depot
73125	E6032	73204	73962	·	Operational	GBRF, St Leonards Depot
73126	E6033	·	·	·	Scrapped	C F Booth, Rotherham, 2009
73127	E6034	73203	·	·	Scrapped	Sims Metals, Halesowen, 2010
73128	E6035	·	·	·	Operational	GBRF, St Leonards Depot
73129	E6036	·	·	·	Preserved	G & WR
73130	E6037	·	·	·	Preserved	Finmere Station
73131	E6038	·	·	·	Scrapped	C F Booth, Rotherham, 2004
73132	E6039	·	·	·	Scrapped	Ron Hull, Rotherham, 2016
73133	E6040	·	·	·	Operational	AFS, Eastleigh
73134	E6041	·	·	·	Stored	GBRF, Loughborough Works
73135	E6042	73235	·	·	Operational	SWR, Bournemouth
73136	E6043	·	·	·	Operational	GBRF, St Leonards Depot
73137	E6044	73202	·	·	Operational	Southern, Stewarts Lane
73138	E6045	·	·	·	Operational	Network Rail, Derby
73139	E6046	·	·	·	Stored	Loram UK, Derby
73140	E6047	·	·	·	Preserved	Spa Valley Railway
73141	E6048	·	·	·	Operational	GBRF, St Leonards Depot
73142	E6049	73201	·	·	Operational	GBRF, St Leonards Depot
·	E6027	·	·	·	Scrapped	BR, Selhurst, 1973

CLASS 73 (Continued)

Class 73/0 (73001 - 73006) Original prototype fleet built at Eastleigh Works
Class 73/1 (73101 - 73142) Production fleet built at Vulcan Foundry
Class 73/2 (73201 - 73235) Modified to become Gatwick Express dedicated locos
Class 73/9 (73901 & 73906) Modified for use on the Merseyrail network
Class 73/9 (73951 & 73952) Rebuilt with a pair of QSK19, 750 hp engines for Network Rail
Class 73/9 (73961 - 73971) Rebuilt with an MTU R43 4000, 1500 hp engine for GBRf

Class 73 Names:

73003	Sir Herbert Walker	73137	Royal Observer Corps
73004	The Bluebell Railway	73138	Poste Haste 150 YEARS OF -
73005	Mid-Hants, WATERCRESS LINE		TRAVELLING POST OFFICES
73100	Brighton Evening Argus	73141	David Gay / Ron Westwood
73101	Brighton Evening Argus | The Royal Alex'		Charlotte
73102	Airtour Suisse	73142	Broadlands
73105	Quadrant	73201	Broadlands
73107	Redhill 1844 - 1994 | SPITFIRE | Tracy	73202	Royal Observer Corps
73109	Battle of Britain 50th Anniversary		Dave Berry
	Force 'O' Weymouth		Gatwick Express
73112	University of Kent at Canterbury		Graham Stenning
73113	County of West Sussex	73204	Stewarts Lane 1860-1985
73114	Stewarts Lane Traction Maintenance Depot		Janice
73116	Selhurst	73205	London Chamber of Commerce
73117	University of Surrey		Jeanette
73118	Romney Hythe and Dymchurch Railway	73206	Gatwick Express | Lisa
73119	Kentish Mercury | Borough of Eastleigh	73207	County of East Sussex
73121	Croydon 1883 1983	73208	Croydon 1883-1983 | Kirsten
73122	County of East Sussex	73209	Alison
73123	Gatwick Express	73210	Selhurst
73124	London Chamber of Commerce	73211	County of West Sussex
73125	Stewarts Lane 1860-1985	73212	Airtour Suisse | Fiona
73126	Kent & East Sussex Railway	73213	University of Kent at Canterbury
73128	O.V.S. BULLEID C.B.E.		Rhodalyn
73129	City of Winchester	73951	Malcolm Brinded
73130	City of Portsmouth	73952	Janis Kong
73131	County of Surrey	73961	Alison
73133	The Bluebell Railway	73962	Dick Mabbutt
73134	Woking Homes 1885-1985	73963	Janice
73136	Kent Youth Music | Perseverance | Mhairi	73964	Jeanette

CLASS 74

Total Built	10	Formation	Bo-Bo	Max TE(D)	40,000 lbf
Date Built	1967-68	Max Speed	90 mph	Max TE(E)	47,500 lbf
Builder	BR Crewe Works	Weight	85 t	P.A.R.(D)	315 hp
Engine	Paxman 6YJXL, 650hp	Brakes	Dual	P.A.R.(E)	2,020 hp
T.M.s	4 x EE532A	Supply	Electric	R.A.	7

74001	E5015	E6101	·	·	Scrapped	Birds, Long Marston, 1978
74002	E5016	E6102	·	·	Scrapped	Cashmore's, Newport, 1977
74003	E5006	E6103	·	·	Scrapped	Cashmore's, Newport, 1977
74004	E5000	E5024	E6104	·	Scrapped	Birds, Long Marston, 1981
74005	E5019	E6105	·	·	Scrapped	Pounds, Fratton, 1981
74006	E5023	E6106	·	·	Scrapped	Cohen's, Kettering, 1977
74007	E5003	E6107	·	·	Scrapped	Birds, Long Marston, 1978

CLASS 74 (Continued)

74008	E5005	E6108	·	·	Scrapped	Birds, Long Marston, 1978
74009	E5017	E6109	·	·	Scrapped	Birds, Long Marston, 1978
74010	E5021	E6110	·	·	Scrapped	BR, Doncaster Works, 1979

Rebuilt from Class 71

CLASS 76

Total Built	58	Formation	Bo-Bo	Max T.E.	45,000 lbf
Date Built	1941-53	Max Speed	65 mph	P.A.R.	1,868 hp
Builder	Doncaster & Gorton Works	Weight	88 t	R.A.	8
T.M.s	MV186	Brakes	Vacuum / Dual / Air	Supply	Steam

76001	E26001		·	·	Scrapped	C F Booth, Rotherham, 1983
76002	E26002		·	·	Scrapped	C F Booth, Rotherham, 1984
76003	E26003	76036*	·	·	Scrapped	C F Booth, Rotherham, 1983
76004	E26004		·	·	Scrapped	C F Booth, Rotherham, 1984
76006	E26006		·	·	Scrapped	C F Booth, Rotherham, 1983
76007	E26007		·	·	Scrapped	C F Booth, Rotherham, 1983
76008	E26008		·	·	Scrapped	C F Booth, Rotherham, 1983
76009	E26009		·	·	Scrapped	C F Booth, Rotherham, 1983
76010	E26010		·	·	Scrapped	C F Booth, Rotherham, 1983
76011	E26011		·	·	Scrapped	C F Booth, Rotherham, 1983
76012	E26012		·	·	Scrapped	C F Booth, Rotherham, 1983
76013	E26013		·	·	Scrapped	C F Booth, Rotherham, 1983
76014	E26014		·	·	Scrapped	C F Booth, Rotherham, 1983
76015	E26015		·	·	Scrapped	C F Booth, Rotherham, 1983
76016	E26016		·	·	Scrapped	C F Booth, Rotherham, 1983
76018	E26018	76035*	·	·	Scrapped	C F Booth, Rotherham, 1983
76020	E26020		·	·	Preserved	National Railway Museum, York
76021	E26021		·	·	Scrapped	C F Booth, Rotherham, 1983
76022	E26022		·	·	Scrapped	C F Booth, Rotherham, 1983
76023	E26023		·	·	Scrapped	C F Booth, Rotherham, 1983
76024	E26024		·	·	Scrapped	C F Booth, Rotherham, 1983
76025	E26025		·	·	Scrapped	C F Booth, Rotherham, 1983
76026	E26026		·	·	Scrapped	C F Booth, Rotherham, 1983
76027	E26027		·	·	Scrapped	C F Booth, Rotherham, 1983
76028	E26028		·	·	Scrapped	C F Booth, Rotherham, 1983
76029	E26029		·	·	Scrapped	Cooper's Metals, Sheffield, 1983
76030	E26030		·	·	Scrapped	C F Booth, Rotherham, 1983
76032	E26032		·	·	Scrapped	Cooper's Metals, Sheffield, 1983
76033	E26033		·	·	Scrapped	Cooper's Metals, Sheffield, 1983
76034	E26034		·	·	Scrapped	C F Booth, Rotherham, 1983
76036	E26036	76003*	·	·	Scrapped	Vic Berry, Leicester, 1983
76037	E26037		·	·	Scrapped	Vic Berry, Leicester, 1983
76038	E26038	76050*	·	·	Scrapped	C F Booth, Rotherham, 1984
76039	E26039	76048*	·	·	Scrapped	C F Booth, Rotherham, 1984
76040	E26040		·	·	Scrapped	Vic Berry, Leicester, 1983
76041	E26041		·	·	Scrapped	C F Booth, Rotherham, 1983
76043	E26043		·	·	Scrapped	C F Booth, Rotherham, 1984
76044	E26044	76031*	·	·	Scrapped	Cooper's Metals, Sheffield, 1984
76046	E26046		·	·	Scrapped	C F Booth, Rotherham, 1983
76047	E26047		·	·	Scrapped	C F Booth, Rotherham, 1983
76048	E26048	76039*	·	·	Scrapped	C F Booth, Rotherham, 1983

CLASS 76 (Continued)

76049	E26049	·	·	·	Scrapped	C F Booth, Rotherham, 1983
76050	E26050	76038*	·	·	Scrapped	C F Booth, Rotherham, 1983
76051	E26051	·	·	·	Scrapped	C F Booth, Rotherham, 1983
76052	E26052	·	·	·	Scrapped	C F Booth, Rotherham, 1984
76053	E26053	·	·	·	Scrapped	C F Booth, Rotherham, 1983
76054	E26054	·	·	·	Scrapped	C F Booth, Rotherham, 1983
76055	E26055	·	·	·	Scrapped	C F Booth, Rotherham, 1984
76056	E26056	·	·	·	Scrapped	C F Booth, Reddish Depot, 1983
76057	E26057	·	·	·	Scrapped	C F Booth, Reddish Depot, 1983
·	E26000	6701	6000	·	Scrapped	BR, Crewe Works, 1972
·	E26005	·	·	·	Scrapped	BR, Crewe Works, 1971
·	E26017	·	·	·	Scrapped	Cashmore's, Reddish, 1971
·	E26019	·	·	·	Scrapped	BR, Crewe Works, 1972
·	E26031	·	·	·	Scrapped	BR, Crewe Works, 1972
·	E26035	·	·	·	Scrapped	Cashmore's, Reddish, 1971
·	E26042	·	·	·	Scrapped	Cashmore's, Reddish, 1971
·	E26045	·	·	·	Scrapped	BR, Crewe Works, 1972

* Renumbered for multiple working purposes after the original locos had been withdrawn

Class 76 Names:

76046	ARCHIMEDES	76051	MENTOR	76055	PROMETHEUS
76047	DIOMEDES	76052	NESTOR	76056	TRITON
76048	HECTOR	76053	PERSEUS	76057	ULYSSES
76049	JASON	76054	PLUTO	E26000	TOMMY
76050	STENTOR				

CLASS 77

Total Built	7	Formation	Co-Co	Max T.E.	45,000 lbf
Date Built	1953/54	Max Speed	90 mph	P.A.R.	2,300 hp
Builder	BR Gorton Works	Weight	102 t	R.A.	8
T.M.s	MV146	Brakes	Vacuum	Supply	Steam

·	E27000	1502	·	·	Preserved	Midland Railway Centre
·	E27001	1505	·	·	Preserved	MOSI, Manchester
·	E27002	1506	·	·	Scrapped	Tilburg Works, Netherlands, 1985
·	E27003	1501	·	·	Preserved	Werkgroep, Netherlands
·	E27004	1503	·	·	Scrapped	Tilburg Works, Netherlands, 1986
·	E27005	·	·	·	Scrapped	Tilburg Works, Netherlands, 1971
·	E27006	1504	·	·	Scrapped	Tilburg Works, Netherlands, 1986

Class 77 Names:

E27000	ELECTRA	E27003	DIANA	E27006	PANDORA
E27001	ARIADNE	E27004	JUNO		
E27002	AURORA	E27005	MINERVA		

3. AC ELECTRIC & BI-MODE LOCOMOTIVES

CLASS 81

Total Built	25	Formation	Bo-Bo	Max T.E.	50,000 lbf
Date Built	1959-64	Max Speed	100 mph	P.A.R.	4,800 hp
Builder	BRC & W, Smethwick	Weight	79 t	R.A.	6
T.M.s	4xAEI 189	Brakes	Vacuum / Dual	Supply	Electric

81001	E3001		·	·	·	Scrapped	BR, Crewe Works, 1986
81002	E3003		·	·	·	Preserved	Barrow Hill
81003	E3004		·	·	·	Scrapped	Cooper's Metals, Allerton, 1992
81004	E3005		·	·	·	Scrapped	MC Metals, Springburn, 1992
81005	E3006		·	·	·	Scrapped	Cooper's Metals, Attercliffe, 1992
81006	E3007		·	·	·	Scrapped	Cooper's Metals, Attercliffe, 1992
81007	E3008		·	·	·	Scrapped	Cooper's Metals, Attercliffe, 1992
81008	E3010		·	·	·	Scrapped	Cooper's Metals, Attercliffe, 1991
81009	E3011		·	·	·	Scrapped	Cooper's Metals, Attercliffe, 1992
81010	E3012		·	·	·	Scrapped	Cooper's Metals, Attercliffe, 1992
81011	E3013		·	·	·	Scrapped	Cooper's Metals, Attercliffe, 1991
81012	E3014		·	·	·	Scrapped	Cooper's Metals, Attercliffe, 1992
81013	E3015		·	·	·	Scrapped	Cooper's Metals, Attercliffe, 1991
81014	E3016		·	·	·	Scrapped	Cooper's Metals, Attercliffe, 1991
81015	E3017		·	·	·	Scrapped	MC Metals, Springburn, 1992
81016	E3018		·	·	·	Scrapped	BR, Crewe Works, 1985
81017	E3020		·	·	·	Scrapped	Cooper's Metals, Attercliffe, 1992
81018	E3021		·	·	·	Scrapped	MC Metals, Springburn, 1992
81019	E3022		·	·	·	Scrapped	Cooper's Metals, Attercliffe, 1991
81020	E3023		·	·	·	Scrapped	Cooper's Metals, Attercliffe, 1991
81021	E3301	E3096	·	·	·	Scrapped	MC Metals, Springburn, 1992
81022	E3302	E3097	·	·	·	Scrapped	BR, Crewe Works, 1990
·	E3002		·	·	·	Scrapped	BR, Crewe Works, 1969
·	E3009		·	·	·	Scrapped	BR, Crewe Works, 1968
·	E3019		·	·	·	Scrapped	BR, Crewe Works, 1971

CLASS 82

Total Built	10	Formation	Bo-Bo	Max T.E.	50,000 lbf
Date Built	1960-61	Max Speed	100 mph	P.A.R.	5,500 hp
Builder	Beyer Peacock, Gorton	Weight	80 t	R.A.	6
T.M.s	4xAEI 189	Brakes	Vacuum / Dual	Supply	Electric

82001	E3047	·	·	·	Scrapped	Vic Berry, Leicester, 1985
82002	E3048	·	·	·	Scrapped	Vic Berry, Leicester, 1984
82003	E3049	·	·	·	Scrapped	C F Booth, Rotherham, 1993
82004	E3050	·	·	·	Scrapped	Vic Berry, Leicester, 1984
82005	E3051	·	·	·	Scrapped	C F Booth, Rotherham, 1993
82006	E3052	·	·	·	Scrapped	Vic Berry, Leicester, 1984
82007	E3053	·	·	·	Scrapped	Vic Berry, Leicester, 1984
82008	E3054	·	·	·	Preserved	Barrow Hill
·	E3046	·	·	·	Scrapped	BR, Crewe Works, 1971
·	E3055	·	·	·	Scrapped	BR, Crewe Works, 1970

CLASS 83

Total Built	15				Formation	Bo-Bo	Max T.E.	38,000 lbf
Date Built	1960-62				Max Speed	100 mph	P.A.R.	4,400 hp
Builder	English Electric Co, Vulcan				Weight	77 t	R.A.	6
T.M.s	4xEE 535A				Brakes	Vacuum / Dual	Supply	Electric

83001	E3024	·	·	·	Scrapped	Vic Berry, Leicester, 1985
83002	E3025	·	·	·	Scrapped	Vic Berry, Leicester, 1984
83003	E3026	·	·	·	Scrapped	BR, Crewe Works, 1975
83004	E3027	·	·	·	Scrapped	BR, Willesden, 1978
83005	E3028	·	·	·	Scrapped	Vic Berry, Leicester, 1984
83006	E3029	·	·	·	Scrapped	Vic Berry, Leicester, 1984
83007	E3030	·	·	·	Scrapped	Vic Berry, Leicester, 1984
83008	E3031	·	·	·	Scrapped	Vic Berry, Leicester, 1984
83009	E3032	968023*	·	·	Scrapped	MC Metals, Springburn, 1993
83010	E3033	·	·	·	Scrapped	Vic Berry, Leicester, 1984
83011	E3034	·	·	·	Scrapped	Vic Berry, Leicester, 1984
83012	E3035	·	·	·	Preserved	Barrow Hill
83013	E3303	E3098	·	·	Scrapped	Vic Berry, Leicester, 1984
83014	E3304	E3099	·	·	Scrapped	Vic Berry, Leicester, 1984
83015	E3305	E3100	·	·	Scrapped	MC Metals, Springburn, 1993

* Converted for use as a static transformer and renumbered with ADB prefix

CLASS 84

Total Built	10				Formation	Bo-Bo	Max T.E.	50,000 lbf
Date Built	1960/61				Max Speed	100 mph	P.A.R.	4,900 hp
Builder	North British Loco Co, Glasgow				Weight	77 t	R.A.	6
T.M.s	4xGEC WT 501				Brakes	Vacuum / Dual	Supply	Electric

84001	E3036	·	·	·	Preserved	Bo'ness & Kinneil Railway
84002	E3037	·	·	·	Scrapped	Texas Metals, Hyde, 1982
84003	E3038	·	·	·	Scrapped	Vic Berry, Leicester, 1986
84004	E3039	·	·	·	Scrapped	Birds, Long Marston, 1985
84005	E3040	·	·	·	Scrapped	Birds, Long Marston, 1985
84006	E3041	·	·	·	Scrapped	Cashmore's, Crewe, 1979
84007	E3042	·	·	·	Scrapped	Cashmore's, Crewe, 1979
84008	E3043	·	·	·	Scrapped	A Hampton, Crewe, 1988
84009	E3044	968021*	·	·	Scrapped	Gwent Demolition, Margam, 1995
84010	E3045	·	·	·	Scrapped	Texas Metals, Hyde, 1982

* Converted as mobile load bank test loco and renumbered with ADB prefix

CLASS 85

Total Built	40				Formation	Bo-Bo	Max T.E.	50,000 lbf
Date Built	1961-64				Max Speed	100 mph	P.A.R.	5,100 hp
Builder	BR, Doncaster Works				Weight	83 t	R.A.	6
T.M.s	4xAEI 189				Brakes	Vacuum / Dual	Supply	Electric

85001	E3056	·	·	·	Scrapped	MC Metals, Springburn, 1989
85002	E3057	·	·	·	Scrapped	MC Metals, Springburn, 1992
85003	E3058	85113	·	·	Scrapped	MC Metals, Springburn, 1992
85004	E3059	85111	·	·	Scrapped	MC Metals, Springburn, 1992
85005	E3060	·	·	·	Scrapped	MC Metals, Springburn, 1993
85006	E3061	85101	·	·	Preserved	Barrow Hill

CLASS 85 (Continued)

85007	E3062	85112	·	·	Scrapped	MC Metals, Springburn, 1992
85008	E3063	·	·	·	Scrapped	MC Metals, Springburn, 1993
85009	E3064	85102	·	·	Scrapped	MC Metals, Springburn, 1992
85010	E3065	85103	·	·	Scrapped	MC Metals, Springburn, 1992
85011	E3066	85114	·	·	Scrapped	MC Metals, Springburn, 1993
85012	E3067	85104	·	·	Scrapped	MC Metals, Springburn, 1992
85013	E3068	·	·	·	Scrapped	MC Metals, Springburn, 1993
85014	E3069	·	·	·	Scrapped	MC Metals, Springburn, 1992
85015	E3070	·	·	·	Scrapped	MC Metals, Springburn, 1992
85016	E3071	85105	·	·	Scrapped	MC Metals, Springburn, 1992
85017	E3072	·	·	·	Scrapped	MC Metals, Springburn, 1993
85018	E3073	·	·	·	Scrapped	MC Metals, Springburn, 1992
85019	E3074	·	·	·	Scrapped	Vic Berry, Leicester, 1990
85020	E3075	·	·	·	Scrapped	MC Metals, Springburn, 1993
85021	E3076	85106	·	·	Scrapped	MC Metals, Springburn, 1992
85022	E3077	·	·	·	Scrapped	MC Metals, Springburn, 1993
85023	E3078	·	·	·	Scrapped	MC Metals, Springburn, 1992
85024	E3079	85107	·	·	Scrapped	MC Metals, Springburn, 1993
85025	E3080	·	·	·	Scrapped	Vic Berry, Leicester, 1990
85026	E3081	·	·	·	Scrapped	MC Metals, Springburn, 1993
85027	E3082	·	·	·	Scrapped	BR, Crewe Works, 1985
85028	E3083	·	·	·	Scrapped	MC Metals, Springburn, 1994
85029	E3084	·	·	·	Scrapped	MC Metals, Springburn, 1993
85030	E3085	·	·	·	Scrapped	MC Metals, Springburn, 1992
85031	E3086	·	·	·	Scrapped	MC Metals, Springburn, 1992
85032	E3087	85108	·	·	Scrapped	MC Metals, Springburn, 1992
85033	E3088	·	·	·	Scrapped	BR, Crewe Works, 1985
85034	E3089	·	·	·	Scrapped	MC Metals, Springburn, 1993
85035	E3090	85109	·	·	Scrapped	MC Metals, Springburn, 1992
85036	E3091	85110	·	·	Scrapped	MC Metals, Springburn, 1992
85037	E3092	·	·	·	Scrapped	MC Metals, Springburn, 1992
85038	E3093	·	·	·	Scrapped	MC Metals, Springburn, 1992
85039	E3094	·	·	·	Scrapped	MC Metals, Springburn, 1989
85040	E3095	·	·	·	Scrapped	MC Metals, Springburn, 1993

Class 85/0 (85001 - 85040) Standard design
Class 85/1 (85101 - 85114) Modified for freight only operations

Class 85 Names:
85101   Doncaster Plant 150 1853-2003

CLASS 86

Total Built	100	Formation	Bo-Bo	Max T.E.	58,000 lbf
Date Built	1965-66	Max Speed	100 mph	P.A.R.	5,900 hp
Builder	EE, Vulcan and BR, Doncaster	Weight	81 t	R.A.	6
T.M.s	4xAEI 282AZ	Brakes	Dual / Air	Supply	Electric

86001	E3199	86401	·	·	Operational	GBRF, Willesden
86002	E3170	86402	86602	·	Scrapped	SCD, Crewe, 2010
86003	E3115	86403	86603	·	Scrapped	C F Booth, Rotherham, 2005
86004	E3103	86404	86604	·	Operational	Freightliner, Crewe Basford Hall
86005	E3185	86405	86605	·	Operational	Freightliner, Crewe Basford Hall
86006	E3112	86406	86606	·	Scrapped	Ron Hull, Rotherham, 2007

86007	E3176	86407	86607	·	Operational	Freightliner, Crewe Basford Hall
86008	E3180	86408	86608	86501+	Operational	Freightliner, Crewe Basford Hall
86009	E3102	86409	86609	·	Operational	Freightliner, Crewe Basford Hall
86010	E3104	86410	86610	·	Operational	Freightliner, Crewe Basford Hall
86011	E3171	86311	86411	86611	Scrapped	HNRC, Crewe Works, 2005
86012	E3122	86312	86412	86612	Operational	Freightliner, Crewe Basford Hall
86013	E3128	86313	86413	86613	Operational	Freightliner, Crewe Basford Hall
86014	E3145	86314	86414	86614	Operational	Freightliner, Crewe Basford Hall
86015	E3123	86315	86415	86615	Scrapped	Ron Hull, Rotherham, 2007
86016	E3109	86316	86416	·	Scrapped	C F Booth, Rotherham, 2005
86017	E3146	86317	86417	·	Scrapped	C F Booth, Rotherham, 2004
86018	E3163	86318	86418	86618	Scrapped	C F Booth, Rotherham, 2005
86019	E3120	86319	86419	·	Scrapped	SCD, Crewe, 2003
86020	E3114	86320	86420	86620	Scrapped	Ron Hull, Rotherham, 2007
86021	E3157	86321	86421	86621	Scrapped	SCD, Crewe, 2013
86022	E3174	86322	86422	86622	Operational	Freightliner, Crewe Basford Hall
86023	E3152	86323	86423	86623	Scrapped	SCD, Crewe, 2010
86024	E3111	86324	86424	009-0~	Stored	FLOYD, Budapest, Hungary
86025	E3186	86325	86425	·	Scrapped	C F Booth, Rotherham, 2005
86026	E3195	86326	86426	·	Scrapped	C F Booth, Rotherham, 2005
86027	E3110	86327	86427	86627	Operational	Freightliner, Crewe Basford Hall
86028	E3159	86328	86428	86628	Operational	Freightliner, Crewe Basford Hall
86029	E3200	86329	86429	·	Scrapped	BR, Crewe Works, 1987
86030	E3105	86430	·	·	Scrapped	C F Booth, Rotherham, 2005
86031	E3188	86431	86631	·	Scrapped	HNRC, Crewe Works, 2005
86032	E3148	86432	86632	·	Operational	Freightliner, Crewe Basford Hall
86033	E3198	86433	86633	·	Scrapped	SCD, Crewe, 2013
86034	E3187	86434	86634	·	Scrapped	C F Booth, Rotherham, 2005
86035	E3124	86435	86635	·	Scrapped	SCD, Crewe, 2013
86036	E3160	86436	86636	·	Scrapped	C F Booth, Rotherham, 2005
86037	E3130	86437	86637	·	Operational	Freightliner, Crewe Basford Hall
86038	E3108	86438	86638	·	Operational	Freightliner, Crewe Basford Hall
86039	E3153	86439	86639	·	Operational	Freightliner, Crewe Basford Hall
86040	E3135	86256	·	·	Scrapped	Ron Hull, Rotherham, 2006
86041	E3118	86261	·	·	Scrapped	C F Booth, Rotherham, 2004
86042	E3154	86255	·	·	Scrapped	Easco, Immingham, 2002
86043	E3139	86257	·	·	Scrapped	Easco, Immingham, 2003
86044	E3136	86253	86901	·	Stored	Network Rail, Crewe Basford Hall
86045	E3137	86259	·	·	Operational	Rail Operations Group, Willesden
86046	E3140	86258	86501*	·	Scrapped	EMR, Kingsbury, 2009
86047	E3142	86254	·	·	Scrapped	C F Booth, Rotherham, 2004
86048	E3144	86260	86702	87702-4^	Operational	Bulmarket, Bulgaria
86201	E3191	86101	·	·	Operational	GBRF, Willesden
86202	E3150	86102	·	·	Scrapped	JT Landscapes, Caerwent, 2005
86203	E3143	86103	·	·	Scrapped	Easco, Immingham, 2002
86204	E3173	·	·	·	Scrapped	Easco, Immingham, 2003
86205	E3129	86503	86701	87701-6^	Operational	Bulmarket, Bulgaria
86206	E3184	·	·	·	Scrapped	Sims Metals, Cardiff, 2004
86207	E3179	·	·	·	Scrapped	Ron Hull, Rotherham, 2006
86208	E3141	·	·	·	Scrapped	SCD, Crewe, 2003
86209	E3125	·	·	·	Scrapped	Boreham Scrap Co, 2005
86210	E3190	86902	·	·	Scrapped	C F Booth, Rotherham, 2016
86211	E3147	·	·	·	Scrapped	BR, Crewe Works, 1987
86212	E3151	·	·	·	Scrapped	EMR, Kingsbury, 2011

86213	E3193	87703-2^	·	·	Operational	Bulmarket, Bulgaria
86214	E3106	·	·	·	Scrapped	Ron Hull, Rotherham, 2006
86215	E3165	005-8~	·	·	Operational	FLOYD, Hungary
86216	E3166	·	·	·	Scrapped	Easco, Immingham, 2002
86217	E3177	86504	006-6~	·	Operational	FLOYD, Hungary
86218	E3175	004-1~	·	·	Operational	FLOYD, Hungary
86219	E3196	·	·	·	Scrapped	Easco, Immingham, 2002
86220	E3156	·	·	·	Scrapped	Easco, Immingham, 2003
86221	E3132	·	·	·	Scrapped	Easco, Immingham, 2003
86222	E3131	86502	·	·	Scrapped	Easco, Immingham, 2003
86223	E3158	·	·	·	Scrapped	EMR, Kingsbury, 2011
86224	E3134	·	·	·	Scrapped	Ron Hull, Rotherham, 2006
86225	E3164	·	·	·	Scrapped	Ron Hull, Rotherham, 2006
86226	E3162	·	·	·	Scrapped	EMR, Kingsbury, 2011
86227	E3117	·	·	·	Scrapped	Ron Hull, Rotherham, 2005
86228	E3167	007-4~	·	·	Operational	FLOYD, Hungary
86229	E3119	·	·	·	Stored	Europhoenix, Long Marston
86230	E3168	·	·	·	Scrapped	EMR, Kingsbury, 2011
86231	E3126	85005-4^	·	·	Operational	Bulmarket, Bulgaria
86232	E3113	003-3~	·	·	Operational	FLOYD, Hungary
86233	E3172	86506	·	·	Stored	Bulmarket, Ruse, Bulgaria
86234	E3155	·	·	·	Stored	Bulmarket, Ruse, Bulgaria
86235	E3194	87704-0^	·	·	Operational	Bulmarket, Bulgaria
86236	E3133	·	·	·	Scrapped	Easco, Immingham, 2003
86237	E3197	·	·	·	Scrapped	Sims Metals, Cardiff, 2004
86238	E3116	·	·	·	Scrapped	Borcham Scrap Co, 2005
86239	E3169	86507	·	·	Scrapped	MRJ Phillips, Crewe, 1997
86240	E3127	·	·	·	Scrapped	Ron Hull, Rotherham, 2008
86241	E3121	86508	·	·	Scrapped	SCD, Crewe, 2003
86242	E3138	008-2~	·	·	Operational	FLOYD, Hungary
86243	E3181	·	·	·	Scrapped	C F Booth, Rotherham, 2004
86244	E3178	·	·	·	Scrapped	Easco, Immingham, 2003
86245	E3182	·	·	·	Scrapped	EMR, Kingsbury, 2010
86246	E3149	86505	·	·	Scrapped	C F Booth, Rotherham, 2018
86247	E3192	·	·	·	Scrapped	SCD, Crewe, 2015
86248	E3107	001-7~	·	·	Operational	FLOYD, Hungary
86249	E3161	·	·	·	Scrapped	JT Landscapes, Caerwent, 2005
86250	E3189	002-5~	·	·	Operational	FLOYD, Hungary
86251	E3183	·	·	·	Stored	Europhoenix, Long Marston
86252	E3101	·	·	·	Scrapped	Easco, Immingham, 2002

Class 86/0 (86001 - 86048) Standard design
Class 86/1 (86101 - 86103) Modified for Class 87 development purposes
Class 86/2 (86201 - 86261) Fitted with 282BZ traction motors and flexicoil suspension
Class 86/3 (86311 - 86329) Modified with resilient wheels
Class 86/4 (86401 - 86439) Modified RES dedicated locos
Class 86/5* (86501 - 86509) Modified for block freight operation with ETH isolated
Class 86/5+ (86501) Modified with revised gearing
Class 86/6 (86602 - 86639) Modified as Freightliner dedicated locos and restricted to 75mph
Class 86/7 (86701 - 86702) Refurbished for spot hire use
Class 86/9 (86901 - 86902) Converted as mobile load bank test locos

~Renumbered when exported to Hungary   ^Renumbered when exported to Bulgaria

Class 86 Names:

86101	Sir William A Stanier FRS	86245	Dudley Castle | Caledonian
86102	Robert A Riddles	86246	Royal Anglian Regiment
86103	Andre Chapelon	86247	Abraham Darby
86204	City of Carlisle	86248	Sir Clwyd County of Clwyd
86205	City of Lancaster	86249	County of Merseyside
86206	City of Stoke on Trent	86250	The Glasgow Herald
86207	City of Lichfield		Sheppard 100
86208	City of Chester	86251	The Birmingham Post
86209	City of Coventry	86252	The Liverpool Daily Post
86210	City of Edinburgh | C.I.T. 75th Anniversary		Sheppard 100
86211	City of Milton Keynes	86253	The Manchester Guardian
86212	Preston Guild 1328-1992	86254	William Webb Ellis
86213	Lancashire Witch	86255	Penrith Beacon
86214	Sans Pareil	86256	Pebble Mill
86215	Joseph Chamberlain | Norwich Cathedral	86257	Snowdon
	Norfolk and Norwich Festival	86258	Ben Nevis | Talyllyn The -
	The Round Tabler		First Preserved Railway
86216	Meteor	86259	Peter Pan | Greater Manchester -
86217	Comet | Halley's Comet | City University		Life & Soul of Britain | Les Ross
86218	Planet | Harold MacMillan	86260	Driver Wallace Oakes GC
	Year of Opera & Musical Theatre 1997	86261	Driver John Axon GC
	NHS 50		The Rail Charter Partnership
86219	Phoenix	86311	Airey Neave
86220	Goliath | The Round Tabler	86312	Elizabeth Garrett Anderson
86221	Vesta | BBC Look East	86315	Rotary International
86222	Fury | LLOYDS LIST 250TH ANNIVERSARY	86316	Wigan Pier
	Clothes Show Live	86328	Aldaniti
86223	Hector | Norwich Union	86401	Northampton Town
86224	Caledonian		Hertfordshire Rail Tours
86225	Hardwicke		Mons Meg
86226	Mail | Royal Mail Midlands	86405	Intercontainer
	CHARLES RENNIE MACKINTOSH	86407	Institution of Electrical Engineers
86227	Sir Henry Johnson | Golden Jubilee	86408	St John Ambulance
86228	Vulcan Heritage	86411	Airey Neave
86229	Sir John Betjeman | Lions Club International	86412	Elizabeth Garrett Anderson
86230	The Duke of Wellington	86413	County of Lancashire
86231	Starlight Express	86414	Frank Hornby
86232	Harold Macmilan	86415	Rotary International
	Norfolk and Norwich Festival	86416	Wigan Pier
86233	Laurence Olivier | ALSTOM Heritage	86417	The Kingsman
86234	J B Priestley O.M.	86419	Poste Haste 150 YEARS OF -
	Suffolk Relax. Refresh. Return		TRAVELLING POST OFFICES
86235	Novelty | Harold Macmillan | Crown Point	86421	London School of Economics
86236	Joseph Wedgewood MASTER POTTER	86425	Saint Mungo
86237	Sir Charles Halle	86426	Pride of the Nation
	University of East Anglia	86427	The Operational Society
86238	European Community	86428	Aldaniti
86239	L S Lowry	86429	THE TIMES
86240	Bishop Eric Treacy	86430	Scottish National Orchestra
86241	Glenfiddich		Saint Edmund
86242	James Kennedy GC | Colchester Castle	86432	Brookside
86243	The Boys' Brigade	86433	Wulfruna
86244	The Royal British Legion	86434	University of London

CLASS 86 (Continued)

86501	Talyllyn The First Preserved Railway		86613	County of Lancashire
86501	Crewe Basford Hall		86614	Frank Hornby
86502	LLOYDS LIST 250TH ANNIVERSARY		86615	Rotary International
86503	City of Lancaster		86620	Philip G Walton
86504	Halley's Comet		86621	London School of Economics
86505	Royal Anglian Regiment		86627	The Operational Society
86506	Laurence Olivier		86628	Aldaniti
86507	LS Lowry		86632	Brookside
86508	Glenfiddich		86633	Wulfruna
86605	Intercontainer		86634	University of London
86607	Institution of Electrical Engineers		86701	Orion
86608	St John Ambulance		86702	Cassiopeia
86611	Airey Neave		86901	CHIEF ENGINEER
86612	Elizabeth Garrett Anderson		86902	RAIL VEHICLE ENGINEERING

CLASS 87

Total Built	36	Formation	Bo-Bo		Max T.E.	58,000 lbf
Date Built	1973-75	Max Speed	110 mph		P.A.R.	7,680 hp
Builder	BREL, Crewe	Weight	83 t		R.A.	6
T.M.s	4xGEC G412AZ	Brakes	Air		Supply	Electric

87001	·	·	·	·	Preserved	National Railway Museum, York
87002	·	·	·	·	Operational	GBRF, Willesden
87003	87003-7*	·	·	·	Operational	BZK, Bulgaria
87004	87004-5*	·	·	·	Operational	BZK, Bulgaria
87005	·	·	·	·	Scrapped	JT Landscapes, Caerwent, 2005
87006	87006-0*	·	·	·	Operational	BZK, Bulgaria
87007	87007-8*	·	·	·	Operational	BZK, Bulgaria
87008	87008-9*	·	·	·	Stored	BZK, Ruse, Bulgaria
87009	87009-4*	·	·	·	Operational	Bulmarket, Bulgaria
87010	87010-2*	·	·	·	Operational	BZK, Bulgaria
87011	·	·	·	·	Scrapped	EMR, Kingsbury, 2011
87012	87012-8*	·	·	·	Operational	BZK, Bulgaria
87013	87013-6*	·	·	·	Operational	BZK, Bulgaria
87014	87014-7*	·	·	·	Stored	BZK, Sofia, Bulgaria
87015	·	·	·	·	Scrapped	JT Landscapes, Caerwent, 2005
87016	·	·	·	·	Scrapped	JT Landscapes, Caerwent, 2004
87017	87017-7*	·	·	·	Operational	Bulmarket, Bulgaria
87018	·	·	·	·	Scrapped	EMR, Kingsbury, 2010
87019	87019-3*	·	·	·	Operational	BZK, Bulgaria
87020	87020-1*	·	·	·	Operational	BZK, Bulgaria
87021	·	·	·	·	Scrapped	EMR, Kingsbury, 2010
87022	87022-7*	·	·	·	Operational	BZK, Bulgaria
87023	87023-5*	·	·	·	Operational	Bulmarket, Bulgaria
87024	·	·	·	·	Scrapped	JT Landscapes, Caerwent, 2005
87025	87025-0*	·	·	·	Operational	Bulmarket, Bulgaria
87026	87026-8*	·	·	·	Operational	BZK, Bulgaria
87027	·	·	·	·	Scrapped	EMR, Kingsbury, 2010
87028	87028-4*	·	·	·	Operational	BZK, Bulgaria
87029	87029-2*	·	·	·	Operational	BZK, Bulgaria
87030	·	·	·	·	Scrapped	EMR, Kingsbury, 2011
87031	·	·	·	·	Scrapped	EMR, Kingsbury, 2010
87032	·	·	·	·	Scrapped	EMR, Kingsbury, 2010

CLASS 87 (Continued)

87033	87033-4*	·	·	·	Operational	BZK, Bulgaria
87034	87034-2*	·	·	·	Operational	BZK, Bulgaria
87035		·	·	·	Preserved	Crewe Heritage Centre
87101		·	·	·	Scrapped	HNRC, Barrow Hill, 2002

Class 87/0 (87001 - 87035) Standard design
Class 87/1 (87101) Originally fitted with thyristor control

* Renumbered when exported to Bulgaria

Class 87 Names:

87001	STEPHENSON	Royal Scot	87019	Sir Winston Churchill
87002	Royal Soverign	The AC Locomotive Group		ACoRP Association of -
87003	Patriot			Community Rail Partnership
87004	Britannia	87020	North Briton
87005	City of London	87021	Robert The Bruce
87006	City of Glasgow	Glasgow Garden Festival	87022	Cock o' the North
	George Reynolds			Lew Adams The Black Prince
87007	City of Manchester	87023	Highland Chieftan	Velocity
87008	City of Liverpool	Royal Scot		Polmadie
87009	City of Birmingham	87024	Lord of the Isles
87010	King Arthur	Driver Tommy Farr	87025	Borderer	County of Cheshire
87011	The Black Prince	City of Wolverhampton	87026	Redgauntlet	Sir Richard Arkwright
87012	Coeur De Lion	87027	Wolf of Badenoch
	The Royal Bank of Scotland	87028	Lord President
	The Olympian	87029	Earl Marischal
87013	John O' Gaunt	87030	Black Douglas
87014	Knight of the Thistle	87031	Hal o' the Wynd	Keith Harper
87015	Howard of Effingham	87032	Kenilworth	Richard Fearn
87016	Sir Francis Drake	87033	Thane of Fife
	Willesden Intercity Depot	87034	William Shakespeare
87017	Iron Duke	87035	Rober Burns
87018	Lord Nelson	87101	STEPHENSON

CLASS 88

Total Built	10	Formation	Bo-Bo	Max T.E.	71,260 lbf
Date Built	2014 -16	Max Speed	100 mph	P.A.R.	
Builder	Vossloh, Valencia, Spain	Weight	85 t	R.A.	7
Engine	Caterpillar 12 cylinder, 950hp	Brakes	Air	Supply	Electric

88001	·	·	·	·	Operational	DRS, Crewe Gresty Bridge
88002	·	·	·	·	Operational	DRS, Crewe Gresty Bridge
88003	·	·	·	·	Operational	DRS, Crewe Gresty Bridge
88004	·	·	·	·	Operational	DRS, Crewe Gresty Bridge
88005	·	·	·	·	Operational	DRS, Crewe Gresty Bridge
88006	·	·	·	·	Operational	DRS, Crewe Gresty Bridge
88007	·	·	·	·	Operational	DRS, Crewe Gresty Bridge
88008	·	·	·	·	Operational	DRS, Crewe Gresty Bridge
88009	·	·	·	·	Operational	DRS, Crewe Gresty Bridge
88010	·	·	·	·	Operational	DRS, Crewe Gresty Bridge

CLASS 88 (Continued)

Class 88 Names:

88001	Revolution		88005	Minerva		88009	Diana
88002	Prometheus		88006	Juno		88010	Aurora
88003	Genesis		88007	Electra			
88004	Pandora		88008	Ariadne			

CLASS 89

Total Built	1	Formation	Co-Co	Max T.E.	46,100 lbf
Date Built	1987	Max Speed	125 mph	P.A.R.	7,860 hp
Builder	BREL, Crewe	Weight	104 t	R.A.	6
T.M.s	6xBrush TM2201A	Brakes	Air	Supply	Electric

89001   ·   ·   ·   ·   Preserved   Barrow Hill

Class 89 Names: 89001   Avocet

CLASS 90

Total Built	50	Formation	Bo-Bo	Max T.E.	58,000 lbf
Date Built	1987-90	Max Speed	110 mph	P.A.R.	7,860 hp
Builder	BREL, Crewe	Weight	84.5 t	R.A.	7
T.M.s	4xGEC G412CY	Brakes	Air	Supply	Electric

90001	·	·	·	·	Operational	GA, Crown Point, Norwich
90002	·	·	·	·	Operational	GA, Crown Point, Norwich
90003	·	·	·	·	Operational	GA, Crown Point, Norwich
90004	·	·	·	·	Operational	GA, Crown Point, Norwich
90005	·	·	·	·	Operational	GA, Crown Point, Norwich
90006	·	·	·	·	Operational	GA, Crown Point, Norwich
90007	·	·	·	·	Operational	GA, Crown Point, Norwich
90008	·	·	·	·	Operational	GA, Crown Point, Norwich
90009	·	·	·	·	Operational	GA, Crown Point, Norwich
90010	·	·	·	·	Operational	GA, Crown Point, Norwich
90011	·	·	·	·	Operational	GA, Crown Point, Norwich
90012	·	·	·	·	Operational	GA, Crown Point, Norwich
90013	·	·	·	·	Operational	GA, Crown Point, Norwich
90014	·	·	·	·	Operational	GA, Crown Point, Norwich
90015	·	·	·	·	Operational	GA, Crown Point, Norwich
90016	·	·	·	·	Operational	Freightliner, Crewe Basford Hall
90017	·	·	·	·	Stored	DB Cargo, Crewe Electric Depot
90018	·	·	·	·	Operational	DB Cargo, Crewe Electric Depot
90019	·	·	·	·	Operational	DB Cargo, Crewe Electric Depot
90020	·	·	·	·	Operational	DB Cargo, Crewe Electric Depot
90021	90221	·	·	·	Stored	DB Cargo, Crewe Electric Depot
90022	90222	·	·	·	Stored	DB Cargo, Crewe Electric Depot
90023	90223	·	·	·	Stored	DB Cargo, Crewe Electric Depot
90024	90224	·	·	·	Operational	DB Cargo, Crewe Electric Depot
90025	90225	90125	·	·	Stored	DB Cargo, Crewe Electric Depot
90026	90126	·	·	·	Stored	DB Cargo, Crewe Electric Depot
90027	90227	90127	·	·	Stored	DB Cargo, Crewe Electric Depot
90028	90128	·	·	·	Operational	DB Cargo, Crewe Electric Depot
90029	90129	·	·	·	Operational	DB Cargo, Crewe Electric Depot
90030	90130	·	·	·	Stored	DB Cargo, Crewe Electric Depot
90031	90131	·	·	·	Stored	DB Cargo, Crewe Electric Depot

90032	90132	·	·	·	Stored	DB Cargo, Crewe Electric Depot
90033	90233	90133	·	·	Stored	DB Cargo, Crewe Electric Depot
90034	90134	·	·	·	Operational	DB Cargo, Crewe Electric Depot
90035	90135	·	·	·	Operational	DB Cargo, Crewe Electric Depot
90036	90136	·	·	·	Stored	DB Cargo, Crewe Electric Depot
90037	90137	·	·	·	Operational	DB Cargo, Crewe Electric Depot
90038	90238	90138	·	·	Stored	DB Cargo, Crewe Electric Depot
90039	90239	90139	·	·	Operational	DB Cargo, Crewe Electric Depot
90040	90140	·	·	·	Operational	DB Cargo, Crewe Electric Depot
90041	90141	·	·	·	Operational	Freightliner, Crewe Basford Hall
90042	90142	·	·	·	Operational	Freightliner, Crewe Basford Hall
90043	90143	·	·	·	Operational	Freightliner, Crewe Basford Hall
90044	90144	·	·	·	Operational	Freightliner, Crewe Basford Hall
90045	90145	·	·	·	Operational	Freightliner, Crewe Basford Hall
90046	90146	·	·	·	Operational	Freightliner, Crewe Basford Hall
90047	90147	·	·	·	Operational	Freightliner, Crewe Basford Hall
90048	90148	·	·	·	Operational	Freightliner, Crewe Basford Hall
90049	90149	·	·	·	Operational	Freightliner, Crewe Basford Hall
90050	90150	·	·	·	Stored	Freightliner, Crewe Basford Hall

Class 90/0 (90001 - 90050) Standard design
Class 90/1 (90125 - 90150) ETH isolated
Class 90/2 (90221 - 90239) Fitted with composition brake blocks

Class 90 Names:

90001	BBC Midlands Today	Crown Point
90002	The Girls' Brigade	Mission Impossible
	Eastern Daily Press -
	SERVING NORFOLK FOR 140 YEARS
90003	THE HERALD	Raedwald of East Anglia
90004	The D'Oyly Carte Opera Company
	City of Glasgow	City of Chelmsford
90005	Financial Times	Vice-Admiral Lord Nelson
90006	High Sheriff
	Modern Railways Magazine / Roger Ford
90007	Lord Stamp	Keith Harper
	Sir John Betjeman
90008	The Birmingham Royal Ballet
	The East Anglian
90009	Royal Show	THE ECONOMIST
	Diamond Jubilee
90010	275 Railway Squadron (Volunteers)
	Bressingham Steam & Gardens
90011	The Chartered Institute of Transport
	West Coast Rail 250
	Let's Go East of England
	East Anglian Daily Times Suffolk & Proud
90012	Glasgow Cultural Capital of Europe
	British Transport Police
	Royal Anglian Regiment
90013	The Law Society	The Evening Star
90014	The Liverpool Phil
	Driver Tom Clark OBE
	Norfolk and Norwich Festival

00016	BBC North West
	The International Brigades Spain
	Colchester Castle
90017	Rail Express Systems -
	Quality Assured
90018	The Pride of Bellshill
90019	Penny Black
90020	Colonel Bill Cockburn CBE TD
	Sir Michael Heron
	Collingwood
	Multimodal
90022	Freightconnection
90026	Crewe International Electric -
	Maintenance Depot
90027	Allerton T&RS Depot -
	Quality Approved
90028	Vrachtverbinding
	Hertfordshire Railtours
90029	Frachtverbindungen
	The Institution of Civil Engineers
90030	Crewe Locomotive Works
90031	Intercontainer
	The Railway Chidren Partnership
90032	Cerestar
90035	Crewe Basford Hall
90036	Driver Jack Mills
90037	Spirit of Dagenham
90040	The Railway Mission
90043	Freightliner Coatbridge

90126	Crewe Electric Depot Quality Approved		90131	Intercontainer
	Crewe International Electric -		90132	Cerestar
	Maintenance Depot		90135	Crewe Basford Hall
90127	Allerton T&RS Depot Quality Approved		90143	Freightliner Coatbridge
90128	Vrachtverbinding		90222	Freightconnection
90129	Frachtverbindungen		90227	Allerton T&RS Depot -
90130	Fretconnection			Quality Approved

CLASS 91

Total Built	31	Formation	Bo-Bo	Max T.E.	43,000 lbf
Date Built	1988-91	Max Speed	125 mph	P.A.R.	6,300 hp
Builder	BREL, Crewe	Weight	84 t	R.A.	7
T.M.s	4xGEC G426AZ	Brakes	Air	Supply	Electric

91001	91101	·	·	·	Operational	LNER, Bounds Green, London
91002	91102	·	·	·	Operational	LNER, Bounds Green, London
91003	91103	·	·	·	Operational	LNER, Bounds Green, London
91004	91104	·	·	·	Operational	LNER, Bounds Green, London
91005	91105	·	·	·	Operational	LNER, Bounds Green, London
91006	91106	·	·	·	Operational	LNER, Bounds Green, London
91007	91107	·	·	·	Operational	LNER, Bounds Green, London
91008	91108	·	·	·	Operational	LNER, Bounds Green, London
91009	91109	·	·	·	Operational	LNER, Bounds Green, London
91010	91110	·	·	·	Operational	LNER, Bounds Green, London
91011	91111	·	·	·	Operational	LNER, Bounds Green, London
91012	91112	·	·	·	Operational	LNER, Bounds Green, London
91013	91113	·	·	·	Operational	LNER, Bounds Green, London
91014	91114	·	·	·	Operational	LNER, Bounds Green, London
91015	91115	·	·	·	Operational	LNER, Bounds Green, London
91016	91116	·	·	·	Operational	LNER, Bounds Green, London
91017	91117	·	·	·	Operational	LNER, Bounds Green, London
91018	91118	·	·	·	Operational	LNER, Bounds Green, London
91019	91119	·	·	·	Operational	LNER, Bounds Green, London
91020	91120	·	·	·	Operational	LNER, Bounds Green, London
91021	91121	·	·	·	Operational	LNER, Bounds Green, London
91022	91122	·	·	·	Operational	LNER, Bounds Green, London
91023	91132	·	·	·	Operational	LNER, Bounds Green, London
91024	91124	·	·	·	Operational	LNER, Bounds Green, London
91025	91125	·	·	·	Operational	LNER, Bounds Green, London
91026	91126	·	·	·	Operational	LNER, Bounds Green, London
91027	91127	·	·	·	Operational	LNER, Bounds Green, London
91028	91128	·	·	·	Operational	LNER, Bounds Green, London
91029	91129	·	·	·	Operational	LNER, Bounds Green, London
91030	91130	·	·	·	Operational	LNER, Bounds Green, London
91031	91131	·	·	·	Operational	LNER, Bounds Green, London

Class 91 Names:

91001	Swallow		91007	Ian Allan | Skyfall
91002	Durham Cathedral		91008	Thomas Cook
91003	THE SCOTSMAN		91009	Saint Nicholas | The Samaritans
91004	The Red Arrows | Grantham		91010	Northern Rock
91005	Royal Air Force Regiment		91011	Terence Cuneo
91006	East Lothian		91012	County of Cambridgeshire

CLASS 91 (Continued)

91013	Sir Michael Faraday		91111	Terence Cuneo
	County of North Yorkshire			For the Fallen
91014	Northern Electric | Saint Mungo Cathedral		91112	County of Cambridgeshire
91015	Holyrood		91113	County of North Yorkshire
91017	Commonwealth Institute | City of Leeds		91114	Saint Mungo Cathedral
91018	Robert Louis Stevenson			Durham Cathedral
	Bradford Film Festival		91115	Holyrood | Blaydon Races
91019	Scottish Enterprise | County of Tyne & Wear		91116	Strathclyde
91021	Royal Armouries		91117	Cancer Research UK
	Archbishop Thomas Cranmer			WEST RIDING LIMITED
91022	Robert Adley | Double Trigger		91118	Bradford Film Festival
91024	Reverend W Awdry		91119	County of Tyne & Wear
91025	BBC Radio 1 FM | Berwick upon Tweed			Bounds Green Intercity Depot -
91026	Voice of the North | York Minster			1977-2017
91027	Great North Run		91120	Royal Armouries
91028	Guide Dog | Peterborough Cathedral		91121	Archbishop Thomas Cranmer
91029	Queen Elizabeth II		91122	Double Trigger
91030	Palace of Holyroodhouse			Tam the Gun
91031	Sir Henry Royce | County of Northumberland		91124	Reverend W Awdry
91101	City of London | FLYING SCOTSMAN		91125	Berwick upon Tweed
91102	Durham Cathedral | City of York		91126	York Minster
91103	County of Lincolnshire		91126	Darlington Hippodrome
91104	Grantham		91127	Edinburgh Castle
91105	County Durham		91128	Peterborough Cathedral
91106	East Lothian			INTERCITY 50
91107	Newark on Trent | SKYFALL		91129	Queen Elizabeth II
91108	City of Leeds		91130	City of Newcastle
91109	The Samaritans | Sir Bobby Robson			Lord Mayor of Newcastle
91110	David Livingstone		91131	County of Northumberland
	BATTLE OF BRITAIN MEMORIAL FLIGHT		91132	City of Durham

CLASS 92

Total Built	46	Formation	Co-Co	Max T.E.	90,000 lbf
Date Built	1993-96	Max Speed	90 mph	P.A.R.	6,700 hp
Builder	Brush Traction, Loughborough	Weight	126 t	R.A.	8
T.M.s	6xBrush 6FRA 7059B	Brakes	Air	Supply	Electric

92001	472 002-1*	·	·	·	Operational	DB Cargo, Romania
92002	472 003-9*	·	·	·	Operational	DB Cargo, Romania
92003		·	·	·	Stored	DB Cargo, Dollands Moor
92004		·	·	·	Stored	DB Cargo, Crewe Electric Depot
92005	472 005-4*	·	·	·	Operational	DB Cargo, Romania
92006		·	·	·	Stored	GBRF, Loughborough Works
92007		·	·	·	Stored	DB Cargo, Crewe Electric Depot
92008		·	·	·	Stored	DB Cargo, Crewe Electric Depot
92009		·	·	·	Stored	DB Cargo, Crewe Electric Depot
92010		·	·	·	Operational	GBRF, Willesden
92011		·	·	·	Operational	DB Cargo, Crewe Electric Depot
92012	472 001-3*	·	·	·	Operational	DB Cargo, Romania
92013		·	·	·	Stored	DB Cargo, Crewe Electric Depot
92014		·	·	·	Operational	GBRF, Willesden
92015		·	·	·	Operational	DB Cargo, Crewe Electric Depot
92016		·	·	·	Stored	DB Cargo, Crewe Electric Depot

92017	·	·	·	·	Stored	DB Cargo, Crewe Electric Depot
92018	·	·	·	·	Operational	GBRF, Willesden
92019	·	·	·	·	Operational	DB Cargo, Crewe Electric Depot
92020	·	·	·	·	Stored	GBRF, Loughborough Works
92021	·	·	·	·	Stored	GBRF, Coquelles, France
92022	·	·	·	·	Stored	DB Cargo, Dollands Moor
92023	·	·	·	·	Operational	GBRF, Willesden
92024	472 004-7*	·	·	·	Operational	DB Cargo, Romania
92025	025-1+	·	·	·	Operational	DB Cargo, Bulgaria
92026	·	·	·	·	Stored	DB Cargo, Dollands Moor
92027	027-7+	·	·	·	Operational	DB Cargo, Bulgaria
92028	·	·	·	·	Operational	GBRF, Willesden
92029	·	·	·	·	Stored	DB Cargo, Crewe Electric Depot
92030	030-1+	·	·	·	Operational	DB Cargo, Bulgaria
92031	·	·	·	·	Stored	DB Cargo, Crewe Electric Depot
92032	·	·	·	·	Operational	GBRF, Willesden
92033	·	·	·	·	Operational	GBRF, Willesden
92034	034-3+	·	·	·	Operational	DB Cargo, Bulgaria
92035	·	·	·	·	Stored	DB Cargo, Crewe Electric Depot
92036	·	·	·	·	Operational	DB Cargo, Crewe Electric Depot
92037	·	·	·	·	Stored	DB Cargo, Crewe Electric Depot
92038	·	·	·	·	Operational	GBRF, Willesden
92039	472 006-2*	·	·	·	Operational	DB Cargo, Romania
92040	·	·	·	·	Stored	GBRF, Coquelles, France
92041	·	·	·	·	Stored	DB Cargo, Crewe Electric Depot
92042	·	·	·	·	Operational	DB Cargo, Crewe Electric Depot
92043	·	·	·	·	Operational	GBRF, Willesden
92044	·	·	·	·	Operational	GBRF, Willesden
92045	·	·	·	·	Stored	GBRF, Loughborough Works
92046	·	·	·	·	Stored	GBRF, Loughborough Works

* Renumbered when exported to Romania   + Renumbered when exported to Bulgaria

Class 92 Names:

92001	Victor Hugo	92016	Brahms	92032	Cesar Franck
	Mircea Eliade	92017	Shakespeare		IMechE Railway -
92002	H.G. Wells		Bart the Engine		Division
	Lucian Blaga	92018	Stendhal	92033	Berlioz
92003	Beethoven	92019	Wagner	92034	Kipling
92004	Jane Austen	92020	Milton	92035	Mendelssohn
92005	Mozart	92021	Purcell	92036	Bertolt Brecht
	Emil Cioran	92022	Charles Dickens	92037	Sullivan
92006	Louis Armand	92023	Ravel	92038	Voltaire
92007	Schubert	92024	J S Bach	92039	Johann Strauss
92008	Jules Verne		Marin Preda		Eugen Ionescu
92009	Elgar | Marco Polo	92025	Oscar Wilde	92040	Goethe
92010	Moliere	92026	Britten	92041	Vaughan Williams
92011	Handel	92027	George Eliot	92042	Honegger
92012	Thomas Hardy	92028	Saint Saens	92043	Debussy
	Mihai Eminescu	92029	Dante	92044	Couperin
92013	Puccini	92030	De Falla | Ashford	92045	Chaucer
92014	Emile Zola	92031	Institute of Logistics -	92046	Sweelinck
92015	D H Lawrence		& Transport		

MaK 0001 - 0005

Total Built	5	Formation	Bo-Bo	Max T.E.	68,600 lbf
Date Built	1991/92	Max Speed	100 km/h	P.A.R.	1,012 hp
Builder	Mak, Kiel, Germany	Weight	90 t	R.A.	CT Only
Engine	MTU 12V 396TC13, 1275 hp	Brakes	Air	Supply	N/A

0001	·	·	·	·	Operational	Eurotunnel, Coquelles, France
0002	·	·	·	·	Operational	Eurotunnel, Coquelles, France
0003	·	·	·	·	Operational	Eurotunnel, Coquelles, France
0004	·	·	·	·	Operational	Eurotunnel, Coquelles, France
0005	·	·	·	·	Operational	Eurotunnel, Coquelles, France

MaK 0006 - 0010

Total Built	5	Formation	Bo-Bo	Max T.E.	65,200 lbf
Date Built	1990/91	Max Speed	120 km/h	P.A.R.	1,012 hp
Builder	Mak, Kiel, Germany	Weight	80 t	R.A.	CT Only
Engine	MTU 12V 396TC13, 1580 hp	Brakes	Air	Supply	N/A

0006	6456	·	·	·	Operational	Eurotunnel, Coquelles, France
0007	6457	·	·	·	Operational	Eurotunnel, Coquelles, France
0008	6450	·	·	·	Operational	Eurotunnel, Coquelles, France
0009	6451	·	·	·	Operational	Eurotunnel, Coquelles, France
0010	6447	·	·	·	Operational	Eurotunnel, Coquelles, France

Re built from Netherlands Railways Class 6400

HUNSLET/SCHOMA 0031 - 0042

Total Built	12	Formation	0-4-0	Max T.E.	
Date Built	1989/90	Max Speed	50 km/h	P.A.R.	
Builder	Hunslet Engine Co, Leeds	Weight		R.A.	
Engine	Deutz, 200 hp	Brakes	Air	Supply	N/A

0031	·	·	·	·	Operational	Eurotunnel, Coquelles, France
0032	·	·	·	·	Operational	Eurotunnel, Coquelles, France
0033	·	·	·	·	Operational	Eurotunnel, Coquelles, France
0034	·	·	·	·	Operational	Eurotunnel, Coquelles, France
0035	·	·	·	·	Operational	Eurotunnel, Coquelles, France
0036	·	·	·	·	Operational	Eurotunnel, Coquelles, France
0037	·	·	·	·	Operational	Eurotunnel, Coquelles, France
0038	·	·	·	·	Operational	Eurotunnel, Coquelles, France
0039	·	·	·	·	Operational	Eurotunnel, Coquelles, France
0040	·	·	·	·	Operational	Eurotunnel, Coquelles, France
0041	·	·	·	·	Operational	Eurotunnel, Coquelles, France
0042	·	·	·	·	Operational	Eurotunnel, Coquelles, France

Re-built to 1435mm gauge by Schoma in 1993-94

Names:

0031	FRANCES	0035	MARY	0039	PACITA
0032	ELISABETH	0036	LAURENCE	0040	JILL
0033	SILKE	0037	LYDIE	0041	KIM
0034	AMANDA	0038	JENNY	0042	NICOLE

CLASS 9 (Le Shuttle)

Total Built	58	Formation	Bo-Bo-Bo	Max T.E.	90,000 lbf
Date Built	1993-2002	Max Speed	100 mph	P.A.R.	
Builder	Brush Traction, Loughborough	Weight	136 t	R.A.	CT Only
T.M.s	6xABB 6PH	Brakes	Air	Supply	Electric

9001	9801	·	·	·	Operational	Eurotunnel, Coquelles, France
9002	9802	·	·	·	Operational	Eurotunnel, Coquelles, France
9003	9803	·	·	·	Operational	Eurotunnel, Coquelles, France
9004	9804	·	·	·	Operational	Eurotunnel, Coquelles, France
9005		·	·	·	Operational	Eurotunnel, Coquelles, France
9006	9806	·	·	·	Operational	Eurotunnel, Coquelles, France
9007		·	·	·	Operational	Eurotunnel, Coquelles, France
9008	9808	·	·	·	Operational	Eurotunnel, Coquelles, France
9009	9809	·	·	·	Operational	Eurotunnel, Coquelles, France
9010	9810	·	·	·	Operational	Eurotunnel, Coquelles, France
9011		·	·	·	Operational	Eurotunnel, Coquelles, France
9012	9812	·	·	·	Operational	Eurotunnel, Coquelles, France
9013		·	·	·	Operational	Eurotunnel, Coquelles, France
9014	9814	·	·	·	Operational	Eurotunnel, Coquelles, France
9015		·	·	·	Operational	Eurotunnel, Coquelles, France
9016	9816	·	·	·	Operational	Eurotunnel, Coquelles, France
9017	9817	·	·	·	Stored	Eurotunnel, Coquelles, France
9018		·	·	·	Operational	Eurotunnel, Coquelles, France
9019	9819	·	·	·	Operational	Eurotunnel, Coquelles, France
9020	9820	·	·	·	Operational	Eurotunnel, Coquelles, France
9021	9821	·	·	·	Operational	Eurotunnel, Coquelles, France
9022		·	·	·	Operational	Eurotunnel, Coquelles, France
9023	9823	·	·	·	Operational	Eurotunnel, Coquelles, France
9024		·	·	·	Operational	Eurotunnel, Coquelles, France
9025	9825	·	·	·	Operational	Eurotunnel, Coquelles, France
9026		·	·	·	Operational	Eurotunnel, Coquelles, France
9027	9827	·	·	·	Operational	Eurotunnel, Coquelles, France
9028	9828	·	·	·	Operational	Eurotunnel, Coquelles, France
9029		·	·	·	Operational	Eurotunnel, Coquelles, France
9031	9831	·	·	·	Operational	Eurotunnel, Coquelles, France
9032	9832	·	·	·	Operational	Eurotunnel, Coquelles, France
9033		·	·	·	Operational	Eurotunnel, Coquelles, France
9034	9834	·	·	·	Operational	Eurotunnel, Coquelles, France
9035	9835	·	·	·	Operational	Eurotunnel, Coquelles, France
9036		·	·	·	Operational	Eurotunnel, Coquelles, France
9037		·	·	·	Operational	Eurotunnel, Coquelles, France
9038	9838	·	·	·	Operational	Eurotunnel, Coquelles, France
9040	9840	·	·	·	Operational	Eurotunnel, Coquelles, France
9101	9711	·	·	·	Operational	Eurotunnel, Coquelles, France
9102	9712	·	·	·	Operational	Eurotunnel, Coquelles, France
9103	9713	·	·	·	Operational	Eurotunnel, Coquelles, France
9104	9714	·	·	·	Operational	Eurotunnel, Coquelles, France
9105	9715	·	·	·	Operational	Eurotunnel, Coquelles, France
9106	9716	·	·	·	Operational	Eurotunnel, Coquelles, France
9107	9717	·	·	·	Operational	Eurotunnel, Coquelles, France
9108	9718	·	·	·	Operational	Eurotunnel, Coquelles, France
9109	9719	·	·	·	Operational	Eurotunnel, Coquelles, France
9110	9720	·	·	·	Operational	Eurotunnel, Coquelles, France
9111	9721	·	·	·	Operational	Eurotunnel, Coquelles, France
9112	9722	·	·	·	Operational	Eurotunnel, Coquelles, France

9113	9723	·	·	·	Operational	Eurotunnel, Coquelles, France
9701	·	·	·	·	Operational	Eurotunnel, Coquelles, France
9702	·	·	·	·	Operational	Eurotunnel, Coquelles, France
9703	·	·	·	·	Operational	Eurotunnel, Coquelles, France
9704	·	·	·	·	Operational	Eurotunnel, Coquelles, France
9705	·	·	·	·	Operational	Eurotunnel, Coquelles, France
9706	·	·	·	·	Operational	Eurotunnel, Coquelles, France
9707	·	·	·	·	Operational	Eurotunnel, Coquelles, France

Class 9/0 (9001 - 9040) Standard design
Class 9/1 (9101 - 9113) Designated as freight only
Class 9/7 (9701 - 9707) Designated as freight only with increased power 9,510hp
Class 9/8 (9801 - 9838) Modified Class 9/0 with increased power 9,510hp

Names:

9005	JESSYE NORMAN		9806	REGINE CRESPIN
9007	DAME JOAN SUTHERLAND		9808	ELISABETH SODERSTROM
9011	JOSE VAN DAM		9809	FRANCOISE POLLET
9013	MARIA CALLAS		9810	JEAN-PHILIPPE COURTIS
9015	LOTSCHBERG 1913		9812	LUCIANO PAVAROTTI
9018	WILHELMENIA FERNANDEZ		9814	LUCIA POPP
9022	DAME JANET BAKER		9816	WILLARD WHITE
9024	GOTTHARD 1882		9817	JOSE CARRERAS
9025	JUNGFRAUJOCH 1912		9819	MARIA EWING
9026	FURKATUNNEL 1982		9820	NICOLAI GHIAROV
9029	THOMAS ALLEN		9821	TERESA BERGANZA
9031	PLACIDO DOMINGO		9823	DAME ELISABETH LEGGE-
9033	MONTSERRAT CABALLE			SCHWARZKOPF
9036	ALAIN FONDARY		9827	BARBARA HENDRICKS
9037	GABRIEL BACQUIER		9828	DAME KIRI TE KANAWA
9801	LESLEY GARRETT		9832	RENTAWA TEBALDI
9802	STUART BURROWS		9834	MIRELLA FRENI
9803	BENJAMIN LUXON		9835	NICOLAI GEDDA
9804	VICTORIA DE LOS ANGELES		9838	HILDEGARD BEHRENS

NOTES

---

5. UNCLASSIFIED LOCOMOTIVES

Main Line Diesel Locomotives

British Railways Type 4

Total Built	1	Formation	2-D-2	Max T.E.	25,000 lbf
Date Built	1952	Max Speed	84 mph	P.A.R.	2,000 hp
Builder	BR Derby Works	Weight	122 t	R.A.	
Engine	4 Paxman 12RPH, 2040hp	Brakes	Vacuum	Supply	Steam

10100	·	·	·	·	Scrapped	BR, Derby Works, 1960

North British Type 1

Total Built	1	Formation	Bo-Bo	Max T.E.	34,500 lbf
Date Built	1950	Max Speed	70 mph	P.A.R.	827 hp
Builder	North British Loco Co, Glasgow	Weight	71 t	R.A.	4
Engine	Paxman 16RPHXL, 827 hp	Brakes	Vacuum	Supply	Steam

10800	800	·	·	·	Scrapped	Loughborough Works, 1976

Rebuilt by Brush Traction in 1962

English Electric Type 3

Total Built	2	Formation	Co-Co	Max T.E.	41,400 lbf
Date Built	1947/48	Max Speed	93 mph	P.A.R.	1,600 hp
Builder	English Electric Co, Vulcan	Weight	132 t	R.A.	9
Engine	English Electric 16SVT, 1600 hp	Brakes	Vacuum	Supply	Steam

10000	·	·	·	·	Scrapped	Cashmore's, Great Bridge, 1968
10001	·	·	·	·	Scrapped	Cox & Danks, North Acton, 1968

English Electric Type 3/4

Total Built	3	Formation	1Co-Co1	Max T.E.	48,000 lbf
Date Built	1950-54	Max Speed	90 mph	P.A.R.	1,300 hp
Builder	BR Ashford & Brighton Works	Weight	135 t	R.A.	6
Engine	English Electric 16SVT, 1750 hp	Brakes	Vacuum	Supply	Steam

10201	·	·	·	·	Scrapped	Cashmore's, Great Bridge, 1968
10202	·	·	·	·	Scrapped	Cashmore's, Great Bridge, 1968
10203	·	·	·	·	Scrapped	Cashmore's, Great Bridge, 1968

BRC&W Type 4

Total Built	1	Formation	Co-Co	Max T.E.	55,000 lbf
Date Built	1962	Max Speed	100 mph	P.A.R.	2,750 hp
Builder	BRC&W, Smethwick	Weight	116 t	R.A.	7
Engine	Sulzer 8LDA28-C, 2750 hp	Brakes	Vacuum	Supply	Steam

D0260	·	·	·	·	Scrapped	Wards, Beighton, 1965

Clayton Type 3

Total Built	1	Formation	Bo-Bo	Max T.E.	
Date Built	1962/63	Max Speed	90 mph	P.A.R.	
Builder	Clayton Co, Derby	Weight	57 t	R.A.	
Engine	Rolls Royce 4xC8TFL, 1500 hp	Brakes	Vacuum	Supply	Steam

DHP1 · · · · Scrapped Clayton Co, Derby, 1967

DELTIC

Total Built	1	Formation	Co-Co	Max T.E.	52,500 lbf
Date Built	1955	Max Speed	106 mph	P.A.R.	3,300 hp
Builder	English Electric Co Preston	Weight	108 t	R.A.	
Engine	Napier Deltic 2xD18-25, 1650 hp	Brakes	Vacuum	Supply	Steam

DP1 · · · · Preserved National Railway Museum, York

English Electric Type 4

Total Built	1	Formation	Co-Co	Max T.E.	50,000 lbf
Date Built	1962	Max Speed	90 mph	P.A.R.	2,700 hp
Builder	English Electric Co, Vulcan	Weight	107 t	R.A.	6
Engine	English Electric 16CSVT, 2700 hp	Brakes	Dual	Supply	Steam

DP2 · · · · Scrapped Vulcan, Newton-le-Willows, 1970

Brush Type 5

Total Built	1	Formation	Co-Co	Max T.E.	61,000 lbf
Date Built	1968	Max Speed	110 mph	P.A.R.	3,353 hp
Builder	Brush Traction, Loughborough	Weight	135 t	R.A.	
Engine	Sulzer 16LVA24, 4000 hp	Brakes	Dual	Supply	

HS4000 · · · · Scrapped Russia, 1993

Gas Turbine Locomotives

GT1

Total Built	1	Formation	A1A-A1A	Max T.E.	31,500 lbf
Date Built	1949	Max Speed	90 mph	P.A.R.	2,500 hp
Builder	Brown, Boveri, Switzerland	Weight	117 t	R.A.	
Engine	Gas Turbine, 2500 hp	Brakes	Vacuum	Supply	Steam

18000 · · · · Preserved Didcot Railway Centre

GT2

Total Built	1	Formation	Co-Co	Max T.E.	60,500 lbf
Date Built	1951	Max Speed	90 mph	P.A.R.	2,400 hp
Builder	Metropolitan Vickers, Manchester	Weight	131 t	R.A.	
Engine	Gas Turbine	Brakes	Vacuum	Supply	Steam

18100 E1000 E2001 · · Scrapped Cashmore's, Great Bridge, 1972

Rebuilt as a 25kv AC electric locomotive in 1959

GT3

Total Built	1	Formation	4-6-0	Max T.E.	38,000 lbf
Date Built	1958-61	Max Speed	90 mph	P.A.R.	2,750 hp
Builder	English Electric Co, Vulcan	Weight	81 t	R.A.	
Engine	EM27L, Gas Turbine, 2750 hp	Brakes	Vacuum	Supply	Steam

GT3	·	·	·	·	Scrapped	Wards, Salford, 1966

Electric Locomotives

ES1

Total Built	2	Formation	Bo-Bo	Max T.E.	
Date Built	1903	Max Speed	25 mph	P.A.R.	
Builder	North Eastern Railway	Weight		R.A.	
T.M.s		Brakes		Supply	

26500	1	6480	4075	·	Scrapped	NRM, Shildon
26501	2	6481	·	·	Scrapped	W Willoughby, Choppington 1966

EB1

Total Built	2	Formation	Bo-Bo	Max T.E.	
Date Built	1915-20	Max Speed	45 mph	P.A.R.	
Builder	North Eastern Railway	Weight		R.A.	
T.M.s		Brakes		Supply	

26502	3	6490	·	·	Scrapped	Wanty & Co, Sheffield, 1951
26503	4	6491	·	·	Scrapped	Wanty & Co, Sheffield, 1951
26504	5	6492	·	·	Scrapped	BR, Darlington Works, 1964
26505	6	6493	·	·	Scrapped	Wanty & Co, Sheffield, 1951
26506	7	6494	·	·	Scrapped	Wanty & Co, Sheffield, 1951
26507	8	6495	·	·	Scrapped	Wanty & Co, Sheffield, 1951
26508	9	6496	·	·	Scrapped	Wanty & Co, Sheffield, 1951
26509	10	6497	·	·	Scrapped	Wanty & Co, Sheffield, 1951
26510	11	6498	·	·	Scrapped	BR, Doncaster Works, 1964
26511	12	6499	·	·	Scrapped	Wanty & Co, Sheffield, 1951

EE1

Total Built	1	Formation	Bo-Bo	Max T.E.	
Date Built	1922	Max Speed	45 mph	P.A.R.	
Builder	North Eastern Railway	Weight		R.A.	
T.M.s		Brakes		Supply	

26660	13	6999	·	·	Scrapped	Wanty & Co, Sheffield, 1951

Shunting Locomotives

D1/1 0-4-0

D2950	11500	·	·	·	Scrapped	Thyssen Ltd, Llanelli, 1983
D2951	11501	·	·	·	Scrapped	C F Booth, Rotherham, 1968
D2952	11502	·	·	·	Scrapped	Slag Reduction Co, Ickles, 1967

D1/3 0-4-0

D2957	11507	·	·	·	Scrapped	Slag Reduction Co, Ickles, 1967
D2958	11508	·	·	·	Scrapped	C F Booth, Rotherham, 1984

D2/1 0-4-0

D2700	11700	·	·	·	Scrapped	BR, Darlington Works, 1964
D2701	11701	·	·	·	Scrapped	Drapers, Hull, 1967
D2702	11702	·	·	·	Scrapped	Drapers, Hull, 1967
D2703	11703	·	·	·	Scrapped	Shipbreaking, Faslane, 1968
D2704	11704	·	·	·	Scrapped	Arnott Young, Carmyle, 1967
D2705	11705	·	·	·	Scrapped	Connels, Coatbridge, 1967
D2706	11706	·	·	·	Scrapped	Slag Reduction Co, Ickles, 1967
D2707	11707	·	·	·	Scrapped	Slag Reduction Co, Ickles, 1967

D2/7 0-6-0

D2500	11116	·	·	·	Scrapped	C F Booth, Rotherham, 1968
D2501	11117	·	·	·	Scrapped	Slag Reduction Co, Ickles, 1967
D2502	11118	·	·	·	Scrapped	C F Booth, Rotherham, 1968
D2503	11119	·	·	·	Scrapped	C F Booth, Rotherham, 1968
D2504	11120	·	·	·	Scrapped	C F Booth, Rotherham, 1968
D2505	11144	·	·	·	Scrapped	C F Booth, Rotherham, 1968
D2506	11145	·	·	·	Scrapped	Steelbreaking, Chesterfield, 1970
D2507	11146	·	·	·	Scrapped	Slag Reduction Co, Ickles, 1967
D2508	11147	·	·	·	Scrapped	C F Booth, Rotherham, 1968
D2509	11148	·	·	·	Scrapped	C F Booth, Rotherham, 1968

D2/10 0-4-0

D2708	11708	·	·	·	Scrapped	Slag Reduction Co, Ickles, 1967
D2709	11709	·	·	·	Scrapped	Slag Reduction Co, Ickles, 1967
D2710	11710	·	·	·	Scrapped	Slag Reduction Co, Ickles, 1967
D2711	11711	·	·	·	Scrapped	Slag Reduction Co, Ickles, 1967
D2712	11712	·	·	·	Scrapped	Slag Reduction Co, Ickles, 1967
D2713	11713	·	·	·	Scrapped	Slag Reduction Co, Ickles, 1967
D2714	11714	·	·	·	Scrapped	Slag Reduction Co, Ickles, 1967
D2715	11715	·	·	·	Scrapped	Slag Reduction Co, Ickles, 1967
D2716	11716	·	·	·	Scrapped	Slag Reduction Co, Ickles, 1967
D2717	11717	·	·	·	Scrapped	Argosy Salvage, Shettleston 1967
D2718	11718	·	·	·	Scrapped	Argosy Salvage, Shettleston 1967
D2719	11719	·	·	·	Scrapped	Slag Reduction Co, Ickles, 1967
D2720	·	·	·	·	Scrapped	Connels, Coatbridge, 1971
D2721	·	·	·	·	Scrapped	Argosy Salvage, Shettleston 1967

D2722	·	·	·	·	Scrapped	Slag Reduction Co, Ickles, 1967
D2723	·	·	·	·	Scrapped	Connels, Coatbridge, 1967
D2724	·	·	·	·	Scrapped	Slag Reduction Co, Ickles, 1967
D2725	·	·	·	·	Scrapped	Machinery & Scrap Wishaw, 1967
D2726	·	·	·	·	Scrapped	P Woods, Queenborough, 1971
D2727	·	·	·	·	Scrapped	Slag Reduction Co, Ickles, 1967
D2728	·	·	·	·	Scrapped	Argosy Salvage, Shettleston 1967
D2729	·	·	·	·	Scrapped	Slag Reduction Co, Ickles, 1967
D2730	·	·	·	·	Scrapped	Argosy Salvage, Shettleston 1968
D2731	·	·	·	·	Scrapped	Argosy Salvage, Shettleston 1968
D2732	·	·	·	·	Scrapped	Slag Reduction Co, Ickles, 1967
D2733	·	·	·	·	Scrapped	Slag Reduction Co, Ickles, 1967
D2734	·	·	·	·	Scrapped	Argosy Salvage, Shettleston 1967
D2735	·	·	·	·	Scrapped	Slag Reduction Co, Ickles, 1967
D2736	·	·	·	·	Scrapped	Birds, Cardiff, 1968
D2737	·	·	·	·	Scrapped	Slag Reduction Co, Ickles, 1967
D2738	·	·	·	·	Scrapped	Alex Smith Metals, Ayr, 1979
D2739	·	·	·	·	Scrapped	Birds, Long Marston, 1967
D2740	·	·	·	·	Scrapped	Slag Reduction Co, Ickles, 1967
D2741	·	·	·	·	Scrapped	Slag Reduction Co, Ickles, 1967
D2742	·	·	·	·	Scrapped	Slag Reduction Co, Ickles, 1967
D2743	·	·	·	·	Scrapped	Slag Reduction Co, Ickles, 1967
D2744	·	·	·	·	Scrapped	Argosy Salvage, Shettleston 1967
D2745	·	·	·	·	Scrapped	Slag Reduction Co, Ickles, 1967
D2746	·	·	·	·	Scrapped	Slag Reduction Co, Ickles, 1967
D2747	·	·	·	·	Scrapped	Argosy Salvage, Shettleston 1967
D2748	·	·	·	·	Scrapped	Argosy Salvage, Shettleston 1967
D2749	·	·	·	·	Scrapped	Argosy Salvage, Shettleston 1967
D2750	·	·	·	·	Scrapped	Connels, Coatbridge, 1967
D2751	·	·	·	·	Scrapped	Connels, Coatbridge, 1967
D2752	·	·	·	·	Scrapped	Slag Reduction Co, Ickles, 1967
D2753	·	·	·	·	Scrapped	Machinery & Scrap Wishaw, 1967
D2754	·	·	·	·	Scrapped	Connels, Coatbridge, 1968
D2755	·	·	·	·	Scrapped	Argosy Salvage, Shettleston 1967
D2756	·	·	·	·	Scrapped	Campbells, Airdrie, 1968
D2757	·	·	·	·	Scrapped	Birds, Cardiff, 1968
D2758	·	·	·	·	Scrapped	Campbells, Airdrie, 1968
D2759	·	·	·	·	Scrapped	Argosy Salvage, Shettleston 1968
D2760	·	·	·	·	Scrapped	Campbells, Airdrie, 1968
D2761	·	·	·	·	Scrapped	Argosy Salvage, Shettleston 1968
D2762	·	·	·	·	Scrapped	Slag Reduction Co, Ickles, 1967
D2763	·	·	·	·	Scrapped	British Steel Co, Landore, 1977
D2764	·	·	·	·	Scrapped	Barnes & Bell, Coatbridge, 1968
D2765	·	·	·	·	Scrapped	Slag Reduction Co, Ickles, 1967
D2766	·	·	·	·	Scrapped	Slag Reduction Co, Ickles, 1967
D2767	·	·	·	·	Preserved	Bo'ness & Kinneil Railway
D2768	·	·	·	·	Scrapped	Shipbreaking, Faslane, 1968
D2769	·	·	·	·	Scrapped	Campbells, Airdrie, 1968
D2770	·	·	·	·	Scrapped	Campbells, Airdrie, 1968
D2771	·	·	·	·	Scrapped	Slag Reduction Co, Ickles, 1967
D2772	·	·	·	·	Scrapped	Slag Reduction Co, Ickles, 1967
D2773	·	·	·	·	Scrapped	Barnes & Bell, Coatbridge, 1968
D2774	·	·	·	·	Preserved	Strathspey Railway
D2775	·	·	·	·	Scrapped	Campbells, Airdrie, 1968

D2/10 0-4-0 (Continued)

D2776	·	·	·	·	Scrapped	Argosy Salvage, Shettleston 1968
D2777	·	·	·	·	Scrapped	Birds, Cardiff, 1968
D2778	·	·	·	·	Scrapped	Slag Reduction Co, Ickles, 1967
D2779	·	·	·	·	Scrapped	Campbells, Airdrie, 1968
D2780	·	·	·	·	Scrapped	Barnes & Bell, Coatbridge, 1968

D2/11 0-4-0

D2999	·	·	·	·	Scrapped	C F Booth, Rotherham, 1968

D2/12 0-6-0

D2510	·	·	·	·	Scrapped	C F Booth, Rotherham, 1968
D2511	·	·	·	·	Preserved	Keighley & Worth Valley Railway
D2512	·	·	·	·	Scrapped	C F Booth, Rotherham, 1968
D2513	·	·	·	·	Scrapped	NCB Cadeby, 1975
D2514	·	·	·	·	Scrapped	C F Booth, Rotherham, 1968
D2515	·	·	·	·	Scrapped	W Hatton Ltd, Bolton, 1968
D2516	·	·	·	·	Scrapped	C F Booth, Rotherham, 1968
D2517	·	·	·	·	Scrapped	Slag Reduction Co, Ickles, 1967
D2518	·	·	·	·	Scrapped	NCB Hatfield Main, 1973
D2519	·	·	·	·	Scrapped	Marple & Gillott, Sheffield, 1985

D3/1 0-4-0

D2900	·	·	·	·	Scrapped	Slag Reduction Co, Ickles, 1967
D2901	·	·	·	·	Scrapped	Slag Reduction Co, Ickles, 1967
D2902	·	·	·	·	Scrapped	Slag Reduction Co, Ickles, 1967
D2903	·	·	·	·	Scrapped	Slag Reduction Co, Ickles, 1967
D2904	·	·	·	·	Scrapped	Slag Reduction Co, Ickles, 1967
D2905	·	·	·	·	Scrapped	Slag Reduction Co, Ickles, 1967
D2906	·	·	·	·	Scrapped	Slag Reduction Co, Ickles, 1967
D2907	·	·	·	·	Scrapped	Slag Reduction Co, Ickles, 1967
D2908	·	·	·	·	Scrapped	Slag Reduction Co, Ickles, 1967
D2909	·	·	·	·	Scrapped	Slag Reduction Co, Ickles, 1967
D2910	·	·	·	·	Scrapped	Slag Reduction Co, Ickles, 1967
D2911	·	·	·	·	Scrapped	Slag Reduction Co, Ickles, 1967
D2912	·	·	·	·	Scrapped	Slag Reduction Co, Ickles, 1967
D2913	·	·	·	·	Scrapped	Slag Reduction Co, Ickles, 1967

D3/3 0-6-0

D3117	13117	·	·	·	Scrapped	Cashmore's, Great Bridge, 1967
D3118	13118	·	·	·	Scrapped	Cashmore's, Great Bridge, 1967
D3119	13119	·	·	·	Scrapped	Cashmore's, Great Bridge, 1967
D3120	13120	·	·	·	Scrapped	Cohen's, Kettering, 1968
D3121	13121	·	·	·	Scrapped	BR, Derby Works, 1968
D3122	13122	·	·	·	Scrapped	Steelbreaking, Chesterfield, 1967
D3123	13123	·	·	·	Scrapped	Cashmore's, Great Bridge, 1967
D3124	13124	·	·	·	Scrapped	Cashmore's, Great Bridge, 1967
D3125	13125	·	·	·	Scrapped	Cohen's, Kettering, 1968
D3126	13126	·	·	·	Scrapped	Cashmore's, Great Bridge, 1967

D3/5 0-6-0

D3152	13152	·	·	·	Scrapped	Slag Reduction Co, Ickles, 1968
D3153	13153	·	·	·	Scrapped	C F Booth, Rotherham, 1968
D3154	13154	·	·	·	Scrapped	C F Booth, Rotherham, 1968
D3155	13155	·	·	·	Scrapped	C F Booth, Rotherham, 1968
D3156	13156	·	·	·	Scrapped	C F Booth, Rotherham, 1968
D3157	13157	·	·	·	Scrapped	Slag Reduction Co, Ickles, 1968
D3158	13158	·	·	·	Scrapped	Slag Reduction Co, Ickles, 1967
D3159	13159	·	·	·	Scrapped	C F Booth, Rotherham, 1968
D3160	13160	·	·	·	Scrapped	Slag Reduction Co, Ickles, 1968
D3161	13161	·	·	·	Scrapped	C F Booth, Rotherham, 1968
D3162	13162	·	·	·	Scrapped	Slag Reduction Co, Ickles, 1968
D3163	13163	·	·	·	Scrapped	C F Booth, Rotherham, 1968
D3164	13164	·	·	·	Scrapped	Slag Reduction Co, Ickles, 1968
D3165	13165	·	·	·	Scrapped	C F Booth, Rotherham, 1968
D3166	13166	·	·	·	Scrapped	C F Booth, Rotherham, 1968

D3/6 0-6-0

12000	7074	·	·	·	Scrapped	BR, Derby Works, 1962
12001	7076	·	·	·	Scrapped	BR, Horwich Works, 1962
12002	7079	·	·	·	Scrapped	BR, Horwich Works, 1956

D3/7 0-6-0

12003	7080	·	·	·	Scrapped	Slag Reduction Co, Ickles, 1968
12004	7081	·	·	·	Scrapped	Cashmore's, Great Bridge, 1968
12005	7082	·	·	·	Scrapped	C F Booth, Rotherham, 1968
12006	7083	·	·	·	Scrapped	Slag Reduction Co, Ickles, 1968
12007	7084	·	·	·	Scrapped	Slag Reduction Co, Ickles, 1968
12008	7085	·	·	·	Scrapped	C F Booth, Rotherham, 1968
12009	7086	·	·	·	Scrapped	Slag Reduction Co, Ickles, 1968
12010	7087	·	·	·	Scrapped	Slag Reduction Co, Ickles, 1968
12011	7088	·	·	·	Scrapped	BR, Derby Works, 1966
12012	7089	·	·	·	Scrapped	W Hatton Ltd, Bolton, 1968
12013	7090	·	·	·	Scrapped	Slag Reduction Co, Ickles, 1968
12014	7091	·	·	·	Scrapped	Slag Reduction Co, Ickles, 1968
12015	7092	·	·	·	Scrapped	Slag Reduction Co, Ickles, 1968
12016	7093	·	·	·	Scrapped	Slag Reduction Co, Ickles, 1968
12017	7094	·	·	·	Scrapped	Slag Reduction Co, Ickles, 1968
12018	7095	·	·	·	Scrapped	Slag Reduction Co, Ickles, 1968
12019	7096	·	·	·	Scrapped	Slag Reduction Co, Ickles, 1968
12020	7097	·	·	·	Scrapped	Slag Reduction Co, Ickles, 1968
12021	7098	·	·	·	Scrapped	Slag Reduction Co, Ickles, 1968
12022	7099	·	·	·	Scrapped	Cashmore's, Great Bridge, 1967
12023	7110	·	·	·	Scrapped	W Hatton Ltd, Bolton, 1968
12024	7111	·	·	·	Scrapped	Cashmore's, Great Bridge, 1968
12025	7112	·	·	·	Scrapped	Slag Reduction Co, Ickles, 1968
12026	7113	·	·	·	Scrapped	Slag Reduction Co, Ickles, 1968
12027	7114	·	·	·	Scrapped	Slag Reduction Co, Ickles, 1968
12028	7115	·	·	·	Scrapped	C F Booth, Rotherham, 1968
12029	7116	·	·	·	Scrapped	BR, Derby Works, 1966
12030	7117	·	·	·	Scrapped	BR, Derby Works, 1964
12031	7118	·	·	·	Scrapped	Cashmore's, Great Bridge, 1968

D3/7 0-6-0 (Continued)

| 12032 | 7119 | · | · | · | Scrapped | Cashmore's, Great Bridge, 1968 |

D3/10 0-6-0

| 15100 | 500 | GWR2 | · | · | Scrapped | Cohen's, Morriston, 1966 |

D3/11 0-6-0

15101	502	·	·	·	Scrapped	Cohen's, Kettering, 1969
15102	503	·	·	·	Scrapped	Steelbreaking, Chesterfield, 1968
15103	504	·	·	·	Scrapped	Steelbreaking, Chesterfield, 1968
15104	505	·	·	·	Scrapped	Steelbreaking, Chesterfield, 1968
15105	506	·	·	·	Scrapped	Cohen's, Kettering, 1969
15106	507	·	·	·	Scrapped	Cohen's, Kettering, 1969

D3/12 0-6-0

15201	S1	·	·	·	Scrapped	Cohen's, Morriston, 1969
15202	S2	·	·	·	Scrapped	Cashmore's, Newport, 1966
15203	S3	·	·	·	Scrapped	Cashmore's, Newport, 1966

D3/14 0-6-0

| 15004 | 8004 | · | · | · | Scrapped | BR, Doncaster Works, 1963 |

BULL1 0-6-0

| 11001 | · | · | · | · | Scrapped | BR, Ashford Works, 1959 |

DES1 0-6-0

15000	8000	·	·	·	Scrapped	R A Kings, Norwich, 1968
15001	8001	·	·	·	Scrapped	Cashmore's, Great Bridge, 1967
15002	8002	·	·	·	Scrapped	R A Kings, Norwich, 1968
15003	8003	·	·	·	Scrapped	Slag Reduction Co, Ickles, 1968

GWR1 0-6-0

| 15107 | · | · | · | · | Scrapped | Cashmore's, Newport, 1958 |

English Electric 0-6-0

| D226 | D0226 | · | · | · | Preserved | Keighley & Worth Valley Railway |
| D227 | D0227 | · | · | · | Scrapped | BR, Darlington Works, 1964 |

North British 0-4-0

| TOM | 27414 | · | · | · | Preserved | Telford Steam Railway |
| TIGER | · | · | · | · | Preserved | Bo'ness & Kinneil Railway |

ABBREVIATIONS

The following abbreviations are used throughout this book:

AC	Alternating Current
AFS	Arlington Fleet Services
BARS	British American Railway Services
BR	British Rail
BREL	British Rail Engineering Ltd
C & PR	Chinnor & Princes Risborough Railway
DB	Deutsche Bahn
DC	Direct Current
DRS	Direct Rail Services
EMD	Electro-motive Diesel Ltd
EMR	European Metal Recycling
EMT	East Midlands Trains
EWS	English Welsh & Scottish Railways
G & WR	Gloucester & Warwickshire Railway
GA	Greater Anglia
GBRF	Great British Rail Freight
GWR	Great Western Railway
HNRC	Harry Needle Railroad Company
hp	Horse Power
lbf	Pound Force
LNER	London & North Eastern Railway
MOSI	Museum of Science and Industry
mph	Miles Per Hour
NCB	National Coal Board
NR	Network Rail
NRM	National Railway Museum
OOC	Old Oak Common
P.A.R.	Powet At Rail
R.A.	Route Availability
ROG	Rail Operations Group
RS & H	Robert Stephenson & Hawthorns
RSS	Railway Support Services
SCD	Sandbach Commercial Dismantlers
SWR	South Western Railway
SYPS	South Yorkshire Preservation Society
t	Tons
T.E.	Tractive Effort
T.M.s	Traction Motors
TOPS	Total Operations Processing System
UKRL	UK Rail Leasing
VT	Virgin Trains
WCRC	West Coast Railway Company
WMT	West Midlands Trains
XC	Cross Country Trains

NOTES

Locofleetshop.co.uk

Loco Fleet List

Loco Fleet Calendar

Metal Signs

Badges

Coasters

Brooches

Cufflinks

DVDs

Mouse Mats

Customised Signs

Ties

Tie Slides

Stationery

Mugs

Travel Mugs

Customised Mugs